User-Centered Computer Aided Language Learning

Panayiotis Zaphiris
Centre for HCI Design, City University, UK

Giorgos Zacharia
Massachusetts Institute of Technology & Open Ratings Inc., USA

Information Science Publishing

Hershey • London • Melbourne • Singapore

Acquisitions Editor:	Michelle Potter
Development Editor:	Kristin Roth
Senior Managing Editor:	Amanda Appicello
Managing Editor:	Jennifer Neidig
Copy Editor:	Julie LeBlanc
Typesetter:	Sharon Berger
Cover Design:	Lisa Tosheff
Printed at:	Integrated Book Technology

Published in the United States of America by
Information Science Publishing (an imprint of Idea Group Inc.)
701 E. Chocolate Avenue
Hershey PA 17033
Tel: 717-533-8845
Fax: 717-533-8661
E-mail: cust@idea-group.com
Web site: http://www.idea-group.com

and in the United Kingdom by
Information Science Publishing (an imprint of Idea Group Inc.)
3 Henrietta Street
Covent Garden
London WC2E 8LU
Tel: 44 20 7240 0856
Fax: 44 20 7379 0609
Web site: http://www.eurospanonline.com

Library of Congress Cataloging-in-Publication Data

User-centered computer aided language learning / Panayiotis Zaphiris and Giorgos Zacharia, editors.
p. cm.
Summary: "This book discusses the basis of a broad framework for the development and management of Computer Aided Language Learning (CALL) environments, covering domains as diverse as education, information systems, psychology, sociology, linguistics, artificial intelligence and e-learning"--Provided by publisher.
Includes bibliographical references and index.
ISBN 1-59140-750-8 -- ISBN 1-59140-751-6 (pbk.) -- ISBN 1-59140-752-4 (ebook)
1. Language and languages--Computer-assisted instruction. I. Zaphiris, Panayiotis. II. Zacharia, Giorgos.
P53.28.U84 2006
418.00285--dc22

2005032113

British Cataloguing in Publication Data
A Cataloguing in Publication record for this book is available from the British Library.

All work contributed to this book is new, previously-unpublished material. The views expressed in this book are those of the authors, but not necessarily of the publisher.

User-Centered Computer Aided Language Learning

Table of Contents

Preface

Overview and Motivation

Computer aided language learning (CALL) has been gaining popularity as computer-based education has been attracting the interest of the business and education sectors.

Due to the increasing popularity of the Internet and the use of multimedia, there has been a recent move of CALL systems from CD-ROM to Web-based systems, making it possible to create systems that can facilitate the emergence of online communities of learners.

CALL allows students to practice language situations interactively, and collaborate and share their learning experiences with other students and teachers in both synchronous and asynchronous communication modes. These new learning opportunities come with a lot of usability challenges that can make the learning experience frustrating and inefficient. Therefore, the ability to design applications that comply with usability standards and offer an easy-to-use, enjoyable learning environment for the students can affect the success of any new CALL effort significantly.

For that reason, the key objective of this book was to look at the topic of CALL in a new direction by focusing on the human-computer interaction elements of learning a language online. The book discusses the basis of a broad framework for the development and management of CALL environments, enriched with contributions from domains as diverse as education, information systems, psychology, sociology, linguistics, artificial intelligence, e-learning and many others.

The book puts the emphasis on the user (learner) and proposes methodologies, strategies and design approaches for designing interfaces that facilitate a user-centered design approach and focus to CALL.

The book's objective is to serve university educators and educators in general; university administrators; researchers; librarians; teachers of foreign languages; e-learning and CALL system managers and designers.

Description of Chapters

A user-centered design approach focuses design activity on the user by employing methodologies that achieve to get a better understanding of the users. This user-centered approach is further broken down into three key activities: analysis, design and evaluation. For that reason, our book is structured in three broad sections. Section I provides some theoretical foundations for CALL. Section II takes those theoretical foundations further by providing chapters that cover analysis and design studies. Finally, in Section III, we include chapters that describe projects that involved extensive evaluation case studies.

The book includes 14 chapters from prominent international authors. The international character of the book is evident in that it includes chapters from authors from Australia, Austria, Brazil, Cyprus, Greece, Ireland, Israel, Japan, Singapore, Spain, the United Kingdom and United States.

The following section presents an overview of each chapter.

Section I: Theory and Analysis

Chapter I, *Developing Enjoyable Second Language Learning Software Tools: A Computer Game Paradigm,* is written by Chee Siang Ang and Panayiotis Zaphiris. It provides a theoretical view of harnessing computer game design for language learning by introducing current academic study on computer games. It proposes a game model that treats games both as play activities as well as narratives. It then demonstrates that a pleasurable CALL application could benefit from both aspects, by presenting two case studies on game-based language learning.

Chapter II, *Culture-Based Language Learning Objects: A CALL Approach for a Ubiquitous World,* is written by Niki Lambropoulos, Martha Christopoulou, and Kosmos Vlachos. It discusses the theoretical rationale of cultural-based language learning on which the construction of culture-based language learning objects (CALLOs) are founded. It makes suggestions on how CALLOs could be designed by second-language teachers for a norm-based and culture-based learning context.

Chapter III, *Situated Task Analysis in Learner-Centred CALL,* is written by Roderick A. Farmer. It examines the roles of user-centered design in CALL design and evaluates and presents Learner-centered design as a theoretical and practical alternative to traditional approaches. The proposed method focuses on a sociocultural task analysis framework for analyzing learner-computer interactions that could be useful in CALL system design.

Section II: Design

Chapter IV, *'Ears before Eyes': Expanding Tutors' Interaction Skills beyond Physical Presence in Audio-Graphic Collaborative Virtual Learning Environments*, is written by Beatriz de los Arcos and Inmaculada Arnedillo Sánchez. It provides an analysis of problems that arise in a virtual language-learning environment in which non-verbal behaviors are absent. It also introduces strategies to deal with certain aspects, such as turn taking and silence, by examining the difficulties of implementing a virtual classroom.

Chapter V, *A Student-Centered Online Writing Course,* is written by Caroline Coit. It demonstrates the design development and implementation of a collaborative writing system, known as peer correction system-tool, which enables students to send academic-style articles to peers and receive feedback from them. The evaluation of the system yields very positive results, and it thus offers an opportunity for other online language courses to adopt this open-source system.

Chapter VI, *Learner-Centered Language Programs: Integrating Disparate Resources for Task-Based Interaction,* is written by Deryle Lonsdale, C. Ray Graham, and Rebecca Madsen. It is centered on the communicative learning environment in which students become first-person participants in language interaction through the use of animated agents and speech technologies. It discusses strategies to design multi-component applications, ranging from appropriate toolkits selection and seamless integration of these technologies.

Chapter VII, *LAPLI - The Language Learning Lab: A Methodological Proposal for a Hybrid Course in a Virtual Environment,* is written by Rita de Cássia Veiga Marriott and Patricia Lupion Torres. It discusses the development of LAPLI, the language lab that implements an integrative CALL methodology, providing language courses in a virtual environment. The language lab provides hybrid activities to students to develop their reading and writing skills by using language as a tool to accomplish tasks in a contextualized way, either individually or collaboratively.

Chapter VIII, *Integrated Micro Learning During Access Delays: A New Approach to Second-Language Learning,* is written by Silvia Gstrein and Theo Hug. It envisages the design of futuristic e-learning projects with the concept of ubiquitous computing. A new learning approach, known as integrated micro learning, has been developed to integrate language learning into the learner's daily routine with the help of electronic devices.

Section III: Evaluation and Case Studies

Chapter IX, *EOI Online Inglés: A Fully Implemented and Operative Online English Language Course,* is written by Pascual Cantos Gómez and Juan García Iborra. It deals with the design of an online English language course as an alternative to the traditional language course and ongoing distance learning course. It offers a full description of the outline, rational and design of the course, ranging from the unit structure to course material development. An evaluation study highlights the benefits and drawbacks of the project, giving an insight of issues to consider for those who work in the same area.

Chapter X, *Metacognition and Learners' Interactions with a Web-Based CALL Grammar Exercise,* is written by Wai Meng Chan. It highlights a qualitative evaluation study that examines the relationship between learners' metacognition and their interactions with a German language CALL grammar exercise. It focused on the metacognitive processes and strategy use while performing the exercise as well as how these affect or are affected by their use of interactive aids.

Chapter XI, *The Effect of a Native-Language Interface vs. a Target-Language Interface on Students' Performance,* is written by Jay Melton. It describes an evaluation experiment on the use of native and target language as the user interface of a course management systems quiz module. A group of Japanese students learning English is studied, and it was found that there is no significant difference in using an English or a Japanese interface.

Chapter XII, *Reading and Learning from Screen,* is written by Miriam Schcolnik and Sara Kol. It studies the mode of electronic text presentation in CALL materials. Factors related to the screen, the reader, the text layout as well as navigation methods might affect reading from the screen. It thus calls for customizable presentation modes in CALL programs.

Chapter XIII, *Evaluating Students' Perceptions of* Online Counselor *for Independent Language Learning,* is written by Yoko Hirata. It outlines the design of a computer program, known as Online Counselor, which assists students who lack independent learning experiences to plan and organize their learning. It argues that a language-learning program should be able to guide learners and at the same time give freedom to them in performing their tasks.

Chapter XIV, *Language Learning and User-Centered Design: The Development of the Electronic European Language Portfolio,* is written by Charalambos Vrasidas, Elena Landone, Niki Christodoulou, and Michalinos Zembylas. It emphasizes the user-centered approach in developing the electronic version of the European language portfolio. It discusses the affordances of technology in serving the need of the electronic environment in supporting language teaching and learning.

Acknowledgments

Many thanks go to the publishing team and especially Kristin Roth for all the support and encouragement in this process. Special thanks go to Chee Siang Ang from City University London for all the help he provided for this project. Finally, we would like to warmly thank all the authors for making this book possible through their very interesting contributions.

Panayiotis Zaphiris (zaphiri@soi.city.ac.uk)
Giorgos Zacharia (lysi@alum.mit.edu)

Section I

Theory and Analysis

Chapter I

Developing Enjoyable Second Language Learning Software Tools: A Computer Game Paradigm

Chee Siang Ang, City University, UK

Panayiotis Zaphiris, City University, UK

Abstract

This chapter attempts to examine computer game theories — ludology and narratology — that explain computer games as play activities and storytelling media. Founded on this theoretical explanation, a game model that incorporates gameplay and narratives is presented. From the model, two aspects of learning in the game environment are identified: gameplay-oriented and narrative-oriented. It is believed that playing computer games involves at least one of these types of learning; thus, this game's nature can be used in designing engaging educational software. In addition, based on Malone's theoretical framework on motivational heuristics, there are two methods of applying computer games in language learning: extrinsic and intrinsic, depending on the integration of game designs and learning materials. Then, two cases of language-learning games are scrutinized, using the game model, in order to demonstrate the use of computer games in language learning.

Introduction

In one of his most influential texts about computer games, *The Art of Computer Game Design*, Chris Crawford (1982) states that schools, but not games, are the untested fad and violator of tradition in education. Game playing is a vital educational function for any creature capable of learning. Hence, games are the most ancient and time-honored vehicle for education. Crawford explores the reasons for people playing games and asserts that the fundamental motivation of game playing is to learn. He also cites an example to support his view by observing the behavior of lion cubs near their mother: the cubs crouch in the grass, creeping slowly toward a butterfly and pouncing on it. The beasts are apparently playing some sort of game and having fun. However, the game is also how lions learn to hunt their prey without being injured. They are learning by doing, with minimum risks. This observation is true not only for animals. Since the dawn of human history, games have been used in the teaching and learning process. Board games, for example, are believed to be the earliest games, and they were battle simulations designed to instruct the young (Murray, 1978).

The ability of computer games to spark interest among players can hardly be denied, and some educators have started to see the capability of these highly engaging games. People play games voluntarily, without asking for external rewards. Besides, the use of computer games in learning is parallel with Piaget's constructivism, in which knowledge is constructed instead of being transmitted. A lot of game-based learning projects have been carried out with an emphasis on this pedagogical epistemology. Nevertheless, most of these projects are centered in science education and mathematics. Not much theoretical work has been done on language learning, although computer games have long been used in this area. This is due to the fact that computer games are too varied and intricate to indicate a clear function in language education. Furthermore, what counts as a game is rather loosely defined. Therefore, a proper study of computer game theories would throw light upon this issue.

This chapter is structured as follows: First, we review the theoretical parts of computer games, which include ludology and narratology. Then, a theoretical model of game is proposed. The next section explains two kinds of learning that occur when playing computer games based on the model. We outline two methods of integrating game designs with language learning. Next, an analysis of two cases of language-learning games is presented. Then, we discuss the future direction of this study; and the final section concludes the chapter.

Theoretical Review on Gaming

Although the use of computer games in learning is gaining attention among educators, there is still a lack of theoretical understanding of the game itself in most studies. Recent literature reveals that the research of computer games falls into two major principles: ludology and narratology. Ludology focuses on the study of computer games as play and game activities, while narratology focuses on the study of computer games as stories. The views between ludologists and narratologists are generally contradictory; the former argues that the pleasure of playing games lies in the gameplay, while the latter treats narrative as the fundamental enjoyment players are experiencing during the play session. In computer games, gameplay is referred to as activities conducted within a framework of agreed rules that directly or indirectly contribute to achieving goals (Lindley, 2002). A narrative is an account of something that happens to someone (Barrett, 1997). It consists of a series of events, from the background setting to the completion of the game. In other words, gameplay is the actions taken by the players, while narratives are an account of these actions. In this section, several kinds of game rules are explicated to better comprehend gameplay. The narrative mechanisms of the game are also scrutinized.

Gameplay and Ludology

The term ludology first appeared in the text of computer game research in 1999. Gonzalo Frasca (1999) points out in his paper, *Ludology Meets Narratology: Similitude and Differences Between (Video) Games and Narrative*, that another dimension has been almost ignored when studying computer games: to analyze them as games. He proposes the term "ludology" to refer to the discipline that studies game and play activities as opposed to narratives, and asserts that ludology should be independent from the medium that supports the activity. Frasca (2001) identifies two kinds of game: ludus and paidea. Ludus refers to the games whose result defines a winner and a loser, while paidea refers to the games whose result does not (Frasca, 2001). Based on this difference, Frasca introduces two types of game rules: paidea rules and ludus rules. Paidea rules are established to play the game as paidea, while ludus rules are established to win or lose the game. In chess, for example, paidea rules describe how each token moves, while ludus rules state a condition to end the match. It is noticed that we can easily switch from paidea to ludus and vice versa. In SimCity (see Figure 1) — a paidea game in which no explicit ludus rules are defined — players can engage in paidea by playing with the buildings. Once they establish a goal, say, to build a city with a population of 10,000, they immediately switch to a ludus activity. Not only can we have several paidea rules, we can also have several ludus rules. In chess, we can define the winner by counting the amount and value of each player's remaining tokens. Table 1 shows some examples of paidea and ludus rules in computer games.

Table 1. Paidea rules and ludus rules

	Paidea rules	**Ludus rules**
SimCity (Paidea game)	If the crime rate is high, the population becomes low	Nil
Tetris (Ludus game)	If the blocks fill a layer, the layer is cleared	To keep the level of block as low as possible

Figure 1. SimCity 4000 (courtesy Electronic Arts, 2003)

Besides rules, ludologists are also keen on understanding gameplay. Jesper Juul (2002) proposes two types of gameplay based on the relationship between the rules of a game and the actual game sessions played. First is emergent gameplay, where a number of simple rules are combined to form an interesting variation of gameplay. In a game of emergence, the game structure is primitive and defined by a set of simple paidea rules with usually only one ludus rule. Chess, for instance, is a game of emergence. It has a set of paidea rules that define how each piece moves, and one ludus rule, which is to take the opponent's King. Driven towards this explicitly stated ludus rule, players might construct more ludus rules (such as to take the Knight) and plan for complicated strategies to achieve the goal. Second is progressive gameplay, where separate challenges are introduced serially for the player to solve. Most adventure games, like Myst (see Figure 2), fall into this category. Players are introduced, one after another, to ludus rules of goals to be achieved that lead to the attainment of the ultimate game goal.

Figure 2. Myst III (courtesy UbiSoft Entertainment, 2001)

Narratives and Narratology

For narratologists, the advent of the computer signifies the birth of a new medium for storytelling. The capability of computers is not limited to performing calculations; computers are a new medium to represent human activities and present narratives in an unprecedented way. In most modern computer games, players can naturalize their actions as the solving of a familiar type of problem (Ryan, 1994). In Myst III, the player needs to track down the villain; in Super Mario Bros. 3 (see Figure 3), the player is trying to save Princess Toadstool; and in SimCity, the player plays the role of the mayor and plans for city development.

Marie Ryan (2001) tries to understand narratives in computer games, and she proposes a definition of narrative based on mental images: A narrative is defined as a mental image, or cognitive construct, that can be activated by various types of signs. This image consists of a world (setting) populated by intelligent agents (characters). These agents participate in actions and happenings (events, plot) that cause global changes in the narrative world. Several useful terms are recognized in this definition: world, character and action, and we would like to know to what extent these exist in computer games. First, a game has a spatial representation, whether real or abstract. Espen Aarseth (1998) has claimed in the article *Allegories of Space* that computer games are essentially concerned with spatial representation and negotiation. Myst, for example, has a rich description of space represented with high-quality pre-rendered 3D images. The player recognizes the space immediately after entering the game world, and knows what and how they should act because it resembles a real social setting. Pong, on the other hand, represents an abstract space, which might not have a referent in the real world. Players might construct their own mental image about the game, though most players would probably relate Pong with table tennis. The space in Pong is symbolic, while in Myst it is narrative. One thing in common is that these two worlds operate within a strict set of rules that define the mechanism of the worlds. Second, most computer games feature explicit characters who will interact with the world or the player. In Myst, the characters are descriptive, and

Figure 3. Super Mario Bros. 3 (courtesy Nintendo, 1988)

players can interact with them as if they are real humans, although the interaction is limited to several chosen aspects. In Pong, even though it does not have an explicit character, the player is apparently playing against an opponent or intelligent agent. The character is not depicted graphically in the game world, but the existence cannot be overlooked. Third, all games involve active actions and reactions of the players. Games are usually discerned from linear narratives by the existence of interaction: the reciprocal actions between players and games. These actions include not only the action of the player, but also the autonomous actions of the characters in the game world.

A Game Model of Gameplay and Narratives

In this section, we propose a game model of gameplay and narratives that attempts to unify the view of ludologists and narratologists, thus advocating the study of computer games that comprises both gameplay and narratives. From the ludological perspective, we know that game rules are significant in understanding the semantics and structure of the game. Though they constitute a very important part of computer games, rules are not always the only thing one needs to learn in order to play. Game playing is more than simply memorizing the rules. Having learned the rules merely establishes the ability to play, and successful play does not necessarily require learning all the rules (Lindley, 2002). We need to understand something more complex that can arise from the rules: the gameplay. Examining the two types of rules and gameplay closely, it has been found that gameplay emerges from and must conform to the paidea rules that describe the semantic of the game. In addition, gameplay is oriented towards the ludus rules that describe the structure of the game. This relation is described in Figure 4.

Usually, paidea rules are fixed and predefined by the game designer. The player cannot breach paidea rules and their planning of strategies should conform to these rules. If the paidea rules state that the game character can only move forward and backward, the player can never move it upward or downward. Ludus rules are more flexible compared to paidea rules. The player may change the ludus rules and get involved in a different

Figure 4. A game model of gameplay and rules

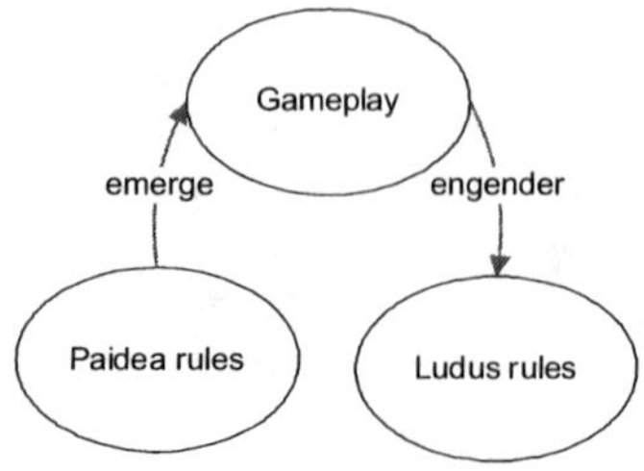

gameplay the game designer has intended, although the player might not be able to win the game. Gameplay emerges from paidea rules; but without ludus rules, there is hardly any gameplay. Paidea rules can be simple, but ludus rules can lead to complex gameplay. If players do not set the ludus rules while playing SimCity, the gameplay does not exist in the play session, because the players' actions are not oriented toward achieving a goal. In Super Mario Bros. 3, if players are only playing around with the world without having the intention to solve the level, gameplay does not exist, although the ludus rules are explicitly defined by the game designer.

If we view from the prism of narratology, it appears that games and narratives are quite similar, as computer games use narrative structures to organize their worlds. Nevertheless, games are not a mental image; they are a system defined by a set of concrete rules. Within this context, players can act freely as long as their actions conform to the rules. The chain of these actions can then be recounted in narrative discourse. In brief, the difference between narratives in computer games and linear narratives is that a linear narrative presents the facts in an immutable sequence, while a game presents a branching tree of sequences and allows the players to create their own story by making choices at each branch point (Crawford, 1982). However, there are sequences of events in games that do not become or form stories (like in Tetris). Therefore, not all games are interactive narratives; rather, some games can be interactive narratives, and these games can be used as a medium for storytelling. In fact, Frasca (1999) has attempted to relate paidea and ludus with narrative elements:

> *If ludus can be related to narrative plot, paidea can be related to the narrative settings. The ability to perform paidea activities is determined by the environment and the actions.*

This statement is quite valuable in analyzing the relationship between rules and narratives in computer games. To perceive this subtle relationship, we would like to derive two narrative components from the narratological framework: spatiality, the space of the narrative; and fabula, the actions and events that might happen in the space. By applying these to the previous model, we have a more descriptive one (see Figure 5). The game space usually consists of compound worlds (Gingold, 2003). In most games, players travel through many locations, and enjoy the exploration of these multiple worlds and the movement between them. Compound worlds are collections of micro-worlds, which are governed by their own sets of paidea rules. These rules influence how the narrative world operates, while the movement of each world is marked by the changes in description and organization. Music, environment and, most importantly, rules change as the player moves between worlds. Ludus rules, on the other hand, are closely related to the narrative events in the narrative world. The player's actions are directly or indirectly affected by the ludus rules which, in turn, are changed according to the players' actions.

The relationship between narratives and gameplay is two-way. As narratives change, the rules become different. Evolving fabula can create new ludus rules, new sources of conflict and even new forms of gameplay. In fact, the best evolving stories can effectively change the rules of the game, something that probably would not be tolerated by a player lacking a story-driven reason. Rules in games need not be static. Narratives provide an

Figure 5. A game model of gameplay and narratives

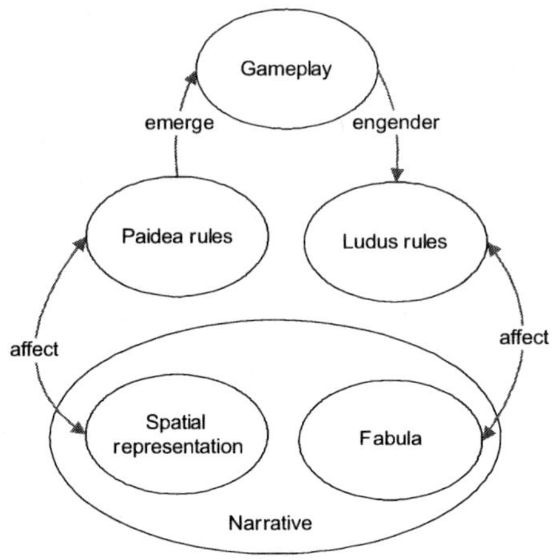

explanation and meaning of the change of rules so that the virtual world is more believable. To exemplify this relationship, let us presume that Mario eats the mushroom and grows up in Super Mario Bros. 3. This event immediately triggers the creation of a ludus rule: to avoid being touched by monsters. It is very likely that in a certain point of the game, a monster will touch Mario and Mario will shrink. This event then again activates new ludus rules: to eat the mushroom.

The Game Model and Learning in Computer Games

The game model that binds both gameplay and narratives reveals something about learning activities when players are engaged in game playing. In most modern computer games, the successfully playing of a game involves at least two types of learning: gameplay and the narrative. In this section, we look into these two aspects of learning in games and how we could use them in designing engaging learning software tools.

Gameplay-Oriented Learning

This relationship between rules and gameplay has a significant implication on designing pleasurable activities, such as learning. In the article *E-Learning as Computer Games: Designing Immersive and Experiential Learning*, e-learning software is interpreted as computer games, and several principles in designing interesting learning environments are outlined (Ang & Rao, 2004). If we look into the definition of paidea and ludus, it is not difficult to conclude that most conventional educational software is actually a loose type of game. It has paidea rules: Click the menu buttons and scroll the text with the mouse button, and so forth. Ludus rules are usually stated as the learning objective: to understand the concept of metamorphosis. Although the definition of game is much more intricate than just having these rules, this software could be seen as paidea or ludus games depending on the existence of an explicit goal. We are interested in investigating why it is not as engaging as commercial games with game rules.

The internal structure of a game can be characterized by its paidea rules, which can further be classified into two types: symbolic and semantic. Briefly, symbolic paidea rules explain the first layer of game interface — the input and output device interactions; while semantic paidea rules describe the narrative layer of interface. Obviously, the paidea rules of most learning software are symbolic, and do not impel learners to search for semantic meaning. The enjoyment of users should not be limited to symbolic paidea rules that define how users interact with computer devices. Learners should engage in gameplay by observing, hypothesizing, testing and updating the semantic paidea rules of the narrative environment. The pleasure of paidea should lie in the exploration of the virtual world and the discovery of paidea rules. Some learners find some educational software interesting when they first play with it. They might have fun interacting with the mouse or keyboard. However, they soon will see through the mechanisms of the system: There is nothing more to explore. Besides, understanding the paidea rules does not let them plan for strategies to achieve the goal. Unlike Super Mario Bros. 3, where players play and observe the causality of their actions and the behavior of the spatial system, most learning software does not contain such qualities. The major "gameplay" of this software revolves around the reading of texts, since the paidea rules are oversimplified: Click and read.

The game designer not only has to design the paidea rules that define how games work, but also must define the goal of the game (ludus rules). We can further derive two kinds of ludus rules: micro and macro. Micro ludus rules contribute indirectly to winning a game, while macro ludus rules contribute directly. Computer games usually have macro ludus rules, which define the ultimate goal; while most micro ludus rules are either predefined by the game designers or created by the players during the play session. Oriented towards macro ludus rules, the player devises individual micro ludus rules in order to achieve the goal. For a game-based learning system, explicitly stated micro ludus rules can be important to scaffold learning. Micro ludus rules also function as guidance in the virtual world that steers players toward the learning objective. Learning objectives are presented as part of the narrative context. Instead of "to understand genetic configuration of animals," we can intrigue the learners "to defeat the monsters by breaking the genetic codes." Besides, this matches task-based learning, while each task is introduced as ludus rules.

Narrative-Oriented Learning

Narrative interfaces have been used in the game industry since its infancy and have successfully enticed a large portion of computer users for decades. Unfortunately, most educational software fails to take advantage of this highly effective design. Spatial design is obviously lacking, as most interfaces of conventional learning software adopt the metaphor of a book. The computer screen should not be a representation of a page of book, but a window to a new world. Learners look through the screen like through a window to a new spatial world of knowledge in which the images of real objects act coherently with virtual models (Morozov & Markov, 2000).

Like paidea rules, the interface of a game is doubled in an interesting way. First is the interface of the computer: the keyboard and the mouse. An additional interface is the narrative metaphor, which illuminates the narrative space in a new dynamic and interactive medium. The spatial design makes the first interface "disappear." Learners are not interacting with the keyboard or mouse, but with the story presented from the computer screen (Jaron & Biocca, 1992). Another issue pertaining to the spatiality of the software is that most educational software structures learning contents linearly, offers textual explanations and gives a particular spatial organization that does not reflect physical experiences. Learners should not regurgitate the context-free facts; rather, they expect to use knowledge in a contextually rich situation.

Apart from these, educational software does not offer narrativity to its users. There is hardly any action except for the clicking of menu buttons, which is hardly conceivable as stories. As Ryan (2001) has pointed out, players do not want to "gather points by hitting moving targets with a cursor controlled by a joystick"; they want to fight terrorists or save Earth from invasion by evil creatures from outer space. It is the same for learning software, which is also a type of game. Learners do not want to click the button to flip through the pages about genetics; they want to defeat monsters by analyzing and breaking their genetic codes.

Language Learning as Extrinsic and Intrinsic Games

We have elucidated two types of learning that might arise when playing a game. But how could these game designs be applied in language-learning software? Malone (1980) has propounded a motivational heuristic of educational games that comprises challenge, curiosity and fantasy. According to his interpretation of fantasy in computer games, two kinds of game design for learning are distinguished: intrinsic and extrinsic games. Intrinsic games rely on the understanding of the subject matter from within the game world, while extrinsic games rely on those external to the game world. Extrinsic games usually consist of a structured series of puzzles or tasks embedded in a game or narrative structure with which they have only the most slender connection. Intrinsic games build in challenges and activities that are more seamlessly integrated, more dependent on the narrative of the game. In brief, extrinsic games are used to attract users to learn a language, while in intrinsic games, the computer game itself becomes the learning activity. Therefore, the game design could be applied in language learning with two methods: the learning of the material as well as the learning of the game itself.

Extrinsic Game Learning

In extrinsic game design, the language learning is superimposed on the paidea rules of an existing game, resulting in new paidea rules. This may and may not engender new gameplay, depending on the quality of the bond between paidea rules and the learning material: Does the game world depend on the learning? In fact, this kind of game design is quite commonly used in language-learning games. Kana Warrior, for example, is a combination of first-person shooter and the learning of Japanese characters (Stubbs, 2003). In this game, the game world is dependent on the language skill. The player must improve in the language to make progress in the game. Often, extrinsic games are regarded as not as good as intrinsic games. They are somewhat the same as conventional e-learning software: Learners are not learning the paidea rules or the narrative of the system, but something external — the textual description of the subject matter. This is rather similar to reading books; we are not learning how the book operates, but the contents in the book. However, an extrinsic game could be effective in making some boring aspects of language learning interesting, such as rote learning of Japanese characters. The key factors that make game-based learning appear more interesting than typical e-learning software are its paidea rules and narratives. It is made enjoyable by binding paidea and ludus rules of computer games and language learning with narratives, creating an imaginary learning space that is engaging and immersive. It is very much like inventing a new form of book, in which every turning of the page yields a more interesting experience to the reader. The paidea is made fun, but it does not help the learning process.

Theoretically, almost every genre of games from the industry — racing games, board games, action games and so forth — could be used for this purpose. Extrinsic game design can be used to develop language-learning games for spelling, character recognition and vocabulary that require memorization and repetitive learning. Extrinsic design can be characterized as drill and practice, in which learning is context-free. Games-based learning has the potential for motivating drill and practice by offering an environment in which learners actually enjoy repetition. To fully utilize this design in learning, the following measures are suggested:

1. Investigate the type of game that target users enjoy. If learners get no delight in the particular genre of the game, it will not be successful in motivating them.
2. Allow learners to switch off the game in the middle of playing. Although the game is used totally as an extrinsic motivation to attract learners, they might become interested in the subject matter and want to focus only on the learning content.
3. Provide strong narratives to create drama effect. Since the bond between paidea and the subject matter is rather weak, narratives are needed to reinforce the connection apart from creating drama effect.
4. The students must be familiar with the game's paidea rules. If the learner is unfamiliar with the game, the paidea rules must be simple so that the learning of paidea rules does not interfere with the learning of the subject matter.
5. Ludus rules must lead to the learning objective. Ludus rules should be stated distinctly and give guidance to the learner.

Narrative-Oriented Intrinsic Game Learning

Unlike extrinsic games, for intrinsic game design, learning contents are seamlessly integrated into either narrative or gaming mechanisms. Hence, intrinsic games provide two ways of learning as derived from the game model previously: narrative-oriented and gameplay-oriented. In narrative-oriented game design, players need to understand the virtual world, the event, the character and, most importantly, the story, in order to proceed. Like a book, the game mechanisms are trivial compared to the narrative mechanisms. The learning material is woven into the game as a story and, strictly speaking, the learning process is almost the same as for extrinsic games. Although the learning content is woven into a narrative context, the learning is explicit because the learners are shown the learning material in the form of text or graphics. Paidea rules merely define how learners should discover and read the material.

This differs from extrinsic game design in that it serves as a complete learning situation. This is most suitable characterized as a computer-based tutorial, in which information is designed to be presented in an effective and interesting way. Material is presented to the student in a narrative structure. This design is useful for learning the cultural aspects of a language by displaying pictorial or animated narratives of social settings, while reading skills could be fostered by exposing learners to textual narratives. In short, in this game design, the learning content or environment is designed as narrative, while paidea is for navigation. To fully utilize this design in language learning, the following measures are suggested:

1. Investigate what fantasy theme the target user is interested in. Narratives are crucial factors in this design. If the user does not like the fantasy theme the designer has chosen, it is likely that the design will be a failure.
2. The learning material is designed in the narrative context. The learning content is not presented as detached items of words or characters, but is connected to form a narrative.
3. The narrative should be able to stimulate the player to know what happens next. Curiosity is incited through the twist of narrative plots.
4. Goals are divided into several sub-goals to scaffold learning. Generally, the sub-goals are gradually presented to lead learners to the learning objective.
5. The control over the program is not as crucial as the control of the flow of the learning content.

Gameplay-Oriented Intrinsic Game Learning

In gameplay-oriented intrinsic games, players learn in a virtual world by interacting with the characters and events with languages. In this game design, paidea rules do not act as a simple interactivity that allows the player to discover predefined material. The learning material is embedded tactfully into the paidea rules of the game. This is used as a game design that prevails, as it demands active experimentation rather than observation, of its subject material. It is also a way to explore, to test models and hypotheses, and to construct and acquire new knowledge in a way traditional media never can. At the extreme end of an intrinsic game for language learning, it would be a computerized conversation game. In fact, a project has been undertaken to develop a language training game in a fully 3D virtual world. The character in the game would be able to respond to what the learner speaks via Natural Language Processing Parser (Johnson, Marsella, Mote, Viljhálmsson, Narayanan, & Choi, 2004).

While in extrinsic games, the learning material is read and understood, in intrinsic games, the learning is experienced. In this design, the game designers — rather than implementing the material for the player to experience — implement a system of parts that come together to form the material in the hands of the player. This design can be used for subjects that require logical thinking, where information is not fact-based but rule- or process-based, such as the grammar of a language. It can be attributed to simulation. This simulation, however, is different from scientific simulations. This design is narrative and context-based, rather than simulating a scenario such as the lab experiment that is not relevant to real-life experiences. It provides an enticing problem-solving environment where students play an authentic role, exploring at will, creating their own ideas of its underlying structure and synthesizing strategies, which reflect their understanding of this structure. To fully use this design, the following measures are suggested:

1. The game should have explicit goals. Unlike scientific simulations, which have no goals, this design should provide clear and unambiguous goals.
2. It should have a narrative theme. This is true for three types of design; as, without narratives, the learner will be just manipulating words and alphabets.
3. The games should be able to stimulate the player to know more about the mechanism of the system by giving clear feedback.
4. The control over the program is crucial. The interaction will determine how the learner observes and infers the rules of the system, which are also the subject matter.

Table 2 is the summary of game-based learning design.

Table 2. The summary of extrinsic and intrinsic game design

	Extrinsic	Intrinsic	
		Narrative-oriented	Gameplay-oriented
Paidea rules	Paidea rules are loosely linked with learning contents	Paidea rules define the navigation of learning contents	Paidea rules define the construction of learning contents
Ludus rules	Fictional learning objectives	Fictional learning objectives	Fictional learning objectives
Narrative	Narrative has little or no connection with learning	Narrative provides a context and contents for learning	Narrative provides a context for learning
Learning	Explicit, Context-free	Explicit, Context-based	Tacit, Context-based

An Analysis of Game-Based Language Learning with the Game Model

In this section, a theoretical view of games in computer-based learning is elucidated based on the game model and method of game-learning integration illustrated in the previous section. Two case studies are presented to demonstrate the implementation of "Slime Forest" in learning Japanese language, as well as how "Alien Language" is used for learning English, Spanish, French and German.

Case Study: Slime Forest

Slime Forest is a game similar to a role playing game (RPG) created to teach three sets of kana (Japanese characters). This is a summary of Slime Forest:

> *The game starts in a cave where the player is required to venture into the world outside to sell potatoes. The player will then be assigned, one by one, several sub-tasks and fight slime monsters in the forest to accomplish the tasks.*

The game features two complete sets of hiragana and katakana, and 200 kanji, the Chinese characters. The aim of this game is to create a learning environment that provides a fun way of memorizing these characters, which are usually learned in a classroom via rote learning. In addition, players are also expected to learn some words borrowed from non-Chinese foreign languages, written in katakana. The instruction of the game is in English; therefore, this game aims at English speakers who wish to learn the Japanese language.

Basically, there are two types of activities: the world, and the battle in which the learning takes place. In the world map, the player plays a role of the game protagonist and explores different locations, such as the cave and the castle. The player needs to gather information about various missions by talking to people in the game. In the forest, the player will get involved in battles to fight slime monsters by typing the Romanized pronunciation of a particular kana that appears on top of the monster. If it is answered correctly, the player gains a chance to attack. Actually, the ultimate goal of this project is to design a game for everyone, even for those who are not interested in learning Japanese.

We would like to examine the game and learning using the theoretical model of gameplay. Based on the definition of paidea and ludus, one can make learning Japanese a form of game by simply adding ludus rules; say, "Those who manage to write down 10 kanas the fastest win the game." In Slime Forest, users are more eager to learn the language because they have an interesting goal in mind: to kill the monsters, so they can progress in the game. However, adding ludus rules to a boring activity merely reduces the boredom. This form of game is not fun enough to engage learners for hours. What would have happened if the rules of "Who Wants to be a Millionaire" were reduced to answering the questions

Figure 6. Screenshots of Slime Forest (courtesy http://lrnj.com/sfa)

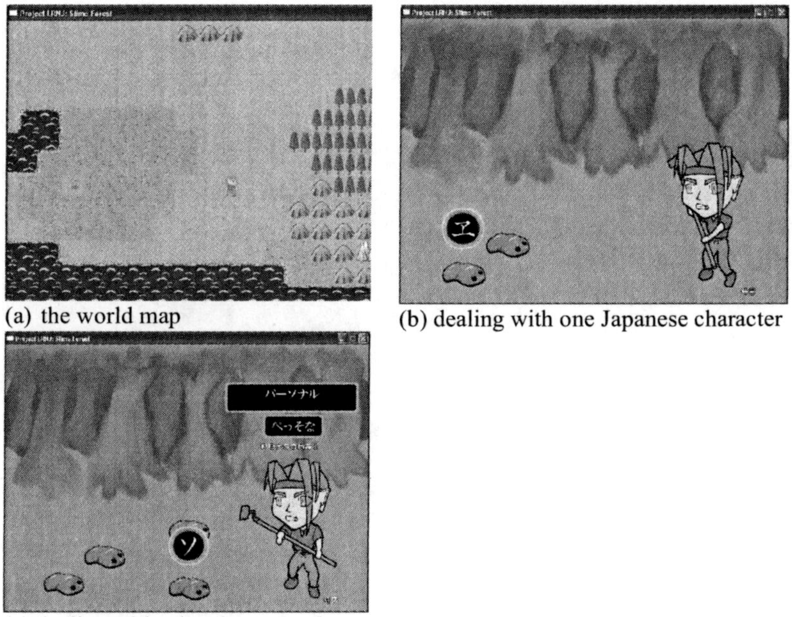

(a) the world map

(b) dealing with one Japanese character

(c) dealing with a katakana word

and wining $1 million without the "safe havens," "lifelines" and so on? Apparently, extra paidea rules are added to make the game really interesting.

It is noted that without the learning part, the game is a complete RPG game system (see Figure 7). The learning of Japanese characters is integrated, though in a loose manner, with the paidea rules of the battle system, resulting in a new form of gameplay oriented toward the ludus rules of the RPG. Besides, the integration of language learning and entertainment would not have been successful if not for narratives. The narrative in Slime Forest has at least two functions: to introduce fantasy learning goals (to fight monsters and save the princess) and to project the game as a complete virtual space with characters and events that retain the learner's interests. The narrative gives an explanation why players have to perform certain tasks. It is unlike certain educational software, in which the user is rewarded with a game playing session after completing learning tasks. By applying a well-integrated narrative, the learning and the game are bound together. Narratives also increase the urgency that pushes learners to complete the learning tasks.

It is concluded that the RPG game used in Slime Forest serves only as an external motivation. The integration of game and learning is extrinsic. It by no means aids the users in understanding the language. Some educators argue that games should not be used

Figure 7. Theoretical view of Slime Forest

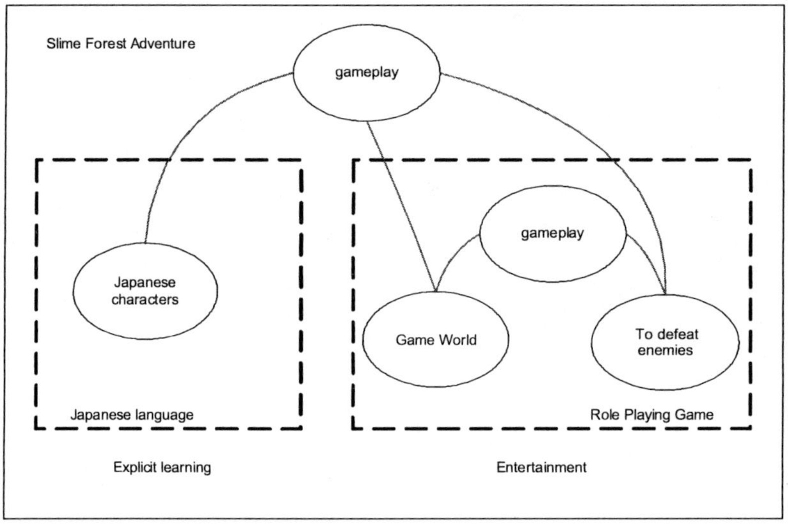

merely as means to motivate students to learn, and that play and learning must be mutually constitutive (Jenson, 2002). Indeed, learning should be made self-motivating, so learners are willing to learn it voluntarily. However, we should realize that not all aspects of language learning are internally motivating. Some are boring and difficult, and we need to help learners learn. In fact, if the learning was motivating, people may have learned them on their own and we probably need not put them in the curriculum (Prensky, 2001).

Case Study: Alien Language

Alien Language is a game distributed over the Internet used to support the teaching of "parts of the body" in four modern languages: English, French, Spanish and German. This is a brief summary of Alien Language:

> *The aliens are on a mission to collect creatures from around the galaxy for the alien zoo. You need to help them transport the creatures, label the specimens and cure the sick aliens.*

The motivation of this project is to create supplementary material for foreign language education based on a particular topic. The key aspects of language learning — spelling, grammar and sentence construction — are the focus of this project. The game can be used in many different combinations; for example, learning English for German speakers,

Figure 8. Screenshots of Alien Language (courtesy www.alienlanguage.co.uk)

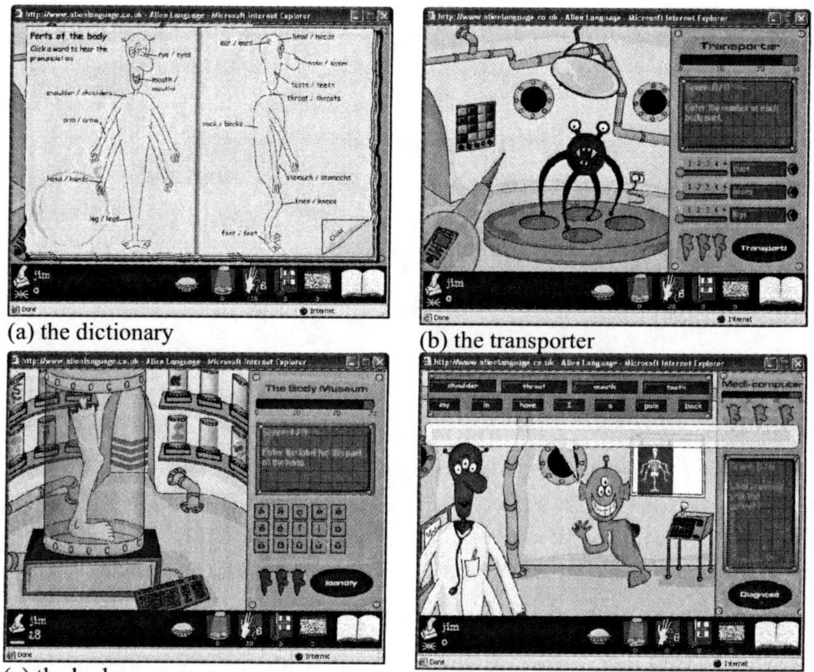

(a) the dictionary

(b) the transporter

(c) the body museum

(d) the hospital

learning Spanish for French speakers and so forth. It assumes that learners have known the basic vocabulary and sentences on the target language. However, if they need help, they can get a translation of the game instruction in their native language by pressing the control button.

Basically, the learners have three major tasks. First, they need to record the number of each body part the alien has and transport it to the alien zoo. Second, they will label the specimen in the museum by typing the name of a body part. Third, they need to construct sentences from a set of given words to identify the medical condition of the alien. The game includes a trivia game — resembling the popular "Who Wants to be a Millionaire" game — that tests the understanding of the learners. It also contains a simple dictionary of body parts.

One of the best ways of learning a language is to use it in daily life. When interacting with people, we are actively receiving what people say, reflecting the meaning in our mind and constructing sentences. Different ludus rules could be introduced to create different scenarios to the language learning environment, hence, creating a game-like learning activity. If we examine Alien Language with the game model, we could see that the learning is designed to be part of the paidea rules. Take the hospital activity, for example: It is actually a micro version of a real-life conversation environment, where the player constructs sentences from words, although the sentence construction activity is far less complex than the real-life conversation.

Figure 9. Theoretical view of Alien Language

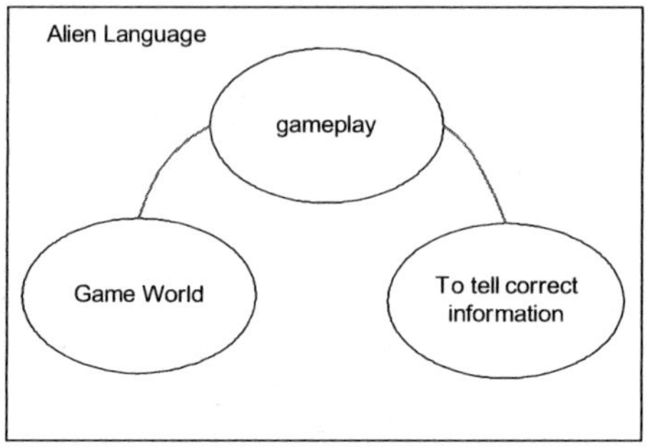

Figure 9 shows a similar gameplay model as shown in the previous section. No external learning material is imposed to this internal structure of game. The paidea rules of the game are, in fact, the grammar rules that the player needs to learn in order to proceed in the game. Predefined ludus rules exist for each activity: to construct a meaningful sentence based on a given context, to construct the word and to count the number of each body part correctly. The use of narrative is also obvious in this case. The game projects a fantasy space with imaginative characters. This creates a more experiential learning environment, as the learners are put in a role within the narrative space. The design is coupled with narrative so the learners are not just manipulating the words and grammar rules, but are solving context-based problems and overcoming challenges.

Unlike Slime Forest, the learning happens in Alien Language itself. The players learn to play the game, and at the same time, they learn the language. The learning happens internally in the game, as the learning content is an integral part of the game structure. It is a gameplay-oriented intrinsic game design. Instead of learning something external to the game, the learner of Alien Language plays an authentic role and carries out interesting tasks.

Cross-Case Analysis

The two cases are examined together to find out what elements differentiate them and what they have in common. The observation is done from two perspectives: ludology and narratology, to derive something about computer game designs for learning. First, it is noted that even if the language learning part is removed from Slime Forest, the game is still a complete RPG on its own. The language learning is superimposed on the paidea rules and can be easily changed to something else, such as answering mathematics questions. Therefore, paidea rules of the RPG are used to attract learners into the learning environment. For Alien Language, however, this is quite different, since the paidea rules are actually designed specifically for language learning. The learning contents cannot be swapped without significant modification of the fundamental structure of the game.

Table 3. Summary of cross-case analysis

	Slime Forest	Alien Language
Paidea rules	The learning material is loosely incorporated as part of the paidea rules of the RPG.	The paidea rules are carefully designed based on the target languages .
Ludus rules	Ludus rules are fantasy objectives, which are not related to the learning (killing monster has nothing to do with learning Japanese).	Ludus rules are fantasy objective, which are related to the learning (reporting illnesses is related to languages).
Narrative	Like paidea rules, the narrative serves no purpose in the learning. It merely makes the game appear more interesting.	The narrative presents a context in which learning takes place.

Second, both have clear and explicit ludus rules that bring about gameplay. The learning objectives are not stated explicitly as the learning of a language. Although both games use fantasy goals, such as defeating monsters and transporting aliens, the goals will eventually lead to language learning, since without leaning the specific language, the goals can never be achieved. Third, both games make full use of the narrative metaphor in designing the user interface. The games are designed as a fantasy world with narrative events. They also feature explicit characters that interact with learners to provide challenges: a fantasy narrative explanation of ludus rules. Some characters in Alien Language also give guidance to the learners regarding language contents. Actions taken by the learner in the game are conceivable and can be recounted as narratives. The following table summarizes the case studies.

Discussion and Future Direction

By studying ludology and narratology, we are able to derive something on how these theories are useful in designing language-learning software applications. It is maintained that computer game theories provide a better framework for designing language-learning software tools, making the experience of learning more immersive and engaging. Computer game-based language learning is expected to be better than its traditional counterpart from two perspectives: learning effectiveness and motivation. It is more effective in the sense that knowledge is constructed instead of being transmitted, especially for intrinsic game designs. It is also motivating, where it challenges the learners, intrigues their curiosity and brings about fantasy. However, an empirical study needs to be conducted to verify the advantages, and these results should help guide designers of educational games to consider how to effectively balance the demands of motivation and learning. Moreover, implementing game-based learning in light of language education needs detailed studies on the nature of language learning, which could be approached from linguistics, psycholinguistics and sociolinguistics. Each of these fields seems to pose an insightful view of language acquisition from different stands. We believe that the understanding of how a language is acquired and learned, either by an infant or an adult, might open up a new door for a more novel use of computer games in language learning.

Summary

We have analyzed two educational games from the perspective of ludology and narratology that explain two important types of game design in language-learning applications. In Slime Forest, computer games are used to attract the learner to learn a language aspect, while in Alien Language, the computer game itself becomes the learning activity. By analyzing both cases with computer game theories, we are able to understand them more closely, and thus derive a better principle of designing learning software based on computer games. Both extrinsic and intrinsic games are suitable for language-learning designs, although the latter is more desirable. It not only creates an engaging learning environment, but also an experiential one in which learners experience the knowledge first hand instead of being told.

References

Aarseth, E. (1998). *Allegories of space: The question of spatiality in computer games.* Retrieved March 2005, from www.hf.uib.no/hi/espen/papers/space/

Ang, C. S., & Rao, R. K. (2004). *E-learning as computer games: Designing immersive and experiential learning.* Pacific Rim Conference on Multimedia, Tokyo, Japan.

Barrett, M. (1997). *Irreconcilable differences: Game vs. story, Gamasutra.* Retrieved March 2005, from www.gamasutra.com

Crawford, C. (1982). The art of computer game design. Retrieved March 2005, from www.vancouver.wsu.edu/fac/peabody/game-book/Coverpage.html

Frasca, G. (1999). Ludology meets narratology: Similitude and differences between (video) games and narrative. Retrieved March 2005, from http://www.ludology.org

Frasca, G. (2001). *Video games of the oppressed: Video games as a means for critical thinking and debate.* Unpublished master's thesis, Georgia Institute of Technology.

Gingold, C. (2003). *Miniature gardens & magic crayons: Games, spaces, & worlds.* Georgia Institute of Technology

Jaron, L., & Biocca, F. (1992). An insider's view of the future of virtual reality. *Journal of Communications, 42*(4), 150-172.

Jenson, J. (2002, April). Serious play: Challenges of educational game design. *Proceedings of the AERA Annual Meeting,* New Orleans, LA.

Johnson, W. L., Marsella, S., Mote, N., Viljhálmsson, H., Narayanan, S., & Choi, S. (2004, June). Tactical language training system: Supporting the rapid acquisition of foreign language and cultural skills. *Proceedings of the STIL/ICALL 2004 Symposium on Computer Assisted Learning.*

Juul, J. (2002). The open and the closed: Game of emergence and games of progression. In F. Mäyrä (Ed.), *Computer game and digital cultures conference proceedings.* Tampere. Tampere University Press.

Lindley, C. A. (2002, June). The gameplay gestalt, narrative, and interactive storytelling. *Proceedings of the Computer Games and Digital Cultures Conference,* Tampere, Finland.

Malone, T. W. (1980, September). What makes things fun to learn? Heuristics for designing instructional computer games. *Proceedings of the 3rd ACM SIGSMALL Symposium and the First SIGPC Symposium on Small Systems.*

Morozov, M. N., & Markov, A. I. (2000, December). *How to make courseware for schools interesting: New metaphors in educational multimedia.* International Workshop on Advanced Learning Technologies: Design and Development Issues. IEEE Computer Society.

Murray, J. J. R. (1978). *A history of board-games other than chess.* New York: Hacker Art Books.

Prensky, M. (2001). *Digital game-based learning.* New York: McGraw Hill.

Ryan, M.-L. (1994). Immersion vs. interactivity: Virtual reality and literary theory, postmodern culture. *Postmodern Culture, 5*(1). Retrieved March 2005, from http://muse.jhu.edu/journals/postmodern_culture/v005/5.1ryan.html

Ryan, M.-L. (2001). Beyond myth and metaphor — The case of narrative in digital media. *The International Journal of Computer Game Research.* Retrieved March 2005, from www.gamestudies.org

Stubbs, K. (2003). E-learning: Kana no senshi (kana warrior): A new interface for learning Japanese character. *The International Conference of Computer-Human Interaction (CHI) 2003 Extended Abstracts* (pp. 894-895).

Chapter II

Culture-Based Language Learning Objects: A CALL Approach for a Ubiquitous World

Niki Lambropoulos, Centre of Interactive Systems Engineering, London South Bank University, UK

Martha Christopoulou, UK

Kosmas Vlachos, University of the Aegean, Greece

Abstract

This chapter presents culture-based language-learning objects (CLLOs) in computer-assisted language learning (CALL), supported by user-centered interaction design. CLLOs' design has been drawn on (a) social constructivist pedagogical theories, (b) self-organised strategies in social contexts, and (c) Scandura's structural analysis and Gange's instructional events. This chapter discusses culture-based language-learning principles and the rationale on which the construction and use of CLLOs are founded on. It also makes suggestions about the ways CLLOs can be constructed by second/ foreign language (L2) teachers. A CLLO example was designed and presented for the context of the Greek Diaspora in the United Kingdom (UK). Furthermore, this chapter introduces the combination of norm-based and culture-based language learning in CALL, the grey zone as the distance between second and foreign language learning, the open nature in Learning Objects with the use of forums or chats. Lastly, it suggests CLLOs networks use in the age of ubiquitous computing.

Introduction

Over the last few years, the possibilities for computer-enhanced language learning have been on the forefront of educational studies. There are two reasons for the increased interest in CALL: the fast-paced technological changes in recent years, and the new methods of teaching/learning languages, one of which is culture-based learning. Ubiquitous computing sees computers not as simple technological tools that facilitate everyday transactions, but as an integral part of contemporary life. One of the main principles of ubiquitous computing is that computers will not be more mobile than they are already, although the information will (Ziveldis, 2004). Hence, interoperability for systems accessibility could suggest new inventions for problems that already exist; for instance, communication among L2 learners. Self-directed learning in L2 environments lifts the barriers of time and space and facilitates the language teacher. Therefore, blended learning, which combines both online and off-line learning modes, can be an approach within the ubiquitous computing framework. Our proposal within the ubiquitous computing and CALL frameworks aim at (a) improving L2 learning, (b) enhancing communication, (c) supporting new forms of creativity and expression, and (d) providing an enjoyable and exciting L2 learning mode.

Taking into consideration that learning always occurs in social contexts (Vygotsky, 1978), the potential of CALL and the advantages of culture-based L2 learning as well as our experience in the Greek Language Classes (GLCs) in the UK, we decided to conduct a questionnaire survey to investigate learners' interests and needs. The questionnaire's findings helped us identify the objectives of CLLOs and, consequently, design an example of a learning object. The objectives of the proposed CLLO regarding scalable ubiquitous computing distributed systems are: (a) to enhance individualistic learning in the particular social context of GLCs; (b) provide access of language learning independent of time and space, and (c) support the design for networks that can expand and handle a growing number of devices, integrated into everyday life. Thereafter, in the proposed design, one part emphasises the theory and other examines engineering.

L2 Learning and CALL

Social constructivist theorists such as Bruner (1966) and Vygotsky (1978) view learning as a process in which students are actively involved and learn through interaction with their peers, assisted by teachers. However, the discovery of knowledge as such springs from their intrinsic motivation and personal past- and present-life experiences.

Kern and Warschauer (2000) claim that the foundations of the social constructivist language pedagogy in CALL and L2 learning have created teaching principles according to which the target language is acquired through both interaction among the learners via computer (the socio-cognitive perspective in CALL) and interaction between the learner and the computer (the cognitive perspective in CALL). Since learners view the computer as a tool of learning and a means of communication, the intrinsic motivational aspect of the computer is seen as an important quality of CALL. Furthermore, research has shown that the socio-cognitive applications of CALL offer learners opportunities to use the target language in meaningful situations. It has also been observed that in these applications, there is an increased language input and output as well as learners' active participation and self-expression (Vlachos, Athanasiadis, & Ganetsos, 2004). Finally, the social constructivist perspective in CALL has created principles, according to which:

- Learners may exhibit *behavioral changes* after being involved in CALL learning processes.
- *Process-based learning* is identified in the context of 'becoming' an energetic member of discourse communities. Mimesis of community members' language may lead to behavioral changes and language learning.
- *Social construction of meaning* occurs as a mode of *internalisation of simulated language forms of communication.*
- Internal reciprocity may result in *creative collaborative textual production.*

CALL applications, which foster the discussed principles, give learners opportunities to define their purpose, learning process and outcome, and reflect on and evaluate them using verbal reasoning. Furthermore, according to Lambropoulos (2004), self-organised learning by observation in social contexts (SOLOS) in CALL environments could occur in two levels:

1. Internalisation of social construction of meaning, via
   - self-observation that aims at the development of the learners' self-awareness regarding learning (Bekoff, 2002)
   - observation of the 'object' (Bandura, 1986). This helps learners enhance their understanding of the semantic and pragmatic aspects of the target language as well as its structure
   - perspective taking, mimesis of the language exemplified in the learning object (Auerbach, 1953)
2. Externalisation for outer self-explanation and self-expression via interaction (Lambropoulos, 2005).

Therefore, social constructivism and SOLOS may create an environment for active learning in which learners can become the constructors of their own knowledge, whereas the teacher has the role of the facilitator, who monitors the learning activities and offers guidance, feedback and support (Vlachos et al., 2004).

Culture-Based Language Learning and CALL

According to Sifakis and Sougari (2003), in many L2 contexts in the past, the norm-based approach was usually adopted. This approach was a rigid procedure, since the target language was mainly taught through specific linguistic rules that helped learners acquire an understanding of each linguistic system (usage), and little attention was paid to the function of the linguistic items in the system of communication (use). However, after the advent of the communicative approach in L2 learning, applied linguists claimed that language and cultural learning cannot take place independent of each other, because culture is an integral part of language and vice versa (Fengyan, 2002; Kramsch, 1993; Byram, 1994). Byram (1994) also states that only if the cultural context is understood can the target language be thoroughly comprehended.

The culture-based approach sees language as an instrument for communication among people and, at the same time, it shields learners from the negative effects of a norm-based approach, such as boredom, disinterest and repulsion (Sifakis & Sougari, 2003). According to Krasner (1999), linguistic competence alone is not enough for learners of L2. Due to the fact that language reflects the cultural values of a society, language learners need to know particular patterns of speaking behavior, such as the use of formal or informal types of questions/answers, associated with cultural behavior appropriate in the community of the target language. For example, they need to be aware of the culturally appropriate ways to address people, express gratitude, make requests and agree or disagree with someone. They also need to be aware of the differences between the language patterns appropriate in the different communities they belong to.

According to Hammerly (1982), culture-based L2 learning can cover three areas, by giving: a) information about the native speakers' society and history and geography of their country, so that learners can get a sense of the world view that native speakers have of themselves and their country (*information culture*); b) information about attitudes, values and so forth, so pupils can acquire particular patterns of speaking behavior associated with cultural behavior appropriate in the community of the target language (*behavioral culture*); and c) information about artistic and literary accomplishments, so pupils can acquire a complete view of the target culture and language (*achievement culture*).

Culture-based L2 teaching and learning could be implemented through CALL, as learners can be engaged in simulations with computer applications through role taking, working on meanings that have cultural associations and making inferences. The facilities CALL offers, such as sound, graphics and multimedia resources, may illustrate the socio-cultural context the target language has and give learners the opportunity to discover more about the target language and culture (Vlachos et al., 2004). Additionally, CALL applications can offer learners the chance to use synchronous and asynchronous online communication with native as well as other speakers of the target language. Thus, they can retrieve cultural and social information directly from native speakers, discuss topics of common interest and expand their knowledge on cultural codes and tolerable and intolerable patterns of verbal behavior in the contexts where the target language naturally occurs.

Based on both the flexibility and interoperability required in ubiquitous computing and on the complexity of the language-learning environment, the CLLOs approach may offer (a) practice in the structure of the target language; (b) information regarding the cultural background in which the target language is contextualised; and (c) the stimuli for individual engagement in the real classroom, online discussions or elsewhere.

Learning Greek as L2 in the UK: Current Practices

According to Karatzia-Stavliotis and Louka-Grann (1999), the majority of learners that attend GLC in the UK are Greek-Cypriot students who are children of second-, third- and fourth-generation immigrants. There are different degrees of language acquisition and use regarding the different generations of immigrants (Damanakis, 1998; Georgoyiannis, 1999). The tendency observed in most of minority communities, as well as the Greek-Cypriot community in the UK, is that in early childhood, children use their parents' mother tongue within the family or community. On the other hand, from the time they enter school and are introduced systematically to the language of the dominant group (English), they mainly start to use this. So, one of the main characteristics of the language of immigrants is that it lacks an immediate space of use (Damanakis, 1998). Lambropoulos and Christopoulou (2004) assert that it could be supported that the learning of the Greek language in the UK takes place in a 'grey zone' between the second and foreign language. They use the 'grey zone' metaphor to indicate the distance between the foreign and second language learning.

According to Karatzia-Stavliotis et al. (1999), the Greek-Cypriot students rely on English for their everyday communication, as it is considered by them to be a language of higher status. This happens because English is used in school exams and it will enable them to acquire upward social mobility. Anecdotal evidence from Greek school teachers shows that Greek-Cypriot students often express their apathy to learning the Greek language, since they perceive it as having no benefit in their lives. In many cases, they find it pointless to learn a language that will have a limited role in their future, especially when this language happens to not be the same one they speak at home. Still, the language Greek-Cypriot students are supposed to learn, if they want to preserve their home-country language, is Modern Greek, which varies from the Cypriot dialect in accent and grammatical and syntactical structure. The Greek language, the Cypriot dialect and the English language compose a 'linguistic triad' that could ideally enable students to build a network of linguistic possibilities on which they would draw upon. However, in practice, this creates more problems, because the students, who only partly speak the Cypriot dialect, feel confused by the different accents and dialects used by their teachers (Karyolemou, 1997). The 'mismatching' between the Greek-Cypriot and standard Greek dialects and the comparison between the two seem to be another impediment, since pupils feel that they do not speak 'proper' Greek and, as a result, they impose themselves into self-censorship.

Greek Diaspora is supported by two main types of educational provision for Greek-Cypriot students: the regular Greek schools and Greek Language Classes (GLCs)[1] (*Τμήματα Μητρικής Γλώσσας*). GLCs are community schools that operate in the afternoons or on Saturdays. According to Karatzia-Stavliotis et al. (1999), age ranges differ in the same GLC, as not all students start attending lessons at the same age; and, incidents of students' sudden interruption, as well as returning in the GLCs, are more than frequent[2] (Karatzia-Stavliotis et al., 1999). Thus, different levels of cognitive development can be found among students in the same class.

Educational materials, such as textbooks and other teaching resources, provided by the Greek and Greek/Cypriot states are not appropriate, because they:

- presuppose a specific language pre-acquisition level, which students most of the time do not possess (Luka-Grann, 1999);
- their authors do not take into account that students have already learned the English structure and grammar, which interferes when learning the grammatical and structural rules of the Greek language (Luka-Grann, 1999); and
- since the particular educational materials have been produced in Greece or Cyprus up to the date this chapter was written, they lack references to pupils' life experiences.

Moreover, they give priority to learning the structure of the Greek language. GLCs' curriculum ignores current trends in teaching and learning L2s that emphasise on helping learners to develop their communicative skills through purposeful and realistic tasks that are embedded in contexts similar to ones in which the target language is used (Kamberi & Vlachos, 2003).

The use of CALL in teaching and learning Greek in the Diaspora is not widely expanded, although it has the potential to create social networks and bring Greeks together. To our knowledge, only one online environment provides access to material and discussion forums regarding learning Greek language based on the theory of distributed constructionism (Zaphiris, Zacharia, & Rajasekaran, 2003). Another project called DiaLogos (Kourtis-Kazoullis, 2003) created asynchronous collaborations between schools in Cyprus, Greece and Canada. Two other projects are focused on e-learning and the use of social contexts as the background of communication: one by the University of Crete (Pedia Omogenon) and the OIKADE project (www.oikade.gr), supported by the Bank of Cyprus. These projects have tried to integrate online material and the use of online (synchronous or asynchronous) discussions. However, they are not based on scalable networks, and the context is independent of students' and teachers' needs and involvement in interaction design processes.

Identification of Users' Needs Suggestions: Discussion of the Questionnaire Survey Findings

Before designing CLLOs, we took under consideration previous CALL applications, constructivist theories, the theory of culture-based learning and the context of Greek Diaspora in the UK. Because the authors had some experience in the ways GLCs operate, they decided to investigate students' needs, interests and preferences towards learning the Greek language before moving on the design of the proposed CLLO. A decision was made to conduct a small-scale questionnaire survey, because this (a) allows generalisations, (b) is a rapid and easy method for collecting data, and (c) ensures anonymity and confidentiality (Bell, 1999; Robson, 1993; Cohen, Manion, & Morrison, 2000). It was anticipated that this kind of research could reveal learners' motivation and suggestions about the means and tools that could be used for learning the Greek language in GLCs.

As GLCs are spread all over London, it was decided to conduct the questionnaire survey in two districts. Turnpike Lane and Friern Barnet were chosen, because distances between schools were short and because one of the authors has worked there and it was easier to obtain permission from the head teachers for conducting the research. Moreover, students of grades five and six were selected, because they had some experience in the operation of GLCs, which could allow them to make suggestions for improvements in the learning procedure. The research was conducted between Sept. 29 and Oct. 3, 2004. Fifty-three students of a total of 61 of the sample population filled in the questionnaires, making a response rate of 87%. The questionnaire had three sections that elicited information about (a) respondents, (b) preferences in learning Greek language and computers, and (c) cultural and language learning.

Ninety-four percent of the respondents said they were born in the UK, and more than half of them (53%) said they were immigrants of third or fourth generations. Fifty-nine percent mainly used the English language at home, while 42% said they used both English and Greek. However, it was not possible to deduce from the findings how often or how well they used the Greek language at home, or to what extent they used mixed code (*switch-coding*) (Georgoyiannis, 1999).

Findings revealed that almost all students (98.1%) used computers at home. More than half said they used a word processor, chat and games, whereas 9.4% said they preferred only playing. Thirteen percent of respondents said they used MSN Messenger. That the vast majority of respondents said they were familiar with information communication technologies was encouraging. Moreover, the competence in the use of the computer and synchronous communication via the Internet could activate students to learn and use the target language both in the physical classroom and through distance-learning modes when they are at home.

Respondents also said that a computer-assisted and culture-based learning would be more interesting (49%) and useful (44%). Moreover, the vast majority (78%) believed that using computers in GLCs would make the lesson more interesting, while 25% said that learning the Greek language would be easier. It seems, therefore, that the use of technologies in the classroom may be motivating and may reduce the boredom that norm-based learning can cause. It also seems that well-designed collaborative activities may give students the freedom to express themselves using the different commands they have in the Greek language.

One question asked respondents to select whether by using computers they would prefer to learn about (a) only the grammar and syntax of the Greek language, (b) only the Greek/Greek-Cypriot culture, or (c) both. Thirty-four percent answered that they preferred to be taught both about Greek language grammar, syntax rules and Greek/Greek-Cypriot culture (arts, history and geography). It can be deduced, therefore, that these respondents recognised the need to be taught the structure of the target language in a contextualised manner so they would be able to use the structures taught in communicative situations. Moreover, because lessons in GLCs are too repetitive regarding their structure and content, these respondents seemed to believe that language learning could be enhanced by cultural learning, as it might be more interesting. More than half of the respondents said they preferred to be taught the cultural elements of the target language without any special attention to its form; that is, grammar and syntax. It seems that cultural knowledge appeared to be essential for these respondents because it can give them the opportunity to achieve the desired level of competence in the Greek language through computer-assisted and culture-based learning.

Respondents were also asked to suggest what they wanted included in a CALL environment. Forty-three percent said they wanted texts, images, sounds and multimedia, and 19% said they wanted only images. It seems that information about language or culture is better provided in different forms, as it may be more motivating for learning. Regarding the help and feedback students would receive in a learning procedure, more than half of respondents (54.7%) said they preferred the combination of teachers' support with automatic, immediate feedback from the computer. On the other hand, 18.9% suggested that they solely wanted teachers' help, while 15.1% said they preferred an automatic and immediate feedback. A significant ratio (11.3%) did not answer the question, which may indicate that these respondents were not sure about the mode of feedback they needed. The fact that students said they preferred use of the Internet (76.9%) and CALL (73.6%) means that CALL activities were preferred online. It can be deduced, therefore, that the dual form of feedback as well as synchronous and asynchronous communication with the use of wikis, chats and discussion forums could provide learners' an immediate space for communication. Finally, 74% of respondents wanted to have an opportunity to send their opinion to CALL developers and criticise the structure and content of the program so that developers can make useful changes.

In conclusion, the majority of respondents:

- recognised the need for learning the culture of Greek language in a communicative environment;
- were familiar with information communication technologies (ICT) and considered that they could be motivated by the use of CALL;

- preferred to receive help and feedback from their teachers in classrooms and feedback from the computers, and
- preferred to have personal online contact with the developers of CALL environments.

It can be suggested, therefore, that integrating cultural and blended learning into the L2 curriculum can motivate students to learn the target language and help them associate the language meanings, functions, structures and codes taught with the communicative situations in which these meanings are used.

Interaction Design for Greek Language in the Greek Diaspora

We attempted to integrate sociability (Preece, Rogers, & Sharp, 2002) and usability (Shneiderman & Plaisant, 2004) in the user-centered design for CLLOs as interactive entities. Bruner's (1966) constructivism, Scandura's structural analysis (2004) for grammatical and syntactical problems and Gagné, Briggs and Wager's (1992) instructional events underpinned the process and design. Structural analysis (SA) (Scandura, 2004) is a methodology used widely in mathematics, authoring tools and software engineering. Based on the minimum capabilities possessed by the learners, SA identifies the rules to be learned for a given topic or class of tasks by breaking them down into their atomic components. The latter is the one of the *learning object* (LO) principles. The sharable content object reference model (SCORM) (2000) suggests a standard definition of a LO: it is modeled as the smallest standalone and meaningful component of a course that is interoperable, modular and discoverable. LOs (Boyle, 2003) are reusable components in knowledge databases that provide flexibility in virtual learning environments for reusability, generativity, adaptability and scalability.

The suggested LOs principles are:

- *Cohesion*: Each unit should explain one thing and only one thing (Sommerville, 2000)
- *Minimised de-coupling*: Each unit should have minimal bindings to other units. The content of one LO should not be used by another LO. In addition, it should use elements that exist in a different LO in order to create necessary dependencies for indexation, based on the structure or function that is taught
- *Motivation* and *interdisciplinarity*: LOs should provide rich and effective learning experiences. The cohesive, decoupled and pedagogically rich LOs could offer the challenge for cross-curriculum activities (repurposability).

Structural learning prescribes teaching the simplest solution path for a problem and then teaching more complex paths until the entire rule has been mastered. According to Bruner (1966), learning is an active process in which learners construct new ideas or concepts based on their current/past knowledge. Bruner's theory of instruction addresses three major aspects:

1. predisposition towards learning,
2. the ways in which a body of knowledge can be structured so that it can be most readily grasped by the learner, and
3. the most effective sequences in which to present material.

Anchored on these propositions, we decided to use Scandura's SA for domain analysis and Gagné et al.'s nine instructional events to create a solid basis for examining the design of the CLLO. In addition, we took into account the findings of the questionnaire survey to establish the design. The events, which underpin the interface of each CLLO, were as follows:

1. Gaining attention (reception)
2. Informing learners of the objective (expectancy)
3. Stimulating recall of prior learning (retrieval)
4. Presenting the stimulus (selective perception)
5. Providing learning guidance (semantic encoding)
6. Eliciting performance (responding)
7. Providing feedback (reinforcement)
8. Assessing performance (retrieval)
9. Enhancing retention and transfer (generalisation)

Moreover, we took under consideration that the necessity of integrating language learning into everyday life demands interoperability between the needed cooperative systems. In ubiquitous computing, interoperability allows connections between the systems by using certain standards. Hence, the wide use of Extensible Mark-up Language (XML) metadata as a standard strategy allows the LO to be received in any Internet-based and mobile device. XML documents are human-legible and reasonably clear, and their design can be easily created and prepared quickly. Therefore, XML contributes to the change of the chaotic Web to a semantic Web. The semantic Web (W3C)[3] provides a common framework that allows data to be shared and reused across application, enterprise and community boundaries. It is based on the Resource Description Framework (www.w3.org/RDF/), which integrates a variety of applications using XML for syntax and URLs for naming (www.w3.org/). As a result, XML metadata allow the LOs to be connected to other LOs to create networks. Following Zaphiris et al.'s example (2003) for Greek language learning, we considered Participatory Design (PD)

(Resnick, Pontecorvo, Saljo, & Burge, 1997) preferable to other human-computer interaction (HCI) design approaches, because it focuses on the intended user of the service or product, and advocates the active involvement of users throughout the design process. As the project was not funded by any organisation up to now, PD is potentially integrated as an aspect of both sociability and usability.

In the search for problem definition and analysis, we followed the steps in SA (Scandura, 2004):

1. select a representative sample of problems;
2. identify a solution rule for each problem;
3. convert each solution rule into a higher-order problem whose solution is that rule;
4. identify a higher-order solution rule for solving new problems;
5. eliminate redundant solution rules from the rule set; and
6. continue the process with each newly identified set of solution rules (steps "c" and "d" are essentially the same as steps "a" and "b"). The result of repeatedly identifying higher-order rules and eliminating redundant rules is a succession of rule sets, each consisting of rules that are simpler individually but more powerful collectively than the ones before.

In order to set intention, gain attention, allow and enhance awareness, and activate information retrieval when teaching L2s, three factors need to be taken into account: (a) the topic areas to be included in the L2 curriculum; (b) the students' motivation for learning the target language and their perspectives toward the culture of the target language; for example, travel abroad, communication with relatives/friends, academic development; and (c) the ways the target language is used by native speakers, which may refer to social codes and formal or informal language. This last factor can provide basic criteria for narrowing the aspects of the target culture to be included in the curriculum by taking into account how native speakers' perceive a certain place (e.g., the Parthenon) or a historical event (e.g., October 1, 1960). According to Fengyan (2002), all the above factors are important for making decisions on the content of L2 curriculum. Students should be given background information so they will be able to incorporate the new information into their world view and work as anthropologists by exploring and understanding the target language and culture in relation to the language they use in their everyday life (Peterson & Coltrane, 2003). As such, cultural activities and objectives carefully organised and incorporated into sequences towards semantic encoding provide meaningful information to learners.

Semantic encoding and presenting stimuli need to be based on authentic material[4] and resources from the native community. Artifacts, films, photographs, literature and so forth can be used as sources of teaching materials. In the case of elementary students, who cannot cope with the complexity of the language of authentic materials, teachers can use semi-authentic material; that is, written or spoken texts that have the characteristics of authentic material but are adapted to the level of language of the students. In the particular CLLO, we used authentic material. Based on aforementioned theories and the survey findings, a prototype of CLLO was constructed. Next, we offer an example of a

CLLO for the Greek Diaspora in the UK, presenting the construction, indexation, packaging and delivery.

LLOs Construction

In most L2 learning contexts, the appearance of common mistakes — for example, in the use of the tenses, cases and so forth — may be used as a guide or map for the creation of learning-language objects (LLOs), which will aim at improving learners' competence in the language components in need of attention. Teachers can design LLO units if they, by using intelligent dynamic enquiry (IDE) methodology (Lambropoulos, 2004b), investigate and identify the common mistakes their students make. IDE is anchored in London and McMillen's work (1992) on a community development project. IDE is headed to result in a successful intervention based on the design of "what would be studied"; the process of inquiry, or "how the information would be collected"; and the interpretation of data, or "how they would make sense of what they discovered." IDE heads toward the articulation of a collective reality that encompasses individual views, problems, underlying causes of the problems and solutions suggested by members of an online community. IDE uses synchronous content management systems software for information tagging and works towards a dynamic structure, hierarchical clustering, non-stationary data learning and the parameter of self-adjustment, especially when data are related to time on the Internet. IDE's bottom-up strategy is needed for three reasons:

1. to identify common mistakes;
2. to suggest ways of helping students understand and correct their mistakes; and
3. to identify LOs' initial basis for indexation.

Since we are seeking a user-centered approach to establish a design, the recognition of patterns should have been coherent and systemised. As each class is a different situation, it is suggested that the teacher of a given class is the most appropriate person for identifying linguistic weaknesses students might have.

Interaction Design: Technical Issues on Building Multimedia CLLOs

The criteria of sociability and usability were anchored in learners' preferences, Scandura's SA and Gagne et al.'s instructional events as well as Boyle's (2003) suggestions for LO construction. The introductory page of our CLLO addresses the topic and informs learners of the objective (expectations). The design and colors are carefully constructed to gain attention without destruction. LOs by design require prior learning (retrieval) so they can be linked and work in a scalable network. The restricted number of cards in a LO and the use of cultural events aim to provide flexible learning guidance and selective perception based on learners' preferences in self-organised activities. The usability design suggested that:

- The size should be the maximum of 720x420 pixels for all monitors
- The navigation bar would better appear at the bottom, so the mouse does not cross over the CLLO
- The buttons for interactivity and information should be located either at the bottom and/or on the right panel. Information, in our opinion, should be limited to only what is necessary because of technical restrictions
- The maximum amount of CLLOs in both a LO and cluster is suggested to be eight
- The colors should not distract or interfere with the CLLOs, but should create a pleasant environment
- The interactive elements would better provide the learner with immediate feedback as well as with explanation and instructions
- A link for more information on the Web regarding the cultural phenomenon can be available
- A link for a discussion forum and/or chat in which learners can have the opportunity to consolidate and expand the linguistic item or language function taught can be available
- An online dictionary for students' reference can be available
- A CLLOs window button can be available

The immediate feedback learners may receive functions as reinforcement and, at the same time, offers opportunities for assessing performance. Discussion forums as social contexts are crucial for learners who may practice what they have learned from the CLLO in real interactions and communication, which reinforces communicative learning.

All media, such as text, sound, video and graphics, can be used to create LLOs and, specifically, CLLOs, provided that the CLLO construction is a one-goal-directed activity in relation to specific linguistic items, cultural codes or language functions. LOs should be arranged in a pre-defined indexation and metadata should be attached, based on the previous indexation. XML metadata can be attached to any kind of file; for example, ppt, doc, jpg, gif, html, avi, wav, simulation and so forth. Building interesting CLLOs is important, because we are dealing with two parameters: cultural and grammatical. Hence, the use of interacting properties with text, image and sound might be a better solution. A multimedia CLLO, technically speaking, needs an html environment to be integrated. The properties to consider are the language (use more than one language) and the design (i.e., size, navigation bar, spaces for the information and amount of information used, maximum amount of CLLOs in a learning cluster, colors and interactive elements).

LLOs' Indexation

Indexation is one of the most difficult parts when deciding the LLOs' design and construction. The suggested sequence of indexation in this CLLO is based on the grammar and structure of the modern Greek language, and it should make LOs searchable in a horizontal and vertical arrangement. As such, the sequence is the following: LOs, learning clusters, learning sets, learning units. Cultural indexation is suggested to take place following the cultural traditions in alphabetical order as well as chronological order. LLOs are one-goal-directed learning activities; for example, feminine, plural, nominative case. *Language-learning clusters* (LLCs) define a specific knowledge sub-domain; for example, cases in nouns. *Language-learning sets* (LLSs) refer to the domain (e.g., feminine nouns). *Language-learning units* (LLUs) describe the overall domain (e.g. nouns). We used the packaging that the European knowledge pool organisation ARIADNE has created.

LLOs' Packaging

LLOs' packaging is the final and equally important step of the procedure described above, because users can find the LLOs they are interested in by using keywords. Educational learning objects metadata approaches (EMD or LOM) can provide the best up-to-date wrappers. LOM generation can be achieved by using metadata software tools based on international standardisation initiatives, such as IEEE LTSC (http://ltsc.ieee.org), IMS (www.imsproject.org), ARIADNE (www.ariadne-eu.org) and CEN/ISSS (www.cenorm.be/isss/Workshop/lt). After issuing a query, XML description that fulfils the query can be downloaded for XML binding. We selected ARIADNE, which we were allowed to use free of charge, as it supports the creation of new metadata files, allows modification of existing LOM in terms of data and is valid in terms of data values (Sampson, Papaioanno,u & Karadimitriou, 2002).

LLOs' Delivery

LLOs' delivery can happen in two ways:

1. *The Internet,* preferably integrated in learning management systems. The latter could support blended learning requirements, coping with increased number of students, supporting communities of practice, and sharing and re-using different kinds of educational material and collaborative work. The use of XML supports CLLOs' delivery for mobile learning.
2. *CD-ROMs*. Language-learning units, sets and clusters as fixed lessons on CD-ROMs.

Having worked with the CLLO, the online/off-line teacher can ask students to find information about the art object(s) in question (Peterson & Coltrane, 2003). It is students' responsibility now to conduct research by using the clues given and submit their understanding in the online discussion group relevant to the specific CLLO. The findings of their research can be presented in the class online or off-line; for example, in the form of a written summary and/or by making an oral presentation in the classroom about the cultural relevance of the art object(s). According to Peterson and Coltrane (2003), these activities can serve for expanding the discussion about larger cultural, historical and linguistic factors that tie with the art object(s).

An Example of CLLO

A prototype of a CLLO that refers to the agreement between adjectives and nouns in the neutral, first case singular is presented below. The CLLO is titled 'The garland for the 1st of May' (*Μαγιάτικο Στεφάνι*). The suggested level is for grade four in GLCs. This could be used in a learning management system; for example, Claroline provided by the Greek University Network (GUNET, htpp://eclass.gunet.gr). In Figure 1, the interface provides the options of agenda, links, documents, video, students' exercises, announcements, users, forum exercises, groups, online chat and the description of the course.

The *learning subject* is Greek grammar. The *learning unit* refers to the 'adjectives.' The *learning set* is about the agreement between nouns and adjectives. According to Tsolakis (2000), adjectives agree with nouns in gender, singular or plural, and case. The *learning cluster* refers to the agreement between neutral nouns and adjectives. The *learning object* is about the agreement between the neutral nouns and adjectives in the nominative singular case.

The CLLO is tied with a specific tradition, which is common in Greece and Cyprus. Greek people celebrate the spring's coming by making garlands from flowers on the May 1. They hang the garlands at the front doors of their homes. The purpose of doing this is to derive energy from nature. In addition, students are shown a painting by Apostolos Geralis (1886-1983). The specific historical period and the influences of Western European art in Greek art can be also examined while students interpret the cultural context in which the artifact was made. In addition, students can be engaged in activities that will introduce them to the traditions, which are celebrated on May 1 in Greece and Cyprus as well as to the grammatical phenomenon examined. Since students and teachers will be

Figure 1. The Garland of May, Apostolos Geralis, 1886 - 1983

working in a blended learning environment, students can be asked to make a garland in their classrooms and search the Internet for relevant information. Moreover, they can be asked to find the significance of making garlands in other cultures, past or present. The findings of the research can be published on the Internet and/or presented in the classroom.

The specific CLLO includes a small text for the tradition of the garland in the Greek language, the painting, an example of the grammatical phenomenon as well as two exercises for assessment.

The Text and Exercises:

Το Μαγιάτικο στεφάνι το φτιάχνουν οι νοικοκυρές την παραμονή της Πρωτομαγιάς. Πριν τη δύση του ήλιου το κρεμούν πάνω από την εξώπορτα. Με αυτόν τον τρόπο καλωσορίζουν την άνοιξη.
Την επόμενη μέρα, όλοι μαζί με τις οικογένειές τους πηγαίνουν στις εξοχές για να γιορτάσουν την Πρωτομαγιά.

Greek housewives make in the evening of 1st of May eve a garland from flowers. They hang them on their front doors. In this way they welcome spring.
The next day everybody along with his/her family goes to the country to celebrate the 1st of May.

Άσκηση 1. Βάζω τις καταλήξεις στα παρακάτω: (Exercise 1: Add the suffixes)
Το μαγιάτικο στεφάνι
Το πράσιν... πάρκο
Το άσπρ... περιστέρ...

Άσκηση 2. Βάζω τις καταλήξεις στα παρακάτω: (Exercise 2: Add the suffixes)
Το λουλούδιν.... στεφάν.... που βάζουμε στην πόρτα του σπιτιού μας την Πρωτομαγιά καλωσορίζει την άνοιξη. Το κίτριν... λουλούδ... του Μάη, λέγεται μαγιολούλουδο στολίζει τα περισσότερα στεφάνια.

Θέμα για συζήτηση: Εσείς πώς γιορτάζετε την Πρωτομαγιά στον τόπο που μένετε; (Topic for Discussion: How do you celebrate the 1st of May in the country you live at the moment?)

Figure 2. Link for discussion forums

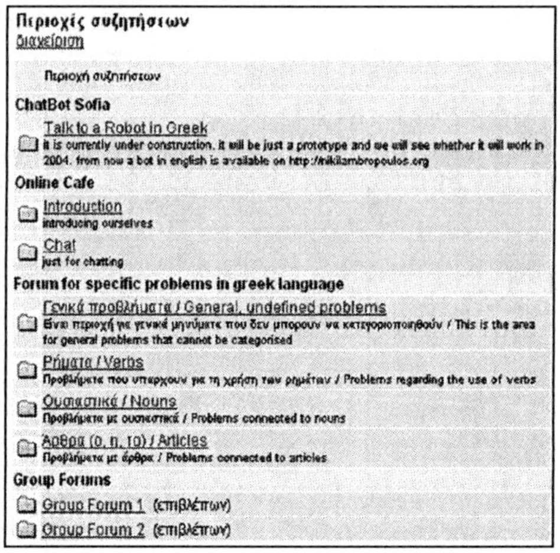

Figure 3. Introductory page

In Figure 2 students and teachers' discussions about the Learning Object will be part of both areas of the nouns or adjectives. The discussion forums are generated according to grammatical and structural phenomena. The use of wikis, chat and discussion fori is stressed as the provision of the immediate space of use.

An Example of the Design of a CLLO

An example for designing a multimedia CLLO is made in Figure 3 by Macromedia FlashMX.

Figure4. CLLO, page 3

Conclusion

The massive use of the Internet and computers has changed the way people communicate, work and learn in their everyday lives. Learning by using digital material in a self-directed and self-organised way, as well as the interaction with the environment and participation and collaboration within virtual learning communities, creates the brand new world of the 21st century. This chapter drew on theories based on these new complex parameters and sees culture as a factor that can enhance L2 learning. It appeared that in the Greek Diaspora in the UK, the majority of students who participated in the questionnaire survey recognised the need for learning the culture of Greek language in a CALL communicative environment. CLLOs can cater for communicative language use, as well as the learning of the structures of a target L2 in mixed-ability classes. CLLOs support students and teachers' online discussion about their design and construction and can identify the structure of important units. In addition, the online environment gives teachers the opportunity to share and reuse the findings of previous discussions/investigations and cooperate and collaborate for new CLLOs' production.

CLLOs' design has focused on the fact that it is essential in terms of L2 learning that learners can work on the structure of the target language and the CLLO can be followed by a free-language production stage. The combination of form and structure teaching with a free-language production stage aims at developing learners' accuracy and fluency in the target language. Further development is required, since this was the first attempt to construct CLLOs for teaching Greek as an L2. For the design and construction of LOs, a systematic inquiry into students' needs and common difficulties in learning the target language is needed. In addition, the cooperation and collaboration for interaction design researchers, teachers, linguists, curriculum developers, artists and multimedia designers is thought to be necessary for the production of high-quality CLLOs.

Acknowledgments

We would like to thank the team of ECLASS GUNET for providing the platform to facilitate our activities, which allowed us to work in the area of research for the Greek Diaspora; Erik Duval and Stefaan Ternier from ARIADNE for giving us access to Silo and their overall help and cooperation; Richard Hayens from Learning Technology Research Institute, London Metropolitan University, for his suggestions on CLLO development; as well as Spyros Themelis, Sophi Danis and Sara Martin for their valuable help and support.

References

ARIADNE. (n.d.). *European knowledge pool and silo*. Retrieved March 14, 2004, from www.ariadne-eu.org and http://rubens.cs.kuleuven.ac.be:8989/silo/

Auerbach, E. (1953). *Mimesis: The representation of reality in Western literature*. Princeton: Princeton University Press.

Bandura, A. (1986). *Social foundations of thought and action: A social cognitive theory*. Englewood Cliffs: Prentice Hall.

Bekoff, M. (2002). Empathy: Common sense, science sense, wolves, and well-being. *Behavioral and Brain Science*, *25*, 26-27.

Bell, J. (1999). *Doing your research project*. Milton Keynes: Open University Press.

Berners-Lee, T., Hendler, J., & Lassila, O. (May 2001). The Semantic Web. *Scientific American*, May. Retrieved April, 4, 2005, from www.sciam.com/article.cfm?chanID=sa006&colID=1&articleID=00048144-10D2-1C70-84A9809EC588EF21

Boyle, T. (2003). Design principles for authoring dynamic, reusable learning objects. *Australian Journal of Educational Technology*, *19*(1), 46-58.

Bricley, D., & Guha, R. (Eds.) (2000). *Resource Description Framework (RDF).* Schema Specification 1.0, W3C Candidate Recommendation. RDF Vocabulary Description Language 1.0: RDF Schema. W3C Recommendation, February 10, 2004. Retrieved September 14, 2004, from http://www.w3.org/TR/rdf-schema/

Bruner, J. (1966). *Toward a theory of instruction*. Cambridge: Harvard University Press.

Byram, M. (1994). *Teaching and learning language and culture.* Bridgend: WBC Ltd.

CEN/ISSS (n.d.). *European Committee for Standardisation*. Retrieved March 14, 2004, from www.cenorm.be/isss/Workshop/lt

Cohen, L., Manion, L., & Morrison, K. (2000). *Research methods in education* (5th edition). London and New York: Routledge Falmer.

Culture-based learning object. (n.d.) Retrieved March 18, 2004, from http://users.ach.sch.gr/nikilambropoulos/ODL/LO/CLO.html

Damanakis, M. (1998). *Repatriated and immigrant students' education in Greece* (original text in Greek). Athens: Gutenberg.

Fengyan, Ch. (2002). *Incorporating culture into foreign language teaching programmes.* Retrieved March 13, 2004, from www.eltexpress.com

Gagné, R., Briggs, L., & Wager, W. (1992). *Principles of instructional design* (4th ed.). Fort Worth: HBJ College Publishers.

Georgoyiannis P. (1999). *Aspects of intercultural education* (original text in Greek). Athens: Gutemberg.

Geralis, A. (1995). The Garland of the 1st of May (Oil on hardboard, 50X31.5). In *The Greek Sale III.* Athens: CHRISTIES & Benaki Museum.

GUNET. (n.d.). *Greek University Network.* Retrieved March 14, 2004, from http://eclass.gunet.gr

Hammerly, H. (1982). *Synthesis in second language teaching.* Washington: Second Language Publications.

IEEE. (2002). *Draft standard for learning object metadata.* Retrieved March 14, 2004, from http://ltsc.ieee.org/doc/wg12/LOM_WD6_4.pdf

IMS Global Learning Consortium. (n.d.). Retrieved March 14, 2004, from www.imsproject.org

Kamperi, K., & Vlachos, K. (2003). Teaching second/foreign languages using the task based approach and online networking. *Proceedings of the 1st International Conference in ICT in Diaspora, Hellenic Education Office of the Greek Embassy & Cyprus Education Mission* (pp. 17-31).

Karatzia-Stavliotis, H., & Louka- Grann, M. (1999). Greek language education in the U.K: Research Findings and considerations (original text in Greek). In M. Damanakis & Th. Michelekaki, *Greek language education in abroad.* Rethymno: E.DIA.ME (pp. 164-170).

Karyolemou, M. (1997). The Greek-Cypriot community in the U.K. (original text in Greek). In *Language education of the Greek immigrants in Europe* (pp. 71-77). Athens: YPEPTH & Greek Language Centre.

Kern, R., & Warschauer, M. (2000). Introduction: Theory and practice of network-based language teaching. In M. Warschauer & R. Kern (Eds.), *Network-based language teaching: Concepts and practice.* Cambridge, MA: Cambridge Applied Linguistics.

Kourtis-Kazoullis, V. (2003). Bilingualism and Information and Communication Technology (ICT). *Proceedings of the 1st International Conference in ICT in Diaspora,* Hellenic Education Office of the Greek Embassy & Cyprus Education Mission (pp. 18-31).

Kramsch, C. (1993). *Context and culture in language teaching.* Oxford: Oxford University Press.

Krasner, I., (1999). The role of culture in language teaching. *Dialog on Language Instruction, 13(*1-2), 79-88.

Lambropoulos, N. (2004a). Greek teachers' online community of practice: Life-long learning in practice. *Proceedings of the 11th International Conference of the Association for Learning Technology (ALT), Blue Skies and Pragmatism: Learning Technologies for the Next Decade* (pp. 102-103).

Lambropoulos, N. (2004b). Intelligent dynamic enquiry for innovation technology: Towards multi-agent systems. *Proceedings of the Artificial Intelligence and Applications, AIA 2004 as part of the 22nd IASTED International Multi-Conference on Applied Informatics* (pp. 183-188).

Lambropoulos, N. (2005, July 22-27). Sociability and usability for contribution based on situated informal learning and consensus knowledge building in online communities (Online communities panel discussion, organised by J. Preece) (in press). *Proceedings of the 1st Conference on Usability and Internationalization, in the 11th International Conference on Human-Computer Interaction,* Las Vegas, NV.

Lambropoulos, N., & Christopoulou, M. (Sept. 29-Oct. 3, 2004). Culture-based learning objects: A framework in Greek Diaspora. In M. Grigoriadou, A. Raptis, S. Vosniadou, & H. Kinigos (Eds.), *Proceeding of the 4th Conference in ICT in Education* (pp. 729-736).

London, A., & McMillen, M.C. (1992). Developing social issues: Organisation development in a multicultural community. *The Journal of Applied Behavioural Science*, *28*(3), 445-460.

Luka-Grann, M. (1999). Educational material for the Greek langauge learning as a second language: Effectiveness - suggestions (original text in Greek). In M. Damanakis & Th. Michelekaki (Eds.), *Greek language education in abroad* (pp. 273-277). Rethymno: EDIAME.

OIKADE Project. (n.d.). *Homeward bound.* Bank of Cyprus. Retrieved September 14, 2004, from www.oikade.gr

Pedia Omogenon. (n.d.). Laboratory of Intercultural and Migration Studies, University of Crete. Retrieved March 17, 2004, from http://ediamme.edc.uoc.gr/diaspora/

Peterson, E., & Coltrane, B. (2003). *Culture in second language teaching.* Retrieved January 26, 2004, from Eric Digest http://www.cal.org/resources/digest/0309peterson.html.

Preece, J., Rogers, Y., & Sharp, H. (2002). *Interaction design: Beyond human-computer interaction.* New York: John Wiley & Sons.

Resnick, L. B., Pontecorvo, C., Saljo, R., & Burge, B. (1997). *Discourse, tools, and reasoning*. Berlin: Springer Verlag.

Robson, C. (1993). *Real world research.* Oxford: Blackwell.

Sampson, D., Papaioannou, V., & Karadimitriou, P. (2002). EM2: An environment for editing and management of educational metadata. *Educational Technology & Society Journal*, ISSN 1436-4522, *Special Issue on Innovations in Learning Technologies*, *5*(4), 98-115. Retrieved November 14, 2004, from http://ifets.ieee.org/periodical/vol_4_2002/sampson_papaioannou.html

Scandura, J. M. (2004). *Structural learning theory: Current status and new perspectives.* Retrieved January 27, 2005, from www.scandura.com/Articles/SLT%20Status-Perspectives.PDF

SCORM (n.d.). Advanced distributed learning initiative. *Sharable Courseware Object Reference Model*, version 1.0. Retrieved January 31, 2000, from www.adlnet.org/

Shneiderman, B., & Plaisant, C. (2004). *Designing the user interface* (4th ed.). New York: Addison Wesley.

Sifakis, N., & Sougari, A. M. (2003). Facing the globalisation challenge in the realm of English language teaching. *Language and Education, 17*(1), 16-27.

Sommerville, I. (2000). *Software engineering* (6th ed.). New York: Addison-Wesley.

Tsolakis, T. (2000). *Modern Greek grammar for grades 5 & 6* (16th edition; original text in Greek). Athens: Publishing Books Organisation for the Greek Schools.

Vlachos. K., Athanasiadis, E., & Ganetsos, T. (2004, Sept. 29-Oct. 3). Online networking and the teaching of English as a foreign language to young learners: The "Euro e-pals project." In M. Grigoriadou, A. Raptis, S. Vosniadou, & H. Kinigos (Eds.), *Proceeding of the 4th Conference in ICT in Education* (Vol. A, pp. 419-424).

Vygotsky, L. S. (1978). *Mind in society*. Cambridge: Harvard University Press.

Zaphiris, P., Zacharia, G., & Rajasekaran, M. S. (2003). Distributed constructionism through participatory design. In C. Ghaoudi (Ed.), *Usability evaluation of online learning programs*. Hershey, PA: Idea Group Publishing.

Ziveldis, A. (2004, Sept. 29-Oct. 3). The 'invisible' technology: Pervasive computing. In M. Grigoriadou, A. Raptis, S. Vosniadou, & H. Kinigos (Eds.), *Proceeding of the 4th Conference in ICT in Education* (Vol. A, pp. 561-566).

Endnotes

1 According to the Greek Ministry of National Education and Religious Affairs, by 1996 there were 523 GLCs in the UK and 5,890 students attending them (cited in Georgoyiannis, 1999, 83-84).

2 Some of the students stop their attendance either because they do not like GLCs or because of the priorities they set in accordance to their English school academic activities.

3 The Semantic Web is an extension of the current Web in which information is given well-defined meaning, better-enabling computers and people to work in cooperation (Berners-Lee, Hendler & Lassila, 2001).

4 According to Fengyan (2002), authentic materials are taken from real life without being adapted, such as radio/TV programs, magazines, newspapers, maps of cities, postcards, train/bus tickets and so forth. These can give learners insights about native speakers' daily lives.

Chapter III

Situated Task Analysis in Learner-Centred CALL

Roderick A. Farmer, The University of Melbourne, Australia

Abstract

This chapter describes the modelling of learner interaction in computer-assisted language learning (CALL) environments. Here, I call for the development and adoption of situated task analysis frameworks in CALL system design and evaluation. The integration of existing CALL, human-computer interaction (HCI) and software engineering techniques constitutes a primary concern for the future of CALL software development. As such, this chapter describes the application of learner-centred design and situated task analysis principles within a flexible and integrative meta-framework: Cognition, Activity, Social Organisation and Environment (CASE). Finally, this chapter demonstrates how application of the CASE framework in CALL contexts leads to the development of more fit-for-purpose and personalized CALL systems.

Introduction

User-centred design (UCD) refers to a myriad of development approaches that emphasize the centrality of user involvement in the development process. Although system design improves when researchers and developers possess a mutual understanding of how users actually use technology (Costabile, 2001; Nardi, 1996a, 1996b; Raeithel & Velichkovsky, 1996), designing well is deceptively complex. This complexity is magnified in CALL contexts: language learning is socially situated and settings vary widely; learners are cast as *novices*; and novel activities abound. Learners themselves may have difficulty describing their experiences with the CALL system (Hémard, 1999) and, indeed, may have differing perceptions of the technology's purpose and meaning depending on the context of use (Gasson, 1999). Hence, creating systems that are *fit-for-purpose* represents a significant challenge to the CALL community.

In this chapter, I critically examine the role of UCD in the context of CALL system design and evaluation. Specifically, I present Learner-Centred Deisng (LCD) as a theoretical and practical alternative to traditional UCD practices. In opposition to the behavioural view of HCI, I promote the need for more *situated*, sociocultural task analysis frameworks for examining learner-computer interaction. Furthermore, I describe the relevance and benefits to CALL of such frameworks when coupled with LCD approaches. This chapter concludes with an exposition of CASE (Farmer & Hughes, 2005a, 2005b), a meta-framework for conducting situated task analysis in CALL system design and evaluation.

User-Centred Design in CALL

Good system design results in technologies that can be used *effectively* and *efficiently* both physically and cognitively (Preece, Rogers, Sharp, Benyon, Holland, & Carey, 1994). A major challenge in the early stages of design is to understand and integrate actual learner behaviour into the software development life cycle (SDLC). Researchers recognise that the need to support existing work practices demands more than simple accounts of a single individual's perception of some *task*[1] (Ackerman, 2000; Gasson, 1999; Bardram, 1998; Bellamy, 1996; Watts & Monk, 1998). Indeed, situating the users' actions within the context of social human praxis has the potential to reshape perceptions of Human-Computer Interaction. To this end, research in CALL is witnessing a transitional shift away from cognitivist 'communicative' CALL (involving drill-and-practice exercises that focus on accuracy and fluency) towards more sociocultural, 'integrative' CALL activities (that address the importance of *agency*) (Gruba, 2004).

Low-level, (cognitive) task-oriented frameworks tend to treat task interaction as a series of linear, sequenced *actions* from which we can derive the sense of an activity and inform system design. High-level, (social) goal-oriented frameworks tend to focus on *situation awareness* rather than on actions. Prominent frameworks within this paradigm include Soft Systems Methodology (Checkland, 1981, 1999), Activity Theory (Leont'ev, 1978, 1981; Engeström, 1987, 1999; Nardi, 1996c), Scenario-Based Design (Carroll, 1994, 1996,

1997, 2000, 2002), Distributed Cognition (Hutchins, 1995a, 1995b; Hollan, Hutchins, & Kirsch, 2001), Situated Action (Suchman, 1987; Bardram, 1998; Lave, 1998) and Cognitive Work Analysis (Vicente, 1999). Collectively, these approaches can be classified as *situated task analysis* frameworks.

Despite this transition towards more situated frameworks, task analysis and UCD principles in CALL continue to focus on traditional cognitivist models of interaction and associated criteria, such as task performance, ease of use and ease of learning (Diaper, 2004; Preece et al., 1994). There is increasing consensus within the HCI community that purely cognitively grounded task analysis methodologies are ill-equipped to capture, model and evaluate computer-mediated activities as they exist within sociocultural communities of practice (Carroll, 1996; Quintana, Carra, Krjcik, & Soloway, 2001). This problem is central to CALL system quality and is commonly referred to as the "social-technical gap" (Ackerman, 2000). Integrative task analysis methodologies capable of addressing both cognitive and sociocultural perspectives in learner-computer interaction are central to overcoming this widening gap within CALL environments.

Developing CALL tools involves design and evaluation of complex systems. Systems are categorised as *complex* due to emergent behaviours and patterns resulting from subsystem interactions and relationships. Complex systems also possess three additional key attributes: openness, accessibility and non-linear relationships. First, information flow and interactions between subsystem boundaries in complex systems are dynamic and in constant flux (openness). Second, elements of the system are restricted to a limited view (or knowledge) of the system as a whole (accessibility). Third, relationships between elements are non-linear, limiting reductionist discussions of cause-and-effect mechanisms in system design and evaluation. Therefore, designing and evaluating CALL systems cannot be reduced to a static, hierarchical, behavioural representation. Rather, more integrative and situated approaches are required (Ackerman, 2000; Bardram, 1998).

Situated task analysis frameworks support the dynamic and emergent nature of social interaction. With the importance of the user being central to the design process, situated task analysis frameworks provide (1) assistance eliciting requirements for effective learner-computer interaction in complex social environments; and (2) provide a way to evaluate how language learning activities unravel *in situ*. Learner-computer interaction can not simply reply on individual user accounts of interaction, rather, it needs to be concerned with problems of participatory construction of learning materials and environments (Bødker, Petersen, & Nielsen, 2000; Crabtree, 1998; Schuler & Namioka, 1993), and impact analysis of shifts in contextual conditions upon human praxis (Beyer & Holtzblatt, 1998, 1999; Holtzblatt & Beyer, 1993).

Faced with the challenges of constructing computer-supported collaborative learning systems, 'integrative' CALL developers, therefore, require an understanding of how people learn in groups and within specific communities of practice. Ideally, such learning systems should support authentic, socially, culturally and historically relevant learning activities (Chapelle, 2001). Progress in this area is, however, limited by several challenges. Learning is highly fluid, non-deterministic and nuanced, requiring extensive negotiation, synchronization and mutual awareness (Hoven, 1999; Ackerman, 2000; Suchman, 1987; Watts & Monk, 1998). According to Lave (1998), these learning traits imply that knowledge is implicitly distributed among all participants in some community ofpractice. Moreover, many salient features oflearner-computer interaction emerge from tool-mediated activity.

One prominent feature is *expertise*, and is especially relevant to CALL environments in which language learns can be modeled as cyclically passing through levels of novice-expert behaviour. First, as learners become increasingly familiar with the system tools, their expertise is likely to grow to a point where previous cognitively demanding tasks become automatic and unconscious through habituation (Bellamy, 1996). Additionally, expert system users are likely to employ a wider range of strategies for completing a task than novice users (Hémard, 1999). As learners gradually acquire second-language competency, the tasks presented should increase correspondingly in complexity (Nunan, 1989; Robinson, 2001). However, this increase in task complexity and learner expertise is likely to affect learner-computer interaction in decisive ways (Farmer, 2005), including focus on form, divided attention and other properties traditionally associated with *usability*, including comprehension, learnability, operability, attractiveness (of task) and compliance (of technology with task demands) (Costabile, 2001). For instance, an attendance rise in task complexity coupled with an increase in tool familiarity could reduce a learner's own perceived level of expertise, negatively impacting motivation and, therefore, goal-oriented behaviour.

Learner-Centred Design (LCD)

CALL and HCI share similar interpretations of LCD. On the one hand, CALL views of LCD have been linked to the importance of self-managed individual learner strategies (Hoven, 1999). As noted by Chapelle (1994), the context of learning and the nature of collaboration between learner agents (human-human interaction) and artefacts of the environment (human-system interaction) impact the production of language in CALL environments. Similarly, Hoven (1999) sees language production as a combination of (agent) *negotiation* (artefact-tool), *mediation* and (agent-artefact) *interaction.* Because these characteristics comprise both cognitive and sociocultural orientations, task analysis in LCD requires an integrative approach (Kumaravadivelu, 1983).

Incorporating a constructivist perspective of learning (Vygotsky, 1986; Lave & Wegner, 1991), LCD promotes individuality and learning potential. This corresponds to current trends in 'integrative' CALL that focus on increasing levels of learner-autonomy and agency (Blin, 1999; Gruba, 2004). Interpreting Hoven (1999), an approach to LCD in CALL should incorporate:

- sociocultural accounts of learning activities;
- recognition of salient task features within the activity;
- support for increased *situation awareness* and autonomous-learner control strategies; and
- task-based design of Second Language Acquisition activities.

On the other hand, HCI perspectives of LCD focus on the specific needs of learners (Brna & Cox, 1998), including identifying those traits that distinguish a learner from a typical user (Quintana et al., 2001; Soloway, Guzdial & Kay; 1994; Soloway et al., 1996). From an HCI perspective, three key characteristics differentiate learners from users: *expertise*, *motivation* and *engagement*[2]. Within HCI, the LCD paradigm attempts to characterise learners according to their expertise in some work practice, and how learners acquire meaning through situated interaction. For instance, language learners are unlikely to develop a high degree of *expertise* in CALL contexts (although this is certainly a goal), as they are frequently exposed to new terminology, changing activities and varying relationships with their peers and local experts. That is, they maintain either a partial or naïve internal representation of the work they try to perform (Quintana et al., 2001). As learners gain experience and expertise in their practices, however, they are likely to demonstrate a higher awareness of goals within the activity. Further, they demonstrate a wider range of metacognitive strategies during computer-mediated activity (Velichkovsky, 1990).

Second, *motivation* is a key affective component of language learning that affects working, procedural and declarative memory systems (Ellis, 1996). Learners are exposed to competing motivations that, if in conflict, may temporarily or permanently impede motivation for some activity. Therefore, a clear design consideration in LCD is providing motivational support during learner-computer interaction.

Third, it must be understood that learners are constantly being asked to *engage* in novel activities, demanding them to gain experience within a possibly foreign work practice. Hence, system design in CALL must grow and adapt to changing interaction strategies as learners gain experience and knowledge. It is now apparent that both perspectives converge through their advocacy of socio-cultural approaches for analysing learner activity.

Learners seek to come to terms with constructing meaning through contextual interaction, self-regulation and reflection. By engaging in an activity, they produce meaningful reconstructions of interaction. Learning is not merely a process of *stimulus and response* that can be quantitatively measured; rather, it involves producing and reproducing cognitive, social and cultural constructs. Culture transforms our activities and social artefacts, and our human praxis reproduces and transforms tools and culture (Farmer & Gruba, 2004; Hollan et al., 2001).

Given our premise of *expertise*, *motivation* and *engagement*, LCD in CALL requires a more appropriate framework for conducting task analysis in learner-computer interaction than is currently afforded by traditional cognitivist task models. As such, future approaches to LCD in CALL must be:

1. Context sensitive;
2. Focused on situated activities framed within a cultural-historic view;
3. Purposeful, motivated and goal-oriented; and
4. Aware of the dynamic flow of information during computer-mediated activity.

Such criteria suggests that task analytic techniques employing LCD principles should explicitly represent the various components that make up a learning activity; represent the relationships (communicative and labeled — such as roles) between actors and artefacts; and capture the *expert* knowledge required by novices in order to participate in the activity (Quintana et al., 2001). This is not a simple task, as the mere integration of new technologies into existing learning environments can cause new tasks, relationships and meanings to emerge (Carroll, Kellogg, & Rosson, 1991).

At present, LCD can be seen as a metaphor for describing principals for investigating learner-computer interaction in CALL. To provide a more rich and detailed account of CALL system design and evaluation, a methodological formulation is required. Developing a robust, flexible and socially oriented task analysis framework is vital to achieving this objective.

Situated Task Analysis

Simply stated, the aim of a task analysis framework is to produce a reliable and procedural account of work for which there is some well-defined practical application. It encompasses the notion of *task* and, as such, represents the specific set of actions that the user may undertake in a goal-directed activity. Task analysis may involve task identification; data collection and analysis; requirements elicitation, analysis and specification; error identification; system design; and process evaluation (Table 1). The type of investigation and context in which a study occurs are crucial determinants in choosing between existing frameworks.

A broader conception of task analysis would seek to establish how people, through the use of socio-technical artefacts, achieve their work goals. This definition applies to both existing and *future* systems (Kieras, 2004). This is an important feature, as many existing task analysis methodologies require an existing system be of any real value (Balbo, Ozkan, & Paris, 2004). Furthermore, the goal-oriented view of task analysis, rather than the cognitive task perspective, is appropriate within CALL system design, as it

Table 1. Key common objectives of task models

Objective	Purpose
To inform	To inform users and designers about potential problems. Common themes involve needs analysis, usability and affordance.
Evaluation of human performance	To establish the impact of new or existing tools upon task performance in some work practice.
System design support	To provide a detailed and structured conceptual model of the task, including behavioral (time, errors, feedback, etc.) and structural modeling (functionality, visibility, etc.).
System generation	To help develop prototypes, user interfaces and elements of the system architecture.

Table 2. Essential components of an integrative task analysis framework

Requirement	Description
Notation system	A common, accessible and formalized notation system, facilitating conceptual modeling and communication of knowledge across interested parties (Balbo et al., 2004; Erickson & Kellogg, 2001)
Proven methodologies	Flexibility in its ability to adopt proven methodologies rather than constantly reinventing the wheel (Whittaker, Terveen, & Nardi, 2000)
Cost-effective practices	Cost-effective practices so as to encourage HCI practices in system design by increasing the *Return on Investment* (ROI) (Stanton, 2004)
Ease of Use	Sufficient express power and a low degree of complexity of use to encourage uptake of the framework by novices and experts in the domain of interest (Balbo et al., 2004)
Whole-of-Lifetime	An ability to be applied across the SDLC, providing integrative mechanisms for inclusion in rigorous software engineering mechanisms (Farmer, Gruba & Hughes, 2004; Costabile, 2001; Flor & Hutchins, 1991; Kazman, Abowd, Bass & Clements; 1996; Sanderson, 2003, Carroll, 1995, Rosson & Carroll, 2002)

corresponds to our previous position that pedagogic tasks must be directed towards some objective, purposeful and motivated outcome.

Despite general agreement that cognitive task analysis frameworks are not appropriate for analysing socially constructed activities (Carroll et al., 1991), post-cognitivist theorists have yet to agree upon the most promising alternatives (Kaptelinin, 1996b). Requirements for constructing an integrative framework capable of modelling cognitive and social phenomena are presented in Table 2. The need for integrative frameworks is especially relevant to CALL practitioners if our goal is to build upon research and not simply technology. Therefore, we need the ability to incorporate and model existing CALL theories and practice (Hubbard, 1992, 1996; Stevens, 1989). At the heart of the post-cognitive, or situated, movement is the search for ecological validity in task analysis of computer-mediated activities. Further, there is a need to know how we can best come to understand task interaction within a larger context than is currently afforded by the cognitivist view (Neisser, 1976).

Situatedness implies that the phenomenon under investigation is situated *within* a spatio-temporal frame of reference. Distinctly an ecological perspective, the term *situatedness* realises the interdependent relationship between context and tool-mediated activity. Situatedness plays a significant role in the construction of learner-centred design methodologies in CALL, as it helps the practitioner focus on how individuals learn to participate with communities of practice, and how their development is shaped by the activities in which they engage. Activities cannot simply be stated or solved by reducing interaction to discrete, static task models (Moran & Carroll, 1996). As learner-computer interaction is typically socially oriented, it follows that design must also be seen as situated (Gasson, 1999).

Situation Awareness

Situation awareness, as described by Erickson and Kellogg (2001), is an understanding of social norms and rules, as well as the immediate state of knowledge about the context, situation and environment in which an activity takes place. Moreover, in collaborative activities, it is possible to view situation awareness as being distributed among individuals and, thus, actionable only within the context of a community of practice (Gasson, 1999). For instance, simply providing similar content and functions to a learner through a CALL system does not guarantee learning, as the learner has the goal of locating the information within his or her current real-world frame of reference (Albers, 1998). Rather, learning is situational, the context essential to comprehending the specific concept at hand (Lave & Wegner, 1991).

Situation awareness does not refer to the actual process of acquiring knowledge; rather, it represents the end result of invoking any number of cognitive and meta-cognitive processes during active participation in a practice (Endsley, 2000). Situation awareness requires that the individual maintain an awareness of the activity as it continuously unfolds *in situ*. According to Endsley (2000), situation awareness entails:

1. Perceiving relevant contextual information;
2. Understanding how the roles and relationships between participants in an activity impact information presentation and comprehension; and
3. An ability to use social cues to assist in planning for future events.

Additionally, Albers (1998) argues that the quality of an individual's situation awareness is governed by an ability to *comprehend*, *integrate* and *reconstruct* new information. This three-step process involves (1) extracting the relevant basic information from the task/activity; (2) integrating the information into the individual's conceptual understanding of the problem; and (3) subsequently generating new rules and beliefs so as to extrapolate the information into future problem-solving situations.

As situations change and new information presented, the learner's awareness of emerging conditions (including new tasks) likely to impact effective participation in the activity, must *a priori*, adapt. Determining the requirements for supporting social processes in CALL system design requires a constant evaluation of system use, including a cyclical process of communicating and validating findings with end users — notably, language learners (Bødker, Grønbæk, & Kyng, 1993).

Experience, goals and motivation are interdependent constructs that produce localised expectations about situated action and, as such, influence situation awareness (Endsley, 2000). Expectations are influential in the division of attention during learner-computer interaction. Expectations primarily act as a selection mechanism, reducing the *resource pool* of cognitive processes available to efficiently respond to new information from the environment (Robinson, 2001). Experience is also influential in the development of automation. Habituated or automatic actions are less cognitively demanding than conscious actions and, thus, require less attention during task interaction. Expert CALL system users, therefore, are expected to demonstrate *better* language-learning skills than novices. Through experience, expert users are likely to have developed greater responsiveness and efficient strategies for overcoming *breakdowns* during interaction (conflicts and contradictions), requiring fewer cognitive resources when automatic actions are brought into consciousness (Engeström, 1999; Endsley, 2000).

Finally, acquiring good situation awareness of some activity does not imply good *task* performance. Situation awareness is a probabilistic construct, making improved performance more likely, yet not assured.

CASE: A Situated Task Analysis Framework for CALL

One of the major challenges facing HCI research in CALL today is the need to integrate existing task analysis methodologies and tools within a holistic system design framework (Kaptelinin, 1996a). CASE is a meta-framework that supports our previously elicited learner-centred design principles (Farmer & Hughes, 2005a, 2005b). The principle aim of the following discussion is to introduce and elucidate this theoretical framework with respect to CALL system design and evaluation, and to describe a minimal set of methodological resources and tools that can be applied within the CASE framework.

Key Principles of CASE

The CASE meta framework is based on the modelling of four key aspects of learner-computer interaction, namely *cognition, activity, social organisation* and *environment* (Farmer & Hughes, 2005a). As such, it is an integrative, descriptive model for analysing, modelling and evaluating learner-computer interaction within complex, dynamic environments. CASE supports a plurality of methodological approaches and, therefore, is flexible, extensible and adaptive to changing contexts. Existing methodologies that can be applied within CASE include: Activity Theory (Leont'ev, 1978, 1981; Engeström, 1987, 1999); Scenario-Based Design (Carroll, 1995, 2000); Cognitive Work Analysis (Rasmussen, Pejtersen, & Goodstein, 1994; Vicente, 1999; Sanderson, 1998, 2003); and various software engineering methodologies, such as the Unified Modelling Language (UML) (Rumbaugh, Jacobson, & Booch, 1999). This practice of methodological reuse avoids the cycle of *radical invention*, which sees the necessity of developing new frameworks to the detriment of a common research focus (Whittaker et al., 2000).

The goal of CASE is to qualitatively improve CALL system design and evaluation. Improving system quality is the result of a range of holistic, context-specific processes and practices that requires correct and unambiguous elicitation and specification of stakeholder requirements (Farmer et al., 2004). Effective requirements engineering demands a robust, adaptive and integrative framework for conducting task analysis and communicating findings throughout the software development life cycle (Balbo et al.,

Table 3. Key LCD criteria in CASE

Principle	Purpose
Negotiation	Concerned with examining conflict within an activity and is essential to understanding degradation in shared-knowledge representation, goal structures and subject motivation (Engeström, 1999). Required for resolving interpersonal and structural conflicts (such as conflicting goals, affordance and embedded cognition). Within the sociocultural paradigm, this process is known as a *breakdown*, which from a situated learning perspectives is seen as a crucial learning opportunity that should be manipulated rather than avoided (Vygotsky, 1986; Leont'ev, 1978; Lave & Wegner, 1991; Engeström, 1999).
Motivation	Central to learner-computer interaction as it dictates to a large extent the nature of the activity itself and the marshalling of appropriate cognitive resources (Robinson, 2001). In collaborative environments, understanding the existing motivational forces (individual and social) greatly contributes to our knowledge of the learning practice (Donato & McCormick, 1994; Nardi, 1996b).
Cooperation and Coordination	Closely linked to work practice synchronization and mutual awareness (Watts & Monk, 1998). Understanding these factors assists with understanding the dynamic nature of individual roles and relationships between actors and their use of tools within an activity (Nardi, 1996b).
Communication	Focuses on stakeholder ability to effectively communicate views and beliefs about an activity, and is central to information flow within any collaborative work practice.

2004). To this end, CASE provides a descriptive framework for isolating salient requirements of learner-computer interaction.

The focus in CASE on holistically describing, rather than decomposing, learner practice stems from a learner-centred design view that says developing *fit-for-purpose* systems requires contextual knowledge of users and activities in which they participate (Soloway et al., 1994). Previously established LCD criteria, such as *negotiation*, *motivation*, *cooperation* and *coordination*, and *communication* (Quintana et al., 2001; Soloway et al., 1994) reflect qualitative rather than analytic attributes of interaction. Table 3 outlines the importance of these attributes within the context of CALL system design and evaluation.

These key characteristics of learner-centred design are simultaneously preconditions and corollaries of increased learner situation awareness. Supporting situation awareness, CASE allows investigators to consider the holistic nature of an activity, investigating all four aspects of the framework or isolating specific areas, such as the social organization of an activity. Additionally, there are no prescribed sequence paths of analysis through the framework, allowing for iterative movement through the major components of analysis. Furthermore, CASE emphasises the importance of descriptive over cognitive analyses. As social information provides the basis for inferences, planning and coordination of activities (Erickson & Kellogg, 2001), analyses of CALL activities should seek to establish a descriptive representation of the activity, gradually tending toward the more analytic/cognitive aspects of interaction.

CASE provides a conceptual framework for describing and evaluating situated language learning activities, and has been applied elsewhere to address the need for increased software reuse and component-based software development in CALL (Farmer et al., 2004). Specifically, CASE has been shown to assist with the examination of both social and physical requirements of learning object design (Farmer & Hughes, 2005a, 2005b).

Theoretical Foundations

The CASE framework (Figure 2) assists in the principle integration of various theoretical methodologies during system design and evaluation. CASE aims to facilitate both macro- and micro-level analysis of the various subsystem components that constitute CALL systems. According to Barnard, May, Duke and Duce (2000), systems or *assemblies* are composed of "interactors," or "subsystems" that interact to form complex behaviours. The impact of these interactors may be examined at different levels of abstraction or layers of granularity. Macrotheories are developed to describe the observable holistic behaviour of systems, whereas microtheories serve to elucidate the low-level behaviours of constituent interactors. For example, the role of multimodal interaction using speech technology in second language acquisition may be described by a particular macrotheory (Farmer, 2005). Specific considerations surrounding system design and evaluation, such as error analysis at the spoken language interface, may be examined by a series of microtheories suited to the nature of each interactor.

Extending the work of Barnard et al. (2000), Figure 1 represents the process by which the holistic system behaviour can be modeled and captured at a particular level of theoretical granularity. CASE consists of four dimensions: Cognition, Activity, Social Organization and Environment. Each of these dimensions can be analysed independently using specific micro-level theories, associated methodologies and research tools. Given their low-level detail, microtheories are typically quantitative and analytical. In terms of research design, *validity* and *repeatability* of findings are central concerns. Investigat-

Figure 1. Macro-, meso- and micro-theories in CASE

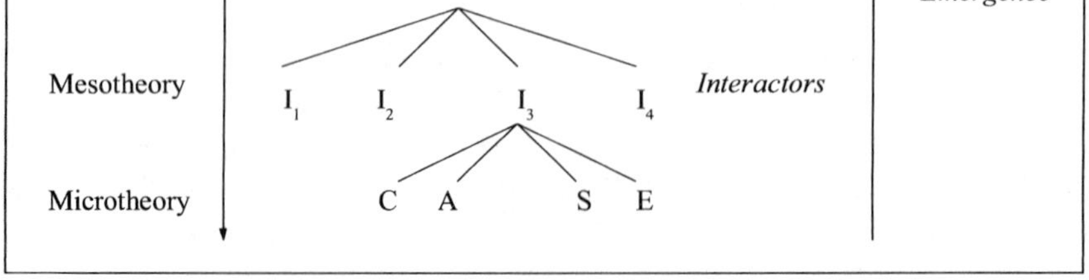

Figure 2. The CASE framework

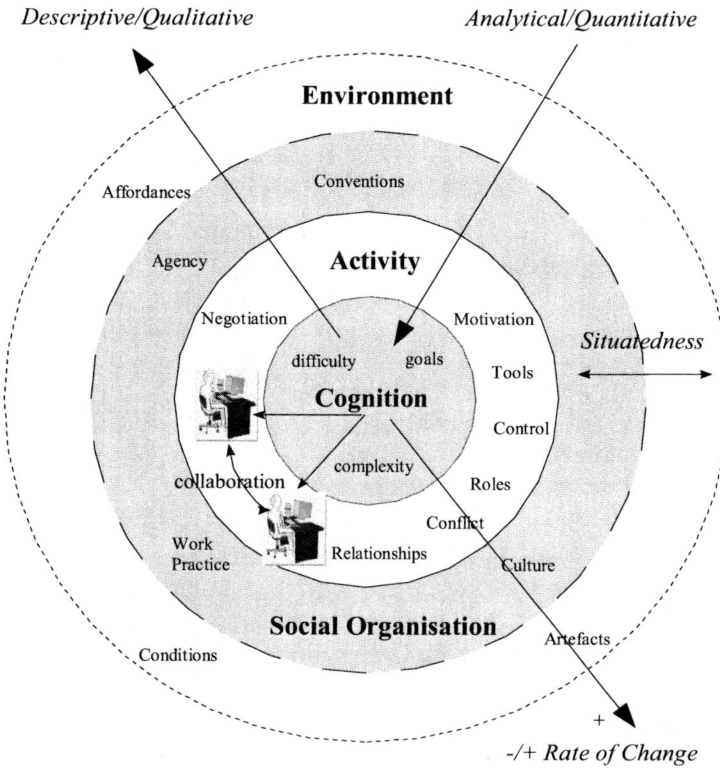

ing the relationship between dimension-centric microtheories within an interactor typically results in the conceptual development of a mesotheory.

Continuing to incorporate analytical methods, mesotheories increasingly tend toward the descriptive and qualitative as the context of interaction becomes more open and dynamic. Being more qualitative, research designs at this level tend to be more concerned with *transferability* and *confirmability* of findings. At the highest level of description are macrotheories. As the sum of observed behaviours of the constituent interactors is likely to be less than that of the whole system due to emergent behaviour (Farmer & Gruba, 2004), macrotheories are generally more descriptive. Hence, macrotheories are often represented as guidelines and are most instructive in the initial design and evaluation phases of an overall system. The CASE dimensions encourages deep theoretical investigation of some phenomenon without sacrificing flexibility and transferability of research and development practices.

Each of the dimensions in CASE represents a layer or level of investigation. The distance of each layer in Figure 2 from the epicentre is inversely proportional to its rate of change. For instance, cognitive processes are expected to change rapidly, while environmental aspects are likely to be relatively stable. Probable influential factors impacting situated activities have been elicited and placed within corresponding levels of the framework. Although some of these factors may inhabit various levels of activity, such as roles and relationships (activity and social organization), their place acts as a mnemonic aid, or checklist, to assist CALL practitioners and developers to direct their attention and resources during system design.

To elaborate on the elements of the CASE framework we briefly examine each of the four principle components within CASE.

Cognition lies at the heart of the CASE framework, as human information processing has the highest rate of change in behaviour and is central to all higher-level metacognitive functioning. In CASE, cognition consists of three primary factors: task complexity (focus on form, divided attention, information priming, construct associativity); conscious subjective goals (motivation, task prioritisation); and task difficulty (reflecting transient qualities, such as intelligence, aptitude, gender, etc.). Modelling activity goals and learner difficulties assists in understanding ill-structured, emergent socio-collaborative practices, whereas cognitive complexity is more relevant to analysing learner-computer interaction in well-structured, fixed scenarios.

Activity is perhaps the most important level within the CASE framework. Here, we are interested in capturing and evaluating tool-mediated, subject-motivated interaction. Informed by Activity Theory, we are concerned with modelling the relationships and roles in agent (actors and artefacts) collaboration, how this polymotivates actions within the activity and how, in turn, conflicts and learner-control strategies impact emerging cognitive tasks. While the environment and social organisation factors are assumed to change at a much slower rate, aspects of an activity are assumed to be highly dynamic and fluid in nature. The socio-collaborative nature of the factors associated with this level is highly likely to be influential in evaluating between-learner variance in learner activity.

Social organisation modelling is primarily concerned with sociological and anthropological questions about the nature of an activity. This is apparent in the emphasis on culture, conventions, work practice and agency. For instance, when developing new computer-mediated communications activities, is communication likely to cross cultural boundaries, requiring varied learner strategies? Are interlocutors constrained by existing cultural conventions and linguistic competencies that are likely to impact discourse structure? Modifying the degree of scaffolding (both social and technological) present within an activity is likely to not only affect agency, but also work practice. For instance, does the learner perceive the learning task as a passive or interactive activity?

Environment modelling is concerned with questions of affordances, artefacts and conditions. Affordances suggest naturally occurring relations between agents in the environment. We may consider the natural affordances of a (instructivist) classroom (many-to-one conversations), which in turn may direct our investigation to the impact of social organization and cultural convention on constructing learner strategies (Donato & McCormick, 1994). Artefacts are those materials and work products used by the learning system (books, microphones, monitors, etc.). Both Activity Theory and Distributed Cognition maintain that artefacts possess cultural residue (Nardi, 1996c). Analysing artefact structure, history and relationships with other agents in the environment may

Figure 3. Locating salient features with CASE

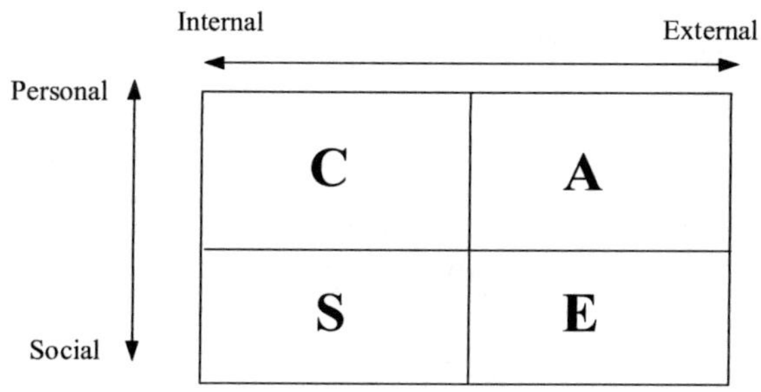

provide key insights into how existing or newly introduced artefacts in the environment influence participation within an activity. This is true of SLA, where modelling changing social conditions has been shown to be an effective indicator of within-learner variance on language-learning tasks (Robinson, 2001).

Each of the CASE dimensions related to a specific interactor can be examined with a particular micro- (or meso-) level theory. For instance, connectionist models could be used to analyse cognitive load and its relation to vocabulary retention. Activity and social organization could be modeled using a combination of Activity Theory and Distributed Cognition, as suggested by Nardi (1996b). Environment modelling could focus on the types of interaction spaces. There are four types of interaction spaces present in which communication occurs: private (interruptions from outsiders is not permitted), privileged (members-only communication), public (anyone can communicate) and hybrid (private communication in public spaces) (Rosenberg, Foley, Lievonen, Kammas, & Crisp, 2005).

Understandably, each of these theoretical models incorporates different techniques for eliciting salient features of interaction, ranging from closed-item response analyses to rich ethnographic methods, such as interviews, direct observation and scenarios.

Once the more salient CASE features of learner-computer interaction have been determined, developers may subsequently locate features along a continuum of social/ personal and internal/external processes (Figure 3). The dimensions of the CASE framework are presented in according to whether they are socially or personally oriented. In addition, the degree to which attributes of each dimension are internal or external can be modeled. For instance, intelligence, gender and aptitude are highly personal/internal attributes or features of cognition. By contrast, task awareness, conscious goals and cognitive load are personal/internal attributes, yet are likely to be influenced by external interaction constraints. Highly personal/external attributes of activity include roles and relationships. Internally oriented attributes of activity include motivation, collaboration and negotiation. Similarly, highly social/internal variables tend to be learners' knowledge and interpretations of social conventions and sense of agency, with more externally oriented attributes including work practice, organizational structure and community of

Figure 4. Areas of proximal influence

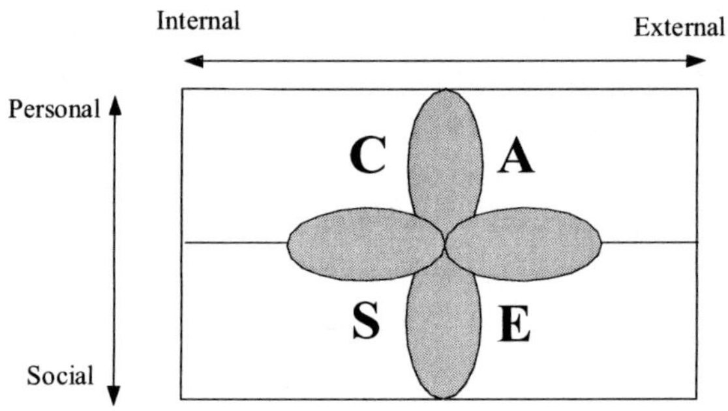

practice. Last, highly external, social attributes of the environment include location and conditions (such as noise), with more internal attributes being affordances and artefacts.

Placing salient features of interaction within a continuum is beneficial, as it respects the dynamic nature and interconnectedness of interaction in socio-technical systems. For instance, artefacts of the environment become tools only when they are used to mediate meaningful activity, therefore acquiring social and personal dimensions. Likewise, cognitive task load may impact goal-orientation, subsequently impacting individual and group motivation within collaborative environments (Robinson, 2001).

CASE proposes that salient features demonstrating the greatest degree of interrelatedness can be represented as *Areas of Proximal Influence*. Figure 4 recognises those dimensional attributes that are most likely to impact interaction, especially within learner-centred domains. Attributes within a dimension may belong to one or more areas. Depending on the type of research questions, investigations can focus on addressing all of the salient features across the four dimensions of CASE or isolate one of them for further research. However, it must be noted that the strength or *degree of influence* of each area is not equivalent. For instance, investigating areas associated most significantly with social organization and environment is unlikely to greatly assist in understanding second-language recall and recognition. In addition, we can classify each of these areas according to some relationship based on the rate and impact of changes in dimensional attributes. These are nominally labeled within CASE as immediate, delayed and eventual. *Immediate* relationships reflect instances whereby variables associated with one dimension are likely to change frequently and have a high impact upon associated dimensions — such as activity type and cognitive load (cognition ↔ activity). Similarly, *delayed* relationships have a high frequency of change, but are less *directly* associated with changes in another dimension — such as classroom vs. home use of learning tools (cognition ↔ social organization). Last, *eventual* relationships involve variables with a slow rate of change that exhibit a highly indirect impact upon other dimensions (cognition ↔ environment). As they are difficult to observe directly, they are less frequently included in research design. One example of an eventual relationship is the changing perceptions of artefact functionality (or affordance) across

Table 4. Degrees of influences

Properties	C	A	S	E
C	-	Immediate	Delayed	Eventual
A	Immediate	-	Immediate	Delayed
S	Delayed	Immediate	-	Immediate
E	Eventual	Delayed	Immediate	-

cultures. For instance, I recall as a teenager while living in Valenciennes (France), my bewilderment when first confronted with the French custom of drinking coffee out of a *bowl* at breakfast. I remember thinking that bowls were for cereal, definitely not coffee. The point here is that the object's properties remained the same — a bowl — yet its *perceived* functionality (or affordance) varied according to different socio-cultural and historic conditions.

In Table 4, we see that the strongest degrees of influences (high rate, high impact) are related to the dimensions of activity and social organization. This is supported by emerging HCI research that establishes the predominance of both activity and social organization in designing and evaluating learning systems (Nardi, 1996b).

Figure 5 provides an example of a typical analysis of salient qualitative features of learner-computer interaction in CALL. From this figure, one can isolate the factors *likely* to have the greatest degree of influence on successful learner-computer interaction. Proceeding from such an analysis, researchers or developers could construct more focused and detailed studies investigating the impact and specific *qualities* of these factors within a particular praxis.

Figure 5. Example analysis of Areas of Proximal Influence

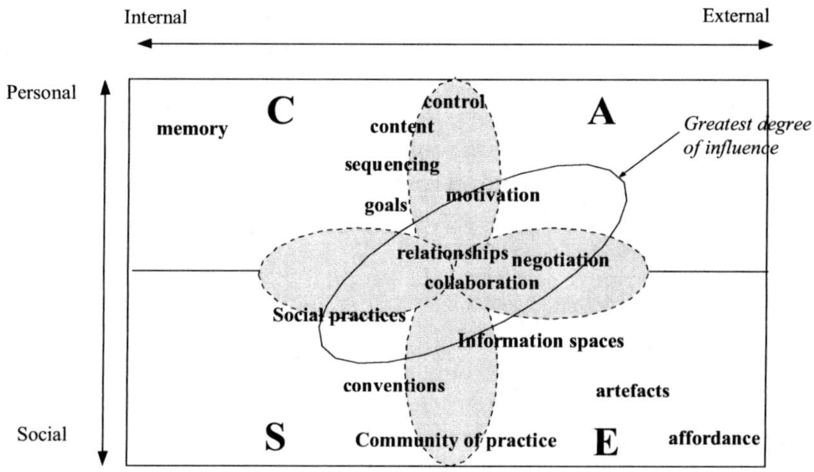

In summary, the benefit of the CASE framework is that it ensures that CALL researchers, practitioners and developers acquire a far more detailed *knowledge of our learners*, their involvement within an activity, their motivations and expectations, and the constraining factors within the situation that possibly limit the *usability* (especially *learnability* and *operability*) of the system. Having established an initial descriptive analysis of the activity under investigation, it would then be possible to either continue with further socio-cultural investigation of the learning environment or conduct a cognitive analysis of an isolated, discrete and well-structured learning task. The CASE framework approach, therefore, maintains that conducting a descriptive analysis prior to conducting empirical analysis of the language-learning activity is likely to provide additional insights into system usage, resulting in more *fit-for-purpose* CALL systems. Despite the descriptive nature of the CASE model, descriptiveness should not be sought at the sake of empirical analyses, without this, developers would find it difficult distinguishing between complex and trivial problems (Whittaker et al., 2000).

Towards CALL Software Quality Improvement with CASE

For the development of quality systems, it is paramount that CALL practitioners and developers realise that understanding the *software ecosystem* associated with any given development effort is important for assuring the quality of the delivered CALL system (Farmer et al., 2004). Although a simplistic definition of the software ecosystem would merely identify the domain of interest for which the system is being produced, a more thorough definition would include the various stakeholders involved in the development and usage of the system, and assert that system design is grounded in a total lifetime view of development (Farmer et al., 2004). Typical stakeholders in software ecosystems include analysts, developers, managers, institutions, end users, instructors and policy makers, to name but a few. The importance of understanding the software ecosystem and its impact upon *quality, cost* and *utility* has previously been reported in Levy (1997), Richmond (1999), and Barson and Debski (1996), who refer to this holistic view of system development as the *design space.*

Given the increased interdisciplinary nature of CALL software development (Debski, 2003; Farmer et al., 2004), the CASE model was developed with several additional software engineering principles in mind to assist in effective collaborative software development (see Table 5). Other critical aspects of continuous software quality improvement include the initial requirements engineering phase and the use of an appropriate SDLC (Farmer et al., 2004; Balbo et al., 2004). This is especially true of interactive systems, whereby the current activity is either highly unstructured or few previous analyses have occurred. *Requirements engineering* (elicitation, analysis and specification) affords a categorisation of possible stakeholders and their level of involvement, provides insight into user and system requirements to be supported, and places the developmental effort within a contextual environment. The major contribution of this stage is its facilitation of future system design projection and its ability to determine the likely impact of design upon end users and any possible (re)divisions of labor. However, considerable differences exist

Table 5. Development properties of the CASE model

Property	Description
Practicality	All tools and processes described by the framework should be practical, not only within the stated context of the user, but for all project stakeholders.
Simplicity	Project stakeholders should not need to undertake extensive training in order to use the methodology. Guidelines and tools should be readily comprehensible and easy to use.
Abstract	The framework should support communication of project knowledge at various levels of granularity, without loss of information. That is, the framework should support abstraction of information where required.
Reuse	The ability to reuse elements of a software project, from requirements elicitation through to system testing and maintenance, is essential to reducing project and organizational costs, and improving quality.
Modifiability	The framework should actively support changes in the development process in a clean and transparent manner.
Extensibility	Additions to the framework should be possible without needlessly re-engineering existing processes and tools.
Traceability	Methodologies should permit the tracing of knowledge (such as requirements constraints and quality goals) through the entire SDLC.
Communicability	The framework should provide a means for all project stakeholders to communicate in a uniform manner all knowledge obtained and transformed by project stakeholders. This is essential as a formal representation of tasks helps to ensure the reliable communication of the joint analyst and user(s) conception of the activity.

between conducting requirements engineering activities within iterative SDLC models, such as the Rational Unified Process (Kroll & Kruchten, 2003) or Win/Win Spiral model (Boehm et al., 1998), and linear sequential models, such as the Waterfall (Royce, 1989) or ADDIE (analysis, design, development, implementation, evaluation) (Colpaert, 2004) models.

Waterfall-based approaches to software development, such as ADDIE, prescribe a linear path through the development effort whereby each phase of development must be completed before the following may commence. However, these frameworks have frequently been shown to be appropriate only for small-scale or trivial software projects (Schach, 1999). Despite this fact, or perhaps in light of it, design methodologies in CALL advocating UCD approaches are mainly based on these inflexible models of software development. Linear SDLC models inexorably lead to increased costs; reduced quality; and poorer software maintenance capabilities (Farmer et al., 2004). Furthermore, Schach (1999) provides a case-based analysis of software development projects, highlighting that the requirements engineering phase of development usually accounts for 60% of all software defects discovered during the maintenance phase. Schach also indicates that the cost of fixing a defect during the maintenance phase, as opposed to the phase in which it occurs, is in the order of 10:1. As the size of the project grows, so do the likely number

Table 6. Purpose of task analysis at various stages of SDLC

Phase	Purpose
Discovery and Definition	To elicit, analyze and specify functional and non-functional stakeholder requirements within the context of use, and the existing limitations and constraints upon the activity. To generate high-level, coarse grained descriptions of the main tasks and objectives that are relevant to the user(s).
Design	Traditionally, the role of this phase has been to develop the user-interface design, however it should also include high-level system architecture specification, documentation and additional resource design. These activities should all occur concurrently. To define and model the generic functionalities of the system, especially *consistency* and *learnability* (affordance, usability) when the system is to be deployed across several platforms.
Development and Deployment	To analyze the implemented functionality of the system in terms of efficiency. To *automatically* generate parts of the architecture and subsystem components related to the functional stakeholder requirements.
Evaluation and Prediction	Through the use of specific task modeling notations, to produce a series of design tests that evaluate user performance and ensure that the final product is *fit-for-purpose*.

of defects. As linear-path models, such as ADDIE, only consider requirements engineering at the start of the SDLC, rather than iteratively throughout, defects are likely to be found later in the SDLC, therefore incurring additional costs (typically, an order of magnitude).

Yet another reason for following an iterative SDLC model in learner-centred design is that requirements are often ill-defined at the start of a project, users only having a partial understanding of the problem and therefore unable to elaborate on their requirements. Instead, the true nature of an activity, and therefore requirements, emerges out of interaction itself (Gasson, 1999), suggesting that not only should we be incorporating rapid prototyping techniques during system design, but that communication between developers and users should be continuing throughout the development process.

Because CASE advocates, both theoretically and practically, an iterative and incremental SDLC, it enables more frequent (and therefore rich) communication between developers and users — a central goal of learner-centred design. This process is likely to be cyclical, requirements elicited from users reflexively instantiated by developers and subsequently (re)validated by the end users themselves (Bødker, Grønbæk, & Kyng, 1993). The assumed benefit of this approach is that the greater the collaboration and cooperation between stakeholders (such as developers and end users), the greater the quality of the system being produced (Farmer et al., 2004). A more detailed discussion of how task analysis may be conducted throughout SDLC is provided in Balbo et al. (2004), and summarised in Table 6.

Using Existing Methodologies within CASE

For CASE to be relevant to CALL, it must support the essential principles of learner-centred design and situated task analysis previously evoked in this chapter. The CASE framework's compliance with these principles is summarised in Table 7.

In addition to complying with the established principles of learner-centred design and situated task analysis, CASE requires a methodological foundation upon which to conduct analyses of computer-mediated activity in CALL. Depending on the level of analysis required (micro, meso, macro) a wide range of existing methodologies and tools could be applied within CASE. As an exposition of this principle, the following brief discussion highlights the integration of Activity Theory and Scenario-Based Design within CASE. The selection of Activity Theory and Scenario-Based Design is principled, as the approaches have previously been found to generate a harmonious relationship, linking theory to practice (Carroll, 1996, 1997; Go & Carroll, 2004; Bødker, 2000). Also, the combination of Activity Theory and Scenario-Based Design satisfies the CASE development properties as specified in Table 5.

Activity Theory examines the importance of tool-mediated construction of meaning; subject-motivated and goal-oriented behaviour; social emergence of user requirements;

Table 7. Common principles of learner-centered design and situated task analysis in CASE

Principles	
• The unit of analysis is *activity*	• Continuous user/developer communication throughout system design
• Activities are subject motivated	• Considers cooperation, collaboration, negotiation and communication
• Tasks are goal-oriented and purposeful	• Considers expertise and engagement as critical factors
• Seeks ecological validity of contextual use	• The principles of situated task analysis are commensurate with those inherent to the *Zone of Proximal Development* (Vygotsky, 1986)
• Supports design within an iterative SDLC	• Activity occurs within a larger socio-cultural context
• Consider motivation, goals, actions and conditions	• Collaboration, cooperation and negotiation are key aspects of learning
• Adheres to the principles of *situatedness*	• Computer-supported activities are *tool-mediated*
• Focus on specific learner needs	• Concerned with modeling emergent social behavior
• Concerned with cognitive and social processes	• Primarily concerned with empirical descriptiveness
• Requirements are fluid and not static	

and dynamic task structure reorientation. As such, it provides a powerful foundation upon which to analyse evolving learner-computer interaction behaviour in CALL. Although Activity Theory can be used during requirements elicitation (Kaptelinin, Nardi, & Macaulay, 1999), it suffers from a lack of systemic methodological tools that can be directly applied by stakeholders to system design (Turner & McEwan, 2004). To assist in rendering the theory more accessible, practical and reusable, Kaptelinin et al. (1999) describe the construction and use of activity checklists. Consisting of questions that may be instructive in understanding the nature of an activity, these checklists assist in the process of system design and evaluations. Through elaboration, checklists may examine a particular phenomenon at various levels of granularity, or abstraction.

Scenario-Based Design promotes the use of scenarios (or structured narratives) in HCI as a way of (1) understanding human activity; and (2) creating computer systems (Carroll, 2000). While natural-language narratives may not be the most scientific notation employed within HCI and software engineering disciplines (because of the innate ambiguity of natural language), Carroll (1996) claims that within collaborative contexts, technical information is often conveyed by means of stories or basic natural language. Scenarios provide a naturalistic means of recording observable behaviour and of capturing subjective accounts of individual experiences (viewpoint analysis). The use of scenarios is not just limited to the initial stages of research and development. They can be used throughout the SDLC, where they facilitate increased communication between project stakeholders and provide additional means of integrating sociocultural accounts of computer-mediated activities into the development process, something CALL practitioners frequently find remiss of software engineering. According to Carroll (2000), there are five principal reasons for advocating the use of Scenario-Based Design in HCI: (1) reflection in design; (2) flexibility in use; (3) multiple views and interpretation; (4) abstraction and categorisation; and (5) work orientation.

In addition, scenarios provide a simple means of implementing *traceability* in software engineering. I will quickly demonstrate this point. Using UML notation, scenarios can be transformed into use-case diagrams. Use-case diagrams can generate sequence, collaboration and class diagrams. Many systems are capable of generating executable code from UML sequence and class diagrams. These same diagrams can be used to generate test cases. Finally, verification of the system before deployment or delivery can make use of the scenarios, use-cases, class diagrams, code and test cases — ensuring traceable functionality throughout the entire SDLC.

Table 8 provides some examples of how Activity Theory and Scenario-Based Design can be used at each of the principle task analysis phases previously described in Table 6.

Although this discussion on Activity Theory, Scenario-Based Design and software engineering has been brief, and assumes a certain degree of background knowledge in software engineering practices, it demonstrates how CASE facilitates a principled integration of existing methodologies for CALL system design and evaluation. This is further reinforced by the final component of the CASE framework; a taxonomy of research design and software engineering methodologies that can be used as a set of *best practices* in CALL system development. That discussion, however, takes us beyond the scope of this chapter.

Table 8. Applying existing methodologies in CASE

Development Phases	**Practices**
Discover & Define	Activity Checklists can be used to examine macrotheories. They act as mnemonic aids to researchers, as well as a means of eliciting and encoding ethnographic data. They are highly useful within Grounded Theory research designs. Coupling each checklist item with one or many scenarios (multiple views) assists in gathering rich, yet discrete, accounts of interaction that can be used directly in system design and evaluation.
Design	Activity Theory can be used to inform developers as to the nature of human-computer interaction. It is highly effective in examining collaboration; negotiation; conflict resolution; and control strategies in interactive environments. Coupled with scenarios, it provides a means of communicating across research disciplines (typically between the social sciences and engineering disciplines).
Develop & Deploy	Scenarios can be used to inform development, generate initial executable code fragments, and provide traceability between practices, system requirements and functionality. This is a critical issue for continuous software quality improvement practices.
Evaluate & Predict	Scenarios and checklists can be used to evaluate existing systems, to validate systems built upon their contents, or to provide a descriptive analysis and evaluation of future systems. These then form an improved means of conducting cost estimation, project planning and requirements engineering.

Conclusion

Developing robust, flexible and holistic frameworks for UCD in CALL is essential to successful system design. However, as demonstrated in this chapter, numerous limitations are inherent in current UCD practices, making the approach incommensurate with the overarching goals of language learning. Addressing this issue, I have described the inadequacies of cognitive task analysis techniques for examining HCI as part of UCD, and instead have argued for the appropriateness of *situated task analysis*. I have demonstrated that there are inherent differences between *users* and *learners* in system design, calling for a learner-centred design paradigm in CALL that advocates the application of socio-cultural theories of language learning and situated task analysis frameworks for analysing learner-computer interaction.

Finally, I have described a flexible, integrative and adaptive framework for CALL system design and evaluation, *CASE*, incorporating the principles of both learner-centred design and situated task analysis. In addition to outlining the theoretical foundations and software quality improvement benefits of applying CASE in CALL, I have described how CASE facilitates the inclusion of existing methodologies and tools, notably activity theory and scenario-based design. I have argued that this process of inclusion rather than occlusion of previous research ensures an integrative approach to developing CALL systems, whereby we are capable of modelling the cognitive and sociological aspects of learner-computer interaction.

Acknowledgments

This work was supported by funding from the Horwood Language Centre, University of Melbourne. I would like to thank Paul Gruba and Baden Hughes for their collaboration on related projects and for volunteering valuable feedback on aspects of this chapter. Last, I wish to thank Simon Goss (Defence Science & Technology Office, Melbourne) for insights gained during our many conversations on cognitive systems engineering.

References

Ackerman, M. S. (2000). The intellectual challenge of CSCW: The gap between social requirements and technical feasibility. *Human-Computer Interaction, 15*, 179-203.

Albers, M. J. (1998). Goal-driven task analysis: Improving situation awareness for complex problem solving. *Proceedings of the 16th Annual International Conference on Computer Documentation* (pp. 234-242). Quebec, Canada: ACM Publishing.

Balbo, S., Ozkan, N., & Paris, C. (2004). Choosing the right task-modelling notation: A taxonomy. In D. Diaper & N. Stanton (Eds.), *The handbook of task analysis for human-computer interaction* (pp. 435-465). Mahwah, NJ: Lawrence Erlbaum Associates.

Bardram, J. E. (1998). Plans as situated action: an activity theory approach to workflow systems. In J. A. Hughes, W. Prinz, T. Rodden, & K. I. Schmidt (Eds.), *Proceedings of the Fifth European Conference on Computer Supported Cooperative Work* (pp. 17-32). Lancaster, UK: Kluwer.

Barnard, P. J., May, J., Duke, D., & Duce, D. (2000). Systems, interactions and macrotheory. *ACM Transactions on Computer Human Interaction, 7*, 222-262.

Barson, J., & Debski, R. (1996). Calling back CALL: Technology in the service of foreign language learning based on creativity, contingency, and goal-oriented activity. In M. Warschauer (Ed.), *Telecollaboration in foreign language learning* (pp. 49-68). Honolulu: University of Hawaii Second Language Teaching & Curriculum Centre.

Bellamy, R. K. E. (1996). Designing educational technology: Computer-mediated change. In B. A. Nardi (Ed.), *Context and consciousness: Activity theory and human-computer interaction* (pp. 123-146). Cambridge: MIT Press.

Beyer, H., & Holtzblatt, K. (1998). *Contextual design: Defining customer-centered systems*. San Francisco: Morgan Kaufmann.

Beyer, H., & Holtzblatt, K. (1999). Contextual design. *Interactions, 6*(1), 32-42.

Bødker, S. (2000). Scenarios in user-centred design: Setting the stage for reflection and action. *Interacting with computers, 13*, 61-75.

Bødker, S., Grønbæk, K., & Kyng, M. (1993). Cooperative design: Techniques and experiences from the Scandinavian scene. In D. Schuler & A. Namioka (Eds.), *Participatory design: Principles and practices* (pp. 157-176). Hillsdale: Lawrence Erlbaum Associates.

Bødker, S., Petersen, M., & Nielsen, C. (2000). Creativity, cooperation and interactive design. In S. Bødker, C. Nielsen, & M. G. Petersen (Eds.), *Proceedings of the Conference on DesigningInteractive Systems: Processes, Practices, Methods, and Techniques* (pp. 252-261). New York: ACM Press.

Boehm, B., Egyed, A., Kwan, J., Port, D., Shah, A., & Madachy, R. (1998). Using the Win/Win Spiral Model: A case study. *IEEE Computer, July,* 33-44.

Brna, P., & Cox, R. (1998). Adding intelligence to a learning environment: Learner-centred design. *Journal of Computer-Assisted Learning, 14*(4), 268-278.

Carroll, J. M. (1994). Making use a design representation. *Communications of the ACM, 37,* 29-35.

Carroll, J. M. (Ed.) (1995). *Scenario-based design: Envisioning work and technology in system development*. New York: John Wiley & Sons.

Carroll, J. M. (1996). Becoming social: Expanding scenario-based approaches in HCI. *Behaviour & Information Technology, 15*(4), 266-275.

Carroll, J. M. (1997). Human-computer interaction: Psychology as a science of design. *International Journal of Human-Computer Studies, 46,* 501-522.

Carroll, J. M. (2000). Five reasons for scenario-based design. *Interacting with Computers, 13,* 43-60.

Carroll, J. M. (2002). Making use is more than a matter of task analysis. *Interacting with Computers, 14,* 619-627.

Carroll, J. M., Kellogg, W. A., & Rosson, M. B. (1991). The task-artifact cycle. In J. M. Carroll (Ed.), *Designing interaction: Psychology at the human-computer interface* (pp. 74-102). New York: Cambridge University Press.

Chapelle, C. (1994). CALL activities: Are they all the same? *System, 22,* 33-45.

Chapelle, C. (2001). *Computer applications in second language acquisition: Foundations for testing, teaching and research*. Cambridge: Cambridge University Press.

Checkland, P. (1981). *Systems thinking, systems practice*. Chichester, UK: John Wiley & Sons.

Checkland, P. (1999). *Soft systems methodology in action*. New York: John Wiley & Sons.

Colpaert, J. (2004). Design methodology in a research-based research-oriented engineering lifecycle approach. In J. Colpaert, W. Decoo, M. Simons, & S. Van Bueren (Eds.),

Proceedings of the 11th International Conference on CALL. Antwerp: Universiteit Antwerpen.

Costabile, M. F. (2001). Usability in the software life cycle. In S. K. Chang (Ed.), *Handbook of software engineering and knowledge engineering* (vol. 1, pp. 179-192). Hackensack, NJ: World Scientific Publishing.

Crabtree, A. (1998). Ethnography in participatory design. In R. Chatfield, S. Kuhn, & M. Muller (Eds.), *Proceedings of the 1998 Participatory Design Conference* (pp 93-105). Palo Alto, CA: Computer Professionals as Social Responsibility.

Debski, R. (2003). Analysis of research in CALL (1988-2000) with a reflection on CALL as an academic discipline. *ReCALL, 15*(2), 177-188.

Diaper, D. (2004). Understanding task analysis for human-computer interaction. In D. Diaper & N. Stanton (Eds.), *The handbook of task analysis for human-computer interaction* (pp. 5-49). Mahwah, NJ: Lawrence Erlbaum Associates.

Donato, R., & McCormick, D. (1994). A sociocultural perspective on language learning strategies: The role of mediation. *The Modern Language Journal, 78,* 453-464.

Ellis, R. (1996). *The study of second language acquisition.* Oxford: Oxford University Press.

Endsley, M. R. (2000). Theoretical underpinnings of situation awareness: A critical review. In M. R. Endsley & D. J. Garland (Eds.), *Situation awareness analysis and measurement* (pp. 3-33). Mahwah: Lawrence Erlbaum.

Engeström, Y. (1987). *Learning by expanding.* Helsinki: Orienta-Konsultit.

Engeström, Y. (1999). Activity theory and individual and social transformation. In Y. Engestrøm, R. Miettinen, & R. Punamaki (Eds.), *Perspectives on activity theory* (pp. 19-39). New York: Cambridge University Press.

Erickson, T., & Kellogg, W. A. (2001). Social translucence: Designing systems that support social processes. In J. M. Carroll (Ed.), *Human-computer interaction in the new millennium* (pp. 324-336). London: Addison-Wesley.

Farmer, R. A. (2005). Multimodal speech recognition errors and second language acquisition: An activity theoretic account. *Sixième colloque des Usages des Nouvelles Technologies dans l'Enseignement des Langues Etrangères (UNTELE 2005).* Compiègne: Université de Technologie de Compiègne.

Farmer, R. A., & Gruba, P. (2004). Critical realism: A philosophical foundation for research in integrative CALL. *Proceedings of the 11th International Conference on CALL.* (pp. 93-102). Antwerp: Universiteit Antwerpen.

Farmer, R. A., Gruba, P., & Hughes, B. (2004). Towards principles for CALL software quality improvement. *Proceedings of the 11th International Conference on CALL* (pp. 103-113). Antwerp: Universiteit Antwerpen.

Farmer, R. A., & Hughes, B. (2005a). A situated learning perspective on learning object design. *Proceedings of the 3rd IEEE International Conference on Advanced Learning Technologies (ICALT'05).* Taiwan: IEEE Computer Society Press.

Farmer, R. A., & Hughes, B. (2005b). A classification-based framework for learning object assembly. *Proceedings of the 3rd IEEE International Conference on Advanced Learning Technologies (ICALT'05).* Taiwan: IEEE Computer Society Press.

Flor, N., & Hutchins, E. (1991). Analysing distributed cognition in software teams: A case study of team programming during perfective software maintenance. In J. Koenemann-Belliveau et al. (Eds.), *Proceedings of the Fourth Annual Workshop on Empirical Studies of Programmers* (pp. 36-59). Norwood: Ablex Publishing.

Gasson, S. (1999). A social action model of situated information systems design. *The DATA BASE for Advanced in Information Systems, 30*(2), 82-97.

Go, K., & Carroll, J.M. (2004). Scenario-based task analysis. In D. Diaper & N. Stanton (Eds.), *The handbook of tasks analysis for human-computer interaction* (pp. 117-134). Mahwah, NJ: Lawrence Erlbaum.

Gruba, P. (2004). Computer-assisted language learning. In A. Davies & C. Elder (Eds.), *The handbook of applied linguistics* (pp. 623-648). Oxford: Blackwell.

Hémard, D. (1999). A methodology for designing student-centred hypermedia CALL. In R. Debski & M. Levy (Eds.), *WorldCALL: Global perspectives on computer-assisted language learning* (pp. 215-229). Lisse: Swets & Zeitlinger.

Hollan, J., Hutchins, E., & Kirsh, D. (2001). Distributed cognition: Toward a new foundation for human-computer interaction research. In J. M. Carroll (Ed.), *Human-computer interaction in the new millennium* (pp. 77-94). London: Addison-Wesley.

Holtzblatt, K., & Beyer, H. (1993). Making customer-centred design work for teams. *Communications of the ACM, 36*(10), 93-103.

Hoven, D. (1999). CALL-ing the learner into focus: Towards a learner-centred model. In R. Debski & M. Levy (Eds.), *WorldCALL: Global perspectives on computer-assisted language learning* (pp. 149-169). Lisse: Swets & Zeitlinger.

Hubbard, P. (1992). A methodological framework for CALL courseware development. In M. C. Pennington & V. Stevens (Eds.), *Computers in applied linguistics: An international perspective* (pp. 39-66). Clevedon, UK: Multilingual Matters.

Hubbard, P. (1996). Elements of CALL methodology: Development, evaluation, and implementation. In M. C. Pennington (Ed.), *The power of CALL* (pp. 15-33). Houston, TX: Athelstan Publications.

Hutchins, E. (1995a). *Cognition in the wild.* Cambridge: MIT Press.

Hutchins, E. (1995b). How a cockpit remembers its speed. *Cognitive Science, 19*, 265-288.

Kaptelinin, V. (1996a). Activity theory: Implications for human-computer interaction. In B. A. Nardi (Ed.), *Context and consciousness: Activity theory and human-computer interaction* (pp. 103-116). Cambridge: MIT Press.

Kaptelinin, V. (1996b). Computer-mediated activity: Functional organs in social and developmental contexts. In B. A. Nardi (Ed.), *Context and consciousness: Activity theory and human-computer interaction* (pp. 45-69). Cambridge: MIT Press.

Kaptelinin, V., Nardi, B., & Macaulay, C. (1999, July/August). The activity checklist: A tool for representing the "space" of context. *Interactions,* 27-39.

Kieras, D. (2004). GOMS models for task analysis. In D. Diaper & N. Stanton (Eds.), *The handbook of task analysis for human-computer interaction* (pp. 83-116). Mahwah: Lawrence Erlbaum Associates.

Kroll, P., & Kruchten, P. (2003). *The rational unified process made easy: A practitioner's guide to rational unified process*. New York: Addison-Wesley.

Kumaravadivelu, B. (1993) The name of the task and the task of naming: Methodological aspects of task-based pedagogy. In G. Crookes & S. M. Gass (Eds.), *Tasks in a pedagogical context: Integrating theory and practice* (pp. 69-96). Clevedon, England: Multilingual Matters.

Lave, J. (1993). The practice of learning. In S. Chaiklin & J. Lave (Eds.), *Understanding practice: Perspectives on activity and context* (pp. 3-32). Cambridge: Cambridge University Press.

Lave, J. (1998). *Cognition in practice: Mind, mathematics and culture in everyday life*. Cambridge: Cambridge University Press.

Lave, J., & Wegner, I. (1991). *Situated learning: Legitimate peripheral participation*. Cambridge: Cambridge University Press.

Leont'ev, A.N. (1978). *Activity, consciousness, and personality*. Englewood Cliffs, CA: Prentice-Hall.

Leont'ev, A.N. (1981). *Problems of the development of mind*. Moscow: Progress.

Levy, M. (1997). *Computer-assisted language learning: Context and conceptualization*. Oxford: Clarendon Press.

Moran, T.P., & Carroll, J.M. (1996). Overview of design rationale. In T.P. Moran & J.M. Carroll (Eds.), *Design rationale: Concepts, techniques and use* (pp. 1-20). Mahwah, NJ: Lawrence Erlbaum.

Nardi, B.A. (1996a). Activity theory and human-computer interaction. In B.A. Nardi (Ed.), *Context and consciousness: Activity theory and human-computer interaction* (pp. 7-16). Cambridge: MIT Press.

Nardi, B.A. (1996b). Studying context: A comparison of activity theory, situated action models, and distributed cognition. In B.A. Nardi (Ed.), *Context and consciousness: Activity theory and human-computer interaction* (pp. 69-102). Cambridge: MIT Press.

Nardi, B.A. (Ed.) (1996c). *Context and consciousness: Activity theory and human-computer interaction*. Cambridge: MIT Press.

Neisser, U. (1976). *Cognition and reality*. San Francisco: W.H. Freeman and Company.

Nunan, D. (1989). *Designing tasks for the communicative classroom*. Cambridge: Cambridge University Press.

Preece, Y., Rogers, Y., Sharp, H., Benyon, D., Holland, S., & Carey, T. (Eds.) (1994). *Human-computer interaction*. London: Addison-Wesley.

Quintana, C., Carra, A., Krjcik, J., & Soloway, E. (2001). Learner-centred design: Reflections and new directions. In J. M. Carroll (Ed.), *Human-computer interaction in the new millennium* (pp. 607-626). London: Addison-Wesley.

Raeithel, A., & Velichkovsky, B. M. (1996). Joint attention and co-construction of tasks: New ways to foster user-designer collaboration. In B.A. Nardi (Ed.), *Context and consciousness: Activity theory and human-computer interaction* (pp. 199-234). Cambridge: MIT Press.

Rasmussen, J., Pejtersen, A. M., & Goodstein, L. P. (1994). *Cognitive systems engineering*. New York: John Wiley & Sons.

Richmond, I. M. (1999). Is your CALL connected: Dedicated vs. integrated CALL. In K. Cameron (Ed.), *CALL: Media, design and applications* (pp. 295-314). Lisse: Swets & Zeitlinger.

Robinson, P. (2001). Task complexity, cognitive resources and second language syllabus design: A triadic theory of task influences on SLA. In P. Robinson (Ed.), *Cognition and decond language instruction* (pp. 285-317). Cambridge: Cambridge University Press.

Rosenberg, D., Foley, S., Lievonen, M., Kammas, S., & Crisp, M.J. (2005). Interaction spaces in computer-mediated communication. *AI & Society, 19*, 22-33.

Royce, W. W. (1989). Managing the development of large software systems: Concepts and techniques. *Proceedings of the 11th International Conference on Software Engineering* (pp. 328-338). New York: IEEE Computing Society.

Rumbaugh, J., Jacobson, I., & Booch, G. (1999). *The unified modelling language: User guide*. Upper Saddle River, NJ: Addison-Wesley.

Sanderson, P. M. (1998). Cognitive work analysis and the analysis, design and evaluation of human-computer interactive systems. *Proceedings of the Australalian Conference on Computer Human Interaction* (pp. 220-227). New York: IEEE Computer Society.

Sanderson, P. M. (2003). Cognitive work analysis. In J. Carroll (Ed.), *HCI models, theories and framework: Toward an interdisciplinary science*. New York: Morgan Kaufman.

Schach, S. R. (1999). *Classical and object-oriented software engineering* (4th ed.). Singapore: McGraw-Hill International.

Schuler, D. & Namioka, A. (Eds.) (1993). *Participatory design: Principles and practices*. Hillsdale, NJ: Lawrence Erlbaum.

Soloway, E., Guzdial, M., & Kay, K.H. (1994). Learner-centered design: The challenge for HCI in the 21st century. *Interactions, 1*(2), 36-48.

Soloway, E., Jackson, S. L., Klein, J., Quintana, C., Reed, J., Spitulnik, J., Stratford, S. J., Studer, S., Jul, S., Eng, J., & Scala, N. (1996). Learning theory in practice: Case studies of learner-centered design. In M. J. Tauber (Ed.), *Proceedings of CHI'96 Conference on Human Factors in Computing Systems* (pp. 189-196). New York: Addison-Wesley.

Stanton, N. (2004). The psychology of task analysis today. In D. Diaper & N. Stanton (Eds.), *The handbook of task analysis for human-computer interaction* (pp. 569-584). Mahwah, NJ: Lawrence Erlbaum.

Stevens, V. (1989). A direction for CALL: From behavioristic to humanistic courseware. In M. C. Pennington (Ed.), *Teaching languages with computers* (pp. 29-43). La Jolla, CA: Athelstan Publications.

Suchman, L. A. (1987). *Plans and situated actions: The problem of human-computer communication*. New York: Cambridge University Press.

Turner, P., & McEwan, T. (2004). Activity theory: Another perspective on task analysis. In D. Diaper & N. Stanton (Eds.), *The handbook of task analysis for human-computer interaction* (pp. 423-440). Mahwah, NJ: Lawrence Erlbaum.

Velichkovsky, B. M. (1990). The vertical dimension of mental functioning. *Psychological Research, 52*, 282-293.

Vicente, K. J. (1999). *Cognitive work analysis: Toward safe, productive, and healthy computer-based work*. Mahwah, NJ: Lawrence Erlbaum.

Vygotsky, L. S. (1986). *Thought and language*. (A. Kozulin, Trans. & Ed.). Cambridge: MIT Press.

Watts, L. A., & Monk, A. F. (1998). Reasoning about tasks, activities and technology to support collaboration. *Ergonomics, 4*(11), 1583-1606.

Whittaker, S., Terveen, L. & Nardi, B. A. (2000). Let's stop pushing the envelope and start addressing it: A reference task agenda for HCI. *Human-Computer Interaction, 15*, 75-106.

Endnotes

1 The term *task* is a polysemous word. The definition we ascribe to it inherently influences our approach to designing language learning systems. In this chapter, I ascribe the following properties to the term: First, a *task* involves purposeful interaction in some activity with the goal to *learn* (implicitly or explicitly) some construct. Second, *task* is defined as incorporating both cognitive and sociocultural elements of interaction, binding human performance to the learner's internal representation of the activity, and their perception of external structure within the environment.

2 Soloway et al. (1994) provide a similar evaluation, highlighting *growth* (task motivation), *diversity* (differing levels of expertise and learning styles) and *motivation* (need for an attractive and engaging interface).

Section II

Design

Chapter IV

'Ears before Eyes': Expanding Tutors' Interaction Skills beyond Physical Presence in Audio-Graphic Collaborative Virtual Learning Environments

Beatriz de los Arcos, The Open University, UK

Inmaculada Arnedillo Sánchez, Trinity College, Ireland

Abstract

This chapter considers how the absence of certain aspects of non-verbal behaviour affects interaction in audio-graphical learning environments. The authors introduce strategies to deal with turn-taking, time lag and other incidences, while observing the difficulty in applying the communicative approach to language teaching in these settings. By highlighting the limited validity of an extrapolation of methodologies between face-to-face and virtual classrooms, we call for research to address the need for a new course of action; one that takes full advantage of the technology in its own right.

Introduction

"Hello, can you hear me?" are the words most likely to greet a participant in an audio-graphic conference. The speaker tries to ensure that, deprived of her eyes, her auditory conduct remains intact. Current approaches in second-language teaching focus on being able to communicate; however, it is seldom we realize how much we rely on information conveyed through the eyes to construct knowledge. Can we function without them? If so, how do we communicate in the dark? It is the aim of this chapter to examine how the absence of certain aspects of non-verbal behaviour affects human interaction in computer-mediated communication (CMC); in particular, in terms of the strategies the tutor needs to develop and incorporate in practice to overcome such loss.

The structure of this chapter is as follows: The literature review establishes the relevance of interaction and collaboration in the construction of new knowledge. It introduces some of the premises of the communicative approach in language teaching and examines to what extent the absence of non-verbal behaviour affects communication in audio-conferencing applications. The design of the learning experience highlights how certain features of the software under consideration facilitate collaboration. It presents the communicative nature of activities to be carried out by learners, and it suggests strategies to deal with important issues, such as turn-taking and awkward silences. A brief explanation of the research methodology and data collection tools serves as a prelude to a short account of the implementation. Findings are discussed and a conclusion put forward: Tandem teaching should be considered a suitable procedure to address the pedagogical shortcomings of audio-graphic collaborative virtual learning environments. The development of new methodologies that concentrate on the importance of oral input in these settings must become a priority among the research community.

Reading for Your Eyes: Literature Review

Illustrating her vision of language learning and teaching online, Felix (2003) borrows the metaphor of the orchestra: competent musicians playing the finest instruments to the guiding baton of a conductor in a milieu of superb acoustics or, as a matter of course, highly motivated students with access to prime equipment and 24/7 technical support, engaged in an endeavor facilitated by an inspiring teacher. It is the partnership of different elements, Felix says, that sustains the performance of an orchestra, a pre-constructed dialog acted out by means of interaction. In a learning/teaching environment, the same interaction occurs: Musicians/learners interact with each other, their instruments/computers and conductor/teacher to display not an already assigned score, but to produce new knowledge.

The concept of collaboration in second language acquisition (SLA) derives from Vygotsky's account that learners construct new language through socially mediated interaction (Brown, 2000). Krashen singled out interaction as the source of input necessary for the development of a second language (Warschauer, 1997). Building on this line of thought, Long formulated his interaction hypothesis, arguing that comprehensible input is the result of modified interaction, thus debunking second language classrooms as platforms for practicing grammatical structures and instead viewing them as contexts for the occurrence of conversation (Brown, 2000). The underlying principle is that language is primarily communication, and communicative competence implies both knowledge and ability to use language (Woodin, 2001). This communicative approach to foreign/second language learning assumes a functional meaning: Learners become more active participants in the class insofar as their learning is a direct response to their needs and subject to partaking in authentic and meaningful interaction. The teacher's role swerves from being a source of knowledge to assisting learners in the process of communicating in the target language (Warschauer, 1997; Woodin, 2001).

This newly bestowed responsibility to promote social interaction has been attenuated for tutors with the advent of CMC. Warschauer (1997) evaluates the potential of online education and concludes that CMC encourages collaborative learning in the language classroom. Hampel and Baber (2003) expand his reliance on the validity of accessing authentic materials and refer to CMC as a medium that lends itself to authentic learning experiences in a multimodal environment. New conferencing technologies complement writing with speech, video and graphics, and make it possible "to offer learners a combination of different modes, which include audio-graphic conferencing, video, text chat, shared writing tools and Web access"; in a sense, to provide for different learners, be these of an auditory, visual or more kinaesthetic type (Hampel & Baber, 2003, p. 174).

Audio-graphic/video conferencing, although not bereft of technical quarrels that occasionally render utterly frustrating any attempt at communicating, defeats most of the disadvantages of using the Web for language teaching. What is required of teachers and learners alike is a generous disposition to adapt their ways to access and exploit the assets these new technologies offer. In audio-graphic conferencing settings, one of the most urgent challenges is interacting with individuals whom we do not see; the anonymity this creates has been positively regarded as a balancing act that reduces clues related to race, gender, age, social and family status, and disability (Warschauer, 1997; Blake, 2000). Nevertheless, the withdrawal of visual contact might also impede communication.

Kellerman (1992) defines non-verbal behaviour as "any behaviour which does not involve language" (p. 239). Lörscher (2003) categorizes non-verbal phenomena according to the channels by which they are communicated: Non-verbal phenomena visually perceived include mimicry (facial expression), direction and movement of gaze, gestures and body movements, and proxemics (interpersonal distance and spatial orientation). Voice quality (pitch, stress, key) and way of speaking (intonation, pronunciation, speed, pauses, turn-taking organization, etc.) account for non-verbal auditory phenomena, while smells, tastes, touches and changes in temperature respond to remaining conducts.

Kellerman (1992) concentrates on visual aspects of non-verbal communication, which she refers to as kinesic behaviour or body movement in her analysis of the influence of these in the decoding of speech in the mother tongue (L1). She observes the regulatory function of kinesic behaviour in interaction: "Body movements maintain and coordinate the flow of speech and turn-taking ... by means of eye contact, direction of gaze, gestures of the hand and arm, and posture" (Kellerman, 1992, p. 244). Jenkins and Parra (2003) sympathize by indicating that participants in interaction use non-verbal behaviour to manage their talk, and thus co-construct knowledge by interpreting kinesic as much as linguistic aspects. In this view, kinesic behaviour enhances communication, and its suppression may very well result in failure to communicate.

To date, researchers have given little attention to the relevance of non-verbal behaviour in SLA. Kellerman (1992) suggests speakers compensate for the absence of information conveyed by the visual channel by overdosing verbal messages with explicitness in an effort to minimize confusion. This also means that too much strain is placed on L2 learners' listening skills, a most difficult ability to achieve outside full immersion in the target language. The question of fatigue presents itself in the most relevant of positions, as evidence has it that learners listening to a foreign language experience less tiredness when all the sensory channels are used to present information. For Lörscher (2003), the question stretches into the theatrics of foreign-language teaching: The communicative approach favors the use of the target language at all times, so it is more often that not a teacher finds herself acting in front of the class, trying to communicate with the help of gestures, mimicry and other non-acoustic phenomena something she knows might not be understood otherwise. Indeed, it has been argued that speakers vary their pronunciation judging by the needs of listeners, and "intelligibility loss is mitigated when listeners look at speakers" (Anderson, Bard, Sotilo, Newlands, & Doherty-Sneddon, 1997, p. 580). Similar support exists in feedback: While a teacher corrects one student, her body language reveals that correction applies to everyone. Lörscher (2003) determines non-verbal behaviour not only is concomitant with speech but can also replace it, and he concludes by calling on researchers to give it the attention it deserves. Kellerman (1992) and Jenkins and Parra (2003) also join this appeal, as learners must be aware of the visual aspects of speech decoding in order to develop appropriate strategies for comprehending L2.

The literature on audio-graphic conferencing tools reports findings cited in connection to the absence of kinesic behaviour in SLA; specifically, a disparity in the duration of online sessions when matched with face-to-face tutorials, and tiredness caused by use mainly of the auditory channel (Newlands, 1996). The tutor needs to be more direct to deal with situations arising from the lack of visual clues in relation to the distribution of dialog; for instance, naming a person to answer a question instead of waiting for a response (Newlands, 1996; Hampel & Baber, 2003). This technique is also meant to address the issue of non-participation; synchronous CMC is a medium where it is very easy to hide and harder to contribute than in a face-to-face classroom. Speech becomes the conscious motor decision of pressing a button to talk, which is often forgotten; it might also be the case that two people speak at the same time, or simply that participants are unable to judge when a speaker has finished her contribution to initiate theirs; either scenario causes substantial confusion, and awkward silences follow. Another quality inherent to the medium is time delay. Hampel and Baber (2003) suggest the lag between a participant speaking and other users receiving the input may be as long as 1 second, and while it does not seriously damage group participation, all parties must get accustomed to it. Due to lack of body language, it is advisable to think of a methodology to guarantee conversation does not languish; for instance, "having the next speaker nominated by the current one, introducing a rotation scheme whereby each student in turn gives their opinion, or using some form of visual signalling to indicate that someone would like to speak next" (Hampel & Baber, 2003, p. 176). Experience confirms that shortcomings are corrected with practice as users become more familiar with these tools, but as students experiencing some degree of difficulty are less likely to be identified at first, it is paramount that the tutor gets everyone as comfortable as possible on the system from day one (Kötter, Shield, & Stevens 1999; Kötter & Shield, 2000; Hampel, 2003). Let us not overlook the certainty that virtual classrooms are places where anonymity is naturally bred and spontaneity subdued, and that "it is possible that the fact that students have to interact orally in foreign language without the usual verbal and visual cues ... can cause increased anxiety and lower motivation in language learning" (Hampel, 2003, p. 29).

A more constructivist task-based approach may be adopted to assist students in their development as autonomous learners, circumstances in which a tutor becomes "a manager of learning resources and an organizer of learning events" (Hauck & Haezewindt, 1999, p. 50). Unequivocally, success of any kind in teaching in an audio-graphic environment depends on the tutors being fully technically confident and willing to accommodate their teaching style to the virtual classroom (Hauck & Haezewindt, 1999). To communicate effectively via CMC, strategies must be developed that overcome the absence of body language. Some of these strategies have already been identified; others have been implemented during the course of this project.

Designing Interaction "in the Dark"

In the design of the learning experience, the authors followed essentially three lines of thought: how the software employed promotes collaboration and interaction; which of its tools can be applied to address the absence of non-verbal behaviour; and how to plan communicative tasks for the students. Strategies to overcome the absence of non-verbal aspects of communication were designed and implemented as incidences occurred. Thus, readers are referred to the discussion section of this chapter to learn more about the cycle of observation of incidences, design and implementation strategies.

The audio-graphic software used for this research allows for real-time many-to-many voice communication over the Internet, a trait that at once unfolds countless possibilities for partnership by making learners independent of time and space. *Learner-content* interaction in Moore's model (Tuovinen, 2000) is based on the learners' consumption of material, a one-way relationship where no input by the former is imprinted on the latter. This common course of events in distance learning, where teaching is primarily done by the books, is revamped by technology enabling two-way interaction between learner and content. Learners' working memory is said to process visual and auditory information separately. Thus, content presented in multimodal form, such as a combination of sound, text and graphics, allows for more information to be managed at once (Tuovinen, 2000). This increased ability to manage information facilitates understanding and could aid language retention (Hampel & Baber, 2003). In addition, multimodal content eases the congestion of the auditory channel.

Figure 1. Multimodal content presentation

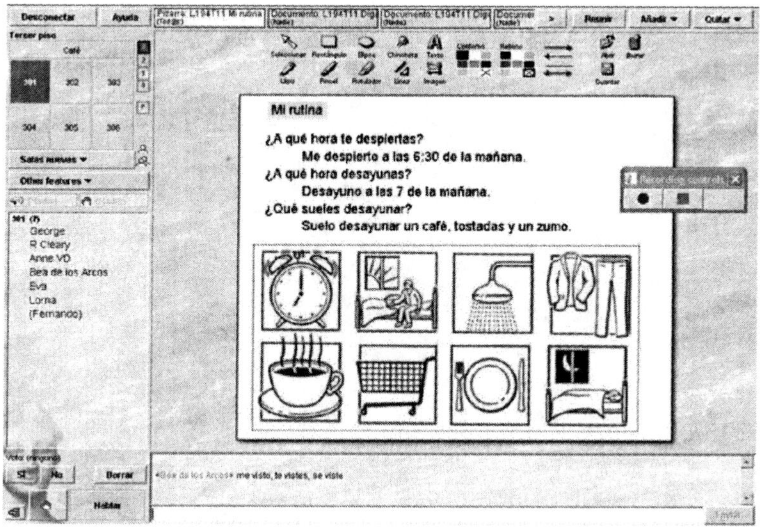

Audio-graphic environments further employ collaboration in as much as they provide for *many learners-content* interaction. Tools such as whiteboards, concept maps and document modules can be manipulated by all the participants in the conference, allowing for shared writing and editing, brainstorming or other activities. One common computer screen becomes a clean canvas for a group to create their work. Most audio-graphic systems provide a tool to fetch real up-to-date information from the Internet. In doing so, learners have access to authentic material at the click of a button, connecting our argument to the interest of researchers in authenticity as a primary source in SLA (Warschauer, 1997). The medium also has the capacity to support students emotionally, as it volunteers a ground for the occurrence of *learner-learner* interaction outside scheduled contact hours with a tutor, therefore helping peer relations.

With regard to turn taking and dealing with awkward silences — an aspect the absence of visual signals is said to affect the most — different audio conferencing software employs a variety of applications. The system under consideration includes a hand-raised button one clicks on when wishing to speak.

Alternatively, the person acting as chair may consider the list of names that appears on the left-hand side of the screen, which corresponds to the order in which participants arrive at the conference. The authors propose the directory feature can be used as a practical tool in terms of providing links for learner interaction, avoiding the pivotal role of the tutor. Otherwise, turn taking may be resolved by directly nominating the person to whom a speaker decides to pass the baton, also sorting out interruptions or any other incidences that may occur from not being able to gauge when a speaker has finished a contribution. Protocol in the conference should have agreed that anyone temporarily leaving the conference during a session should click the "away" button, to avoid being invited to speak in their absence. Overall, it is the authors' recommendation that

Figure 2. Requesting the floor

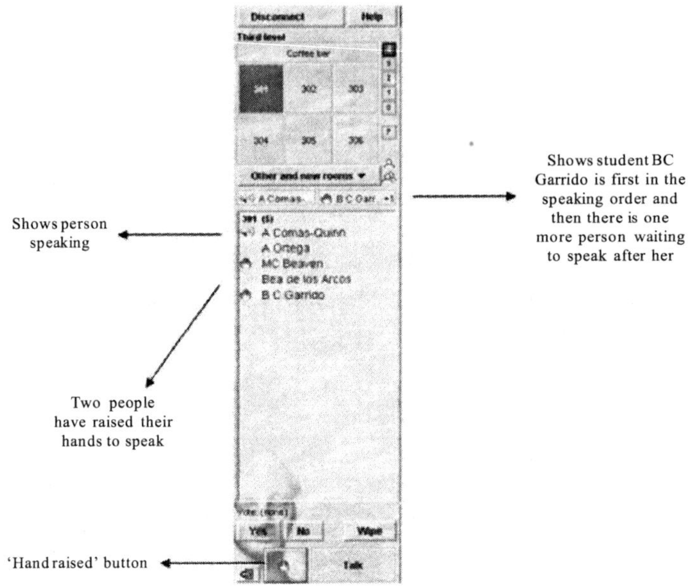

participants are vocal in extreme, so as to compensate for the visual information lost in the medium. In relation to this, given the difficulty to verify whether instructions have been understood correctly, we envisage the voting buttons to be very useful for quick comprehension checks: students click on "yes" or "no," and either a "tick" or a "cross" appears beside their names, giving the tutor instant feedback — equivalent, for instance, to a nod of the head.

The software also allows for the creation of an unlimited number of temporary "breakout rooms" with full audio-graphic capacity. The tutor can ask students to go to these sub-conferences to do pair or small-group work, and facilitate *learner-learner* interaction away from direct tutelage.

As tools for interaction and collaboration, audio-graphic conferencing systems compel language tutors to embrace the communicative approach and incarnate their role of "guide on the side," facilitating learners' communication in the target language (Warschauer, 1997; Woodin, 2001; Felix, 2003). In this light, planning for activities to be carried out by students in the virtual environment at hand is informed by several communicative principles, as stated by Woodin (2001). First, the need for contextualization of the learning experience was addressed with the provision of opportunities to practice the target language — in this case, Spanish — in situations likely to be encountered in real life (such as, you are going on holidays and join an agency to help you find a travel companion; you are looking for a new property in Spain and contact an estate agent, and others). Likewise, tasks mirrored those likely to be necessary in dealing with others in the target culture (booking a hotel room, asking for prices, making and accepting

Figure 3. Protocol in the conference

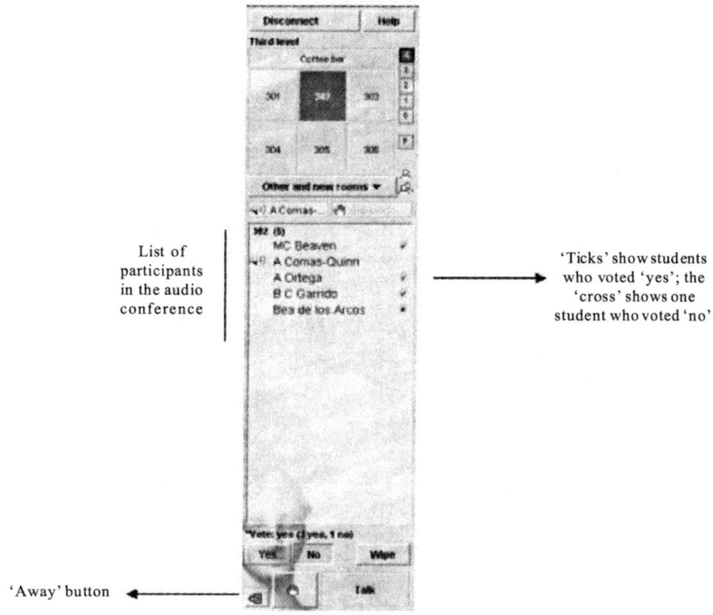

invitations, buying food in a market, etc.). Cultural understanding was equally considered, as learners must be made aware of cultural differences among communities. In this sense, ground was laid to learn about very simple facts, like meal times or opening and closing hours, but also to expose some of the most deeply rooted misconceptions about Spanish life. Overall, the design of activities is briefed by the characteristics of a communicative class, whereby the emphasis is on the students to create language relevant to them in an authentic context, rather than regurgitating previously learned conversations (Woodin, 2001).

Following Kötter et al. (1999), Kötter et al. (2000) and Hampel (2003) in their recommendation to familiarize participants in an audio-graphic conference with the various applications of the software, it was a conscious decision to gradually introduce students to some of the tools (saving and opening modules, grabbing images from the Web and so on) in a bid to eliminate the extra anxiety caused by having to speak a foreign language and use state-of-the-art technology at the same time.

Some Considerations of Method

We considered action research to be the most suitable method for the investigation of the learning experience reported here. Once established non-verbal behaviour is paramount in the process of communication, a priority was to generate hypotheses as to what strategies may be implemented to overcome the absence of mimicry, gestures, body movements and proxemics from audio-graphic conferences. The proposed strategies were implemented through an audio-graphic collaborative learning environment and validated through the authors' own practice. The ultimate objective was to help all participants in audio conferences — tutors and students alike — to gain a better understanding of the medium in order to learn how to best deal with its functionality in deficiency.

To complete this research, data collection of a qualitative nature was favored over quantitative information, as all interest was attached to providing an insight into the process, rather than an end product. For triangulation purposes, more than one method for data collection was used: An electronic questionnaire, linked to a database, was designed to gather reflections of the tutor on the outcomes and procedure of each session. In an effort to eliminate the bias of subjectivity, an independent observer was asked to be a non-participant at the conferences and compare notes with the tutor at a later stage. Chat logs were stored, and audio and video recordings of each tutorial were kept for observation and transcription of significant interaction. The tutor's reflections and initial unstructured observations were used to generate hypotheses to be subsequently put in place for analysis in a cycle of action-observation-action. Structured observations provided the researchers with the coding of silence and overlapping in discourse. To cross-check findings, questions were posted via e-mail to the respective asynchronous conferences for tutors and students on the course.

Implementation of an Ears-Tuned, Eyes-Shut Approach

The project involved a group of adult learners taking a distance course of ab-initio Spanish with Open University (OU). Tutorials took place over an audio-graphic conferencing system by the name of Lyceum, developed by OU to offer language students more opportunities to practice their oral and aural skills without having to travel long distances to their tutorial venues. The group under consideration was initially formed by 16 individuals, four of whom withdrew from the course in the first 3 months for reasons either unknown or not relevant to our study. The rest attended regular tutorials in Lyceum, approximately twice a month each time for about 1 hour, although the number of participants on each session varied much, from a maximum of eight to a minimum of three. This is not surprising, due to the non-compulsory policy of attendance to tutorials adopted by OU. All participants except one were novice in joining in audio-graphic conferences, but expressed confidence in their technical skills to use e-mail and the Internet. Prior to the beginning of the course, tutor and students alike were asked to run through an animated tutorial explaining the basics of the software's functions. Training was also provided for tutors in three 1-hour sessions over a period of 3 weeks.

Listening with Your Ears, Speaking without Your Eyes

In this section, the authors discuss instances that occur in the absence of non-verbal behaviour (mimicry, gestures and body movements) in *tutor-learner*, *learner-learner* and *learner-content* interactions in audio-graphic collaborative virtual learning environments. Strategies aimed at overcoming this deficiency are implemented primarily in areas concerning the tutor's input, turn taking and dealing with silence.

Input of the Tutor

It was noted in early observations that, although devised to last approximately 45 minutes, the duration of each session on the system generally surpassed the 1-hour mark, the longest running into 1 hour and 20 minutes. A considerable amount of time, especially during the first tutorials, was spent in sound checks and working out minor technical problems arising from the participants' lack of experience in operating the software's applications. Nevertheless, the chief agent in failing to keep time allocated was the tutor. The literature review, which precedes this section, stated that in the absence of visually perceived non-verbal phenomena, such as mimicry, gaze, gestures and body movements, the speaker compensates by increasing verbal input (Kellerman, 1992). In our case, such a scenario is accurately replicated: The tutor is articulate in excess, for instance, describing the screen to participants when everyone can see what she sees. This maneuver may be explained by the tutor's zeal to ensure students clearly follow her instructions, say saving a screen or adding a new module, but it becomes unnecessary in successive visits to the conference. As instant acknowledgment of communication is not possible, repetition comes as a surrogate and frequent comprehension checks are mandatory: Two buttons to vote "yes" or "no" provide an easy response to questions such as "Is that clear?" or "Does anyone have a problem?," but more often than not, one query immediately follows the other; thus, a situation generates whereby both a positive and negative answer are valid. The tutor needs to be aware of the confusion he or she is creating and avoid this type of utterance by being absolutely clear and precise in prompting.

Similar occurrences can be related to emphasize the need for over-explicitness on the tutor's part: A limitless number of temporary sub-conferences or breakout rooms can be built in Lyceum for pair or group work. Common practice impelled students to head into these as soon as they were mentioned, without waiting to find out from the tutor what to do once they got there. Other instances led to comparable behaviour under the tutor's responsibility, as the tutor forgot to set a task while totally occupied explaining how to access these separate areas. Different strategies were subsequently arranged to revert the chaos: First, the tutor adopted a very assertive tone in her instructions: "Nobody moves until I say so, please," "Do not touch anything yet"; which decreased thereafter as participants grew more comfortable inside the system and realization came of the need and the benefits of listening before acting when working a collaborative tool. It is essential the tutor understands students will act upon every word uttered; hence, the tutor must carefully plan the sequence of events as he or she wants them to happen, and communicate these in such a way that aborts any undesired movements that may boycott interaction. The tutor must define the objectives of an activity, attentively explain the motions needed, say the group will break out for pair work, remind them to return to the plenary room as soon as they finish, and only then proceed to distribute participants into sub-conferences. Clarity, explicitness and order must rule each of the tutor's interventions.

Observations recorded that the tutor's use of English (L1) as prime language of communication contravened the recommendations of the communicative approach. However, let us be reminded that the tutor is bereft of the gestures that in a face-to-face setting support her conversation in the target language (L2) at all times. Audio-graphic conferencing systems completely subdue the theatrics of language learning; as the tutor has no assurance of being understood, he or she has no option but to abandon Spanish in favor of the language most familiar to learners. In this regard, we register the comments of a tutor after her first tutorial in Lyceum: "The only bad thing was that I spoke too much English; I couldn't use body language, so to make sure everybody followed, I had to translate everything I said." Translation of input means longer speeches, which, considered concurrent with reiterative and unnecessary explanations, justify the prolonged duration of sessions.

Turn-Taking

The arbitration of turn-taking in audio-graphic environments is difficult, to say the least, due to the deficiency of those visual clues which accompany physical presence in face-to-face classrooms. In Lyceum, at the click of a button, a little hand appears beside the name of the person who wishes to speak, informing the tutor of who is to be given the floor first. As the system also registers who raised their hand next, it is rather uncomplicated to maintain a right level of participation. The gimmick proves very effective, for example, in brainstorming exercises, where the tutor invites responses to an open question and takes names to avoid two individuals speaking at the same time or interrupting each other. However, it was found in certain circumstances the tutor abused the role as moderator. With all the group gathered in the main conference room, the tutor's position is pivotal to the production of interaction, as all exchanges bounce back to him or her. Note this exercise where students have to call out the objects they can see in a bar pasted onto a whiteboard [translation in square brackets]:

Tutor:	Jim, eres el primero, you are first on the list, ¿qué hay en el bar? [*What's in the bar?*]
Student 1:	Hay unas mesas. [*There are some tables*]
Tutor:	Vale, muy bien. Fiona, ¿qué hay en el bar? [*Ok, very good. Fiona, what's in the bar?*]
Student 2:	Hay unos taburetes. [*There are some stools*]

Tutor:	Vale, muy bien. Peter, ¿qué hay en el bar? [*Ok, very good. Peter, what's in the bar?*]
Student 3:	Hay un camarero. [*There is a waiter*]
Tutor:	Estupendo. Ann, ¿qué hay en el bar? [*Great. Ann, what's in the bar?*]
Student 4:	Hay un periódico. [*There is a newspaper*]

This routine of directly nominating the person to talk is explained as the tutor's strategy to secure contributions from all attending the conference; virtual presence makes it very easy to overlook a participant, so bearing in mind the main purpose of the tutorial is the delivery of opportunities for the learners' rehearsal of oral and aural skills in the target language, the tutor can not afford to leave anyone behind. It can be argued that the moment is suitable for the very straightforward question, "Have I not asked anyone?," but as the medium feasts in anonymity, such a personal course may only aggravate matters. By restricting their options to select an interlocutor, the tutor hampers the students' development as autonomous learners. An alternative methodology must then be implemented, involving the tutor relinquishing control over nominations to the students, while equal participation can still be watched by the tutor ticking names off as they speak. Intended as a solution, it resulted exactly in students being unsure of who had or had not partaken in the conversation (Student: "I'm not sure if Fiona was asked already"). The unsatisfying position is best resolved by means of working with the technology, exploiting the strengths of the application in hand: For collaborative exercises on the modules, the software displays the name of the user on the screen after an action has been taken (for example dragging a box, editing text, placing pins and others), thus facilitating tracking down the most active and passive patrons.

In similar fashion, as participants log on to the conference, their username is listed in a window. This sequence of arrival can be of service to establish a chain of turn taking, as the first person on the list interacts with the second, the second with the third and so on. Unfortunately, there were occasions when this tactic was rendered unproductive, given the fact that, for reasons unknown, different users would view different permutations of the same names on the directory. Therefore, conclusion has it that, in the context of technology distrust, sharing direct nomination of the addressee comes as best strategy to regulate turn taking.

A positive aspect of this pattern of interaction between tutor and learners, whereby the tutor functions as a kingpin of communication, is that the tutor gradually moves from L1 to L2, allowing students to get used to instructions in the target language. In the following transcript, the tutor successively nominates two people to perform a dialog about travelling to South America.

Tutor:	Kate, why don't you ask Jenny where she is going?
Student 1:	Sí, Jenny ¿adónde vas? [*Where are you going?*]
Student 2:	Voy a Uruguay. [*I'm going to Uruguay*]
Student 1:	¿Dónde está Uruguay? [*Where is Uruguay?*]

Student 2:	Está entre Argentina y Perú, no, sorry, Brazil.
	[*It is between Argentina and Peru*]
Tutor:	Muy bien, muchas gracias. Jenny, why don't you ask Darren now, please?
	(...)
Tutor:	Muy bien; Darren, ¿puedes preguntarle a Orla? [*Can you ask Orla?*]
	(...)
Tutor:	Vale. Orla, ¿hablas ahora con Jim? [*Would you talk to Jim?*]

From the preceding exercise, discourse in a virtual setting can be observed not to deviate much from the ubiquitous three-phase I-R-F structure — initial move by the tutor, response by the student, follow-up move by the tutor — which dominates teacher-centered classrooms. The variation here is that the tutor initiates interaction (I) by designating two people to talk to each other (i-r-i-r) before completing the cycle with feedback (I-i-r-i-r-F):

Tutor:	(I)	Kate, why don't you ask Jenny where she is going?
Student 1:	(i)	Sí, Jenny ¿adónde vas? [*Where are you going?*]
Student 2:	(r)	Voy a Uruguay. [*I'm going to Uruguay*]
Student 1:	(i)	¿Dónde está Uruguay? [*Where is Uruguay?*]
Student 2:	(r)	Está entre Argentina y Perú. [*It is between Argentina and Peru*]
Tutor:	(F)	Muy bien, muchas gracias. [*Very good. Thank you very much*]

Note that feedback is always a reassuring comment, an acknowledgment of the effort made ("Very good, thank you very much") prior to indicating any weaknesses in pronunciation or other aspects, assuming they have been covered in the course materials. This can be seen as a reinforcement not so much of the learners' progress in the target language, but of their capacity to perform well in the medium, a procedure aimed at minimizing the anxiety caused by the technology itself. As we do not see the person we are talking to, audio-graphic conferencing has been branded a cold intermediary of interaction, mounting high-tech apprehension on the already tangible unease of communicating in a language other than L1. Hence, feedback must be embraced by the tutor as an instrument to cater for the affective needs of the learners. It is a prerogative, nonetheless, that initially does not emerge in learner-learner interaction, which in the beginning is simply a very prosaic exchange of questions and answers (i-r-i-r). Hypothesis establishes the reason for this lack of emotional support of peers in their stoic embodiment of their role as passive receivers of information, their original expectations as beginner learners to talk only when personally asked to do so and not to venture beyond the necessary. Students do not come to terms with the modus operandi of the software as swiftly as is required of the tutor in his or her position of manager of the learning experience. As sessions on the system progress, the divide is shortened and feedback from peers begins to surface in interactions that imitate the input of the tutor, and ultimately live on collaboration. The short conversation we reproduce next takes place in one of the breakout rooms, immediately after the tutor draws the students' attention to the masculine and feminine features of the Spanish language; student 1 disregards the tutor's indications and repeatedly mistakes gender agreement of adjectives; student 2 subtly marks her words to correct her partner and finally empathizes with his plea:

Student 1:	¿Qué es? [*What is it?*]
Student 2:	Es una iglesia. [*It is a church*]
Student 1:	¿Cómo es? [*What is it like?*]
Student 2:	Es antigua y fantástica, can you say that? [*It is old and wonderful, can you say that?*]
Student 1:	Alto [*Tall*]
Student 2:	Sí, alta, and would you say is antigua? [*Yes, tall, and would you say it is old?*]
Student 1:	Sí, antigua, alta y ... ¡precioso! [*Yes, old, tall and ... beautiful!*]
Student 2:	Yes, that's a good one, es preciosa. [*Yes, that's a good one, it is beautiful*]
Student 1:	I'm getting mixed up with feminine and masculine.
Student 2:	Yes, I know, it is an easy mistake.

The type of interaction reproduced here does not conform to the mechanical repetition of the initiation-response model previously observed in learner-learner exchanges; it actually unfolds in a more intricate pattern brought upon by collaboration and negotiation of meaning, which at the same time mirrors closely a real-life situation. Negotiation of meaning does exist in audio-graphic environments, despite the absence of non-verbal behaviour: In instances where all participants are present in the main conference, the tutor must not dwell in the limelight, but include learners in sharing answers to queries coming from the floor. If a student cannot think of an item of vocabulary, the opportunity to help must be passed on to everybody; relation of peers is then encouraged and learning autonomy pushed to the front. On a one-to-one basis, for negotiation of meaning to take place, an accord on who will speak first must already stand.

Dealing with Silences

Although Lyceum allows for a maximum of three people to talk as a group, it is standard procedure that only one speaker takes the floor at a time. The OU has compared the experience of talking using Lyceum to talking in a room in complete darkness. The authors would add that it is more like being inside a void, the only background noises being your own or those coming from your own environment. Nothing is heard inside Lyceum that is not meant to be heard. As talking is then a deliberate action, silences occur very often: In a plenary session, the tutor nominates and puts a question to a student, waiting for the system's inherent time lag; when no response comes from the nominee, the tutor is prompted to check there are no technical sound difficulties — it may very well be the case of not having pressed "speak" — and reattempt communication, maybe through the text chat facility; if silence persists, it can only be assumed that the person has left the conference but has not clicked on the "away" button to indicate so, or simply that the person is still present but, for whatever reason, has no intention of participating. In this situation, the tutor is absolutely powerless, as without any visual contact it is impossible to determine a reason for the failure in communication. It is then sensible, for the sake of the rest of the participants, to abandon further efforts and to leave to the tutor's discretion the task of privately contacting the person in question.

Brainstorming exercises produce a different type of silence: Students tend to shy away from speaking too much; having contributed once, they are willing to give somebody else a chance, even being aware of the silence this generates. The following are a participant's thoughts on the matter: "I hate 'silences' to develop; I always want to jump in there, and sometimes it seems to me that I'm taking part more than my fair share." This, of course, is very hard to gauge when you do not see your classmates; hence, it is the tutor's responsibility to amalgamate the forum, acknowledging the interest of those who take part freely and directly addressing the quiet ones, as the tutor would normally do in a face-to-face setting.

In learner-learner interactions inside sub-conferences, turn negotiation is essential if awkward silences want to be avoided. In the following sample, two students struggle to get on with an exercise before settling on who is to speak first.

Student 1:	Have you got the screen in front of you?
Student 2:	I have, did you open it?
Student 1:	I did. Ok, I think we start. Do you want to start?
Student 2:	{overlap} Ok Ann, you can start.
{silence}	
Student 2:	Will I start Ann?
Student 1:	¿Dónde trabajas? [*Where do you work?*]
Student 2:	Trabajo en una oficina. [*I work in an office*]
{silence}	
Student 2:	¿Quién es tu jefe? [*Who is your boss?*]
{silence}	
Student 2:	Is that ok, Ann? Did you not hear me?
Student 1:	I thought I answered. I ask you and you answer and ask me, and I answer.

In the fourth line of this transcript, an instance of discourse overlapping is caused by Student 2 coming in over the initiating move of Student 1; they immediately realize they are both talking at the same time, so they stop; a few seconds of testing silence follow until finally Student 2 restarts interaction; Student 1 does not act upon her partner's cue, but initiates conversation herself. The problem we confront here is not so much judging when a speaker has finished her contribution, as the literature review points out, but agreeing on a beginning. Let us not forget that under consideration for this study is a group of beginner learners of Spanish, and their performance in interaction is very much limited by their intake of the language (at the time approximately 16 hours of oral and aural exposure, plus an unestimated amount of personal dedication). Advanced learners are better equipped for expressing their thoughts in terms of having the linguistic structures and vocabulary not only to communicate more freely, but also to say more. Thus, while the absence of visual information becomes an issue in determining the end of a particular speech in advanced exchanges, the matter of contention for beginners is negotiating a starting turn.

As previously mentioned, the strategy to employ is to spare one's blushes and be as direct as possible, either taking the initiative or nominating a next speaker; on certain occasions, it is also desirable that the speaker is extra-vocal: As the tutor arranges modules on the screen, for example, students are most aware of the void that surrounds them; they wait in silence for a new exercise, but because they do not see their classmates and therefore do not share the body language of that waiting period, silence becomes a short-lived encounter with isolation. This feeling can be easily prevented if the tutor keeps talking through his or her actions; to aid this Lyceum allows for the transmission of voice also by holding the "control" and "shift" keys together, in which case the mouse is free to do work on the screen. The tutor can manipulate the software's applications while at the same time describe his or her steps to the students, and must deliberately do so to defeat the system's emotional wasteland. This is once more contributing to the over-compensation of information conveyed through the auditory channel due to the loss of certain features of non-verbal behaviour in audio-graphic conferencing systems.

Other Aspects

In analyzing learner-content interaction, it was observed that when content is presented on a digital support, learners tend to deal with it as two separate learning experiences: On the one hand, it is about coming to grips with the technology; on the other, managing to communicate in the target language. Note in the following transcript the amount of negotiation it takes from learners to sort out the technology — in this case, opening a previously saved module in one of the breakout rooms — before turning their attention to Spanish.

Student 1:	Peter, can you hear me?
Student 2:	Yes, I can hear you.
Student 1:	Do you want to open the document or ...?

Student 2:	Yeah, I'm just trying to figure out how to open it. Do you have the Lyceum screen in front of you?
Student 1:	Yeah, that's all I have. I'm trying to remember how to ... was it "añadir," was it, we had to press?
Student 2:	I'll just try that now, hang on a second, mmm I'm not sure...
Student 1:	Don't you go ...? Oh, brilliant, we have it!
Student 2:	Oh, you can see that!?
Student 1:	What did you do after "añadir"?
Student 2:	Eh, I just clicked on ... I think it was I went into "documento" and I chose the one I saved as "Saturday tutorial."
Student 1:	Anyway, brilliant, brilliant. Do you want to start? Will I?

The joy of getting technology right can be as uplifting as it is frustrating to get it wrong. In the beginning of the course, many were the instances where technology got in the way of the course subject: When trying to construct a dialog in the target language by moving text boxes on a concept map, the difficulty was not knowing which line of discourse followed, but dragging the box to its correct position. Likewise, the authors have identified the "nervous finger" syndrome, which compels participants on an audio-graphic conference to click anywhere at any time, either accidentally or in complete disregard for the tutor's efforts to keep smooth-running affairs. Indeed, the best strategy to handle the enmity of the system in such terms is patience in capital letters, for it is also a very grateful medium for carrying exceptional quantities of good manners and humor. A participant likened the "Buenas tardes, ¿qué tal? [Good evening, how are you?] Can you all hear me?" sound check that opens each conference to the "Hello Dublin, Vilnius calling" in the Eurovision telephone round of scores. Spontaneity, however, is not naturally achieved when transmitted other than orally: Subsequent analysis of the logs found that some comments written on the chat, for example, were missed during the tutorial, thus denying the whole group a light moment of relief from the tension of the virtual class. One's voice becomes the sole tool for communicating what on the tutor's part should primarily be friendliness and understanding. A student on the course says, "I do wonder what everybody looks like, but it is easy to recognize voices. I attach personalities to the voices and feel I know the people." After all, there has to be something to relate to as human beings, a substitute for the bonding of a smile, a sigh or a tap in the back in a face-to-face situation: Learners must be encouraged to look for that warmth in the voices of fellow classmates, to get to know them as best they can by chit chatting at the beginning and end of each session.

It is still a very hard and exhausting experience to put to work all that helps one cope with the room in darkness. Nevertheless, it is true that audio-graphic conferences serve well their purpose of supplying learners with the flexibility to access and benefit from as many opportunities to listen to and speak in the target language: "To be able to attend a tutorial from home without having to travel, without having to be stuck in traffic, etc., is worth a lot"; "I love Lyceum, [it] means I don't have to drive to a class, get distracted by somebody's new shoes, etc.". This last comment brings to the fore one of the positive aspects of teaching and learning in audio-graphic conferences: By not having any visual information of fellow participants, there are also fewer distractions and one tends to concentrate more and listen carefully. To find out whether speaking without seeing brings added anxiety to learning a second language, we addressed the question directly to the learners and received mostly very cordial responses, as these quotes show: "I would find it quite embarrassing in a face-to-face tutorial but feel quite comfortable online," "How can you make a fool of yourself if no one can see you?," "It is better than face-to-face for shy people and people who dislike speaking in public." Negative reactions to the medium came from the technological side of the experience, particularly with regard to time wasting: "For some unknown reason, I could hear everyone but could not be heard, and it is extremely frustrating, as I knew I was delaying the activities and wasting everybody's time."

Conclusion: Ears to the Future

At the time of writing, teaching in Lyceum is still taking place twice a month. The identification and subsequent implementation of strategies to overcome the absence of some aspects of non-verbal behavior in communication over audio-graphic conferences is also still in progress. As each session brings about new episodes, the authors cannot declare this study concluded. A positive judgement can be drawn from experience in the last session covered in the research, whereby time allocation was kept as originally scheduled, the tutor communicated mainly in the target language and learners' interaction showed an ease within the system that had not been witnessed before to such an extent. That there were only three participants in the conference prompts us to speculate whether the medium at a beginners' level may be best exploited in small numbers. It is paramount that tutors and learners alike are aware that for interaction to be successful in audio-graphic collaborative virtual environments, there has to be a mutual understanding of what the medium requires of the user for the user to benefit fully from the medium. A compromise of adults must follow a previously agreed protocol to function with technology. In short, there is much to be done before getting to the stage where the learner can concentrate on the course subject; then, to the tutor's advantage, tandem teaching should be considered, with one tutor managing the technical side of the experience while a second one focuses attention on facilitating interaction in the target language. Teaching a language over an audio-graphic conferencing system is a completely different experience from teaching a language in a face-to-face environment; any attempt at comparing the two should be disregarded as futile. That the tutor finds him or herself in a virtual classroom doing what he or she knows should not be done in a communicative lesson should highlight the need for a new methodology to be applied in these new settings; a methodology that makes full use of the technology, informed by research into how oral input adds to the graphic environment. For our ears tell us a story that the eyes cannot follow.

Acknowledgments

The authors would like to thank their colleague Fernando Rosell Aguilar at Open University for his invaluable help and support in this research.

References

Anderson, A. H., Bard, E. G., Sotilo, C., Newlands, N., & Doherty-Sneddon, G. (1997). Limited visual control of the intelligibility of speech in face-to-face dialogue. *Perception & Psychophysics, 59*(4), 580-592.

Blake, N. (2000). Tutors and students without faces or places. *Journal of Philosophy of Education, 34*(1), 183-196.

Brown, H. D. (2000). *Principles of language learning and teaching*. White Plains: Longman.

Ellis, R. (1994). *The study of second language acquisition*. Oxford: Oxford University Press.

Felix, U. (2003). An orchestrated vision of language learning online. In U. Felix (Ed.), *Language learning online: Towards best practice* (pp. 7-18). Lisse: Swets & Zeitlinger.

Hampel, R. (2003). Theoretical perspectives and new practices in audio-graphic conferencing for language learning. *ReCALL, 15*(1), 21-36.

Hampel, R., & Baber, E. (2003). Using Internet-based audio-graphic and video conferencing for language teaching and learning. In U. Felix (Ed.), *Language learning online: Towards best practice* (pp. 171-191). Lisse: Swets & Zeitlinger.

Hauck, M., & Haezewindt, B. (1999). Adding a new perspective to distance (language) learning and teaching — the tutor's experience. *ReCALL, 11*(2), 46-54.

Jenkins, S., & Parra, I. (2003). Multiple layers of meaning in an oral proficiency test: The complementary roles of nonverbal, paralinguistic, and verbal behaviors in assessment decisions. *The Modern Language Journal, 87*(i), 90-107.

Kellerman, S. (1992). "I see what you mean": The role of kinesic behavior in listening and implications for foreign and second language learning. *Applied Linguistics, 13*(3), 239-258.

Kötter, M., & Shield L. (2000). *Talk to me! Real-time audio-conferencing and the changing roles of the teacher and the learner in a 24/7 environment.* Retrieved February 10, 2004, from http://collaborate.shef.ac.uk/nl2000.html

Kötter, M., Shield, L., & Stevens, A. (1999). Real-time audio and e-mail for fluency: promoting distance language learners' aural and oral skills via the Internet. *ReCALL, 11*(2), 55-60.

Lörscher, W. (2003). Nonverbal aspects of teacher-pupil communication in the foreign language classroom. *Web Proceedings of 2nd International Conference "Knowledge & Discourse: Speculating on Disciplinary Futures."* Retrieved February 17, 2004, from http://ec.hku.hk/kd2proc/proceedings/fullpaper/Theme3Fullpapers/LorscherWolfgang.pdf

Newlands, D., & McLean, A. (1996). The potential of live teacher supported distance learning: A case-study of the use of audio conferencing at the University of Aberdeen. *Studies in Higher Education, 21*(3), 285-297.

Tuovinen, J. E. (2000). Multimedia distance education interactions. *Educational Media International, 37*(1), 16-24.

Warschauer, M. (1997). Computer-mediated collaborative learning: Theory and practice. *The Modern Language Journal, 81*(iv), 470-481.

Woodin, J. (2001). Approaches to language teaching. In L. Arthur & S. Hurd (Eds.), *Supporting lifelong language learning: Theoretical and practical approaches* (pp. 49-57). London: CiLT & The Open University.

Chapter V

A Student-Centered Online Writing Course

Caroline Coit, University of Münster, Germany

Abstract

This chapter looks at a student-centered online writing course, where peer corrections were the sole source of feedback. Using the peer correction system-tool (PCS-tool), designed especially for the course, students wrote one text a week and sent their texts to anonymous readers for corrections. The study described here evaluated students' texts from 25 randomly chosen portfolios, looking at, among other aspects, the number of unreturned texts and false repairs as well as the amount of improvement in the students' writing over the semester. Based on the very positive results of the study, the author hopes that other universities will adopt the PCS-tool for their courses so that their students, too, can have the advantage of using this non-threatening environment to practice and improve their academic writing. The PCS-tool is open-source and available to all interested parties.

Introduction

Foreign language learners are aware that their classrooms do not truly reflect the foreign language as it is used in the real world. For this reason, many learners yearn to try out what they have learned in their classes on people in real-world situations. It is always exciting when strangers actually understand and respond to what a student has learned and when mistakes are not responded to as critically as in a classroom setting. However, finding opportunities to practice oral skills in real-world situations is not always easy, and depends on many circumstances; for example, the number of foreign visitors in the area where the student lives and the distance a student has to travel to visit another country. On the other hand, finding opportunities to practice written skills in real-world situations is not as difficult. Today, the Internet provides students with countless opportunities to practice their written skills outside of the classroom. Students can easily participate in e-mail exchanges or in chat rooms to practice their second language.

Despite the valuable practice these real-world online exchanges offer students, they lack two important criteria necessary to assure that students can become successful writers in an academic setting. The style of writing carried out in these real-world exchanges does not help students practice the type of formal writing that they will need for academic and career purposes. In addition, these exchanges offer little or no feedback to the writers concerning their errors. Consequently, we have designed an online writing course that offers students the opportunity to practice their academic-style writing techniques in a real-world setting where they also receive feedback. For this purpose we have developed the PCS-tool, which enables students to send academic-style texts to peers whom they do not know and receive feedback from them.

Collaborative Learning

Over the past several decades, research has substantiated the benefits peer collaboration can bring to the learning environment. When students' academic and social behaviors become more interactive, this results in a higher level of thinking (Hertz-Lazarowitz, 1992). Students who are given responsibility for their own learning and that of their peers are more motivated to perform better and more supportive of their fellow students (Johnson, Johnson, & Smith, 1991). Student-centered learning, therefore, encourages learners to be more autonomous and to take charge of their own learning (Abrami, Chambers, Poulsen, DeSimone, d'Apollonia, & Howden, 1995). In a non-threatening and non-competitive collaborative learning atmosphere, learners feel less fear, which enhances the affective aspects of learning (Johnson et al., 1991). As a response to this paradigm shift from the teacher-centered classroom toward a student-centered classroom (He, 1993), many writing instructors have begun to use peer-response groups in their writing classes.

Peer Review in Writing Classes

Using peer review in writing classes can especially benefit the learners' developmental processes. Vygotsky (1978) defines the distance between the learner's actual developmental level and the level of potential development as the zone of proximal development (ZPD). Because the level of texts written by peers is likely to operate within this zone, learning is likely to take place. This idea is also supported in the field of foreign language learning by Krashen's input hypothesis theory, which states, "in order for acquirers to progress to the next stage in the acquisition of the target language, they need to understand input language that includes a structure that is part of the next stage" (Krashen & Terrell, 1983, p. 32). A study by Kuhn (1972) also found that a small difference in the learners' cognitive levels was more conducive to cognitive growth than a large difference. By reading and working within this level of proximal development, learners are more likely to pick up vocabulary, grammatical structures and structural devices used by the students than when modeling is done at a higher level.

Peer-response groups in writing classes are also beneficial for students from the cognitive-processing point of view. One aspect of peer review that often remains unarticulated is that it can increase opportunities for students to practice the material to be covered in a class (Slavin, 1992). Because the number of texts that can be corrected is no longer dependent solely on the teacher finding time to correct them, but is put in the hands of many, students are able to write more (Peckham, 1978). Research in the cognitive processes of writing has shown that through practice, learners are able to become more proficient writers (Flower, Hayes, Carey, Schriver, & Stratman, 1986). Practice improves learners' abilities to write texts that are more grammatically correct and leads to better word choices to depict their ideas. With more opportunities to generate ideas and construct written thoughts, students' abilities to write more coherent and unified texts also increase.

Receiving Feedback

Research has consistently shown that students want error feedback (Ferris, 1995; Leki, 1991; Hedgcock & Lefkowitz, 1996). Research suggests that students appreciate negative comments that show them their problems (Nelson & Carson, 1998). But much research has focused on students' inattentiveness to teacher feedback. Researchers blame vague comments, a lack of positive encouragement and a reliance on error correction for negative student attitudes toward and inattention to feedback (Robb, Ross, & Shortreed, 1986; Cohen & Cavalcanti, 1990; Leki, 1991). A study by Cohen (1987) reported that 20% of students had not attended to their teacher's comments and that most of them had only "made a mental note" (Cohen, 1987 p. 63) of their teacher's feedback. More recent research in the field of process writing has led to the discovery that students look at corrections more carefully when they are carried out on papers to be revised than when the corrections are made on the final product (Ferris, 1995; Chandler, 2003).

However, research is inconclusive regarding the types of feedback that are most effective. In the multiple-draft context, some researchers have found that idea-based, meaning-level feedback can be more effective in promoting student revision (Hillocks, 1982; Kepner, 1991). Others found a mismatch between the type of teacher feedback that students expect and the type of feedback actually given, with students expecting a more error-correction approach (Cohen & Cavalcanti, 1990; Leki, 1991). According to Ferris and Roberts (2001), students want error feedback, such as underlining with descriptions, direct corrections or simply underlining, although research has found that cues more than corrections can help improve learners' abilities to self-correct (Makino, 1993). In another study, however, even though students thought they had paid most attention to grammar corrections, the feedback that students remembered most were the positive comments made by the teachers (Ferris, 1995).

Research specifically looking at peer review feedback has mainly concentrated on the benefits of peer feedback as a collaborative learning tool or on its potential to become an unproductive experience for L1 learners (Mangelsdorf & Schlumberger, 1992). However, research has begun to look at the effect peer review has for English-as-a-foreign-language (EFL) students (Paulus, 1999). Some researchers feel that because students may not think their peers are qualified to critique their writing and may distrust their recommendations (Nelson & Murphy, 1993), they may prefer teacher feedback (Nelson & Carson, 1998). But this does not mean that students do not like peer review. Mendonça and Johnson (1994) found that 53% of revisions made in students' essays were a result of peer feedback being incorporated into their work, and 69% of the students in a study by Mangelsdorf (1992) reacted positively to peer reviews. However, when comparing the influence of peer feedback to teacher feedback on revisions incorporated into revised essays, Connor and Asenavage (1994) found that most revisions did not even occur as a result of peers (5%) or teachers (35%), but from some other source (60%), which they speculated was probably the writers themselves.

Giving Feedback

Receiving feedback is not the only advantage peer review has for students. Peer reviewers can also gain competencies as givers of feedback (Keh, 1990). Taking responsibility for the learning of others is practice for later careers, one that many students feel they do not get enough practice in while at a university, despite the fact that many EFL students will become teachers or editors, where giving feedback is almost a daily task. Many researchers also cite social and cognitive advantages that giving feedback can have on reviewers. Through giving feedback, students' social and interpersonal skills can be rehearsed. By being both the receiver and giver of help, students learn to take the perspective of another, which is critical to social maturity (Hertz-Lazarowitz, Kirkus, & Miller, 1992). In the role of teacher, peer reviewers gain from articulating and reconstructing their own knowledge (Webb, 1989). Cognitive-elaboration perspectives (Dansereau, 1985) suggest that the help-giver must engage in some sort of cognitive restructuring if information already in memory is to be related to new material. Doing so may reveal gaps in the help-givers' understanding, which may cause them "to search for new information, resolve inconsistencies and learn the material better" (Abrami et al., 1995, p. 38).

Research on giving feedback has also looked at the types of feedback teachers and peers give (Paulus, 1999; Connor & Asenavage, 1994). Based on the taxonomy of revisions by Faigley and Witte (1981), revisions can be categorized into two types: surface level and meaning level. Although in general, teachers make more corrections than peers, both peers and teachers tend to make more surface-level corrections than meaning-level corrections (Hedgcock & Lefkowitz, 1992; Villamil & Guerrero, 1996; Coit, 2004). However, this depends on the draft and type of treatment being used. Meaning-level corrections are more likely to be made on earlier drafts, while surface-level corrections are more likely to be made on later drafts (Connor & Asenavage, 1994). In oral revisions, students tend to make more meaning-level corrections than when the revisions are made in writing.

And finally, being able to read other students' texts takes away the myth that shrouds writing in many classrooms and lets writers "see" how their peers write and deal with similar subjects. Students no longer remain passive recipients of a teacher's grades, only to wonder why one student's paper was judged as better than another. Peer review empowers students to become active, critical readers looking for characteristics that make texts powerful and characteristics that may hinder. By becoming objective critics themselves, they are more likely to learn from and adopt those styles of writing they find "good" and to learn to accept critique from different sources, both students and teachers, as they advance through their academic careers.

Significance of the Study

In most of the studies on peer review mentioned above, peer revision was carried out as a part of the writing process, which was done prior to a teacher's corrections. Most teachers view peer-response groups as students sharing their preliminary drafts with others before they hand them in to the teacher (Nelson & Murphy, 1993; Hayes & Flower, 1980; Saunders, 1989). Consequently, students are aware that they are not truly responsible for the corrections they make, knowing the teacher will be the final evaluator. Very little is known about what changes and effects may occur during peer review when students are empowered to be the final evaluators. Some educators even fear that these final student corrections, if left unchecked, could do more harm than good. False repairs and missed corrections are cited as the main reasons for not using peer reviewers as final correctors. If research can determine the effectiveness of student-empowered peer correction system (PCS), this can influence the way teachers and universities incorporate such practices into their programs. Therefore, to determine the efficacy of the use of such an approach in a student-centered online writing course, this class-based study analyzes the feedback given by student reviewers and looks at changes that take place in the student writing over the course of one semester.

The Study

Course Procedures

The study was conducted with 94 students who were enrolled in two separate online writing courses for the 2004 summer semester at two German universities. All subjects were EFL majors or minors in their first to fourth semesters. The course consisted of weekly writing assignments that were given via Internet. All in all, the students wrote a total of 12 texts. When the students completed their assignment for the week, they requested the e-mail address of a peer reviewer to send their text to for corrections. The peer reviewers were chosen randomly by the program while keeping the number of times a student was chosen within a limit of one more than the others. Due to the size of the departments and number of participants in the course, the students did not know their peer reviewer in most cases. In addition to sending their text to a peer reviewer, each student also received a text from a different student that they were to correct.

An introductory meeting was held at the beginning of the semester to explain the objectives and procedures to be followed in the course, after which all other correspondence took place virtually. Since most students are acquainted with informal writing through e-mails and chat rooms, it was explained that the idea of the course was to give them the opportunity to practice formal styles of writing in a similarly non-threatening atmosphere with the added benefit of receiving feedback on what they wrote. The requirements for earning credit in the course were completing all of the written assignments and doing their share of peer corrections. Both the corrected drafts and the final drafts were to be collected in a portfolio, which would then be shown to the teacher at the end of the semester to receive credit.

To assure the PCS would run smoothly and efficiently, students were asked to take it as seriously as they did their own writing. For editing, the teacher asked the students to use the reviewing tool available in Microsoft *Word* or any other word processing program. This would not only make it easier for the reviewers to edit the texts, but it would also make it easier for writers to revise their texts. A time limit of 1 week was set for returning the corrected texts, so the flow of feedback would be constant and up to date. The students were also made aware of the dangers of making false repairs. It was suggested that when they felt unsure about a correction, it would be most advisable to simply put a question mark next to the area rather than to insert a correction. And finally, the students were reminded that positive comments are an essential part of any feedback.

To determine the effects this student-empowered online course had on student writing, feedback and attitudes, data was collected at the end of the semester. The portfolios of 25 students were randomly chosen for evaluation in the study. Other data was also collected by asking students to fill out a questionnaire made available to them on the Internet at the end of the semester. To assure that it remained anonymous, the students were asked to drop it into the teacher's post box rather than sending it back by e-mail. Fifty of the questionnaires were randomly chosen for final evaluation.

Data Analysis

Problems with Unreturned Texts and False Repairs

In a completely student-centered online environment, new problems that do not occur in traditional classrooms may arise. Simply setting up the possibility for students to work cooperatively "does not mean that learning will be maximized" (Johnson et al., 1991, p.

2). Students' behaviors can have a negative as well as a positive impact on each other's learning. How the students interact depends on how the teacher structures their interdependence in the learning situation (Johnson et al., 1991). In an online course where the teacher does not monitor whether everyone has done all of the work on time, the possibility that students will not get their corrected texts back on time or even at all is an ever-present concern for both teacher and students.

The reasons for texts not being returned on time are numerous. For one, it can never be certain that every e-mail reaches its destination due to a lack of available memory space, spam filters and other hindrances. To alleviate the uncertainty about whether the text arrived at its destination, reviewers are asked to quickly e-mail a reply saying they have received the text; but even then, some students do not check their e-mails more than once a week, and so the writers remain uncertain as to whether it has reached its destination. In addition, some students are not reliable about doing their work on time. Therefore, if after 1 week, writers have not received their corrected text back, the instructor has set up several alternatives the students can carry out to assure that they get a corrected text back: The students can write an e-mail to their designated peer reviewer reminding them about their text, they can choose a new reviewer or they can send the text to the instructor for corrections. In order to estimate the severity of this potential problem, a questionnaire was used to find out whether the students had received their texts back on time and, if not, what actions they had carried out to see to it that they did get them back.

Unreturned texts are not the only area of special concern in an online student-centered environment. Students are aware that some of the corrections they receive may not be correct. False repairs can be very misleading for students and are considered one of the greatest drawbacks in a course where the teacher does not have a final look at the corrections made by peers. But how serious is this problem for EFL students studying English? To find this out, the corrected versions of the second and penultimate texts were scanned for false repairs made by peer reviewers. The number of false repairs was compared to the total number of corrections made by the peer reviewers on those texts.

Learning from Feedback

Considering the problems students may have had getting their feedback returned on time and their concern about false repairs, it is important to find out what the students thought about the feedback they received from their peers. Did they consider it helpful? Did they feel they were able to learn from the corrections? To what extent did they attend to their peer corrections? We put four questions on the questionnaire to learn the answers to these questions.

In addition to the regular corrections inserted directly into the text using the reviewing tool, reviewers were asked to write a brief comment at the end of each text they corrected. Because the type of teacher feedback students tend to remember most are the final comments, we evaluated the types of final comments made by the student reviewers.

The final comments on the second and penultimate texts in the 25 portfolios were first read and categorized based on whether they were neutral, positive or negative. A comment was considered neutral if no remark concerning the quality of the text was made or when the number of negative comments was equal to the number of positive comments. (It should be noted that two of the texts had been corrected by the teacher and were therefore not counted, leaving 48 for the study.) The following example illustrates a neutral comment:

"Nice story, a little confusing, but very interesting. (I have to admit that I had to read it twice to understand everything.)"

	Comment	Rated as:
1.	Nice story	Positive
2.	a little confusing	Negative
3.	but very interesting	Positive
4.	(I have to admit that I had to read it twice to understand everything.)	Negative

The final comments were then once again read and each phrase in the comments was categorized according to its purpose. The final categories decided upon were as follows. Did the peer reviewer:

1. Compliment the writer on the text
2. Mention what made the text good
3. Suggest ways to improve the text
4. Suggest areas the student should work on
5. Demonstrate uncertainty regarding corrections
6. Explain corrections
7. Make comments pertaining to the content of the text
8. Make personal comments

Below are some examples from the peer revisions to illustrate the categories.

1.	Complimented the writer on the text	All in all, fantastic!
2.	Mentioned what made the text good	Excellent vocabulary. It was fun to read your essay.
3.	Suggested ways to improve the text	To make it a little bit better, you could have mentioned something about your hobbies.

4.	Suggested areas the student needs to work on	I think you should look into the use of adverbs and adjectives, as you seem to have mixed that up a bit.
5.	Demonstrated uncertainty regarding corrections	I don't know if the corrections are of any use to you, or if they are always 100% right.
6.	Explained corrections	Almost all the other corrections are simply my own esthetical feeling of right or wrong.
7.	Made comments pertaining to the content of the text	Your description is very funny and exceptional. Darth Vader would have been proud.
8.	Made personal comments	Are you a dark metal fan, by the way ☺

Since giving feedback is also an important learning experience, three questions on the final survey dealt with this aspect. The students were asked if they felt they had learned from giving feedback and whether they had felt insecure about making corrections. If they were uncertain about a correction, they were asked what measures they took.

Changes in Writing Skills

It was postulated that as students began to feel more comfortable and secure in their writing, their texts would become longer. To check whether this was true, the length of the texts the students wrote in their second and penultimate assignments were compared. These texts were used as a basis for comparison because they were the most similar in topic. The difference between the number of words in the two tests was determined and a repeated measures t-test was performed to determine if there was a significant change.

In addition to the texts getting longer throughout the semester, it was also postulated that the quality of the texts would improve as a result of regular writing practice with peer feedback. To determine whether the students' writing improved over the course of the semester, the second and penultimate texts were again used for comparison. They were rated and scored, based on a score of one (lowest) to 10 (highest). Because the students were asked to focus on both structure (which was a part of every assignment) and surface errors, such as vocabulary and grammar (an important aspect for EFL learners), a separate score was given for each of these criteria. The scores were averaged together for a final score for each text. To determine if there was a significant improvement made, a repeated measures t-test was performed.

Table 1. Unreturned texts

	YES	NO
1. Did you always get your text back on time?	13	37
2. If not, how many times?		
a. Once?	15	
b. Twice?	16	
c. Three times?	6	
d. More than three times?	0	
3. If not, what did you do?		
a. Wrote to the person	32	
b. Asked the teacher for help	22	
c. Requested another peer editor	8	
d. Nothing	4	

Results

Unreturned Texts

Table 1 summarizes the results of the questionnaire on how frequently the students did not receive their corrected texts back on time. Thirty-seven students, or 74% of those surveyed, reported not having received at least one text back on time. Of those students who did not receive their texts back on time, six (16%) reported not having received three texts back on time. Although 4 students (10%) reported having taken no action, the other 90% reported having at least written the peer, asked the teacher for help or requested another peer reviewer in an attempt to get their corrected versions back.

False Repairs

Table 2 lists the number of total corrections and false repairs made on each of the 25 texts. Analysis shows that of the total 475 corrections made, the number of false repairs was 25, or 5.26% of all corrections for the second text. This decreased to 2.54% of all corrections (275) on the penultimate text.

Table 2. Percentage of false repairs

Text	Total Number of Corrections	Number of False Repairs
2nd	475	25 (5.26%)
11th	275	7 (2.54%)

Receiving Feedback

Did the students learn from the feedback they received, and to what extent did they attend to the corrections they received? Summarizing the answers to those questions from the questionnaire, Table 3 shows that although 43 (86%) students said they had not always agreed with the corrections they received, 44 (88%) felt they had learned from the peer corrections. And most impressive was that all 50 students said they had gone over the corrections their peers made for them. Of the 43 students who answered that they had not always agreed with their corrections, 40 of them (93%) said they had either looked up the material and/or asked someone else. Only 3 (7%) did nothing.

Table 4 looks at whether the final peer comments the students received were neutral, positive or negative. The data shows that from the 50 corrections evaluated, nine (18%) were neutral in nature. Forty (80%) were ranked as positive (see samples below) and only 1 of the 50 was considered negative. The negative comment consisted only of suggestions for ways to improve the text and made no positive comments.

Table 3. Learning from feedback

	YES	NO
1. Were you able to learn from the corrections you received?	44	6
2. Did you always go over the corrections from the peers?	50	0
3. Did you always agree with the corrections?	7	43
4. If not, what did you do?		
a. Looked it up?		40
b. Asked someone?		9
c. Nothing?		3

Table 4. Final peer comments

Peer Corrections	Neutral Comments	Positive Comments	Negative Comments
50	9	40	1

Table 5. Final peer comments categorized

Type of Comment Made by Peer Reviewer	Number of Times
1. Complimented the writer on the text	36
2. Mentioned what made the text good	35
3. Suggested ways to improve the text	15
4. Suggested areas for the student to work on	6
5. Demonstrated uncertainty regarding the corrections	10
6. Explained the corrections	16
7. Made comments relating to the contents of the text	15
8. Made personal comments	24
Total number of types of comments	**157**

To get an in-depth understanding of the types of remarks peers make in their final comments, each phrase was categorized and counted. Table 5 summarizes the number of times the eight categories were used in the final comments.

The following are sample scripts of student comments with the categories in parentheses:

> "Dear Katja!
>
> I really liked reading your text. It was very fluent and I found it very interesting because I have never been on such an event. I have just marked some mistakes in vocabulary. Nevertheless you have done a great work!
>
> Well done!" (1, 2, 6, 8)

> "Hi, I did not find many mistakes only the few I marked.
>
> Sorry it took me so long, but my life was a catastrophe the last three weeks!
>
> Karina" (8)

"Hello Birgit,

Basically, your text was well written. A few times I wasn't sure exactly what was wrong (or if it was), that's why I put a question mark in those places. I hope you are getting the corrections on time. I wish you a nice vacation.

Maren" (1, 5, 6, 8)

"Dear Anne!

I liked your paragraph very much. There was nothing to complain about! You have written an exiting and entertaining text. Thank you for such a pleasure.

Well done, Linda" (1, 2)

"It was great fun to read your text. And I only found these two little things. Very good – go on like that." (1, 2, 8)

"Very well done. Few minor spelling mistakes, but a very elaborate style. A great read!" (1, 2,6)

"Congratulation! Rather good!! I couldn't find any mistakes at all." (1)

"Hey Kati!

I just read your text. And in my opinion it was good. I marked some things. Just look at it. I don't know if I correct it right." (1, 5)

"I like your text! It's funny and it has a punch line.

I think it's good how you describe the situation in the bus — I can feel what it must be like to drive by bus every morning, though I fortunately have a bike J" (1,2, 8)

"Good job! There were no serious mistakes in your essay and it was easy to read. The only thing you could maybe think of is connecting your sentences a little more, as you had some real short sentences. Other things I marked are just expressions you could think over or some typing mistakes, I guess. Nevertheless, a nice essay! Keep on writing!" (1, 2, 3, 6, 8)

"Your description was really funny. The mistake you make most often is to translate exactly from German to English, e.g., There stands a bottle." (2, 6)

"It was a lot of fun reading your story! Sometimes your sentences are rather long, thus not immediately easy to comprehend. But nevertheless, I think it is a quite good text — I admire your brilliant English expression!

With best wishes

Kathi" (1, 2, 3)

"Dear Andrè,

Wow — I am really impressed after having read your paragraph! The first time I really just read it, without searching for mistakes, and I fully enjoyed it. The way you develop your thoughts and arguments is clearly structured and so, for the reader, easy to follow (If I got it right, one could divide the text in the following parts: 1) your enthusiasm for philosophy and therefore your aim to make it you profession, therefore: spend some time abroad, 2) your first contact with philosophy, 3) further experiences = civilian service, 4) present situation in Münster and aim for future = frame with beginning = aim to study abroad.)

Moreover, your style contributes to the convenient reading, as your sentences are clearly structured, too. I had the impression that almost every sentence helped as a support for your general topic and thus made the text appear as a unit, coherent and enjoyable as a whole. In two cases I was not sure what you exactly meant->see ???.

I really find it hard to correct your and texts in general. I always try my best but often I ask myself if one can say something in that way or better not ...

So, whenever I put something in brackets, it is just an advice how it might sound better – in my opinion. When I crossed out something, I was sure that it had to be corrected. As a general statement, I would say that there are almost no serious mistakes, one wrong if-sentence maybe, and that you really did an excellent job! Go on this way!

If you have any questions or critics, please let me know ...

Have a nice Sunday

Sonja" (1, 2, 5, 6, 7, 8)

Giving Feedback

Table 6 below summarizes answers relating to how the students felt about giving feedback. When asked whether they learned from giving feedback, 96% responded with "yes." All of the students admitted to having felt unsure about some of the corrections they made, but only 8% reported not doing anything when that was the case. The other 92% said they either looked the material up and/or asked someone else.

Table 6. Giving peer feedback

		YES	NO
1.	Did you learn from giving feedback?	48	2
2.	Were you sometimes unsure about a correction?	50	
3.	If so, what did you do?		
	a. Looked it up?	46	
	b. Asked someone?	27	
	c. Nothing?	4	

Changes in Writing Skills

Did the texts become longer as the semester progressed? Table 7 compares the average number of words students wrote in the second and penultimate texts. On average, the number of words increased by 106.24 words, which was an increase of 131%. The repeated measures *t*-test was found to be -5.601, significant at p = .000 (df = 24), indicating a statistically significant increase in the number of words from the second to the penultimate texts.

Did the students' writing improve over the course of the semester, despite the lack of teacher feedback? Table 8 shows the average scores in each of the areas judged and their final scores. On average, student writing improved by a score of 3.166 on a 10-point scale. The repeated measures *t*-test for structure was found to be -15.477, significant at p = .000 (df = 24); and for vocabulary and grammar -.734, significant at p = .000 (df = 24), both indicating statistically significant improvements in writing skills from the second to the penultimate texts.

Table 7. Average length of texts

Average number of words for text 2	334.80
Average number of words for text 11	441.04
Average difference between the two texts	106.24

Table 8. Average results of text scoring

	Text 2	Text 11	Difference
Structure	4.096	8.104	4.008
Vocabulary and Grammar	4.528	6.852	2.324
Average	4.312	7.478	3.166

Overall Course Rating

If students are going to be made responsible for managing their own writing and for the corrections of their peers, it is helpful to know exactly what students think about working in such an environment and to know which areas of the course the students liked the best and the least. The final two questions on the questionnaire gave students the opportunity to express these likes and dislikes. From the 50 questionnaires, the students

Table 9. Course rating

What did you like least about the course?		What did you like best about the course?	
Feedback			
Not getting the text back on time	6	Getting valuable feedback	4
Not getting enough feedback	2	Reading the other students' texts	4
The difficulty of giving feedback	2	Being able to practice giving feedback	2
		Not knowing the students when getting and giving feedback	2
Writing Process			
Not knowing what to write about	5	Being able to write so much	16
Structure of the Course			
Not knowing the others	2	Doing the assignments whenever they wanted	7
		Getting to know each other better than in class	2
Total	**17**	**Total**	**37**

responded 17 times to what they liked the least and 37 times to what they liked the best about the course. Table 9 summarizes their answers, which have been grouped by feedback, the writing process and the structure of the course.

The area of feedback was mentioned most frequently in the negative course ratings, showing just how important feedback is, even in a completely student-reviewed course. Regarding what the students liked best about the course, all of the areas received a good sampling of comments. However, being able to "write so much" was mentioned almost half the time.

Discussion

Feedback

The results show that in this student-empowered online writing course getting feedback returned on time was a problem. Seventy-four percent of the students did not get at least one text returned on time, and this was an apparent problem for many students, causing them unnecessary concern and effort. Despite these results, however, all 50 texts that had been randomly chosen for the study were corrected, showing that the students not only took initiatives to make sure their texts were returned but that they were also successful in their attempts.

On the other hand, false repairs, one of the major reasons for teachers being skeptical about using PCS, did not prove to be as great a problem as in previous studies (Cho & Schunn, 2003). There could be several reasons for this. This study was carried out with students of English, many of whom want to become English teachers. Therefore, they probably had a greater interest in practicing what they would later be doing in their professions than students of other fields. Another contributing factor may also be that the students were asked to simply put a question mark next to structures they were uncertain of rather than to try and correct them. This may have avoided many pitfalls. They also may have felt more responsible for correcting their peer's text well, knowing the teacher would not correct it later. That the number of false repairs decreased by more than half over the course of the semester also shows that with extended practice students can improve in their feedback techniques.

The extent to which the students found peer feedback helpful is comparable to findings in studies on teacher feedback (Ferris, 1995). All of the students reported going over their corrections, which is a higher percentage than in most studies. However, 93% of the students also reported taking an extra step and looking up the material when they were not sure if it was right, something they may not have done if the corrections had been made by the teacher, where they would have been less likely to question the corrections. Another factor that may have motivated students to attend to their corrections is the editing tool with which the students made their corrections. The tool makes it very easy for writers to either accept or reject the corrections their peers have made, and thus motivates the writers to revise their texts and think about their corrections while deciding whether to adopt them. Another contributing factor could have been the detailed final comments they received, in which they were given tips on how to improve their text and areas they should focus on. This is information that many teachers do not regularly find time to include when they correct papers of an entire class.

Although the participants considered receiving feedback extremely important, they did not look upon giving feedback quite as eagerly. In fact, on the questionnaire, two students wrote that "giving feedback" was what they liked the least about the course. This could be due to the insecurity that all of the students reported having sometimes felt when making corrections, which is also reflected in many of the final comments the students made in their corrections. Despite this uncertainty, 96% of the students responded that they felt they had learned from giving feedback, and two students even said that "practicing giving feedback" was what they had liked most about the course. As all but 8% of the students reported having looked up or asked about material they were unsure of led the students to the feeling that they had learned from giving feedback.

That the students did not know the person they sent their texts to or the person whose text they corrected was also mentioned by several students. Two of the students rated not knowing the other course members as what they liked least about the course. However, two other students said that was what they liked most about the course. In conversations with students, many referred to the anonymity as being an intriguing factor in the course and that, despite not knowing the students, they had had a better feel for their audience than when writing for only the teacher (Hedgcock & Lefkowitz, 1994; Huff & Kline, 1987). Others said they had appreciated not knowing the students when writing their texts or giving feedback. They felt less shy about what and how they wrote than if they had known the person and felt more free and open to make corrections than if the person were sitting across from them (Etheris & Tan, 2004). Some also mentioned that they had gained confidence when a "stranger" was able to understand their text and felt "very pleased" when they liked it.

Changes in Writing Skills

The increased length in the student texts and the average improvement of more than 3 points on a 10-point scale show that as the semester progressed the students not only felt more comfortable with writing but they had become better writers. In conversations, some students also reported spending less time while writing the same amount as the semester progressed. This finding is consistent with other long-term studies on teacher feedback (Chandler, 2003).

Despite these positive changes in writing skills, it is hard to say which of the factors, peer feedback or extended writing practice, may have had the greatest influence on them. Possibly, it depends on the student and the experiences he or she had. In the final course rating, the most responses concerning what the students liked best about the course had to do with writing. Sixteen from 37 students responded that what they liked best about the course was "being able to write so much." Seven other students responded that they appreciated being able to do the assignments whenever they wanted and not having to go to class, which left them more time to write. Only four students responded that receiving feedback was what they liked most. However, a total of 12 students mentioned feedback in one way or another as being what they liked most about the course. Possibly a synergetic combination of these two factors was responsible for the improved writing skills of the students. Without the corrective and essentially positive feedback, there would have been little motivation to complete the weekly assignments. And without the weekly assignments, there would have been no feedback.

Limitations and Recommendations for Further Research

The current study looked at advanced students of EFL who were studying English as one of their major subjects. Future research could enhance the reliability of the findings by studying EFL students who are not studying English but, for all practical purposes, need to be able to write academic-style papers in English.

Since this study looked only at the results of PCS on the students' first drafts, another possible area of investigation is to study the number and types of corrections the writers incorporate into their final revisions. Particularly interesting here would be to look at how many of the false repairs are taken over and incorporated by the writers.

Further studies could also look at the types of revisions made by peer reviewers and those incorporated by the writers based on the taxonomy of revisions by Faigley and Witte (1981). This would offer teachers and researchers a better comparison of the types of revisions made as a result of student-empowered peer feedback compared to teacher feedback. A deeper analysis of the effects of PCS on students' writing will have a profound influence on to what extent teachers and universities adopt such a tool.

Conclusion

The positive results in this course using PCS should motivate teachers and researchers to look at the advantages technology offers students to take charge of their own learning and of their peers'. Through the use of the PCS-tool, students are able to gain the much-needed real-world writing practice lacking in their regular writing courses and still receive valuable feedback on what they write. The results show that in such an environment, students value the peer feedback they receive and attend to it as much as, if not more than, teachers' corrections. This technology-oriented environment is familiar to students, and students adapt quickly to the social-supportive aspect of giving feedback to writers they do not know. Because they are not writing for the teacher, whose corrections are considered more threatening, many writers say they feel freer to experiment with new styles of writing, grammar structures and vocabulary. As one student's final comment read: "At last, a course which lets one think about new vocabulary, test structures and enjoy the language!!"

Further Uses

The tool described in this online writing course can be adapted for use in other courses where writing and feedback are important. This tool can be used in a completely student-centered environment as well as in courses in which the instructors are unable to "check" as many assignments as they would like, allowing students to continue writing and receive feedback (Mackworth, 1970) on what they have written, despite large and overfilled classrooms. Anyone interested in taking advantage of the existing course or creating their own similar environment is invited to write the author for information.

References

Abrami, P. C., Chambers, B., Poulsen, C., DeSimone, C., d'Apollonia, S., & Howden, J. (1995). *Classroom connections: Understanding and using cooperative learning.* Toronto: Harcourt Brace.

Chandler, J. (2003). The efficacy of various kinds of error feedback for improvement in the accuracy and fluency of L2 student writing. *Journal of Second Language Writing, 12*, 267-296.

Cho, K., & Schunn, C. D. (2003). Validity and reliability of peer assessments with a missing data estimation technique. *Proceedings of ED-Media.*

Cohen, A. D. (1987). Student processing of feedback on their compositions. In A. Wenden & J. Ruben (Eds.), *Learner strategies in language learning* (pp. 57-69). Englewood Cliffs: Prentice-Hall.

Cohen, A. D., & Cavalcanti, M. C. (1990). Feedback on compositions: Teacher and student verbal reports. In B. Kroll (Ed.), *Second language writing: Research insights for the classroom* (pp. 155-177). Cambridge: Cambridge University Press.

Coit, C. (2004). Peer review in an online college writing course. *Proceedings of IEEE International Conference on Advanced Learning Technologies,* 902-903.

Connor, U., & Asenavage, K. (1994). Peer response groups in ESL writing classes: How much impact on revision? *Journal of Second Language Writing, 3*, 257-276.

Dansereau, D. (1985). Learning strategy research. In J. W. Segal, S. F. Chipman & R. Glaser (Eds.), *Thinking and learning skills: Vol. 1. Relating instruction to research* (pp. 209-239). Hillsdale: Erlbaum.

Etheris, A. I., & Tan, S. C. (2004). Computer-supported collaborative problem solving and anchored instruction in a mathematics classroom: An exploratory study. *International Journal of Learning Technology, 1*(1), 16-39.

Faigley, L., & Witte, S. (1981). Analyzing revision. *College Composition and Communication, 32*, 400-414.

Ferris, D. R. (1995). Student reactions to teacher commentary on student revision. *TESOL Quarterly, 31,* 315-339.

Ferris, D. R., & Roberts, B. (2001). Error feedback in L2 writing classes. How explicit does it need to be? *Journal of Second Language Writing, 10*(3), 161-184.

Flower, L., Hayes, L., Carey, L., Schriver, K., & Stratman, J. (1986). Detection, diagnosis, and the strategies of revision. *College Composition and Communication*, 37, 16-55.

Hayes, J. R., & Flower, L. S. (1980). Identifying the organization of writing processes. In L. W. Gregg & E. R. Steinberg (Eds.), *Cognitive processes in writing* (pp. 3-30). Hillsdale: Erlbaum.

He, A. (1993). Language use in peer review texts. *Language in Society*, *22*(3), 403-420.

Hedgcock, L., & Lefkowitz, N. (1992). Collaborative oral/aural revision in foreign language writing instruction. *Journal of Second Language Writing, 3*, 141-163.

Hedgcock, J., & Lefkowitz, N. (1994). Feedback on feedback: Assessing learner receptivity to teacher response in L2 composing. *Journal of Second Language Writing, 3*, 141-163.

Hedgcock, J., & Lefkowitz, N. (1996). Some input on input: Two analyses of student response to expert feedback in L2 writing. *Modern Language Journal, 80*, 287-308.

Hertz-Lazarowitz, R. (1992). Understanding interactive behaviors: Looking at six mirrors of the classroom. In R. Hertz-Lazarowitz & N. Miller (Eds.), *Interaction in cooperative groups: The theoretical anatomy of group learning* (pp. 71-101). Cambridge: Cambridge University Press.

Hertz-Lazarowitz, R., Kirkus, V., & Miller, N. (1992). Implications of current research on cooperative interaction for classroom application. In R. Hertz-Lazarowitz & N. Miller (Eds.), *Interaction in cooperative groups: The theoretical anatomy of group learning* (pp. 253-280). Cambridge: Cambridge University Press.

Hillocks, G. (1982). The interaction of instruction, teacher comment and revision in teaching the composing process. *Research in the Teaching of English, 16*, 261-278.

Huff, R., & Kline, C. (1987). *The contemporary writing curriculum: Rehearsing, composing, and valuing*. New York: Teachers College Press.

Johnson, D., Johnson, R., & Smith, K. (1991). *Active learning: Cooperation in the college classroom.* Edina: Interaction Book Company.

Keh, C. L. (1990). Feedback in the writing process: A model and methods for implementation. *ELT Journal, 44,* 294-304.

Kepner, C. G. (1991). An experiment in the relationships of types of written feedback to the development of second-language writing skills. *Modern Language Journal, 75*, 303-313.

Krashen, S. D., & Terrell, T. D. (1983). *The natural approach: Language acquisition in the classroom.* Oxford: Pergamon.

Kuhn, D. (1972). Mechanism of change in the development of cognitive structures. *Child Development, 43*, 833-844.

Leki, I. (1991). The preferences of ESL student for error correction in college-level writing classes. *Foreign Language Annals, 24,* 203-218.

Mackworth, J. (1970). *Vigilance and habituation.* Harmondsworth: Penguin.

Makino, T. Y. (1993). Learner self-correction in EFL written compositions. *ELT Journal, 47,* 337-341.

Mangelsdorf, K. (1992). Peer reviews in the ESL composition classroom: What do the students think? *ELT Journal, 46,* 274-284.

Mangelsdorf, K., & Schlumberger, A. (1992). ESL student response stances in a peer-review task. *Journal of Second Language Writing, 1,* 235-254.

Mendonça, C. O., & Johnson, K. E. (1994). Peer review negotiations: Revision activities in ESL writing instruction. *TESOL Quarterly, 28,* 745-769.

Nelson, G. L., & Carson, J. G. (1998). ESL students' perceptions of effectiveness of peer response groups. *Journal of Second Language Writing, 7,* 113-131.

Nelson, G. L., & Murphy, J. M. (1993) Peer response groups: Do L2 writers use peer comments in revising their drafts? *Tesol Quarterly, 27*(1), 135-141.

Paulus, T. M. (1999). The effect of peer and teacher feedback on student writing. *Journal of Second Language Writing, 8*(3), 265-289.

Peckham, L. (1978). Peer evaluation. *English Journal, 67,* 61-63.

Robb, T., Ross, S., & Shortreed, I. (1986). Salience of feedback on error and its effect on EFL writing quality. *TESOL Quarterly, 20,* 83-95.

Saunders, W. M. (1989). Collaborative writing tasks and peer interaction. *International Journal of Educational Research, 13*(1), 101-112.

Slavin, R. E. (1992). When and why does cooperative learning increase achievement? Theoretical and empirical perspectives. In R. Hertz-Lazarowitz & N. Miller (Eds.), *Interaction in cooperative groups: The theoretical anatomy of group learning* (pp. 71-101). Cambridge: Cambridge University Press.

Villamil, O. S., & Guerrero, M. (1996). Peer revision in the L2 classroom: Social-cognitive activities, mediating strategies, and aspects of social behavior. *Journal of Second Language Writing, 5,* 51-76.

Vygotsky, L. S. (1978). *Mind in society: The development of higher psychological processes.* Cambridge: Harvard University Press.

Webb, N. (1989). Student interaction and learning in small groups. *International Journal of Educational Research, 13*(1), 21-31.

Chapter VI

Learner-Centered Language Programs: Integrating Disparate Resources for Task-Based Interaction

Deryle Lonsdale, Brigham Young University, USA

C. Ray Graham, Brigham Young University, USA

Rebecca Madsen, Brigham Young University, USA

Abstract

In this chapter we first discuss three factors believed to be important for success in second-language learning: comprehensible input, comprehensible output and noticing discrepancies. We then discuss our current research work in integrating various components of human language technology to address these three language acquisition factors. Our efforts involve creating a wide spectrum of interesting language-learning applications, including question answering and pronunciation tutoring. These applications show the potential of combining speech processing with other important natural-language tools, such as external knowledge sources and dialog move engines. The applications we have developed not only show that this integration can be successful in creating non-trivial applications, but that there is much work that can be done to build on what we have accomplished thus far.

Introduction

Recent reviews of computer-assisted language learning (CALL) (Pennington, 1996; Beatty, 2003; Zhao, 2003) suggest that while developers and learners are often enthusiastic about CALL programs, there is little empirical evidence that shows they are effective in helping learners develop oral communication skills, particularly speaking skills. This lack of evidence is, in part, due to the fact that researchers have simply failed to conduct the needed research with the myriad of software programs available for teaching such skills. A great deal of the fault, however, must be placed at the feet of program developers, who have failed to create programs that enable learners to practice oral interaction skills as part of their learning activities.

When one examines the nature of software programs reviewed in such journals as *CALICO* and *Language Learning & Technology,* or online at the CTI Centre for Modern Language Resources and the CALL@ChorusSoftware Reviews, one is struck by the fact that, with few exceptions, software programs provide learners with very little opportunity to go beyond a rather mechanical reproduction of oral language. While many programs may provide learners with some high-quality listening opportunities and lots of graphic support and enhanced input, opportunities for oral interaction are very limited. In fact, most of these programs require that students activate the learning materials by clicking on buttons to watch actors participate in oral interactions that serve as models for them to repeat and memorize. Thus, the learner becomes a third-person participant in the interaction. Instructions are most often presented in written form and often in the native language, and learners interface with the program via keyboard and/or buttons with clicks of the mouse. In some programs, learners are encouraged to insert their names into structured dialogs that they have seen enacted by others and to participate in presenting alternate lines following previously given models. In some, they are encouraged to record their own voices performing the dialogs and then compare them with the native speaker model. These exercises are much more akin to dialog memorization than they are to communicative interaction.

The major goal of our work is to show how non-communicative learning activities in conventional CALL programs can become part of a communicative learning environment where the student becomes a first-person participant in language interaction through the use of animated agents and speech technology. We show that animated conversational humanoid agents can direct the language experience of the learner through verbal communication and that the learner can interact both verbally and non-verbally with the agent. Our strategy has been to develop complex, multi-component applications — selecting appropriate toolkits supporting existing technologies and integrating them together as seamlessly as possible.

This chapter will discuss: 1) a theory of language learning that supports the interactive nature of our learning activities; 2) core technologies that serve as the foundation for our work; and 3) novel applications we have developed to engage the learner in simulated communication with agents. Finally, we will conclude with possible further work.

Background: A Theory of Second Language Acquisition

It has long been recognized that input plays a crucial role in language acquisition (Krashen, 1985; Gass, 1997). Comprehensible input can be presented to learners in a variety of ways, including an agent speaking directly to the learner, video segments of native speakers performing real-world tasks, video and audio segments of presentations and monologs, and so forth. The comprehensibility of the input can be enhanced by using visual aids and pre-listening schema-building exercises, presenting crucial vocabulary items prior to the listening exercise, providing the written form of the text to accompany the listening exercise and providing a glossary of difficult words, to mention only a few methods.

However, for input to get incorporated into the learner's interlanguage, it must not only be comprehensible but comprehended (Gass, 1988, 1997, 2003). Verification of comprehension requires interaction on the part of the learner. Long's (1996) Interaction Hypothesis claims that attention, achieved through interaction, is a crucial part of the mechanism of acquisition. Thus, one of the contributors to the effectiveness of second-language instruction is the degree to which it provides the learner with input comprehended by the learner. We believe that this can be done most effectively in CALL by having an animated agent speak directly to the learner, giving instructions and interacting with the learner regarding instructional contents and by engaging the learner in verbal exchanges.

A second factor that has been shown to contribute to the development of language is comprehensible output (Swain, 1985). Not only does interaction increase the comprehensibility of input for a given learner, but attempts to produce language that is comprehensible to interlocutors contributes to the acquisition process in other ways. Recently, Swain (1995) has claimed that the mechanism behind the influence of output on language acquisition is that it moves the learner from a general nondeterministic semantic processing mode for comprehension to a complete grammatical processing mode necessary for production. Thus, as learners are required to formulate novel utterances in a communicative task, they are forced to focus on the more temporal and structural aspects of the forms and process them in much greater detail. Hence, task-based approaches to second-language instruction, in which learners are required to participate in communicative interactions, are widely considered to be the most efficient way to develop interlanguage skills (Bygate, Skehan, & Swain, 2001; Lightbrown & Spada, 1999; Swain, Brooks, & Tocalli-Beller, 2002; Hall & Walsh, 2002). We attempt to create this interaction via animated agents using speech recognition and synthesis.

A third factor hypothesized to contribute to acquisition is that of "noticing." Many researchers in second-language acquisition believe that for the learners' interlanguage system to evolve toward more native-like forms, the learner must notice, either through positive or negative evidence, that their system is at variance with the native speaker forms. This is believed to be accomplished through various mechanisms, including those already discussed. As mentioned above, Long's (1996) Interaction Hypothesis claims that attention to form is accomplished through negotiated input. As interlocutors use strategies such as confirmation checks, comprehension checks, clarifications requests, recasts and overt corrections, learners are made aware that their interlanguage needs modifying. This, along with positive modeling, enables learners to make corrections in their interlanguage system.

An example of how noticing with negative evidence is accomplished in our program is illustrated by one of our pronunciation activities, discussed in detail below. In the activity, the animated agent describes a situation involving a character performing a certain action (for example, a blacksmith heating metal with a fire or hitting the metal with a hammer). If the agent tells the learner that the blacksmith is hitting the metal, the learner must respond that it is with a hammer. If the learner misperceives what the agent has said and chooses the fire instead of the hammer, the agent gives corrective feedback, but always in the context of communicating the correct meaning. When it becomes the learner's turn to tell the agent what the blacksmith is doing, he or she must pronounce "hitting" and "heating" well enough for the agent to correctly identify the object. If the agent chooses the wrong object, the learner knows that he or she has not pronounced it correctly and must try again. It is expected that by reducing the redundancy of language to a minimum so that miscommunication results from a mispronounced sound, the learner will be induced to notice and begin the process of modifying the interlanguage phonological system, especially if the experience is repeated with several situations involving the same sound.

Core Technologies: Issues and Solutions

Speech Recognition and Synthesis

Our work incorporates two fundamental technologies: speech recognition and speech synthesis. Although both are familiar, we deem it necessary to mention some of the criteria and features that make these technologies desirable for language learning, as well as some of the difficulties that preclude their widespread use in current educational applications.

Speech recognition is a complex problem that relies on various architectures instantiated in several developer toolkits and end-user programs. While work has been progressing on increasing the versatility of such technology, its performance is still far short of the widely sought-for ideal: large-vocabulary, high-accuracy, speaker-independent continuous speech recognition for any language. Still, speech recognition technology can be a viable option for educational applications when pragmatically implemented and integrated with other components, particularly when developers are able to adapt system components to the particular issues being addressed. For an application to be successful, the questions developers must ask themselves are, "What do we want to use it for?" and "How do we get it to perform the task?" (Ehsani & Knodt, 1998). Pursuing technological tradeoffs via available toolkits becomes the central question for the use of speech recognition.

A speech synthesis component is equally important for highly interactive speech processing systems. Most widely used speech synthesis systems use text-to-speech (TTS) processing. Although the quality of TTS spoken output is improving, all existing systems produce unnatural-sounding voices to varying degrees. The use of diphone concatenation techniques seems the most promising solution to phonetic and phonological variation. However, significant progress remains to be made in the area of suprasegmental properties: intonational contours, stress, rhythm and so on. It has been observed that the "speech synthesis component is the one that often leaves the most lasting impression on users" (Glass, 1999, p. 7).

In the rest of this section, we indicate how our work has involved selecting and developing interactive speech-based tasks that build on the strengths of existing speech technologies.

Pronunciation Modeling

For adults, proper pronunciation is one of the most difficult areas to achieve in learning another language (Ellis, 1994; Gass & Selinker, 1994; Lightbrown & Spada, 1999). To this end, various pronunciation tutors have been developed to assist language learners in their pronunciation (Bernstein et al., 1999). One system (Knoerr, 1994) even allows students to view and compare waveforms from their own utterances with those of an idealized native speaker (for example, the teacher).

On the other hand, the use of animated humanoid agents as pronunciation tutors has increased lately. Whereas traditional animated agents were not designed to show fine-grained articulatory movements (Ladefoged, 1993), newer articulatorily correct animated agents have been developed specifically for visually modeling correct pronunciation in three-dimensional space. Some agents even allow for control of such properties as intonational patterns, speech rate and pitch levels.

Our pronunciation tutor relies on such an agent to model pronunciation in a communicative environment in which the negotiation of meaning is at the center of all practice.

Conversation Agents

Beyond pronunciation tutors, language-based agents are becoming more useful in carrying out linguistic interactions with human users (Mostow & Aist, 1999; Hatless et al., 1999). Some interact with users in a virtual-reality environment for specific tasks. Though the earliest conversational agents were purely textual, more recent ones interact via speech with users.

When conversational interactions take place, considerably more attention must be paid to pragmatic factors: discourse participants, context, previous utterances, participants' goals and assumptions, and so forth. This nontrivial aspect of interaction is often implemented via a dialog manager.

A dialog manager is the component of conversational agents that controls the flow of the dialog, the higher-level decisions of how the agent should proceed in the conversation — what questions to ask or statements to make and when to ask or make them (Rees, 2002). A dialog agent can interact and communicate with other agents in a coherent way, with coordinated utterances serving to accomplish the same end goal or collaborate on the same topic.

The previously discussed core technologies all have been developed in different ways by various research groups. Their products span a wide range of components and associated functionality. In this section, we discuss the specific components we have chosen to use in our work, along with the rationale behind their selection.

The Speech Toolkit

We use the CSLU/OGI Speech Toolkit (Cole, 1999) as our speech-processing platform of choice for several reasons. First, this toolkit supports both speech recognition and text-to-speech synthesis. It has also included Baldi, an articulatorily correct animated humanoid agent (a "talking head") whose movements can be closely controlled.[1] We have found Baldi's articulation modeling capabilities to be useful in modeling pronunciation in applications described shortly. Another benefit of using the OGI toolkit is that the programming environment consists of a user-friendly Rapid Application Developer (RAD) component. This is an object-oriented graphical interface consisting of different widgets that can be placed on a canvas to create various interactive speech-based dialog scenarios. RAD also allows adjustment of numerous low-level aspects of the speech recognizer and synthesizer performance via menu-driven environment. With RAD, the developer can specify the linguistic properties of an interactive scenario: context-free phrase-structure grammars for recognizing utterances, lexicons and vocabularies for word spotting, and user-specifiable phonemicizations for any desired words. Finally, the toolkit is freely available, widely used and actively supported.[2]

It should be mentioned, though, that while the OGI toolkit has been used extensively for our research and pedagogical work, our work involves the development of additional resources that are as general as possible so that our results could be implemented on other platforms if necessary.

The Dialog Move Engine

Dialog move engines (DMEs) are increasingly popular in designing and implementing conversational scenarios. One approach, Trindi, addresses task-oriented instructional dialog (Larsson et al., 2000). Its associated toolkit, TrindiKit, enables developers to build and experiment with dialog move engines and information states. It supports the design of a general dialog system architecture: information state formats, update rules, algorithms and dialog moves. The system developer must define task-specific update rules, discourse moves and utterance structure. The common ground between discourse participants is tracked by the system as much as possible, including agendas, shared assumptions and shared referents.

Typical approaches to dialog managers include finite state models, form fillers and belief-desire-intention models. The finite state approach uses a different node to represent each possible state in the conversation. Each node then precisely dictates the system output used at that point in the conversation — the system's response. The finite state model uses user input to determine which transition to follow, from the current state to some new state in the system. This produces "canned" dialogs, in effect, because the programmer must predetermine acceptable input and what output will be generated. This type of approach makes the dialog managers grow exponentially large as the desired complexity for conversations grows. It does have the advantage of being a quick system to build, though it does not allow for much human user control over the flow of the conversation.

The use of forms extends the finite state model to allow mixed-initiative dialogs (both the human user and the system could help decide the next state in the dialog). Instead of specifying all states in the system, developers specify a set of inputs desired from the user. For example, if the user is asking about airplane flight information, the set of inputs might include: destination, departure city, dates, whether there will be a return flight and the class. A form-based approach to dialog management would accept as much information at once from the user as the user desired (user control), but would also generate questions (system control) based on the next empty element in the set of desired inputs until all the slots were filled. This allows for a more robust system than the finite state model, but does not explain the motivation for each step in the dialog.

Belief-desire-intention models were developed to give context to a dialog and provide an explanation of the human user's goals in communicating. Trindi (Larsson, 2004) is an example of this type of dialog manager. Based on the observed exchanges in the conversation, dialog move engines update the current information state in the dialog manager and select the next appropriate move. The information state is the dialog manager's method of modeling its perception of both the system and user goals in conversing. It can model information as it becomes apparent what both participants understand in the course of a dialog. This gives a richer capability to modeling context and motivation in dialog management techniques. Other approaches to dialog management include discourse plans and recipes (Green, 2002).

With DMEs, it is possible to implement various kinds of conversations. System-initiated conversations put the system in charge, and the human participant is relegated to simple answers to questions. Human-initiated conversations put the system in the role of question answerer or respondent to actions requested of the user. In mixed-initiative interactions, both participants (i.e., the system and the human) share the initiative as the conversation unfolds. Clearly, mixed-initiative discourses are the most engaging to a human to the degree that they can be coherent and sufficiently constrained. On the other hand, they are the most difficult to implement with a high degree of success. In this chapter, we discuss systems we have developed with various types of initiative.

Prolog

The Prolog programming language was instrumental in providing some of our applications the ability to do high-level knowledge-rich processing. Some advantages to using Prolog are that it can be used to do forward inferencing; it can efficiently encode relationships and rules between sets of data; and it can efficiently match queries to those sets of data regarding relationships that might exist. Also, Prolog components of a multi-modal application can be tested prior to integration, thus aiding in the discovery of programming errors. Certain Prolog systems, such as SICStus, also come packaged with added functionality, including more built-in predicates and a library of modules for interfacing with other programming languages such as Java or Tcl/Tk. This greatly increases the power of Prolog to be used for a myriad of different types of applications.

External Knowledge Sources

To support a dynamic, realistic interactive environment, real-world knowledge about such topics as language, geography and events of interest to a user is necessary. Extensive hand coding of such resources for one-time applications is prohibitive and tedious. On the other hand, appropriate resources are becoming increasingly available for public use. The applications that we have developed make use of some well-structured databases and other knowledge sources.

The UCI zoo database contains information for about 100 animal instances, with features for salient properties like number of legs, fur or feathers and so forth. Though used primarily for machine-learning applications, this database is useful (as are others in this repository)[3] for dialog purposes in our applications.

The freely available CIA World Factbook[4] is a rich source of information about different countries of the world: each country's bordering countries, major industries and climate.

Genealogical information is rich with low-level data, such as dates, names, locations, family relationships and documentary references. A GEDCOM file is a standardized format for encoding and exchanging such information[5].

WordNet (Fellbaum, 1998) is a freely available lexical database[6]. It provides large-scale coverage of lexical relationships such as synonymy, homonymy, hyponymy and meronymy for words and their various senses.

Our university's online events calendar is an example of Web-based information we have used in our applications. The calendar lists such events as music concerts, sporting matches and theater productions. The information is semi-structured and, hence, can be fairly easily queried to access data. Its domain-specific, closed-world nature makes it ideal for the applications discussed below.

The Internet itself is a large-scale repository of usable information for conversational tasks. Content concerning almost any topic can be freely accessed, manipulated and organized in a form that will allow for easy integration into conversational applications.

Applications: Integrated Solutions

In this section we survey applications that reflect our integration of the core technologies, components and knowledge sources mentioned above. As with any software integration effort, issues of modularity, interface mechanisms and data structures have been paramount. Fortunately, our calculated choice on which toolkits and knowledge sources to use have minimized the amount of integration work necessary.

For example, the Toolkit command language (Tcl) is widely used to integrate various computer applications and toolkits, acting as "glue" between the various software components and knowledge sources. Tcl is used in the OGI toolkit and is supported by the dialog move engine we used. Given our use of various engines and Web-based knowledge sources, the use of sockets is also critical for establishing interprocess communications.

Pronunciation Tutor

Our pronunciation tutor application combines the OGI Toolkit with multimedia images in interactive practice in which the learner must be able to hear and produce certain sound distinctions in a second language to perform a communicative task. It is based on a technique for teaching second-language pronunciation, developed originally by Bowen (1972) and expanded by Henrichsen, Green, Nishitani and Bagley (1999). The learner is introduced to a sound distinction through a brief story presented in narrative form with pictures. Through the story, a plausible but ambiguous sentence (e.g., "The blacksmith

Figure 1. RAD canvas showing automaton for minimal pair pronunciation drill

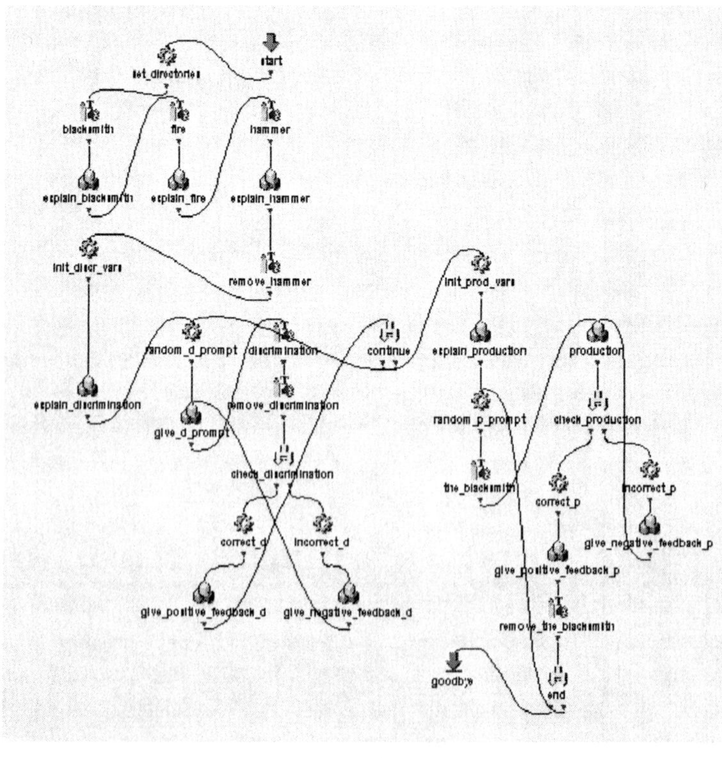

hits/heats the metal.") is introduced, in which two meanings are possible based on the sound distinction in question.

After telling the story, the agent articulates one member of the sentence pair while displaying two pictures and the learner must choose the appropriate picture to represent the meaning of the sentence. Then the learner must produce (i.e., speak) the appropriate sentence as the agent displays one of the two pictures. The system recognizes the user's answer and the agent comments on its (in)correctness. The system then starts an interactive activity where images are presented to the user, who must describe them to the system. Correct responses are met with congratulations and positive feedback, while incorrect responses are met with hedging, requests for clarification, reformulations and so forth. Clearly, this approach assigns all discourse initiative to the system. Figure 1 shows a dialog structure automaton for a task that helps learners distinguish between the vowels in "hit" and "heat." We have created dozens of such pronunciation stories teaching a variety of sound contrasts in English and Spanish. In our experience, current speech technology is capable of discriminating between most, but not all, of the sound contrasts of interest.

Empirical research in pronunciation instruction, whether with live teachers or with CALL tutors, suggest that there is a vast difference between developing mechanical articulation skills in a drill environment and producing correct pronunciation in a communicative context. What is needed, then, is not more sophisticated ways of drilling students in the articulation of particular segmental or even suprasegmental features in isolation. Such practice must be integrated into a communicative context in order for it to get instantiated in productive spontaneous speech. (Morley, 1987; Celce-Murcia, Brinton, & Goodwin, 1996) This is what we attempt to do with our pronunciation tutor. As mentioned earlier, comprehensible input is provided through the narrative by the agent, accompanied by visuals. The learner interacts with the system both verbally and non-verbally, and receives both positive and negative evidence to help in noticing and, thus, in reformulating the interlanguage system.

Language Pedagogy Task Scenarios

Besides the pronunciation tutor, we have developed a number of scenarios for teaching English using an animated agent and speech processing, as well as some external sources, such as WordNet. Following is a brief summary of some scenarios of various types.

One such activity involves practicing buying tickets for various modes of transportation. The learner is guided through an interactive task-oriented scenario in which he or she learns how to accomplish different subtasks relevant to buying a ticket, such as differentiating amounts of money, telling time and recognizing different places and types of transportation. An animated agent guides the learner through the entire activity, giving feedback regarding the interaction of the user. The activity culminates in an information gap activity, in which the learner negotiates the ordering of a ticket from the agent. Again, we have attempted to bridge the gap between conventional CALL activities, in which learners practice form in a rather mechanical way, and real communication, in which they apply those forms in a simulated communicative context with an agent. Again, all the conditions for language acquisition are met in that learners receive comprehensible input specific to the task being learned. They then have the opportunity to practice producing the forms, first in a mechanical way with feedback. Then they are given the opportunity to employ those forms in a communicative activity in which the agent, which controls discourse initiative, recognizes their negotiations and responds in an appropriate way.

Another activity is a 20-questions game. For this, we use the hierarchical relations from WordNet to pursue increasingly specific semantic/hierarchic goals. An agent interacts with the learner regarding certain predefined topics (e.g., languages of the world, animals, plants, etc.) and tries to guess which item a user has chosen. Meanwhile, the user answers "yes" or "no" to increasingly specific questions posed by the agent. Or, if the user fails to understand a term used by the agent, he or she can ask for clarification. The game ends when the agent guesses the pre-selected object the user has chosen. For example, the agent might say, "Think of a language and I will guess what language you are thinking of." The participant may choose any artificial or natural language and the agent will ask yes/no questions until it is able to identify the language. This activity is designed primarily to provide comprehensible input and the opportunity to manifest comprehension by responding to yes/no questions. We have developed a limited number of applications of this game in which roles are reversed, so the learner is asking the yes-no questions and the agent is responding. Initiative, then, can be implemented as either user-driven or system-driven.

Another task-oriented scenario involves learning how to give directions. In the directions scenario, users are shown a map consisting of various streets and corresponding city blocks. The goal is to have a user guide a friend from a starting point on the map to the user's house, located at a different spot on the map. As correct directions are given, progress is shown on the map (see Figure 2). After a number of refinements were made to the system, an overall interaction success rate of 93% was achieved. In this scenario,

Figure 2. Direction-giving exercise display at start (left) and after one utterance (right)

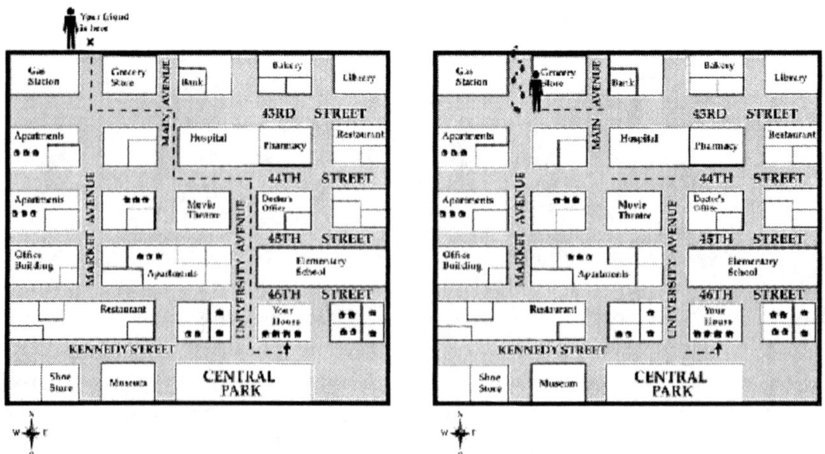

we have found the need to develop a hedging function to avoid giving false feedback to learners as they improve in their ability to give directions.

Another task involves interacting with an agent in a lost-and-found-booth scenario. Here, the user plays the role of a person who works in such a booth. The agent approaches and asks a series of questions to ascertain whether a given item (e.g., a large purple backpack) that it has lost has been turned in. The user must decide whether, among the items in the booth, one matching the agent's description is present. Each time the scenario is run, the booth is populated with a random set of items of various descriptions, assuring a novel situation each time. Sometimes the sought item is present in the booth and sometimes it is not. In this scenario the system controls the initiative, though we intend to implement the inverse scenario, where the learner must seek an item from the booth and thus control the initiative.

Country Talk

This application has an agent ask questions and make comments to a user concerning a specific country. The application makes use of the OGI toolkit, the CIA World Factbook and WordNet. The system asks users where they are from; after they respond with a specific country, the system retrieves appropriate information, enabling it either to ask a question concerning a specific fact about that country or to make comments about it. Users then may answer any questions asked of them and the system may respond with either another question or a comment. The mixed-initiative nature of this task allows for interesting, realistic conversation, albeit on a narrow topic. An interesting challenge in this task was that some country names overlap with common nouns (e.g., Turkey). WordNet was employed to help distinguish the correct sense in such cases. Another issue was that because of the amount of data listed in the Factbook, a comprehensive vocabulary would have been prohibitively large. Accordingly, we implemented a dynamic recognizer in the system. The dynamic recognizer allows the system to anticipate what kind of vocabulary would be needed by the speech recognizer at a given stage in the conversation (i.e., when a given country was chosen). This implementation has increased the accuracy of the system significantly. A similar discussion engine on the topic of animals leverages the zoo database mentioned earlier.

GEDspeak and GEDquiz

GEDspeak is a speech-based application designed to enable a user to query information contained in GEDCOM files. The OGI toolkit along with its RAD canvas was used to structure the dialog and specify requisite vocabulary and grammar for spoken interactions. Middle-level functionality in the system was supplied by data-specific interface routines. They allow the system to receive and formulate queries from the user, and then send those queries to a library of Tcl routines that directly access the GEDCOM file for relevant information. The correct answer is then sent back to the dialog level for response generation. In GEDspeak scenarios, the initiative belongs to the user of the system. A related system called GEDquiz focuses on how GEDCOM data can be used to drive an

Figure 3. GEDquiz system architecture: The engine mediates between genealogical and real-world knowledge sources, the conversational agent and a dialog move engine

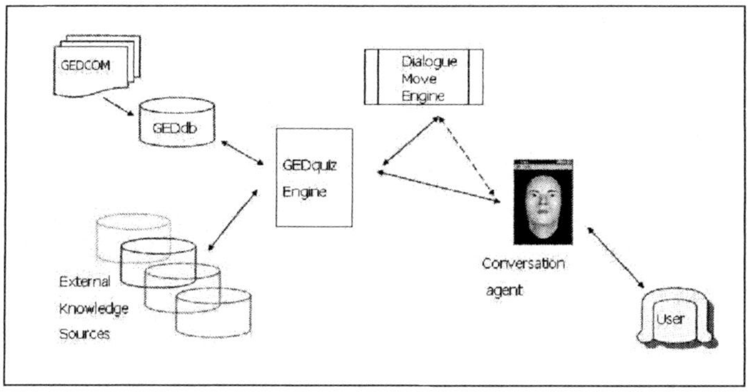

interactive natural-language game, where the system has the initiative. The goal was to develop a system that allows a user to assimilate, in a fun way, a global impression from the myriad of low-level facts contained in a typical GEDCOM file.

A GEDCOM file is supplied to the engine, which then parses out the file's contents and stores it as a database of Prolog assertions. Then, a set of pre-specified inferential relationships is automatically generated by the system. Questions might involve specific data items about an individual (e.g., "Where was your paternal grandfather born?") or might be of a very global nature (e.g., "Name two of your ancestors who immigrated to America.").

At run time, a minimal amount of information about the user was also supplied to situate the user with respect to information in the file, and to ascertain the level of expertise of the user with respect to the data in question (e.g., minimal = very little, average, expert = very knowledgeable). This helps the system set an appropriate level of specificity and difficulty for the interaction.

Once the system has been initialized and the data compiled, the engine enters into an interactive, goal-directed dialog with the user. The system presents the user a series of family history questions for which one or more alternative answers have been determined from the fact base. The system employs the GoDIS/TrindiKit dialog move engine to track the multi-participant goal-directed discourse. Questions are generated from propositional content of the knowledge base via phrase-structure grammar designed specifically for the task. The system gauges the correctness of the user's response(s) for each question and responds accordingly.

Set-a-Date Program

The set-a-date program combines our university's events calendar, a Prolog database of closed-world knowledge and a dialog move engine. With this application, a user can query a database of campus events using speech. The dialog move engine keeps track of specific event times, types and locations. The user answers queries by the system about suggested possible events based on cost, preferences, time constraints and so forth.

For this system-initiated application, we coded specific domain-dependent information into a Prolog database that provided a core set of common-sense knowledge available to the system. This included such facts as where particular rooms and buildings were located on campus, time scheduling conventions and different categories of events (e.g., sports, lectures, musical events).

Another application allows students to listen to weather reports and practice saying numbers and times of the day. It begins by asking the learner for a U.S. ZIP code. The system then accesses a Web site for weather information for that ZIP code, parses out the information and returns to the user. The user is then asked for a time frame (e.g., Friday afternoon), and the system reports the weather forecast for that time period. Again, the learner is subject to system initiative in this type of interaction.

Future Work

The applications discussed in this chapter show how integrating speech, dialog and knowledge representation technologies can result in highly interactive, dynamic, knowledge-rich and realistic scenarios. These scenarios can be used in task-oriented applications for question answering and language instruction, as well as many other possible uses. Our work has sought a pragmatic balance between the current limited state of the art in these technologies on the one hand and the unlimited possibilities for instruction and data access that spoken-language dialog can provide.

We expect to pursue current directions in future work, such as the following: 1) developing increasingly complex task scenarios; 2) developing foreign-accented English acoustic models; 3) integrating learning tasks and speech engines for other languages (including less-commonly taught ones); 4) integrating speech components with richer off-the-shelf language tutoring environments; and 5) developing and supporting more complicated dialog structure: multi-person conversations, more interaction error recovery, and other text-, corpus- and Web-driven interactions. All of these technologies are becoming viable as separate language-processing paradigms, and we believe that our novel implementations will leverage the strengths of each approach. Each type of processing resource mentioned in this chapter either models or directly interacts with a human user, and the integrated solution we propose and are developing addresses many of the pitfalls of current CALL approaches.

Our work in the immediate future involves going beyond simply bundling these components together to create a new systems architecture. We are also integrating these resources into a fully functional large-scale CALL system (Elzinga, 2000) that, while innovative in its user feedback mechanisms (Parry, 2000), only uses the traditional, limited user-interaction modalities (mouse clicks, icons and keyboard input). We expect to see substantial gains in student learning due to this synergistic combination of proven and innovative practices and technologies.

Conclusion

In this chapter, we outlined a theory of second-language acquisition consistent with learner-centered task-based instruction. We have argued that three essential features of current SLA theory must be incorporated into such a program: 1) it must provide ample opportunity for the learner to receive comprehensible input; 2) it must provide opportunities to interact both at the comprehension level and at the production level; and 3) through modeling and feedback, it must provide both positive and negative evidence that will enable learners to incorporate new patterns into developing interlanguage.

We have attempted to show how current technologies lend themselves to the construction of activities that meet the demands of such a theory. In particular, we have shown that by having a humanoid agent speak directly to learners and guide them through activities rather than having them activate multimedia material through clicking on a series of buttons, the learner becomes a first- or second-person participant in the communication process. This enhances opportunities to demonstrate that input is not only comprehensible but also comprehended. In addition, we have shown that current technologies can provide interesting and motivating opportunities for learners to participate in the negotiation of meaning with humanoid agents through the use of speech recognition, speech synthesis, dialog move engines and external knowledge sources. We have shown how such interaction can provide learners not only with large amounts of comprehended input and appropriately modeled speech, but also that it can give them significant opportunities to interact verbally and receive feedback regarding the correctness of their attempts to communicate.

While most of our learning activities are currently in prototype form, we anticipate that in the near future we will incorporate them into a full-blown instructional system that will enable us to examine empirically the extent to which the activities achieve the intended goals.

References

Beatty, K. (2003). *Teaching and researching computer-assisted language learning.* Longman: London.

Bernstein, J., Najmi, A., & Ehsani, F. (1999). Subarashii: Encounters in Japanese spoken language education. *CALICO Journal, 16*, 361-384.

Bowen, J. D. (1972). Contextualizing pronunciation practice in the ESOL classroom. *TESOL Quarterly, 6*(1), 83-94.

Bygatc, M., Skehan, P., & Swain, M. (2001). *Researching pedagogic tasks: Second language learning, teaching, and testing. Applied linguistics and language study*. New York: Longman.

Celce-Murcia, M., Brinton, D., & Goodwin, J. (1996). *Teaching pronunciation: A reference for teachers of English to speakers of other languages*. New York: Cambridge University Press.

Cole, R. (1999, August). Tools for research and education in speech science. *Proceedings of the International Conference of Phonetic Sciences,* San Francisco.

Ehsani, F., & Knodt, E. (1998, July). Speech technology in computer-aided language learning: Strengths and limitations of a new CALL paradigm. *Language Learning and Technology, 2*(1), 45-60.

Ellis, R. (1994). *The study of second language acquisition*. Oxford: Oxford University Press.

Elzinga, C. B. (2000). *Technology assisted language learning*. Provo: Brigham Young University Department of Instructional Psychology and Technology MS Project.

Fellbaum, C. (1998). *WordNet: An electronic lexical database*. Cambridge, MA: MIT Press.

Gass, S. (1988). Integrating research areas: A framework for second language studies. *Applied Linguistics*, *9*, 198-217.

Gass, S. (1997). *Input, interaction, and the second language learner*. Mahwah: Lawrence Earlbaum Associates.

Gass, S. (2003). Input and interaction. In C. Doughty & M. Long (Eds.), *The handbook of second language acquisition* (pp. 224-255). Madsen: Blackwell Publishing.

Gass, S., & Selinker, L. (1994). *Second language acquisition: An introductory course*. Hillside: Erlbaum.

Glass, J. (1999, December 12-15). Challenges for spoken dialogue systems. *Proceedings of the 1999 IEEE ASRU Workshop,* Keystone, CO.

Green, N., & Lehman, J. F. (2002). An integrated discourse recipe-based model for task-oriented dialog. *Discourse Processes*, *33*(2).

Hall, J. K., & Walsh, M. (2002). Teacher-student interaction and learning. *Annual Review of Applied Linguistics*, *22*, 186-203.

Harless, W. C., Zier, M. A., & Duncan, R. C. (1999). Virtual dialogs with native speakers: The evaluation of an interactive multimedia method. *CALICO Journal, 16*(3), 313-337.

Henrichsen, L. E., Green, B. A., Nishitani, A., & Bagley, C. L. (1999). *Pronunciation matters: Communicative, story-based activities for mastering the sounds of North American English.* Ann Arbor: University of Michigan Press.

Knoerr, H. (1994). *Elaboration d'un didacticiel pour l'enseignement de l'intonation en Français Langue Seconde*. CIRAL: Quebec.

Krashen. S. (1985). *The input hypothesis: Issues and implications*. New York: Longman.

Ladefoged, P. (1993). *A course in phonetics* (2nd ed.). New York: Harcourt, Brace and Jovanovich.

Larsson, S., Berman, A., Bos, J., Grönqvist, L., Ljunglöf, P., & Traum, D. (2000). *Manuarl for Trindikit 2.0.* Retrieved November 2005, from www.ling.gu.se/research/projects/trindi

Lightbrown, P. M., & Spada, N. (1999). *How languages are learned.* Oxford: Oxford University Press.

Long, M. (1996). The role of the linguistic environment in second language acquisition. In W. Ritchie & T. Bhatia (Eds.), *Handbook of second language acquisition* (pp. 413-468). San Diego: Academic Press.

Morley, J. (Ed.). (1987). *Current perspectives on pronunciation: Practices anchored in theory.* Washington, D. C.: TESOL.

Mostow, J., & Aist, G. (1999). Giving help and praise in a reading tutor with imperfect listening because automatic speech recognition means never being able to say you're certain. *CALICO Journal, 16*(3), 407-424.

Parry, K. (2000). *Improving implementation fidelity of large scale, distributed, computer assisted learning systems using scalable automated feedback* (PhD dissertation). Provo: Brigham Young University Department of Instructional Psychology and Technology.

Pennington, M. C. (Ed.). (1996). *The power of CALL.* Houston: Athelstan.

Rees, R. D. (2002). *Investigating dialog managers: building and comparing FSA models to BDI architectures, and the advantages to modeling human cognition in dialog.* Provo: Brigham Young University Department of Physics Honors Thesis.

Swain, M. (1985). Communicative competence: Some roles of comprehensible input and comprehensible output in its development. In S. Gass & C. Madden (Eds.), *Input in second language acquisition* (pp. 235-253). Rowley: Newbury House.

Swain, M. (1995). Three functions of output in second language learning. In G. Cook & B. Seidlhofer (Eds.), *Principle and practice in applied linguistics: Studies in Honour of H.G. Widdowson* (pp. 125-144). Oxford: Oxford University Press.

Swain, M., Brooks, L., & Tocalli-Beller, A. (2002). Peer-peer dialog as a means of second language learning. *Annual Review of Applied Linguistics, 22,* 171-185.

Zhao, Y. (2003). Recent developments in technology and language learning: A literature review and meta-analysis. *CALICO Journal, 21*(1), 7-27.

Endnotes

1 Recently, Baldi has been replaced by a collection of other animated agents.

2 See http://cslu.cse.ogi.edu/toolkit/

3 See www.ics.uci.edu/~mlearn/MLRepository.html

4 See www.cia.gov/cia/publications/factbook

5 See http://homepages.rootsweb.com/~pmcbride/gedcom/55gctoc.htm

6 See www.cogsci.princenton.edu/~wn

Chapter VII

LAPLI - The Language Learning Lab: A Methodological Proposal for a Hybrid Course in a Virtual Environment

Rita de Cássia Veiga Marriott,
Pontifícia Universidade Católica da Paraná, Brazil

Patricia Lupion Torres,
Pontifícia Universidade Católica da Paraná, Brazil

Abstract

The teaching of languages to higher-intermediate and advanced-level students requires a distinct methodology. Many of these students are, or will be, language teachers and need to be motivated to continue learning the foreign language, practice the acquired knowledge, and develop teaching and researching skills. Aiming at challenging them to go beyond their limitations, LAPLI — the language learning lab: a methodology of integrative CALL using the Internet — is made of 12 activities in which the students, based on authentic material selected by them, are stimulated to develop fluency and accuracy in the foreign language, focusing on the development of their reading and writing skills, but also promoting their oral skills. Students use the language as a tool to accomplish tasks in a contextualized way, being involved in individual and collaborative learning, natural learning, meaningful learning and discovery-based learning, by means of the new technologies in a virtual learning environment.

Introduction

The rapid technological transformations that have taken place in recent years in the fields of communications and information technology (IT) have brought changes to the paradigms of education both in the education of the student and in his or her professional development. In Poland, the educational reforms of 2000 included the use of computers and IT for material preparation and teaching, both as an incentive for English language teachers to retrain and as a prerequisite for their professional promotion. (Krajka, 2002). In research conducted by the American Department of Education in 2001, it was proven that the preparation of educators with a proficiency in IT — which allows them to meet the necessities of the 21st century — is "an educational challenge," since "more than two-thirds of current teachers will be replaced with new teachers during the next decade" (Bell, 2001, p.1).

To meet this challenge, it is necessary to change the current paradigm, centered on the teacher, to one centered on the student that promotes responsibility, critical analysis and autonomy. For this, as Behrens (2000) said, it is important to:

(a) gradually reduce the number of theoretical lessons, increasing the time available to do research, to access databases, to give support in the construction of activities and the students' own texts;

(b) encourage students' development in both well-planned individual and collective group work activities with defined responsibilities;

(c) organize differentiated activities, events that require creativity, challenging projects that provoke cross-referencing, dialogue with authors and own production; and

(d) promote the use of electronic devices, of IT, of multimedia and telecommunications with all the available resources of the school campus. (pp.121-122)

The use of new technology can assist with collaborative work, discovery-based learning and in the production of knowledge. Besides, the changes that were brought about by the technology-innovator paradigm — which itself is still resisted by many professionals in different sectors of education — remind us of the warning words of McCarthy, "Professors will not be substituted by technology, they will be substituted by professors who use technology" (2001). We are, as each day goes by, closer to the time to rethink our current practices in teaching/learning and search for new paths to teach, where we will benefit from information and communication technology.

LAPLI has been developed based on the activities proposed by the Online Learning Lab (LOLA), a methodology created for distance learning by Torres in 2002. LOLA (which was awarded 1st place in 2003 by the Brazilian Association for Distance Learning and by EMBRATEL Brazilian telephone communications company in the category "Research" (Torres & Marriott, 2004)) is made up of six activities based on Bochniak's *Pedagogy of Research* (1993) exercises for face-to-face teaching. One of the main objectives of these three methodologies is to overcome the learning/teaching model of reproduction and accumulation of knowledge by developing students' responsibility and autonomy. All 12 activities that form LAPLI are explained later in this chapter.

What LAPLI Is and Who It Is For

LAPLI is a methodology for practicing and developing language skills based on educational theories, principles and practices, which makes use of CMC, a VLE and the Internet. It is a language development course designed for students of a higher-intermediate level and above (students/teachers taking language degree courses, language courses in private/state schools, teacher training/refresher courses) who not only want to further their studies in the target language, developing fluency and accuracy in reading and writing skills, practicing oral skills and increasing vocabulary and knowledge in areas of interest, but also want to develop teaching and researching skills using the resources of the Internet and those of a VLE.

LAPLI is a carefully planned course whose framework is provided by the teacher, but whose material is produced by the students. When developing the activities, students construct knowledge by constantly exchanging information, points of view, questions, solutions to problems and evaluations.

The collaboration among individuals and group members allows for a coherent and unique production of the class, as all work is shared and published in the VLE. This collaboration is not meant to create standardization, but it respects the students as different individuals who, in their heterogeneity, produce and grow together. In the management of this heterogeneity, students handle conflicts, propose alternatives, review concepts and ideas, discuss positions, share authorship, negotiate and are responsible for their own actions.

LAPLI's activities give meaning to the action of the group while at the same time energizing it. They challenge students to become more autonomous and a researcher. Moreover, they are planned to have a spiral movement, a succession of balance and counterbalance, being open to what is new, reasoning between old and new meanings. Their objective is to promote creativity, questioning, paradoxes and discussions, all to enhance the production of knowledge. To handle these activities, members organize themselves, interact, discuss ideas and positions, share roles and define subtasks. The educational and linguistic theories that support LAPLI's activities are presented below.

Methodologies Involved in LAPLI

LAPLI promotes a shift from rote-mode to meaningful-mode learning through task-based learning activities in which students use language for a communicative purpose; they do things and exchange meaning in order to achieve an outcome (Willis, 1996). They develop their reading and writing skills by being exposed to a rich but comprehensible input (Krashen, 1981) of real written language in a low-anxiety situation. When selecting and reading the texts and engaging in LAPLI's activities, students activate their previous knowledge and background information (Brown's Schema Theory, 1994) and practice skimming, scanning, intensive and extensive reading (Brown, 1994); develop cognitive and meta-cognitive strategies, prediction and inference (Nicholls, 2001; Bastos, 1998); as well as get involved in process writing (Brown, 1994) with strategies like brainstorming, planning, outlining, writing, re-writing, editing, peer-editing, proofreading and feedback.

LAPLI's activities encompass the input hypothesis (Krashen, 1981), output hypothesis (Swain, 1985, as cited in Dubravak, n.d.) and interaction hypothesis (Long, 1996, as cited in Dubravak, n.d.), stimulating cognitive development and the development of both language acquisition and fluency (in Part 1) and language accuracy (in Part 2). The activities provide an opportunity for reflection (individual work) and collaborative learning (group work), encouraging students to learn to do, learn to know, learn to live together and learn to be (Delors, 1998). By working together to accomplish tasks, learners gain more knowledge through the help of more capable students (Vygotsky's social interaction and zone of proximal development (ZPD), as cited in Moreira, 1999). They get involved in natural learning and discovery-based learning when offered opportunities to question, to explore the resources of the Internet and to practice their initiative. Meaningful learning and constructivism are stimulated in activities, such as working with texts selected by the students themselves and in their area of interest, and the construction of concept maps, lexical lists and group articles.

LAPLI falls into Warschauer's third phase of CALL, named as integrative CALL, and the Internet, which uses the computer as a tool and enables the student to use and understand the target language, making use of word processors, spelling and grammar checkers, desktop presentation programs and concordancers, using CMC (Warschauer, 1996). Being connected to the Internet allows students to access authentic material and publish their own material.

LAPLI's Activities

LAPLI is made of 12 activities developed in the following sections of a VLE: *message board* (where instructions about the class and important information about the course are published by the teacher); *info* (information about course participants); *chat* (for synchronous communication); *mail* (for asynchronous communication, allowing mes-

Table 1. LAPLI's 12 activities

1. *Inserting Links and Comment (Link + C);*
2. Questioning (Q);
3. Construction of Concept Maps (CM);
4. Construction of Lexical List (Lex List);
5. Answering (A);
6. Adding details to Concept Map (CM+);
7. Elaborating list of Linking Words (LW);
8. *Commented Reading (CR);*
9. Research on the Internet on grammar topics, theoretical explanation and exercises, and presentation of findings/exercises to colleagues (GT);
10. *Production of Group Article (Ind_R, Ind_RGR & Group_Art);*
11. Evaluating (Evaluation);
12. Preparation and presentation of group article (only in the second cycle).

sages to be replied to or forwarded and for attachments to be included); *content* (where both students and teacher can upload classroom work and reference material); *forum* (allowing students several levels of asynchronous reply); and *links* (where participants contribute with their favorite links/Webliography for the course). In the table below, we have LAPLI's 12 activities, highlighting Bochniak's (1998) three original activities in normal writing, Torres' (2002) three extra activities in italics and LAPLI's six new activities in bold.

Activities 1 to 8 make up Part 1, when students develop their fluency and communicative skills (Message Oriented), whereas activities 9, 10 and 12 form Part 2, focusing on accuracy (Language Oriented). Activity 11 is done in the students' mother tongue.

The balance between individual and group work (see Table 2) allows students to experience both situations, as they are completely different and equally enriching. Table 2 shows how the activities are split between individual and group work.

When students work individually, in cycle 1, they make their choices and do not have to express themselves verbally to justify or defend a point of view. They simply follow their own criteria. On the other hand, in cycle 2 (when they form new work groups based on similar interests that arise from specific activities), they need to share their choices and negotiate with other members, thus exercising their fluency (oral or written), linguistic, social and communicative skills.

LAPLI uses the resources of a VLE and can be delivered fully in distance learning, face-to-face or a hybrid mode. We recommend that it be used in a hybrid mode (50% distance learning and 50% face-to-face), as it encompasses the best of both worlds (Murphy, 2003; Young, 2002; Matthews, 2002; Spannier, 2003). It maximizes student learning, developing/enhancing "time management, critical thinking skills, problem solving skills, computer skills — increasing opportunities for academic and professional success — promote[ing] self-directed learning" (*Hybrid Courses*, 2003) and contributes to the development of autonomy, self-trust, responsibility and collaboration.

Table 2. Individual and group work in LAPLI

Activity	First Cycle	Second Cycle
1. Link + C	Individual	Group 1
2. Q	Individual	Group 2
3. CM	Individual	Group 2
4. Lex List	Individual	Group 2
5. A	Individual	Group 1 or Group 3
6. CM +	Individual	Group 1 or Group 3
7. LW	Individual	Group 1 or Group 3
8. CR	Individual	Group 4
9. RGT	Individual	Group 5
10a. Ind R	Individual	Individual
10b. Ind RGR	Individual	Individual
10c. Group Art	Group 1	Group 1
11. Evaluation	Individual – in the forum Class – face-to-face or videoconference	Individual – in the forum Class – face-to-face or videoconference
12. Presentation	- - - - - - - - - - - - - - - - - -	Group 1

Legend	
Individual	Individual work
Class	Everybody together
Group 2, 3, 4 & 5	Newly formed work groups based on common themes of interest

Inserting Links and Comment (Link + C)

In this activity (cycle 1), students choose a theme/topic of their interest related to their course, and select an article/text from the Web that they find interesting and/or informative to publish. (In traditional methods, it is the teacher who selects the scientific truth to be memorized by the students.)

For this text selection, students scan several texts, brainstorming and comparing their previous knowledge against the "new information" for content and level of English, making a judgment whether to keep or discard the text. Once they have found a suitable text, they need to write a comment on it; to do that, they read the text extensively, inferring or looking up the meaning of new words, to express their view on that piece of information to the group. When link and comments are published in the VLE, they can receive more comments that are themselves open to more contributions.

This activity promotes active thinking and the development of the students' intellectual autonomy and, as Fialho says, "autonomy increases students' possibility of self-motivation to create new knowledge" (2001, p. 34). Montessori (1965) pointed out that, "To serve somebody is to withdraw his/her independence" (pp. 42-55) and, although her pedagogical proposal was developed for children, in this work this idea is used in the context that LAPLI students are not "fed" with information and knowledge. Instead, information and knowledge are not only not supplied by the teacher (as in activity 8) but are mainly provided by the students, allowing them to develop themselves as researchers and play an active, collaborative and reflective role in the construction of knowledge, discovering an independent way that takes them to more autonomous learning.

The authentic texts selected at this stage form the base for the development of LAPLI's activities, which aim to broaden students' lexical, syntactical, semantical, textual and world knowledge, making it a unique course for these students.

In the second cycle, the students in their groups from cycle 1/activity 10 repeat this activity from a group point of view, taking the final group article work from activity 10c as the subject area.

The following activities — "questioning," "construction of concept maps" and "construction of lexical lists" — form a mini-sequence of collaborative activities. Students work on a text selected by a colleague, which is also in their area of interest, called the secondary text. They go back to work on their main text in subsequent activities (activities 5, 6, 7 and 10). In the second cycle, students need to form a different group (Group 2 — see Table 2) to collaborate in this mini-sequence of activities.

Questioning (Q)

Students are again encouraged to play an active role, using the foreign language as a tool to practice interrogative structures motivated by the content/subject. They choose a secondary text to work on (one of the other students' primary text) and formulate two or three questions on it. According to Widdowson (1978), questions can be classified as being by "reference to form," evaluating students' understanding of the text and leading them to practice scanning; or by "reference to function," encouraging students to think and express their ideas, leading them to practice top-down reading strategies. The latter type of questions is stimulated.

Traditionally, it is the teacher's responsibility to ask questions concerning the content of the subject being studied. Students basically only ask clarifying questions to the teacher and, as mentioned by Shor and Freire (1986):

> *Students are excluded from searching, from the activity, from the demand. Answers are given to them to memorize. Knowledge is passed to them like a corpse of information — a corpse of knowledge — and not as a live connection to their own reality. Hour after hour, year after year, knowledge is nothing but a monotonous task from an official syllabus.* (pp. 14-15)

In LAPLI, it is the students' responsibility to elaborate content questions to each other, making them an active and reflective participant in the process. As in LOLA, when students need to form new groups while developing the fluency activities, they have a chance to experience different roles in each group. At school, students usually "elect" their work group and do not want to work in another group, establishing interpersonal links among themselves, which are accepted by the institute without any questioning or analysis of their implications. This permission impoverishes the process, for each member of the group "specializes" in a role: the spokesperson, the writer, the researcher, the one that prepares the presentation and so on. When the groups are constantly altered, a change of roles is automatically promoted.

Construction of Concept Maps (CM)

The construction of concept maps is a powerful learning technique, implemented in many schools and universities in countries such as Australia, China, Spain, the United States (U.S.), the United Kingdom (UK), Brazil and Italy. Companies such as NASA use them to represent and organize information visually.

To make a concept map, students have to read the secondary text carefully, employing skimming, scanning, top-down and bottom-up reading techniques, identifying keywords and supporting ideas, to create a summary of the text. This exercise promotes the understanding of micro and macro structures in the text, helping them identify the framework of the text and how the ideas are related, knowledge that is useful when writing their own texts later. By using keywords in the reconstruction of the meaning of the text, students deepen their active vocabulary and develop their grammar. They also practice word transformation to construct the map, taking their proficiency in the foreign language one step higher. The guidelines suggested for creating a map are:

> *... concepts are written in boxes, which are organized in a hierarchical form —from top to bottom or from the centre to the sides – and are linked to each other by lines, which include linkage words (like prepositions, verbs, linking words) that express the relationship between these concepts.* (Torres & Marriott, 2004, p. 606)

Concept maps can be produced using pen and paper, a word processor with drawing facility or CmapTools (a software application available online with free download for pedagogical purposes). We recommend the use of CmapTools, because it is user-friendly and it facilitates the dragging, deleting and/or re-writing of concepts. It allows the work to be done at a distance, as the maps are saved on the server in Florida, U.S. students can work with each other online, collaborating, interfering, modifying, doing research, inserting annotations, documents, links and pictures and setting up discussion threads. By engaging in the construction of concept maps, students think about both content and form. The organized visual representation of content also helps in the transfer of knowledge from short-term to long-term memory, anchoring new concepts to previously acquired ones.

To create a map, students need time, concentration and understanding of the concepts being exposed or discussed in the text. For those who are only used to "ticking" the correct answer or to answering unchallenging questions, this activity seems too difficult, complicated and demanding. The building of concept maps requires a change of attitude. Once again, students are encouraged to become more active and responsible for their learning.

Construction of Lexical List (Lex List)

At this point, students list the vocabulary related to the theme, preferably in alphabetical order, providing the meaning of the word if they feel the need. This gives cohesion to the text. The thematic list of words can receive further contributions by other students working on newly selected texts related to the same theme in subsequent cycles, and provides a good resource for writing their individual and collective articles. The relationship between these concepts can be visualized in the corresponding concept maps.

This is the last activity in the mini-sequence of collaborative activities. Now, students go back to work on the main (primary) text they chose, and get involved in individual or collaborative group work with the objective of constructing the group article.

Answering (A)

This activity is linked to the "questioning" activity. Students have freedom to choose two or three questions (as stipulated by the teacher) to answer, about their research theme or not, although the tendency is to answer the questions formulated based on the articles they selected. In cycle 2, if they find questions based on their main text, they get together in their Group 1 group to answer them. However, if no questions have been asked about their topics, they answer questions on another subject(s) (which are, in turn, different from those that they have just worked on) and form another group, Group 3 (see Table 2), with the students interested in answering those questions. The teacher is informed about the formation of this group.

To elaborate these answers, students practice fluency in the target language, using and adapting the structures and vocabulary of the main/source text in their answers in a meaningful and communicative way. Good questions motivate more research, and students have the freedom to search for new information.

The mere activity of choosing which question to answer from the many options published, and the discussion — oral or written — on the criteria for the selection, is already a research activity, as the arguments used to accept or reject a question often constitute knowledge being constructed collectively, and sometimes are in themselves the answer to the question. According to Torres (2002), students select the questions based on two criteria: interest or usefulness and ease or difficulty. This individual or group choice on which questions to answer and how detailed an answer to give makes them, once again, responsible for their learning. These choices, which result from the criteria established by the learners, imply an acceptance of the consequences when the "evaluation" activity is undertaken. This emphasizes the importance of choosing questions that promote more growth in the construction of knowledge (and, in turn, foster the use of the target language in a contextualized way).

One of LAPLI's aims is to provide students with all these insights, highlighting the importance of the process over the product, developing students' critical sense and initiative, and making them more responsible for their learning process.

Adding Details to Concept Map (CM+)

Here, students work on the concept map constructed by their colleagues based on their own text/article, trying to capture the meaning of the text from the information conveyed in the map, referring back to the text for more details to add to the map to make it more complete.

The aim of this activity is to develop students' reviewing, critical, analytical and concentration skills by engaging them in a deeper and more careful reading of the main text in order not only to compare it with the information already mapped but also to add more details to make the map more complete. This exercise aids in the assimilation of new vocabulary and grammatical structures, taking students' proficiency in the target language a stage further both in terms of linguistics and specific knowledge.

When in the second cycle, as in the previous activity, students either continue working with Group 1 or with the newly formed group 3.

Elaborating List of Linking Words (LW)

To elaborate a list of linking words, students look back to the main text to detect and list the linking words used by the author to express a point of view, an opposing idea, an explanation or a sequence of events, and all the expressions that establish coherence and cohesion within phrases, sentences and paragraphs in a text, with the objective of using them later when writing their own texts.

The act of listing words of the same category helps transfer vocabulary from short-term to long-term memory, and this organized anchoring facilitates recovery in future situations (Dias, 1996). Students work individually in cycle 1; in cycle 2, they work with Group 1 or Group 3, as in the previous two activities.

Commented Reading (CR)

The goal of "commented reading" is to provide students with more time for oral practice, based on the reading of texts selected and supplied by the teacher, that help them in the construction of their articles. This activity can be developed face-to-face or using resources like videoconferencing or a Web camera. Students read all the texts provided but come to class or to the videoconference prepared to initiate discussion on a particular text selected for/by him/herself (or for/by the group). In cycle 2, students work with other class members according to their interests, forming Group 4.

This activity is fundamental to the course, for it is the channel of communication the teacher has to deliver theoretical content on the new methodology/activities being implemented or on the construction of their articles.

Research on the Internet on Grammar Topics, Theoretical Explanation and Exercises, and Presentation of Findings/Exercises to Colleagues (RGT)

This is the first activity in Part 2 — language oriented. Students have, once again, the opportunity to act as a researcher, responsible for the "production of knowledge, with a critical, autonomous and investigative approach" (Behrens, 2000, p. 87); the teacher's role is, as in the other activities, to be a mediator both in the face-to-face and distance-learning classes. Students do research on grammatical issues (with which they have encountered problems when expressing themselves in earlier activities) and then prepare interactive, challenging and meaningful exercises, making use of the technology available (VLE and Internet). The explanation of the grammar point and the exercises (which should be targeted just above their peer group level of fluency) are presented, using software such as Microsoft PowerPoint, and should take no longer than 10 minutes. The answers are provided in a separate document. Students' work should be carefully prepared and should not contain any grammar, vocabulary or spelling mistakes.

In cycle 2, students form yet another work group (Group 5) based on their linguistic difficulties or research interests. It is important that they are made aware at the beginning of the course that they will be working in different groups in cycle 2, and that it is important they do this for the development of their communicative, social, negotiation and management skills.

Production of Group Article (Ind_R, Ind_RGR, & Group_Art)

This activity is made of three distinguishable and complementary phases: *production of individual review* (Ind_R), *production of individual reflection on group review* (Ind_RGR) and *production of group article* (Group_Art).

Students (who have in the previous exercises done research on subjects of personal interest related to the course — cycle 1) now exchange ideas, via chat or forum, to select the topic of their article. Group 1 is then formed according to the similarity of interests in their research topic. If they want, they can (and are encouraged to) combine two topics, concentrating their research on more specialized themes, such as *bilingualism* and *deaf children*, exploring the linking threads between them.

Once the groups are formed, students refer to the articles inserted in the Links section (either their main text or a secondary one, if their main text is completely different or cannot offer a different insight to the newly chosen topic), compile all the work done on them (questions, concept maps, answers, lexical list) and work on the first individual review (this task is always done individually), sending the finished product to the teacher by e-mail. Once feedback is received from the teacher, each student produces an Ind_RGR by skillfully joining together the entire group's Ind_Rs, making his own review of the group's work.

Group_Art is the group's chosen Ind_RGR (this could be the best marked review), which then receives new contributions from other members of the group to make it even better or to make it complete. The second Group_Art (in cycle 2) always incorporates the output of the first Group_Art and the current Ind_RGRs.

At this stage, students are encouraged to consult online concordancers (like *The British National Corpus* or *Just the Word*) to help them express their ideas more clearly because, as Raimes (2002) said, "Writing is for discovery of learning, not just demonstration of learning" (p. 309).

For each one of the three steps mentioned above there is a chart in which colors are used to highlight the ambiguities. Core aspects such as content (ideas developed), form (introduction, development and conclusion) and use of English (vocabulary, grammar and punctuation) are pointed out, taking into account the peculiarities of each phase (for example, the use of linking words when joining the Ind_Rs together). Students' color-coded work, explained in the chart "Key to Marking," also receives personal comments on its strengths and suggestions on how to improve its weaknesses.

In LAPLI, writing is understood as a process. Students are encouraged to edit their own work, sending it back to be (re)marked as many times as they want, but always making sure to publish the updated version in the VLE so it is available for the collaborative activities.

In this exercise, the individual and collective mix at all moments. Their personal universe merges with a new universe discovered by the group in LAPLI. Each member of the group can interact with any of the colleagues, establishing a communications network. In this process, everybody assumes the role of writer, researcher, reviewer and critic.

Evaluating (Evaluation)

At this stage, students reflect on LAPLI's activities and issues, such as their criteria for choosing the links, questions to answer, difficulties encountered during the process and how they were overcome. This sharing and exchanging of information is done orally with the whole class (face-to-face or by videoconference, for group feedback) and individually, in writing, in the Forum (for individual feedback). It takes place in the students' mother tongue at the end of each cycle, allowing them to express themselves fully.

Students reflect on the process, not on the product, thinking about the methodology developed, the course itself, the interaction and collaboration among themselves, and the process of learning a foreign language. They discuss the communication within the groups and difficulties in managing conflicts made more difficult by the type of communication (mainly written); their commitment to success, made evident by the publication of their work; the time/space relationship determined by synchronous or asynchronous communication; the roles performed when working in (different) groups; and mainly the fact that everyone — individuals or groups — belongs to the same large group, a feeling emphasized by the fact that their work is published so it can be used as a reference by any member, and is thus owned by everyone.

Preparation and Presentation of Group Article (Only in the Second Cycle)

In this last activity, students create a 20-minute presentation in groups (Group 1) for the whole class (face-to-face or by videoconference), summarizing their work in no more than 10 slides, work that is the product of the collaboration and insight of all participants. This is a relaxed but formal situation, in which pupils show what they have learned, demonstrating proficiency in the foreign language and incorporating the new vocabulary both in written and oral delivery.

How LAPLI was Developed: The Research Methodology

LAPLI was created with the objective of developing a methodology to promote meaningful and collaborative learning for use with students of a higher-intermediate level of proficiency and above in a foreign language, which focused on improving reading and writing skills but also catered to speaking skills by means of a VLE and the Internet, in a hybrid mode. The following methodological procedure was followed for its development: review of the literature; construction of a methodological proposal for CALL; implementation of the methodological proposal for CALL; monitoring of students during the process; adjustments; analyses of students' production; construction of a questionnaire for data collection; validation of the questionnaire; application of the questionnaire for data collection; analysis and discussion of results; and conclusion.

To develop this methodology, we worked with a group of pre-service teachers taking their fourth semester towards a degree (total of eight semesters) in English and Portuguese languages at the Catholic University of Paraná in Brazil from August to December 2002, subject *English Language Intermediate I*, and adopted one type of descriptive research called *case study*.

Descriptive Research was chosen because it allows observation and description of the process without interfering in the flow of educational development. According to Preti, descriptive studies describe the facts and characteristics present in a specific population or area of interest systematically and observe the facts spontaneously as they occur

(Preti, 2002). Knupfer believes this method has an important place and meaning in the field of IT research. For him, unlike other methods, it allows the observation and description of processes without interfering with the ongoing educational process. He says that in this method, which has elements of both qualitative and quantitative research and can also include ethnographic aspects, the cause-and-effect relationships are not presumed and what happens is described accurately. (Knupfer, 1996).

As we wanted to study students' achievements and reactions in detail, we thought the choice of a case study would be appropriate, as Preti explains that, in this type of research the background, present situation and interactions of a social unit, event, group of people and even only one subject are studied intensively (Preti, 2002). Furthermore, although Trivinos says that in this type of research the results are only valid for the case in question, he states that the results achieved allow the formulation of hypotheses for the development of other studies (Trivinos, 1987).

Of the 23 initial pre-service teachers that formed the group in which LAPLI was implemented, 15 finished the course. The reasons given by the students who gave up were basically five: lack of time to dedicate to studies, as they worked full time; difficulty in gaining access to a computer with Internet; lack of willingness to participate actively in the activities; lack of IT knowledge; and lower level of target language compared with the level of the group.

Before the course started, 10 of the 15 students said they had studied English as a foreign language in private institutions for between 4 and 9 years, but at the end of the course, although six of them said they did not have any difficulty with the level of English, nine students felt understanding authentic texts to be rather difficult. In terms of their IT knowledge, before the semester started, three of them stated that they were proficient in the use of computers (the tasks listed were: do research, send e-mails with attachments, do uploads and downloads from VLE, take part in forums and chats) whereas at the end of the term this number rose to 10.

The qualitative and quantitative data was collected throughout the semester during the evaluation activity published in the forum of the VLE, and by a questionnaire consisting of 30 closed questions, with the possibility of justification, applied face-to-face at the end of the course.

Results

A methodology for a languages course using collaborative learning, CMC, a VLE and the Internet can be considered an innovation in the teaching of languages. The implementation of just one of these features into a language course would cause a significant change in the teaching/language process. However, the combination of these four variables, which gave birth to the LAPLI methodology, seems to foster positive results among students.

Thirteen out of the 15 (87%) students (pre-service teachers) who formed the group in which LAPLI was implemented believe that using the LAPLI methodology increases their world knowledge and improves their linguistic skills in the target language. For 93% of them, the course develops reading comprehension. Both for the students who said that it "improved a lot" (33%) as well as for those who said that it "improved" (60%), it is evident that the need to read to accomplish the tasks during the semester contribute to this improvement: "The more you read, the easier it gets," "We had to read a lot," "I feel I understand the ideas in a text better now and I have assimilated some sentence construction" and "I've learned to want to read." The research and selection of texts were also highlighted as important factors that helped increase their reading comprehension: "The research on the Internet helped" and "I learned to look for and select good texts."

Ninety-three percent of the pupils said that LAPLI develops their writing skills ("I pay more attention to linking words, etc. ...") along with increasing their vocabulary (87%) ("... because I read so many different texts, I learned many new words," "I had to consult dictionaries, very important to acquire vocabulary"). Ninety-three percent of pre-service teachers believe that a VLE contributes to the acquisition of knowledge (33% of them said "significantly") and that it increases their knowledge of IT — whereas 20% said they were proficient in the use of computers in the beginning of the course, this percentage rose to 67% at the end of the course. The collaborative activities have caused some discomfort to a number of pupils (47% said they found it "a bit difficult") because of the need to wait for other students' contributions to continue their work. Nevertheless, the alternation between face-to-face and distance-learning classes was said to be beneficial (87%; 60% said "very beneficial") and for 80% of them, the course should always be offered in a hybrid mode because it develops "autonomy," "self-trust" and "responsibility."

To ensure effective continuity, the teacher needs to provide established guidelines for naming and saving files, and students need to follow them to ensure effective continuity. It is also important to note that developing online activities takes time, and it is both the individual's and the group's responsibility to be on time once delivery dates have been agreed on. Ideally, the teacher is advised to receive some prior training in the LAPLI methodology to successfully manage the course.

Future Trends

From the world scenario of constant changes resulting from the globalization of economies and technological evolution — in which knowledge is the basis — one of the greatest challenges to education emerges: the access to life-long education made easy to all segments of society. Even technologically prepared countries face difficulties when dealing with social transformation forces, and both developed and developing countries have been seeking to qualify their professionals so they can respond to the demands and changes of the market, products and processes. To learn a second, third or even fourth language, which is now being required by some companies in today's global world, every professional needs and has the right to continue his or her studies, keeping up to date, as the knowledge learned at school is nowadays nearly always insufficient and, in many cases, obsolete.

Companies also need to realize that it is through the ideas generated by these professionals that businesses grow, and that they have to be encouraged to feed on the knowledge available. All this can be achieved by motivating the workforce to do computer-assisted courses when they are at work or at home. As Bill Gates (1995) says, "The highway [Internet] will alter the focus of education from the institution [school or company] to the individual" (p. 204).

At the same time, as the world is becoming global, it is important to preserve peoples' cultural and linguistic identities. Incentives need to be given to the learning of foreign languages, ensuring linguistic diversity, for use both at the national and supranational levels, as well as catering to the demands of a society in evolution.

To meet these educational, cultural and company demands, it is necessary to develop new mechanisms and methodologies that allow for flexible formal and informal educational processes and increase the efficiency of communications.

LAPLI's methodology represents a step forward in language teaching methodologies. Nevertheless, more research needs to be carried out into its use in companies; and the benefits of its use when developed in virtual-reality worlds should be investigated. The linguistic barriers to progress need to be overcome and more opportunities of life-long education need to be offered.

Conclusion

The need for educational and professional refinement brought about by the technological evolution and the need to keep abreast of and adapt to changes calls for the development of new methodologies that promote learning and knowledge production to meet constantly renewed demands.

The learning/teaching of languages has a lot to gain from this revolution. LAPLI — a methodology that uses integrative CALL and the Internet — approaches language learning through activities based on collaborative learning, discovery-based learning, natural learning and meaningful learning by means of a VLE.

Students need to become active participants in the learning process, learning to interact, work collaboratively, solve problems and learn together. As expressed by Gabrielatos (2003), "The ultimate goal of teaching is for learners to no longer need the teacher; not because they have learnt everything, but because they can keep learning on their own" (p. 4). LAPLI's activities stimulate autonomy, creativity, responsibility, research and the adaptation of material, providing opportunities for individuals to work by themselves or in groups, allowing them to reflect, interact and collaborate with questioning, ideas and feedback using the target language as a tool to achieve their objectives.

By removing the spotlight from the formal learning of a foreign language, students are involved in activities that encourage them to be researchers, readers, writers, editors and proofreaders, and to develop their reading, writing, analytical, critical, evaluative, social, communicative and collaborative skills. Dialog with authors is encouraged, through the questioning of established knowledge and the writing and re-writing of texts, thus fostering their own production (and breaking away from the philosophy of "cut and paste"). All this exercise empowers students and allows them not only to become more proficient in a foreign language but also to develop as a student, a professional and a human being.

References

Bastos, H. M. (1998). A escrita no ensino de uma língua estrangeira: Reflexão e prática. In V. L. M. Paiva (Ed.), *Ensino de língua Inglesa: Reflexões e expressões*. Campinas: Pontes.

Behrens, M. A. (2000). Projetos de aprendizagem colaborativa num paradigma emergente. In J. M. Moran, M.T. Masetto, & M.A. Behrens (Eds.), *Novas tecnologias e mediação pedagógica* (pp. 67-132). Campinas: Papirus.

Bell, L. (2001). Preparing tomorrow's teachers to use technology: Perspectives of the leaders of twelve national education associations. *Contemporary Issues in Technology and Teacher Education.*

Bochniak, R. (1998). *Questionar o conhecimento. A interdisciplinariedade na escola e fora dela* (2nd ed.). São Paulo:Loyola.

Brown, D. (1994). *Teaching by principles: An interactive approach to language pedagogy*. NJ: Prentice Hall Regents.

CmapTools (2003, v. 3.3). *IHMC – Institute of Human and Machine Cognition* (computer software application). Retrieved August 4, 2003, from http://cmap.ihmc.us

Delors, J. (1998). *Report to UNESCO of the International Commission on Education for the twenty-first century*. Retrieved March 22, 2003, from www.unesco.org/delors/

Dias, R. (1996). A incorporação de estratégias ao ensino-aprendizagem de leitura em inglês como língua estrangeira. In V.L.M. de O. Paiva (Ed.), *Ensino de língua Inglesa – Reflexões e experiências* (pp. 137-160). Campinas: Pontes Editores.

Dubravak, S. (n.d.). *Current theories in electronic media and second language acquisition.* Retrieved July 1, 2004, from www.dubravac.fau.edu/5876/read/chap4.doc

Fialho, F. A. P. (2001). Gestão estratégica do conhecimento. In *Apostila da disciplina de mestrado em gestão estratégica do conhecimento da FAE.* Curitiba: FAE.

Gabrielatos, C. (2003, April-May). My methodology. *Iatefl Issues, 172,* 3-4.

Gates, B. (1995). *The road ahead.* UK: Viking.

Gates, B. (n.d.). *Hybrid courses: The best of both worlds*. Retrieved May 26, 2003, from http://courses.durhamtech.edu/tlc/www/html/Special_Feature/hybridclasses.htm

Knupfer, N., & McLellan, H. (1996). Descriptive research methodologies. In D. Jonassen (Ed.), *Handbook of research for educational communications and technology.* New York: Macmillan.

Krajka, J. (2002). Training online teachers of English: The biggest challenge to online learning. *Teaching English with Technology: A Journal for Teachers of English. Iatefl Poland Computer Special Interest Group. 2.1, Special Post-Conference Issue*. Retrieved January 30, 2002, from www.iatefl.org.pl

Krashen, S. (1982). *Principles and practices in second language acquisition.* New York: Pergamon.

Marriott, R. C. V. (2004). *Do LOLA – Laboratório online de aprendizagem — ao LAPLI – Laboratório de Aprendizagem de Línguas: Uma proposta metodológica para o ensino semi-presencial em ambiente virtual* (Master's Thesis). Paraná: Pontifícia Universidade Católica do Paraná.

Matthews, H. (2002). *Hybrid courses and the future of teaching and learning at UC.* Retrieved April 30, 2003, from www.uctltc.org/news/2002/12/matthews.html

McCarthy, M. (2001, July 15). Words, words, words: Vocabulary acquisition. *Proceedings of the 4th Southern Cone Tesol Convention – Integrating for the growth of ELT,* Curitiba, BR.

Montessori, M. (1965). *Pedagogia científica: A descoberta da criança.* São Paulo: Flamboyant.

Moreira, M. A. (1999). *Teorias de aprendizagem.* São Paulo: EPU.

Murphy, P. (2002). *The hybrid strategy: Blending face-to-face with virtual instruction to improve large lecture courses.* Retrieved April 30, 2003, from www.uctltc.org/news/2002/12/feature.html

Nicholls, S. M. (2001). *Aspectos pedagógicos e metodológicos do ensino de inglês.* Maceió: EDUFAL.

Preti, O. (2002). *A aventura de ser estudante: Um guia metodológico.* Cuiabá: EDUFMT.

Raimes, A. (2002). Ten steps in planning a writing course and training teachers of writing. In J. C. Richards & W. A. Renandya (Eds.), *Methodology in language teaching – An anthology of current practice* (pp. 306-314). Cambridge: Cambridge University Press.

Shor, I., & Freire, P. (1986). *Medo e ousadia - o cotidiano do professor.* Rio de Janeiro: Paz e Terra.

Torres, P. L. (2002). *Laboratório On line de Aprendizagem: Uma proposta crítica de aprendizagem colaborativa para a educação* (Doctoral Dissertation). Santa Catarina: Universidade Federal de Santa Catarina.

Torres, P. L., & Marriott, R. C. V. (2004). The contribution of concept maps to LOLA – the online learning lab. *Proceedings of the First International Conference on Concept Mapping* (pp. 603-610).

Trivinos, A. N. S. (1987). *Introdução à pesquisa em Ciências Sociais: A pesquisa qualitativa em educação.* São Paulo:IBRASA.

Warschauer, M. (1986). Computer-assisted language learning: an introduction. In S. Fotos (Ed.), *Multimedia language teaching.* Tokyo: Logos International. Retrieved July 1, 2004, from www.ict4lt.org/en/warschauer.htm

Widdowson, H. G. (1991). *O ensino de línguas para a comunicação* (J. C. P. de Almeida Filho, Trans.) Campinas: Pontes. (Original work published in 1978.)

Willis, J. (1996). *A framework for task-based learning*. UK: Longman.

Young, J. (2002, March 22). "Hybrid" teaching seeks to end the divide between traditional and online instruction: By blending approaches, colleges hope to save money and meet students' needs. *The Chronicle of Higher Education Information Technology*. Retrieved April 30, 2003, from http://chronicle.com/free/v48/i28/28a03301.htm

Chapter VIII

Integrated Micro Learning During Access Delays: A New Approach to Second-Language Learning

Silvia Gstrein, Research Studios Austria, Austria

Theo Hug, University of Innsbruck, Austria

Abstract

Time pressure and lack of motivation are often seen as obstructive factors in second-language (L2) learning. In fact, L2 learning is much more of an ongoing process than just taking a course. In response, a new approach to learning has been developed, called integrated micro learning (IML), based on a patent-pending technology that allows integrating language learning into a learner's daily routine with the help of electronic devices. It thus helps to envisage a new mode of information technology-assisted L2 learning as part of vocational and educational training. In this chapter, we introduce the concept of IML in general and with regard to L2 learning in particular. We also report on the first prototypical representation as well as the first experience.[1]

Introduction

In the last couple of years the broadening of the scope of technological feasibility has entailed the assimilation of computers and computer-based technology into every aspect of our lives. Recent advances in microprocessor, communication and sensor/actuator technologies envision a whole new era of telecommunication, in many papers referred to as "ubiquitous computing."[2] Researchers in this field strongly believe that in the near future, appliances and objects of everyday use (personal digital assistants, smartphones, active badges and wearable computers, to name a few) will deliver services adapted to the person, the time, the place — in other words, the context — of their use.

In such contexts, the electronic device recedes more and more into the background and the individual human being is brought to the forefront. Wireless "small intelligent objects" replace the "static" wired computer of the past and constitute a setting of ubiquitous access to information processing units. The appearance of computing devices will become invisible, networked, spontaneously responsive and inherent in everyday environments with "hidden" services (Ferscha, 2004).

The main aim of "ubiquitous computing" lies in designing, drafting and developing systems of information technology (IT) that support the individual in mastering daily routines and offer alternative ways to solve posed problems. The challenge is to assign extra functionality to gadgets of everyday use and at the same time make them "sensitive" enough to react to certain context-based situations autonomously, intelligently and — above of all — invisibly.[3] Among others, pilot projects are being developed in terms of "smart homes" (e.g., intelligent fridges and heating systems), intelligent offices and learning environments.

In the following sections, we focus on a new approach to learning with the help of electronic devices. While concepts of "ubiquitous computing" will be taken into consideration in future e-learning projects, our approach makes use of ongoing processes of medialization. Along with media changes, life worlds are changing, as well as media cultures, socio-economic spheres and knowledge dynamics. In this context, new forms of learning are being developed. As a future-oriented example, a method to seamlessly embed learning activities into an individual's everyday life and work will be put forth. IML[4] is an effective realization of blending daily life and IT for learning purposes, foreshadowing "ubiquitous learning," so to speak.

This new method has been developed to combine the learning process with the use of electronic devices (e.g., personal computer/PC or mobile phone), thus integrating bits and pieces of learning into our daily lives. IML works by integrating small learning tasks into the initial processes of any electronic device or digital application, thus harnessing both extrinsic and intrinsic motivation.

Background

Most recent figures (CEDEFOP, 2003; Eurobarometer, 2001) emphasize an eagerness to learn among a broad range of individuals for private or professional advancement. On the other hand, many participants drop out of traditional courses due to lack of time and motivation. According to Kloyber (2002, p. 15), it is the "rigidity of structures in time and place" [our translation] that makes people decide to leave. On the other hand, even in traditional distance education and computer-assisted courses, where learners can at least partially choose time and place, it has been shown that drop-out rates are particularly high (Wang, Foucar-Szocki, & Griffin, 2003). They range from 26% (Wang et al., 2003) to 85% (Fritsch, 2003) of initial enrollment figures.

Up to the present, new media elements have often been used in traditional lecture-oriented courses without paying special consideration to the new opportunities of, as well as threats to, learning in these surroundings. Much too often, text-based material is digitized in the form of simple replication without promoting the inherent multi-medial, interactive and hyper-textual qualities e-learning can offer (e.g., Issing & Klimsa, 1997). Additionally, the employment of e-learning has not always contributed to making learning more flexible, since wired desktop computing has simply replaced regular attendance in the classroom. This is why we, and others (e.g., Keegan, 2002), tend to look critically at the inclusion of e-learning elements into vocational training if they do not enhance flexible learning "anytime, anywhere, anybody."

Finally, we want to stress that conventional e-learning tends to be more efficient for experienced learners than for beginners. Without special amendment and adjustment, new-media learning demands a high degree of self-organization, self-motivation and media competence of the individual learner, who struggles to master both the subject and the context in which learning takes place (Rösler, 2004).

Based on this experience of common e-learning settings not being as efficient as they could be, we describe an alternative method of learning. The aim of IML is to bridge the gap between the individual's willingness to learn and the frustration resulting from contexts that do not support learning but, rather, impede it. This is achieved by using information and communication technologies of *everyday use* for didactic purposes. We think that, in the future, not just traditional desktop computers and mobile phones, but actually any electronic device, can serve a didactic aim and play an integral part in the learning process.

What is IML, Then?

IML is designed to empower the learner with a tool that embeds learning activities into daily life according to a user-dependent pattern. Therefore, in addition to the learning that takes place either in institutionalized or e-learning courses as well as in auto-didactic efforts, IML accompanies learning on an individual basis.

The following contains what we consider to be the characteristic features of IML. IML works on the basis of dividing the learning process into small activities ("micro activities") embedded in everyday life. Learning takes place parallel to professional and domestic commitments and, as such, is in strong contrast to "artificial" learning found in conventional course settings.

Figure 1. Example of daily microlearning unit of a language calendar (Langenscheidt, 2004)

Strictly speaking, micro learning is not an entirely new invention. In general, it takes place all the time, as every human being is confronted with tiny bits of knowledge all day long that construct our vision of the world in one way or another. In a more narrow sense, however, it should be understood as a conscious process of learning with a particular goal in mind taking place within short attention spans. Well-known examples of this mode of learning are language calendars, for example, which segment content according to the space provided on a single page (see Figure 1), or computer pop-ups, which appear to explain hidden functionalities once the user has started a certain program.

Micro learning, in fact, presupposes the fragmentation of knowledge and information. It takes place in a network of interwoven learning objects that allow the user to actively partake in the process. Due to recent findings, it has caused controversial discussions among researchers (Gerdes, 2003). While some stress its advantages in view of mobile "learning on demand" (Crosman, 2004), others are more critical towards this kind of fragmented learning (Keegan, 2002).

In *integrated* micro learning, though, learning is made accessible through information and communication technology devices already used routinely in working and private lives, such as PC, laptop or mobile phone. The microlearning activities are "posted" to the daily use of certain functionalities of these devices (such as activating the computer after the screensaver has turned on, opening the Web browser or activating the key lock on the mobile phone, etc.). We believe this makes systematic learning possible.

IML supports learning because the user can select the daily tasks to which the interpositions are added, a feature supported by the so-called "Knowledge Pulse"® (Gassler, Hug, & Glahn, 2004). This possibility of self-configuration also fosters the

Figure 2. Daily routines – schematically (©ARC Seibersdorf Research GmbH — RSA Studio eLearning Environments)

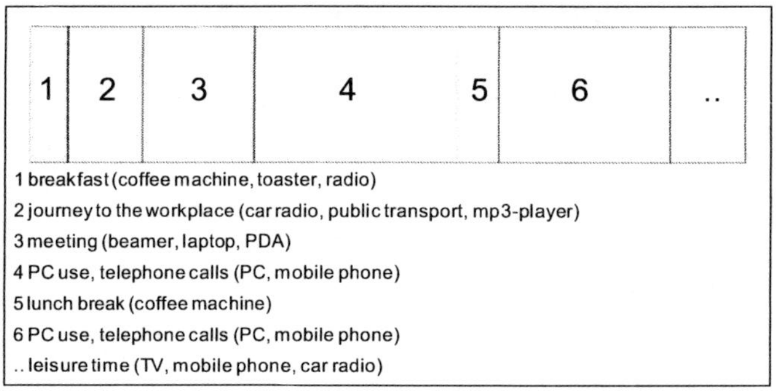

aspect of intrinsic motivation instead of only being "the system," to force the learner to undergo learning activities.

In this context, it is important to consider the two aspects of time and motivation. Our daily routines are structured by various activities. Consider 1 day in the life of Ms. Smith: In the morning she has her breakfast, goes to work, then attends a meeting and deals with various tasks. While doing so she has been routinely using her coffee machine as well as her laptop and mp3 player. All the while, at the beginning or the end of an activity, time slots are created by retardation of the service, which she could fill with "something useful and profitable" (Gassler, Hug, & Glahn, 2004).

Using these time slots constructively for learning purposes is the goal of IML. For learning to take place, active concentration is necessary, requiring a period of undivided attention, however short it may be. Consequently, the interference with work in progress must be avoided. We believe that attempts to introduce learning activities as regular time-based interruptions (e.g., pop-ups), regardless of the present activity, fail because they impede learning rather than promote it.

Traditionally, many learners find it difficult to structure learning activities themselves. Usually, self-regulated learning software both on CD-ROM (computer-based training/CBT) or the Internet (e.g., Web-based training/WBT) requires a high level of independence and meta-competence on the part of the learner, because he or she has to decide which aspect of language to study anytime he or she loads the software, and find sufficient motivation to do so. Traditionally, then, the learner approaches the educational setting. With IML, things are approached from a different direction. It makes the setting in which learning takes place more dynamic by having the individual prompted to undergo learning processes at the instigation of a task. Here, the learning task manifests itself to the user at predetermined time slots.

Practically speaking, how does this kind of learning work?

Figure 3 illustrates a typical workflow of a PC user where IML is embedded into the daily work routine. The use of other electronic devices, such as mobile phones, could be shown in a similar way. In this example, the learning activities are bound to the use of the PC.

Figure 3. PC workplace as example for IML (©ARC Seibersdorf Research GmbH—RSA Studio eLearning Environments)

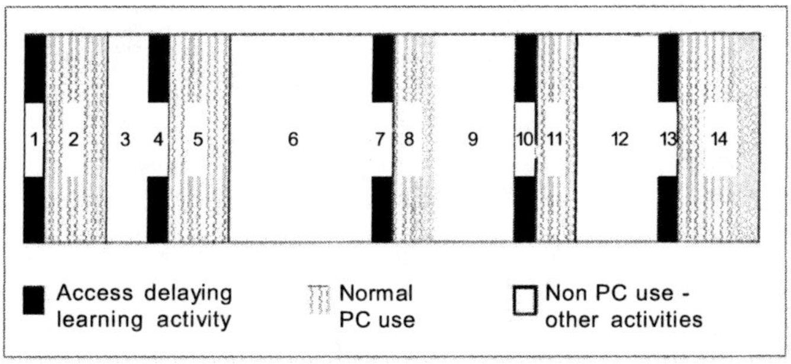

Whenever the user wants to continue working on the PC after he or she has given attention to other commitments, he or she is presented with a learning activity— and cannot proceed until the learning activity is completed.

Basically, each beginning or end of a committed activity creates candidate time slots for possible microlearning units. Since there is no single answer to which of these time slots is the most suitable for learning, the choice depends on the respective situation of the user and his or her preferences.

L2 Learning with IML

Speaking a foreign language is a gateway into a new world; learning a language is a requirement in an ever-changing society. In the process of globalization and technological progress, mastering languages other than one's mother tongue has become a key factor for promotion and success at work, as well as for one's own personal development.

In the course of the 20th and 21st centuries' psychology, linguistics and education have contributed their share to the multitude of theories on L2 learning. Many of these are related to each other in some way or another, some working from previous approaches and refining them, others refuting earlier findings and bringing a new perspective into play. Generally speaking, modern theories on L2 learning are now stressing social and intercultural skills rather than grammatical accuracy, incorporating the various approaches and adapting them to the individual learner as well as to a particular situational context (Altmayer, 2002).

The following model of L2 learning is based on Edmondson (2000) and Ellis (1994), showing that learning a second language takes place on a variety of levels, apart from the actual items of the language. All spheres are closely interdependent and contribute to the degree of success in mastering a foreign language. We have adapted the model to fit the special requirements of IML.

Figure 4. Model of L2 learning, adapted, based on Ellis (1994) and Edmondson (2000)

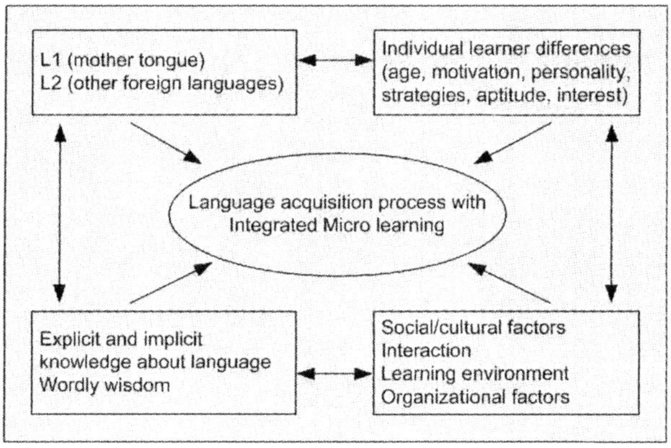

Language Learning and "Small Units"

As we see above, many internal and external factors contribute to the success of L2 learning. L2 learning is a multidimensional process; all factors are interdependent. Hence, language learning never proceeds as a simple linear cause-action principle (Bleyhl, 2000).[5]

How can L2 learning be enhanced by integrated micro activities, then? Given the multidimensional model of L2 learning above, what are the advantages, prerequisites and boundaries of integrated microlearning settings? IML, in fact, means highly fragmented learning – the time between two learning activities cannot really be predicted in advance. Additionally, the seamless inclusion into life requires brevity as a feature. These are some crucial questions that need further investigation in future studies:

- How can the results of L2 acquisition research be put into practice in IML scenarios? In what form should individual activities be designed? How can the four language skills be promoted best by this mode of learning?
- How should the learning environment be designed to make this approach to learning possible? (Organization, workplace, objectives, content, equipment, etc.)
- How can individual learner differences be taken into account? What can be done to motivate learners? What is the relationship between extrinsic and intrinsic motivation in this context?

As far as the educational design is concerned, we consider the following points fundamental in employing IML for language-learning activities. Research on foreign-language learning and computer-assisted language learning (CALL) suggests the formulation ofcommon minimal standards for L2 learning:

1. Experience has shown that learning vocabulary without providing meaningful cotext and context does not contribute to achieving reasonable language competence and performance (Bleyhl, 2000).
2. A study of the use of mobile phones in language learning shaped our view that mobile learning is a highly fragmented experience (*Mobile Learning*, 2001). Consequently, reframing of fragmented knowledge is essential for IML settings (Hug, 2003). Anchors are needed to bridge the gap between the working and learning environments. Naturally, the learning application must be designed with this in mind.[6]
3. In IML settings, the context cannot only be provided in written form (e.g., by contextualization through narration or dialog), but also by using imagery and animation (Rampillon, 1989). Visual appearance, furthermore, plays a central role to promote intrinsic motivation in the learner. Most studies of L2 learning in electronic environments make it clear that the combination of text and images is crucial for language learning success because images, animations and videos refer to an authentic context close to reality. Nyíri (2002) highlights the special importance of pictures in mobile learning settings in general.
4. Listening comprehension is essential for mastering a language (Bleyhl, 2000). Therefore, sound must be incorporated into any successful form of microlearning activities. What should be borne in mind, however, is that the learner does not always find him or herself in a situation able to listen to sound overtly or where headphones are available. Generally, the learner will not want to disturb colleagues sharing the same office. In other situations, the learner might find him or herself in a situation where learning is impeded by the surroundings; for example, on a bus or train packed with passengers. Sound in IML settings, therefore, must always be optional rather than obligatory.
5. Learning is a personal and emotional process. Language learning in particular requires opportunities to practice in an emotionally safe and supportive environment, which can be supported by an attractive interface design and, above all, differentiated feedback. In particular, the latter is still a major problem in CALL (Rösler, 2004).
6. If IML accompanies a course book, the learning management system (LMS) working in the background should visualize the individual activities in the form of a "learning path" and connect them to the respective off-line materials to avoid the risk of getting lost in a vast array of seemingly unconnected tasks (Rösler, 2004).
7. The individual activities should be as authentic as possible, which means they must be designed according to what is really needed at the workplace or in the field in which the target language is to be used. Authenticity can best be safeguarded by carefully pre-selecting the learning activities or tagging them with metadata.

L2 acquisition is a comprehensive process that requires IML to embed the training of individual skills into an overall design of learning, which should be structured by thematic unity as well as by personal objectives. At best, such a design incorporates elements of collaborative learning that go beyond the scope of purely individual learning activities and encourages the establishment of interpersonal networks (Godwin-Jones, 2004).[7]

Moreover, we recommend that IML not be used exclusively in stand-alone settings but, rather, be used as a component of a blended learning concept, where it supplements face-to-face settings (Sauter, 2004). Between these settings, microlearning activities support the learner in his or her individual learning process.

How can individual learner differences be taken into account?

Learning differs from individual to individual. Our suggestions for how IML could be adjusted to the special needs of individual learners include the following:

- First, the learner's level of competence should be assessed and feedback given about the preferred type of learning channel. The learner should also be pointed to those language skills that need special training. According to this assessment, a well-adjusted set of micro-activities is presented to the learner (contextualization).[8] From these, the learner chooses those activities he or she wants to have activated.
- The learner could be given the possibility to decide which micro-activities will be activated at which specific points in his or her daily routine and workflow, and when they will occur. Specifically, the latter fosters concentration and combats distraction, as some periods during the day are less apt for learning than others, depending on the individual biorhythm and office timetables. Studies looking at the relationship between IML-assisted learning and the special conditions of work and leisure environments, however, still need to be carried out.

Implementing IML

Recently, the first prototypical implementation of IML has been made publicly available in the form of a client-server implementation for PCs with Internet connection only.[9] In the near future, it is planned to run on other electronic devices — above all, mobile phones.

At present, the Web version enables brushing up vocabulary in five languages. In keeping with its status as a prototypical realization and demo version, it is kept didactically and technologically at a simple level. At the moment, it offers the possibility to contrast individual sentences with mother tongue utterances according to the principle of the "file-card box" (Leitner, 2003). Furthermore, the appearance of microlearning objects is bound to that of the screensaver only, rather than other functions (e.g., start-up, starting e-mail-program, starting other software applications, etc.) as foreseen in future implementations.

Figure 5. IML-screensaver has started

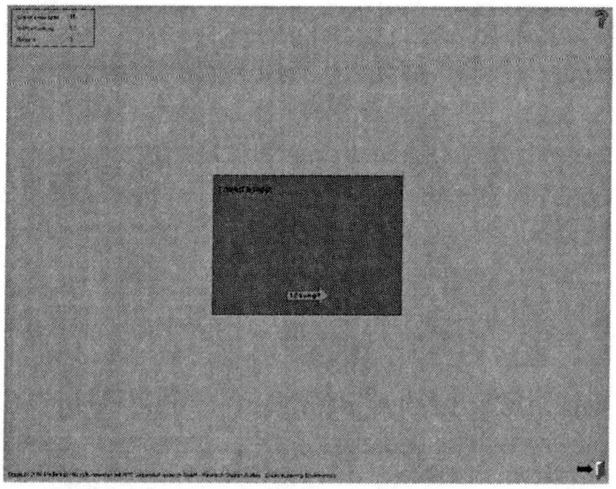

Figure 6. IML-screensaver with model solution

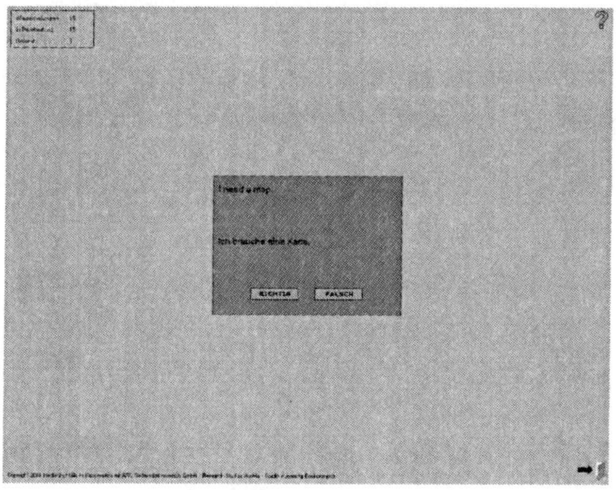

In Figure 5, the screensaver has been turned on after some time of non-activity, and IML activities are retrieved from the server. Here, the user is given a sentence in the mother tongue and is asked to translate into the target language. The button "Lösung" (solution) reveals the model solution as shown in Figure 6.

Now the learner compares the model solution with what he or she has come up with. In an effort of self-assessment, the learner then evaluates the correctness of his or her answer by choosing "richtig" (right) or "falsch" (wrong). On the basis of the user's answers, a learning management system pre-selects future learning objects in a dialectic process. Technically, the algorithm used in the prototypical version runs according to common flashcard index systems (Leitner, 2003).

After evaluation, the IML screensaver closes automatically and the PC is again accessible for "ordinary" use. But even during performing the various micro activities, the user is free to cancel at any time and return to the original service. The learner just needs to click the exit symbol (bottom right-hand corner of the screenshot) or press the escape key.

Learning thus remains a free act on the part of the user, who is instigated to fulfill a certain task but is never forced to do so. Moreover, successful learning always requires full concentration and preparation (*Mobile Learning*, 2001). Experience has shown that if the user is not prepared to learn, he or she will just "click through" the presented activities rapidly to return to the original service as fast as possible.

First Experience in Practice

At present, about 300 people have registered to use the first implementation of IML for L2 learning in the form of the screensaver. Conclusions drawn from this small sample can, of course, by no means be exhaustive or allow us to make an overall assessment. But they can — and do — give some first impressions as to the usability of this new mode of learning.

1. Acceptance of the proposed learning time frames is very high. In about 75% of cases, the present sample group voluntarily accepts the instigation to learn.
2. An "ordinary" IML lcarner using the "IML-Screensaver" on average performs a maximum of 15 learning units per day. Assuming about 200 workdays per year, this makes roughly 3,000 learning activities per user, per year.
3. Feedback from users shows a high degree of acceptance of IML. This is best illustrated by their desire for extra units to be provided, which they can activate themselves whenever inclined (Gassler, Hug, & Glahn, 2004). Learning "on demand," hence, supplements instigated learning — the heterogeneous user group showed high motivation to go beyond the impulses offered by IML in the first place.

In spring 2005, we carried out a more comprehensive empirical analysis of http://schonendlernen.at in practice to find out if our first impression of IML was justified or needed modification. We decided to do an anonymous, summative evaluation of the 300 people then using IML for language-learning purposes. Out of the 300 IML users, 35 learners returned their feedback, contributing to a qualified sample of more than 11%.

The sample is made up of 63% male and 37% female learners, the majority of which are between 41 and 50 years old. More than 70% have attended high school or possess a university degree. As this distribution, *eo ipso*, constricts the range of general deductions, further investigation into other segments of society are needed to gain a more complete picture.

In the following section, we will report the findings of this survey as to the general acceptance of the IML screensaver setting within this particular group, its modes of inclusion into daily life and suitability for language learning. Room will be also provided for discussing suggested improvements and possible future trends, relying mainly on the actual experiences of those using IML. By doing so, we hope to prepare the ground for future research as well as to help define more precisely which direction further field studies and applications should go.

General Acceptance

Learning is an active process and, as such, requires motivational behavior. It can only work if the individual contributes to it and believes his or her endeavors will succeed and pay off in the end. New modes of learning, therefore, sometimes conjure up skepticism as learners walk "untrodden paths," causing them to fear their efforts will go unrewarded. To check the level of general acceptance, the first question was thus directed at assessing the overall impression learners had of IML. In a scale of 5 possible "marks," about 50% of the users attest to a "rather good" impression of IML, and almost 30% indicated a "good" one. Less than 5% estimate IML as "rather bad" and no respondents regarded it as bad (see Figure 7). Asked if they have recommended IML to their friends and colleagues, almost 70% of the users answered positively (Figure 8).

Interestingly, acceptance of learning with the screensaver depends on the amount of computer work learners habitually do. The more learners are used to working with the computer, the more critically they look at learning in an IML fashion and vice versa (see

Figure 7. General acceptance

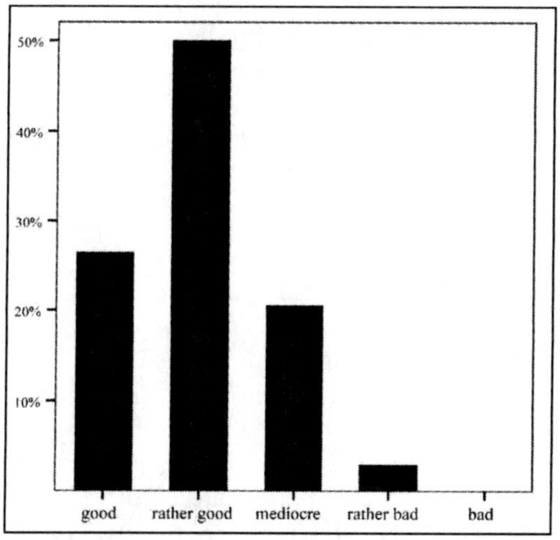

Figure 8. Application recommended?

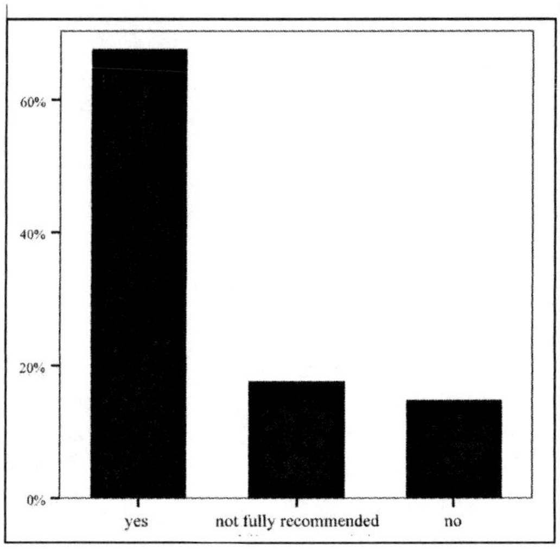

Figure 9). However, this could be interpreted as a negative sign towards the IML approach. On the other hand, however, it might also support the claim for diversification of vehicles of learning. We believe that people used to spending a lot of time with one single electronic device (here, the PC) may be inclined to look for alternatives to avoid virtual overload.

Experience has shown that handling is a central aspect for the acceptance of CALL settings and, as such, a motivating factor to learn (Rösler, 2004). Learners were asked to download a file and install it on their PC. Afterwards, they had to configure the screensaver according to their individual preferences and determine the number of learning objects. The results of this survey draw an interesting picture with regard to user friendliness. We looked at both the technical installation on the PC and the handling of the IML screensaver. Returned feedback points to a high degree of satisfaction with keeping the IML screensaver as simple as possible. This proves our assumption that complex virtual structures do not support learning but may even impede it. Design, the third constituting factor, needs some serious reconsideration, as it is seen as only "mediocre" by most testers.[10]

Inclusion into Daily Life

As IML works by presenting small learning objects at the instigation of clearly predefined functionalities, the length of these activities is in itself a decisive factor. How do the participants experience learning within small concentration spans? Questioned about the duration of performing one presented task, the vast majority of learners expressed their belief that the activity is "just of adequate length." Less than 20% state that an individual task is either too short or too long (see Figure 11). This corresponds with the

Figure 9. Relationship of amount of PC work and general acceptance

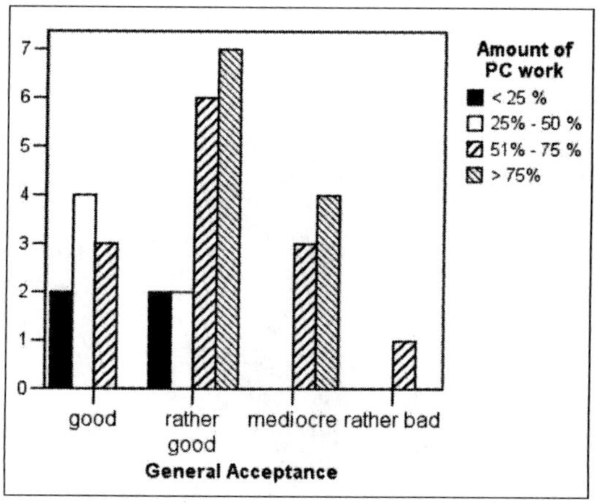

Figure 10. Installation, handling and design of schonendlernen.at

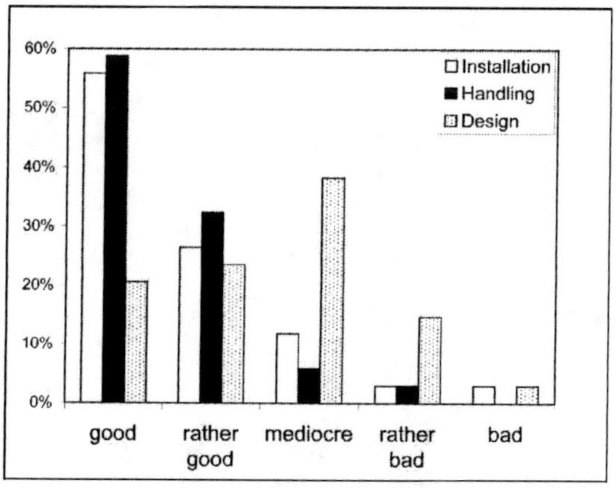

fact that the majority of learners are only prepared to spend less than 5 minutes on more complex learning objects (see Figure 12).

The following graphs (Figure 13) show that the majority of users are presented with 6 to 10 micro activities per day, depending on the time configuration of the screensaver, as well as the frequency and continuity of computer use (horizontal line). The vertical bars represent the number of conscious terminations of the service prior to learning. The combination of both criteria signifies the interdependence of frequency of pop-ups and the level of acceptance. It seems as if the fewer activities appearing during a certain period of time, the more prepared the learners are to accept and perform them. It must be added,

Figure 11. Length of an individual micro-activity

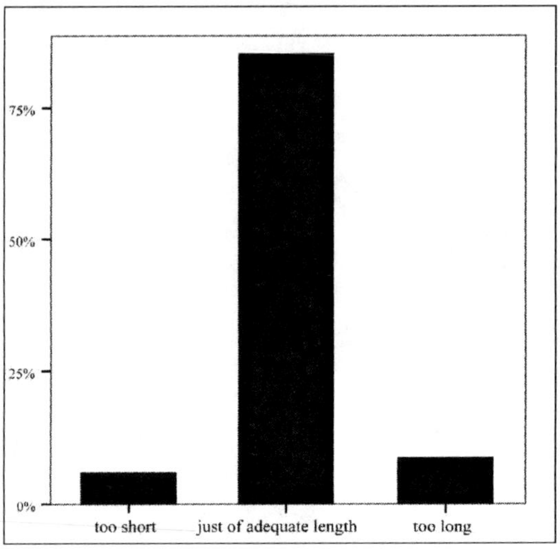

Figure 12. Extra time for more complex activities

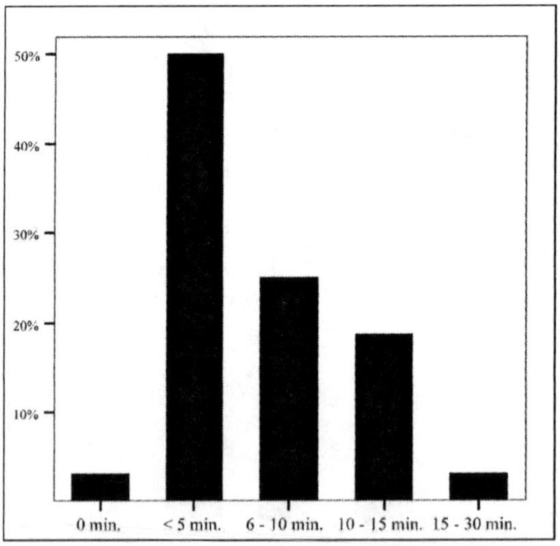

however, that the amount of untimely terminations does not allow for any inferences whatsoever with the success and efficiency of learning at the end of the day.

Under what circumstances do learners tend to call off a microlearning activity, then? In this respect, the collected feedback points to the problem of commitments of various kinds rather than innate computational or didactic shortcomings. The category "other work urgently to be done" features most prominently, with more than 70% of all

Figure 13. Relationship of automatic instigations and untimely terminations

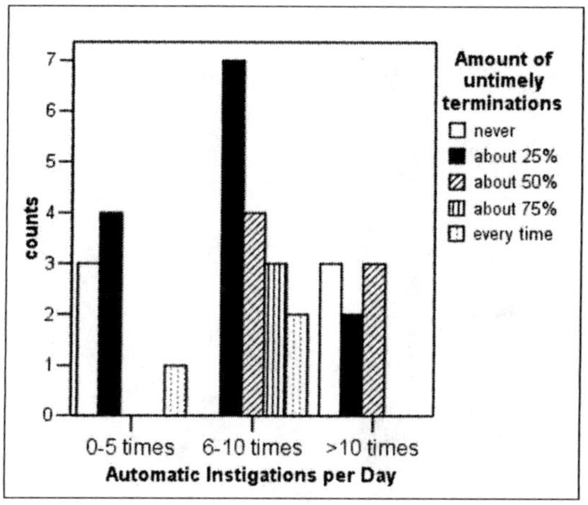

responses. Other explanations, such as inadequacy of material or technological complications, are, by contrast, statistically insignificant (less than 3.5%).

Although other commitments was the prime reason for turning away from learning, at the same time, the majority of users testify to the easiness of embedding microlearning objects into their daily routines. A possible explanation for this discrepancy could be that the users were "led astray" by some other commitment, thus calling off what they were doing. At a later point in time, this very same activity is reloaded by the system, so users do not lose out on anything.

Suitability for Language Learning

The use of IML for language learning is the key factor within the scope of this chapter; therefore, this aspect deserves close investigation. At present, the application http://schonendlernen.at supports the learning of five foreign languages contrastively with German: English, French, Italian, Spanish and Polish. Users can choose if they want to study one particular language, more than one or all of them together. About 52 of the participants selected English, followed by Spanish (21%), French (15%) and Italian (12%).

We get an initial, overall impression of the practicability of IML for language purposes when we ask users to assess the quality of the material offered to them. Within the given framework of marking from 1 to 5, a relative majority attach "rather good quality" to the input provided, and 27% evaluate it as "good." Almost 20% are not content with the language, assessing its quality as "rather bad" or "bad" (Figure 14). Moreover, there is a close interrelation between the qualitative assessment of language input and the overall impression of IML. In other words, the quality of the material determines the level of acceptance of the whole microlearning setting (Figure 15).

Figure 14. Content L2 learning

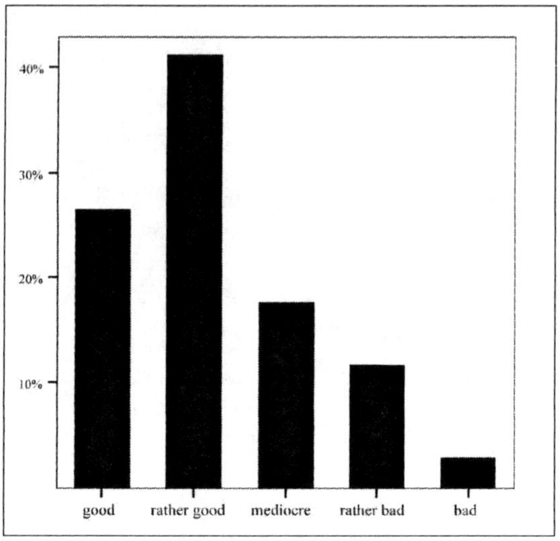

Figure 15. Relationship of general acceptance and content

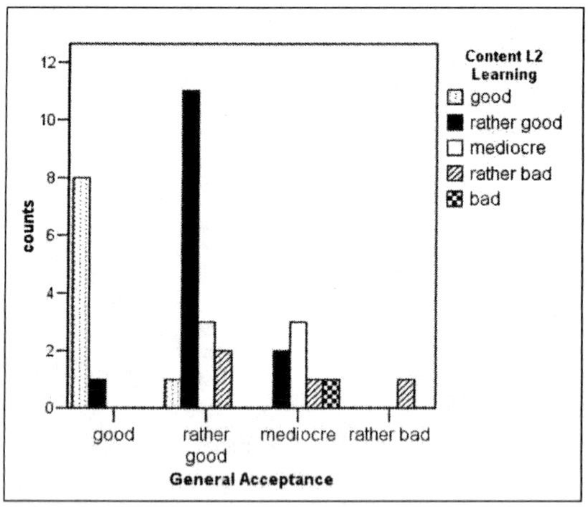

Integration into Daily Life

IML aims to make learning part of everyday life, thus revoking the separation between settings deliberately designed for learning and real-life contexts. As far as integration into daily routines is concerned, the questionnaire offers food for thought. A total majority of almost 90% of learners report having used IML during habitual work or leisure routines in an unconscious and smooth way (Figure 16).

Figure 16. Assessment of integration into daily routines

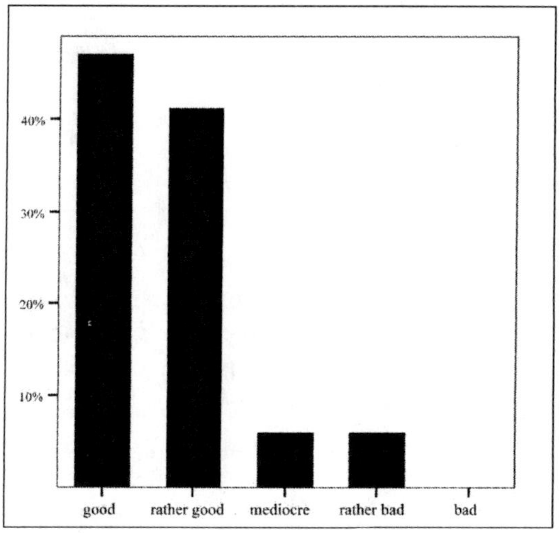

After having investigated the three central fields of acceptance, suitability and aptness of inclusion into daily life, it is time to summarize what can be said so far. The evidence gained leads to the following conclusions:

1. IML seems to have been accepted by the sample group as an alternative mode of learning. Simplicity of design and shortness of duration are of great importance — users do not seem to be prepared to spend too much extra time solving problems of handling or doing additional learning.
2. The IML screensaver is suitable for language-learning purposes, even if the provided microlearning objects themselves still need to be worked on. Suggestions on improvements will be discussed next.
3. Users testify that IML can be embedded into habitual actions at work and home relatively easily. Even if disturbances from other commitments occur from time to time, they do not seriously affect motivation and general acceptance.

Suggestions on Improvements

In the course of evaluating the IML Screensaver, we asked participants to describe the recurring problems during language learning. As a next step, they suggested improvements on the technology, content and didactic framework of http://schonendlernen.at based on their experiences. Multiple suggestions were welcomed and are included in the following survey. The list below contains the proposed refinements in categorical order:

(a) Content:

1. Including more languages, especially Czech and Slovakian. This suggestion is in line with the growing demand for mastering Eastern-European languages within the European Union.
2. Concentrating on supra-segmental structures in language (e.g., texts), not just provision of individual words and isolated sentences. This response needs to be weighed against brevity, which still remains the prevailing principle, as a great many users showed they are not prepared to invest too much extra time for learning.
3. Installing a dictionary to look up unfamiliar words and phrases (63%). This could be realized in a variety of ways; for example, shortcuts, extra buttons to activate pop-ups containing a complete dictionary, direct linking of each word to its dictionary entry and so forth.
4. Including pop-ups explaining certain aspects of grammar (53%); for example, according to the help-button feature in Microsoft Office programs.
5. Providing an editor for users to build up relevant content themselves (47%). Above all, vocabulary could be easily personalized by employing copy/paste features.

(b) Didactics:

1. Preparing divergent learning paths through hypertext structure.
2. Installing open structures for assessing language progress; for example, answering sheets that allow for multiple solutions to posed problems.
3. Fostering interaction through installation of fields for manual input. This suggestion is only applicable for PC use, though, because typing words or whole phrases with mobile phones is very tenuous and, therefore, impedes learning.
4. Structuring language according to thematic criteria. Users are keen on choosing the relevant topics and the level of difficulty. To make this possible, metadata must first be tagged to each learning object. Afterwards, individual preferences and language competences are matched with these data by using either a profiling interface (thematic correlation) or classification quiz (mastery of language) or both together.
5. Including self-definable points of time in which acquired language patterns are automatically recycled and condensed (43%). To safeguard this, an internal learning path is needed to help the system remember which micro activities have already been presented.
6. Contextualizing microlearning objects through textual (43%), figurative (66%) or auditory elements.
7. Including audio elements to support imitation of pronunciation (67%).

(c) Technology:

1. Simplifying installation rights and access which, at the moment, require the status of an administrator.

2. Including self-regulated presentation by the system of extra learning objects once the chosen ones have all been performed, instead of moving on within the same circle.

Potential

Finally, users were asked to express their visions for the future potential of the IML Screensaver as far as L2 learning is concerned. The range of given answers is generally in line with what learners have seen and experienced by using the prototypical model. Thus, more than 90% believe the system is the most suitable for acquiring and building up vocabulary. In turn, 45% vote for learning grammar and effective reading comprehension with the help of IML, whereas just 35% see potential to improve listening and communication skills.

As IML is designed to put forth a more flexible and ubiquitous mode of learning in the future, it is also essential to find out which device users can imagine learning with, apart from the PC. Evidence from our sample group (82%) identify the mobile phone as the PC's closest ally for installing IML services in the coming years, followed by PDAs (50%). Alternative technologies, such as coffee machines or car radios, seem to be too far out of the scope for learning to present real options for the time being. They might, however, become emergent as the digitization of devices such as these continues.

At present, IML on the PC is bound to the functionality of the screensaver and, as such, pops up any time the computer is used after a pre-configured time of non-activity. Which other interconnections could be imagined? It seems as if this group of learners had difficulties envisioning unprecedented forms of interaction. A minority of users advocated micro activities tied to the opening of an Internet browser or unlocking of the PC.

As far as IML on mobile phones is concerned, a similar picture unfolds. Here, too, most users see microlearning objects in combination with the screensaver (84%), followed by activating and deactivating the key-lock or checking the e-mailbox (21%-37%).

What is evident for PCs and mobile phones alike is that most users prefer the learning prompts to be tied to functionalities that are not invoked too frequently. It seems as if learning in an "offensively" permanent way is not what users are very keen on. Learning obviously takes time, as does micro learning.

Conclusion and Outlook

Conventional e-learning approaches have not always proven to be as satisfactory as they could have been. In the future, new technologies and didactic settings can be used to increase efficiency. In both ways, IML suggests real improvements to learning in general and L2 learning in particular. IML, therefore, is designed to be highly adaptable to "blended learning" arrangements, where it accompanies and instigates learning scenarios in daily life and work.

Having advocated IML in the field of language learning, we would like to emphasize that this concept is not limited to this area. Generally speaking, it can be made to fit various learning purposes and to accommodate a wide range of educational or organizational settings.

The 21st century offers technological possibilities on an unprecedented scale. People will be growing up in an ever-more mobile, flexible and interconnected way of life, handling devices such as PDAs, mobile phones, mp3 players seemingly naturally and effortlessly. New forms of learning should go beyond the instruments of learning we can imagine today and make use of the new possibilities created by more and more powerful electronic devices. Perhaps at some time in the future, it will be possible for someone to stand at the coffee machine waiting for the coffee to brew while doing a micro activity, finally "learning anytime, anywhere."

References

Altmayer, C. (2002). Lernstrategien und autonomes Lernen. Teilaspekte eines "konstruktivistischen" Fremdsprachenunterrichts? *Babylonia, 2*, 7-13.

Bleyhl, W. (2000). Fremdsprachenlernen konstruktiv. In M. Wendt (Ed.), *Konstruktion statt Instruktion. Neue Zugänge zu Sprache und Kultur im Fremdsprachenunterricht* (pp. 103-118). Frankfurt a. Main: Lang.

CEDEFOP (2003). *Lifelong learning. Citizens' views. European Centre for the Development of Vocational Training.* Luxembourg: Office for Official Publications of the European Communities. Retrieved October 10, 2004, from www2.trainingvillage.gr/etv/publication/download/panorama/4025_en.pdf

Crosman, P.L. (2004). *E-learning for short attention spans*. Retrieved November 7, 2004, from www.transformmag.com/showArticle.jhtml?articleID=22101169

Edmondson, W., & House, J. (2000). *Einführung in die Sprachlehrforschung*. Tübingen: Francke.

Ellis, R. (1994). *The study of second language acquisition*. Oxford: Oxford University Press.

Eurobarometer (2001). *Eurobarometer Report 54. Europeans and languages. Executive summary*. Retrieved October 10, 2004, from europa.eu.int/comm/public_opinion/archives/elo/ebs)147-summ_en.pdf

European Commission (2004). *Förderung des Sprachenlernens und der Sprachenvielfalt.* Luxemburg: Amt für amtliche Veröffentlichungen der Europäischen Gemeinschaften.

Ferscha, A. (2003). Pervasive computing. *Datenbank Spektrum, October 2003,* 48-51. Retrieved November 6, 2004, from www.soft.uno-linz.ac.at/research/publications/_documents/pervasive_computing_ferscha.pdf

Ferscha, A., Hechinger, M., Mayrhofer, R., dos Santos Roch, M., Franz, M., & Oberhauser, R. (2004, April 18-23). Digital aura. In A. Ferscha (Ed.), *Pervasive computing,*

Second International Conference. Vienna: Springer Verlag. Retrieved November 6, 2004, from *www.soft.uni-linz.ac.at/Research/Publications/_Documents/digitaleAura.pdf*

Fritsch, H. (2003). *Contrasting distance learning education drop out experience*. Retrieved November 6, 2004, from www.fernuni-hagen.de/ziff/contract.htm

Gassler, G., Hug, T., & Glahn, C. (2004). Integrated micro learning – An outline of the basic methods and first results. In M. Auer, & U. Auer (Eds.), *International Conference Villach/Austria "Interactive computer aided learning" ICL 2004. The future of Learning*. Kassel: Kassel University Press.

Gerdes, H. (2003). Aufbereitung von Lehrmaterial für Online-Seminare. In H. Apel & S. Kraft (Eds.), *Online lehren* (pp. 76-90). Bielefeld: Bertelsmann Verlag.

Godwin-Jones, R. (2004). Emerging technologies. Learning objects: Scorn or SCORM? *Language Learning & Technology. 8(2)*, 7-12. Retrieved August 26, 2004, from http://llt.msu.edu/vol8num2/emerging/

Hug, T. (2003). Unsere Gegenwart: Fragmentierung des Wissens und Wissensintegration. In T. Hug & J. Perger (Eds.), *Instantwissen, Bricolage, Tacit Knowledge. Ein Studienbuch über Wissensformen in der westlichen Medienkultur* (pp. 111-122). Innsbruck: Studia Universitätsverlag.

Issing, L., & Klimsa, P. (Eds.). (1997). *Information und Lernen mit Multimedia*. Weinheim: Psychologie Verlags Union.

Keegan, D. (2002). *The future of learning: From e-learning to m-learning*. ZIFF-Papiere 119. Hagen: Zentrales Institut für Fernstudienforschung. Retrieved November 11, 2004, from *www.fernuni-hagen.de/ZIFF/ZP_119.pdf*

Kiernan, P., & Aizawa, K. (2004). Cell phones in task-based learning. Are cell phones useful language learning tools*? ReCALL, 16*(1), 71-84.

Kloyber, C. (2002). Marktplatz der Sprachen. In Bundesministerium für Bildung, Wissenschaft und Kultur. Abt. Erwachsenenbildung V/B/15 (Ed.), *Marktplatz der Sprachen. September 17-22, 2001. Dokumentation einer Initiative des Bundesministeriums für Bildung, Wissenschaft und Kultur zum Europäischen Jahr der Sprachen 2001* (pp. 7-17). Vienna: Bundesministerium für Bildung, Wiss. u. Kultur, Abt. V/B/15 – Erwachsenenbildung.

Langenscheidt (2004). Langenscheidt Sprachkalender. Retrieved November 13, 2004, from www.langenscheidt.de/deutsch/sprachspass/sprachkalender/today.html?2004-11-12_1100217600000

Leitner, S. (2003). *So lernt man lernen*. Freiburg i. Br.: Herder.

Mobile Learning Explorations at the Stanford Learning Lab. (2001, January 8). In E. Brown (Ed.), *Speaking of computers. A newsletter for the Stanford academic community, 55*. Retrieved November 14, 2004, from http://web.archive.org/web/20010505021814/http://acomp.stanford.edu/acpubs/SOC/Back_Issues/SOC55/#3

Nyíri, K. (2002, August 29-30). *Towards a philosophy of M-learning*. Paper presented at the IEEE International Workshop on Wireless and Mobile Technologies in Education (WMTE 2002), Växjö University, Växjö, Sweden. Retrieved November 10, 2004, from 21st.century.phil-inst.hu/eng/m-learning/nyiri_m-learn_philas.htm

Rampillon, U. (1989). *Lerntechniken im Fremdsprachenunterricht. Handbuch.* Munich: Hueber.

Rösler, D. (2004). *E-learning Fremdsprachen – eine kritische Einführung.* Tübingen: Stauffenburg Verlag.

Sauter, A. (2004). *Blended learning. Effiziente Integration von E-learning und Präsenztraining.* Munich: Luchterhand.

Wang, G., Foucar-Szocki D., & Griffin, O. (2003). *Departure, abandonment and dropout of e-learning: Dilemma and solutions. Final report.* James Madison University. Retrieved August 26, 2004, from www.masie.com/researchgrants/2003/JMU_Final_Report.pdf

Weiser, M. (1991). The computer for the 21st century. *Scientific American, September,* 94-104. Retrieved November 10, 2004, from www.ubiq.com/hypertext/weiser/SciAmDraft3.html

Endnotes

1 Research leading to the publication of this chapter has been part of an action program of the Austrian Federal Ministry of Economics and Labour and has been supported by the Tyrolean Future Foundation.

2 This term was first introduced by Weiser in his article, *The Computer for the 21st Century* (1991). Other researchers attach different names to the same idea. One of the most widely used terms is "pervasive computing" (Ferscha, 2003, p. 48).

3 "The most profound technologies are those that disappear. They weave themselves into the fabric of everyday life until they are indistinguishable from it." (Weiser, 1991, p. 94)

4 We use the term "Integrated Learning" as an umbrella term for integrating small learning activities into a person's daily routines. It should by no means be understood in the way as it is used in the concept of Content and Language Integrated Learning (CLIL) (European Commission, 2004).

5 In the German version, it says: "Insgesamt ist Fremdsprachenlernen ein multidimensionales Geschehen. Jede Dimension, ob die sprachliche, die lernpsychologische, die didaktisch-methodische oder die allgemein-pädagogische, ist von Bedeutung. Jede hat einen Einfluss, der im Einzelnen aber nie genau bestimmbar ist. Alles steht mit allem in Wechselwirkung, weshalb der Sprachlernprozess auch nie ein triviales Geschehen sein kann, das nach einem einfachen Ursache-Wirkungs-Prinzip verläuft. Der Fremdsprachenlernprozess ist eben ein nichtlineares bio-psycho-soziales Geschehen, das — wie die Organisation des Gehirns insgesamt — ein Prozess der Selbstorganisation ist." (Bleyhl, 2000, p. 105)

6 Gerdes (2003, p. 78f) in this respect suggests structuring the material according to predesigned categories of information, thus combining hypertextual and linear elements.

7 See Kiernan and Aizawa (2004) for one of the first studies on using mobile phones in collaborative L2 learning.

8 See Ferscha (2003) for context-sensitivity in "ubiquitous computing."

9 See http://schonendlernen.at

10 In the meantime, the layout of the IML-screensaver demo-application hs been improved — Figures 5 and 6 already represent the enhanced version.

Section III

Evaluation and Case Studies

Chapter IX

EOI Online Inglés: A Fully Implemented and Operative Online English Language Course

Pascual Cantos Gómez, Universidad de Murcia, Spain

Juan García Iborra, Universidad de Murcia, Spain

Abstract

This chapter outlines the rationale and design of an online English language course as an alternative to the traditional attendance language course and distance-learning course offered by the Escuelas Oficiales de Idiomas *(EOI) in Spain. It describes the goals of the EOIs, and explains how these vocational language courses are organized and structured. The authors offer a full description of the unit structure and course materials designed and developed: topics, communicative functions and situations, linguistic skills (reading, speaking, reading and writing) and language levels (phonology, morphology, syntax, semantics and basic pragmatic features) dealt with. The chapter then presents some preliminary conclusions highlighting the benefits of the project as well as drawbacks, focusing on how to profit from this experience in ongoing work.*

Introduction

This chapter starts with a brief description of the aims and philosophy of EOI — publicly run vocational language schools with a unified 5-year syllabus — and explains how these vocational language courses are organized and structured.

The main thrust of the chapter is towards the outline, rationale and design of an online English language course — *EOI Online-Inglés* — as an alternative to traditional attendance language courses and ongoing distance-learning course *That's English* offered by EOIs throughout Spain.

The first course performance of *EOI Online-Inglés* was carried out during the academic year 2003-'04, and students were invited to anonymously assess the course by means of an online questionnaire. The results are displayed and discussed in order to improve course contents, structure and interface in forthcoming editions.

The main objectives of this chapter concentrate on: 1) the need for time-flexible, distance language-learning courses, such as online ones; 2) the significance of continuous online tutoring by highly qualified language teachers; and 3) the importance of designing and structuring online language courses offering optional attendance sessions to practice oral skills (listening and speaking).

In brief, this chapter puts together the challenging experience carried out by the EOI of Murcia in designing and implementing an online distance-learning language course with exactly the same syllabus and course contents as its equivalent attendance-learning course, to ensure the same official recognition. However, the main motivation for this online course was to give response to 1) the high number of people who, year after year, find it impossible to access the EOI of Murcia as demand clearly exceeds the actual offer; and 2) people who either live in remote or rural areas or who have a rigid working schedule and cannot attend the EOI of Murcia.

Background and Motivation

In Spain, there are 203 EOIs, within which most European languages, including Spanish for foreigners, are taught together with Arabic, Japanese and Chinese. The present system of official Language Schools was established in 1979 as one of the first education measures of the first Spanish democratic government. The four most-studied languages are English, French, German and Italian, with English covering nearly 60% of all the students attending lessons at the EOIs. Students' ages range from 14 and older, yet 70% of all the students are adults between 18 and 40 (university students, young professionals, teachers and housewives). The average fee to attend classes is 60€ a year, which means virtually free, state-covered studies. We teach, certify and occasionally give refresher courses for teachers. The advanced-level title enables holders to teach the certified language in primary and secondary schools.

This type of school runs five courses (130 hours each year/course) divided in two levels: elementary (3 years) and advanced (2 years). When students conclude each of the two levels, they obtain a certification officially recognized throughout the Spanish territory by the Spanish Ministry of Education and Science (MEC). The curriculum and structure of these types of schools are managed by the MEC. The official curriculum was published in 1988[1] and the academic structure of the schools in 1986.

However, the curriculum and present structure of these studies are undergoing a process of renovation and academic change that will be implemented in September 2005. First, the MEC, following the guidelines of the Council of Europe and its linguistic project, which resulted in the *Common European Framework for Languages: Teaching, Learning, Assessment*[2], is to change the official curriculum, establishing three levels of 240 hours each (elementary, intermediate and advanced). Along with this, the structure of the studies will consist of 6 years instead of 5, offering two academic courses for each level. These levels correspond to A1 and A2 for elementary, B1 and B2 for intermediate and C1 and C2 for advanced. At the same time, the EOIs will be giving three certificates, one for each level successfully finished.

Learning languages in the global village world is becoming a must for people in all areas of society. The European Union (EU) is continuously developing new tools and providing more means to help people acquire new languages within the European context. In the *White Paper on Education* (WPE) (1995)[3], a report made by the EU on the needs of teaching and learning, the European Commission believed that it "is necessary to make proficiency in at least two foreign languages at school a priority" (WPE, 1995, p.13). In this report, four main objectives are put forward regarding education, the fourth being what they called "the three languages proficiency"(WPE 1995, p. 50)[4]; that is, the European Commission considers it a priority for the citizens of the EU to reach, in the near future, the mastering of at least two foreign languages. Besides encouraging the learning of languages, the EU promotes the use of Information and communication technologies (ICT). In the International Certificate Conference[5], the main conclusions given were drawn upon the improvement of the usage of ICT in the language-learning context:

The new technologies are breaking down borders and barriers at a faster rate than is possible in physical terms. Sudden, unexpected encounters with other languages and cultures confront European citizens with new choices, opportunities and challenges. Thanks to the WWW, access to authentic materials has never been easier; vast linguistic resources and an exhaustive range of materials are available in all languages of the European Union and beyond, ready for immediate exploitation ... Research also indicates that European teachers seem to be overwhelmingly open to technological change with an enormous reservoir of potential Internet users amongst EU teachers. Although there are few specific statistics for language teachers, what information is available indicates that, apart from ICT subject specialists, language teachers are the most open to use of the new media. (WPE, 1995, pp. 4-5)

In the EOI of Murcia, due to the increasing uneasiness over the number of people left out every year and the urge to attend as many applications as possible, we concluded that it was necessary to offer a structure available to most people in our region (Comunidad

Autónoma de la Región de Murcia) so as to have access to the Elementary level in English, which is the one applicants requested most. We believed that such a tool fitted perfectly in the networked new society, so we thought of implementing an experimental online course that could be modified and flexible in real time. Thus, teachers and administrators could change and adapt the course to their needs and physical social context. We also came across with the claim that many professionals found it difficult to attend classes at a fixed time. At the same time, we could give access to disabled people and others that have difficulties leaving their homes or driving long distances to come to school.

Previously, in the EOI of Murcia there was another English distance-learning program that had been running since 1992. The program, first called *That's English*[6] (launched by the Ministry of Education and Science) and from 1997 *Open English*[7], consisted of a 1-hour weekly class, self-study book and 1/2-hour free tutorial per week with a teacher. This program, though being a solution in its time, presented a great drawback, as the exposure to the target language was only 1 hour a week and students had to do the rest on their own without further tutoring during the week. As the academic results worsened each year and Internet technologies were developing fast in the educational world due to broadband access and multimedia resources[8] at home, we believed that an online program, at least in the first stages of learning a language, could be a solution for those people who had little or no possibility of attending a regular language course.

We should point out that from the early stages of our work on this program, our final goal was to integrate a number of people who could not attend regular courses, but by no means was it to substitute the present system. We also realized that home technology in Spain would not allow us to go further than A1 and A2 and that we would need at least 5 more years working with students to implement further levels (B1 and B2). The starting point with the educational authorities of the Region of Murcia was to create an English distance-learning program able to replace, in the long run, other distance programs (*That's English* and *Open English*).

During the academic year 2002-'03, we worked on the program as an experiment with 50 students. All of them were older than 18 and had finished at least secondary school. Most of them were university students or had a degree. During the academic year 2003-'04, A1 (*Inglés online 1*) was offered among the different English teaching programs of the school and had 210 students, which was the maximum allowed by authorities. During the same academic year, we experimented A2 (*Inglés online 2*), with 25 students; in 2 years' time, we will try to continue the experiment with B1, since the regional government is on its way to launching a program to facilitate access to Internet broadband to everyone at a very low cost. We know that the higher the level we try to reach, the better the technology that is needed by users. In the 2004-'05 academic year, we had 250 students in A1 and 100 in A2, and the academic results are better than those reached by the traditional distance-learning programs, as we shall explain later.

EOI Online Inglés 1 and *2* is a unique experience in Spain at the moment and is having excellent results, as it provides access to English learning to a wide variety of people who prefer this way of learning. We are sure that the experience will expand in coming years to other schools, as traditional distance-learning programs are becoming obsolete in many ways and do not meet the needs of the new society immersed in the information and technology world.

Our program is tutored by fully qualified teachers who have participated in the creation of the activities, revision of the curriculum and elaboration of final evaluation tests. The average time response for queries is 12 hours and there is also a Web page updated by tutors with other learning resources for students, such as dictations, further grammar practice and many links to help them in the process of solving uncertainties.

During the first year we experimented, the program tutors realized some of the students lagged behind in the oral expression skill. Although the rest of the skills were fully covered and satisfactory dealt with by students, the results in this skill were worse than the others, though this fact also takes place in regular courses. However, in this type of learning, students did not have the opportunity to practice oral skills. So we decided to offer those students who freely wished a weekly class exclusively based on oral practice. Twenty-five percent of students registered attended this class more than 10 times during the year, and 50% of the students never attended, probably not needing it.

Students are given a login (access number) and password to access the course; a guiding tutorial can be found in the school Web page if they have any technical problems. Moreover, there is a presentation of the program at the beginning of each academic year in which the use of the course relying on the Internet is explained in detail. Students under this program can register, follow their course and make use of tutorials through the Internet, and it is only once (or twice if they fail) that they need to come to the EOI of Murcia. This time is in June, to sit for the final evaluation test that certifies their learning. If they fail, the course is left pending, and students can work during the summer holidays and have another opportunity to pass the evaluation tests in September. Tests, following the guidelines of the *Common Framework for Languages*, cover the four skills in a balanced way and are exactly the same tests regular attendance students take. Tests are taken at the same time, under the same physical conditions and follow the same guidelines as the regular students. Finally, it is important to mention that these tests are made and marked by the English department, and tests are experimented with beforehand in other EOIs in the state to obtain reliable results.

EOI Online Inglés

Syllabus Design and Course Contents

In this section, we shall concentrate on level 1 (*Inglés 1*), which corresponds to A1 according to the EU Portfolio. In the 2003-'04 academic year, the EOI of Murcia already started this level together with level 2 (*Inglés 2*; A2) and is presently working on level 3 (*Inglés 3*; B1).

The syllabus of *EOI Online Inglés 1*[9] and its contents are the same as those of the official attendance-learning course[10]. Succinctly, it is structured in 10 content units: two blocks of 5 units with each block followed by a revision unit, which makes 12 units altogether. Figure 1 shows the unit display, once students have successfully logged on to the system[11].

Figure 1. Units of EOI Online Inglés 1

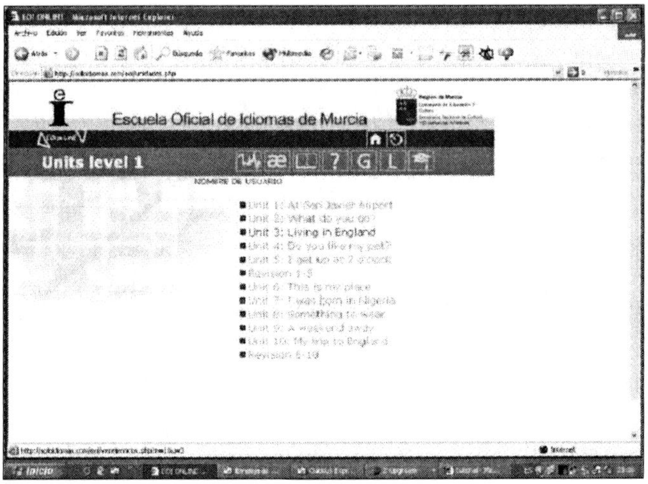

Table 1. Linguistic contents of Unit 1

Unit	Grammar	Functions	Vocabulary	Pronunciation
1 *At San Javier Airport*	• Present simple: *to be* • Subject pronouns • Possessives (singular): *my/your/his/ her*	• *Excuse me/sorry* • *Please/thank you* • *Hello/hi/welcome/ (good)bye/see you* • *How do you do?/Nice to meet you* • *Where are you from /I'm from...*	• Numbers: *1-30* • Alphabet • Countries and Nationalities • At the airport	• The alphabet

Each unit concentrates on a specific topic and all linguistic and communicative contents appearing in that unit are organized around and linked to the topic. These contents are explicitly organized in four sections: grammar, functions, vocabulary and pronunciation. For example, unit 1 focuses on arriving at an airport (*at San Javier Airport*). The dialog introduces basic communication functions, such as *excuse me*, *welcome* and so forth; greetings with starting vocabulary (numbers 1-10, alphabet, countries, etc.); and the fundamental grammatical contents needed at this first stage (present simple of the verb *to be*, some subject pronouns and possessives). Table 1 below shows the full contents for unit 1.

We have tried to keep more or less the same unit outline also for the end-user interface, substituting *Functions* for *Communication* and adding a final revision section (see Figure 3). Once users have logged on, they can either choose to navigate at will across

Figure 2. Learning paradigm

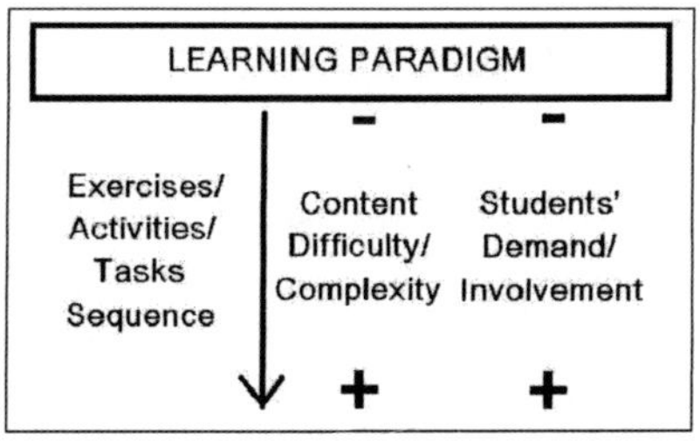

Figure 3. Overview of exercises, activities and task for Unit 1

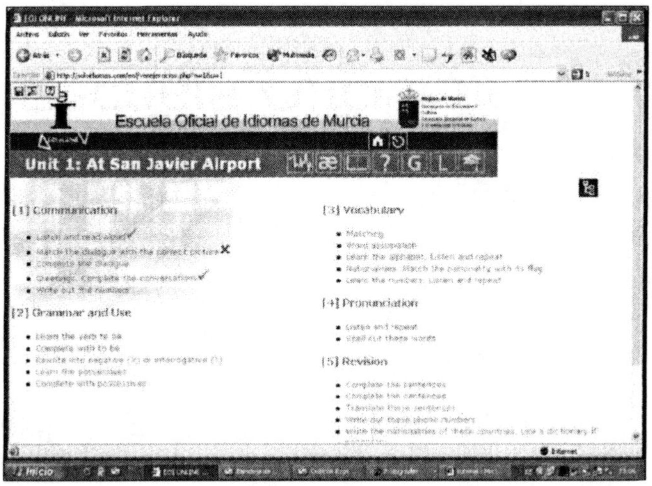

the exercises and activities or can opt for the established "standard" learning path — this is what happens by default. The "standard" learning paradigm refers to the content-graded difficulty each unit has been sequenced into. This sequence moves from easier to more complex contents, introducing new contents and/or adding already learned ones. Special care has also been taken in not only sequencing the contents present in each unit, but also in establishing a plausible learning paradigm that gradually progresses from implicit content presentations (grammatical, lexical, communicative, etc.) with less demanding exercises to more content-explicit and demanding exercises and activities. As students progress in the unit, it becomes not only more complex, but also more demanding. The exercises in the unit start with simple comprehension activities[12] with simple ticks and ends up with significantly more complex reading comprehension tasks. Consequently, the learning paradigm pays special attention to both the content difficulty and the students' demand for involvement. The last exercises, activities or tasks of each unit invite students to practice all contents learned, not in isolation but in meaningful communicative contexts. Students are left, by means of more open-ended tasks, to activate and use those linguistic issues learned, and practice them on their own in real and significant contexts. This learning path, designed by the language teachers, ensures a positive, realistic and plausible learning process in a very similar way to regular attendance courses. The learning paradigm itself is highly elaborated, based on the two intrinsically interwoven principles outlined above: content difficulty and demand for students' involvement. Therefore, the materials of each unit (texts, exercises, activities and tasks) are also organized following these learning paradigm principles. Visually, the learning paradigm can be summarized as shown in Figure 2.

To see how this is done in *EOI Online-Inglés 1*, observe Figure 3. This figure displays the contents of Unit 1 (*At San Javier Airport*). Each of the contents refers to a particular activity, exercise or task. As already stated, students can navigate freely.

However, if they choose to start with the very first exercise (*Listen and read aloud* in the *Communication* section), they will be "guided" along the unit, following the established learning paradigm. Table 2 shows the established sequence for Unit 1 (learning paradigm).

Once a student is working on any exercise, activity or task, the system displays two navigation arrows (see Figure 4), allowing the student to go back to the previous exercise — if he or she has any doubts with the present exercise or does not feel confident enough — or move on to the next one. This is not a free navigation but a fixed one, following the established learning paradigm.

Table 2. Learning paradigm of Unit 1

Sequence order	Content block	Exercise/Activity/Task
1	[1] Communication	Listen and read aloud
2	[1] Communication	Match the dialogue with the correct picture
3	[1] Communication	Complete the dialogue
4	[2] Grammar and Use	Learn the verb *to be*
5	[2] Grammar and Use	Complete with *to be*
6	[3] Vocabulary	Matching
7	[4] Pronunciation	Listen and repeat
8	[3] Vocabulary	Word association
9	[2] Grammar and Use	Rewrite into negative (X) or interrogative (?)
10	[1] Communication	Greetings. Complete the conversations
11	[3] Vocabulary	Learn the alphabet. Listen and repeat
12	[4] Pronunciation	Spell out these words
13	[3] Vocabulary	Nationalities. Match the nationality with its country flag
14	[2] Grammar and Use	Learn the possessives
15	[2] Grammar and Use	Complete with possessives
16	[3] Vocabulary	Learn the numbers. Listen and repeat
17	[1] Communication	Write out these numbers
18	[5] Revision	Complete the sentences
19	[5] Revision	Complete the sentences
20	[5] Revision	Translate these sentences
21	[5] Revision	Write out these phone numbers
22	[5] Revision	Write the nationalities of these countries. Use a dictionary if necessary

Figure 4. Exercise navigation facilities

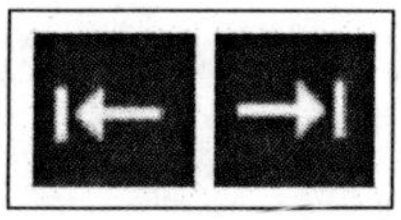

If a student wants to navigate freely, he or she can do so by going straight to the unit exercise display screen (see Figure 3) and click on any exercise, activity or task. Once the student has completed the exercise, he or she can go back to the unit exercise display screen by just clicking on the highlighted icon of Figure 5.

Similarly, students can move to a different unit at any time by clicking on the highlighted icon in Figure 6.

Exercise, Activity and Task Typologies

This online course points towards autonomous learning. With this premise in mind, we have tried to design the interface and course functions in a simple but consistent way. This applies not only to the interface, but also to the exercises, activities and tasks students have to perform. Consequently, we decided to limit the types of exercises available to ensure functionality without necessarily penalizing creativity. The exercise typology has been limited to seven, though some of them are open-ended and/or can be combined with others. The basic typology is explained below:

1. Text associated with a recording (Figure 7). Students can read and/or listen to a recorded text. Additional visual information (picture, drawing, video, etc.) can be added.
2. Text associated with visual information (picture, drawing, video, etc.; Figure 8). Students are required to match the most appropriate picture or drawing with the text displayed. Optional recorded material can be added.

Figure 5. Exercise display icon

Figure 6. Unit display icon

Figure 7. Text associated to a recording

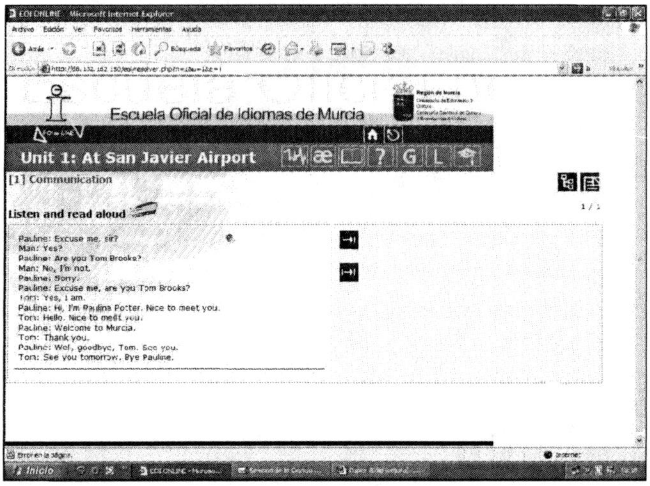

3. Text completion (Figure 9). Students have to complete the missing word of a sentence, end a sentence, rewrite a sentence, complete a text (close), write a sentence or text and so forth. Additional aural and visual information (picture, drawing, video, etc.) can be added.
4. Display of learning boxes (Figure 10). Students are required to learn specific linguistic contents (grammar, vocabulary, communicative situations, etc.). Additional visual information (picture, drawing, video, etc.) can be added.

Figure 8. Text associated to visual information

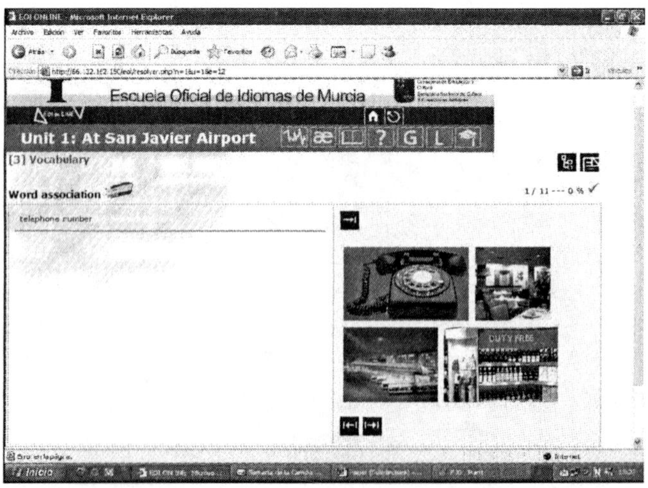

Figure 9. Text completion

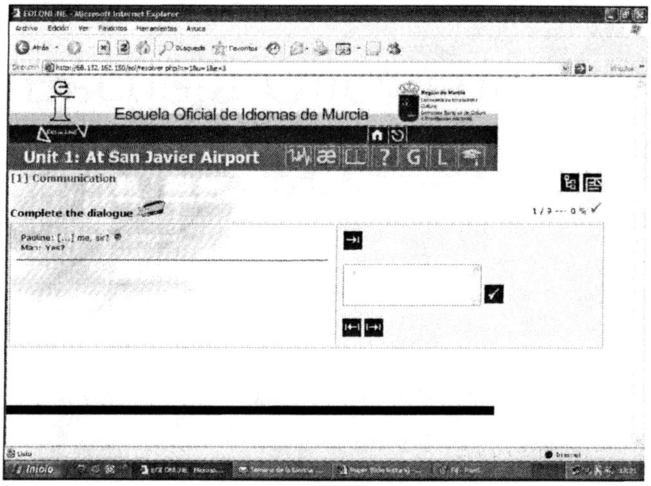

5. Multiple choices (Figure 11). Students have to choose the most appropriate answer from a limited number of options. Students' output is just a click on the answer chosen.
6. Text completion associated with a recording (Figure 12). Students have to read and/ or listen to a recorded text and answer questions or fulfill some other task. Additional visual information (picture, drawing, video, etc.) can be added. In contrast to type 1 above, students are expected to input data.

Figure 10. Learning box

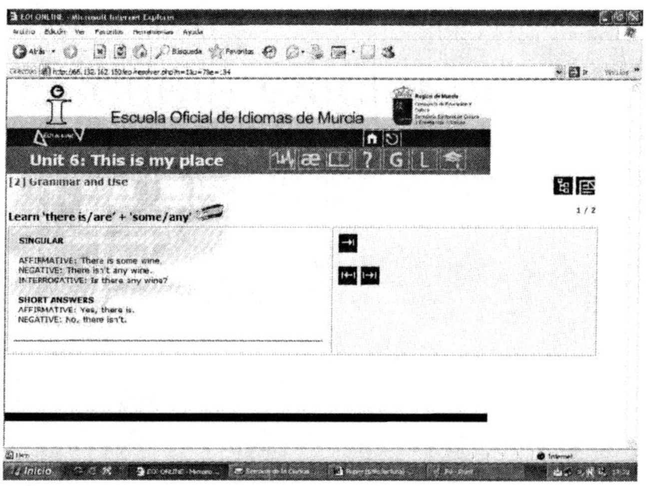

Figure 11. Multiple choice exercises

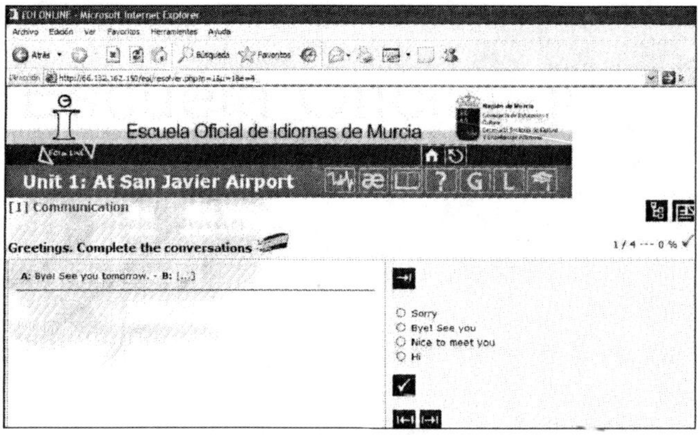

Figure 12. Text completion related to a recording

Figure 13. Translation activity

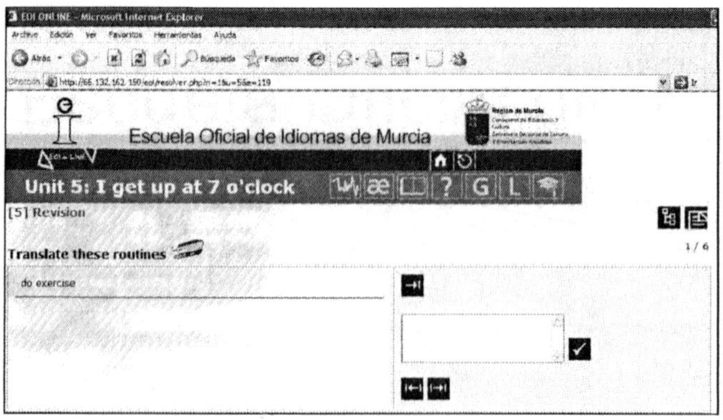

7. Translation exercise (Figure 13). Students are asked to translate a number of words, expressions, sentences or full text.

Exercise, Activity and Task Solving

Students are always provided with immediate feedback to their responses and answers. Students' output can be of various types (none, click or write) depending on the exercise. After each answer, students have to confirm their input by means of clicking on the validation button (Figure 14) and, once the system has displayed the adequate feedback[13], students move on to the next question within the same exercise (Figure 15) or move on to the next exercise or activity (see Figure 4) — if they have finished the one they were working on.

The different types of exercise, activity or task solving depend on the kind of activity:

1. Text associated with a recording. No response output is required. Once they have read and/or listened to a text, students move on to the next exercise. The reading and/or listening is essential for forthcoming exercises.
2. Text associated with visual information. Students have to match the most appropriate picture or drawing with the text displayed by means of a simple click on the pictures. Students get immediate feedback on the correctness of their answers (if the answer is wrong, the right answer is displayed).
3. Text completion (Figure 16). Students have to write the required information (immediate response on answer correctness; if the answer is wrong, the right answer is displayed).
4. Display of learning boxes. No students' output required. The learning and understanding of these boxes is very important for forthcoming exercises and activities.
5. Multiple choices. Students have to click on the right answer (if the answer is wrong, the right answer is displayed).

Figure 14. Answer validation

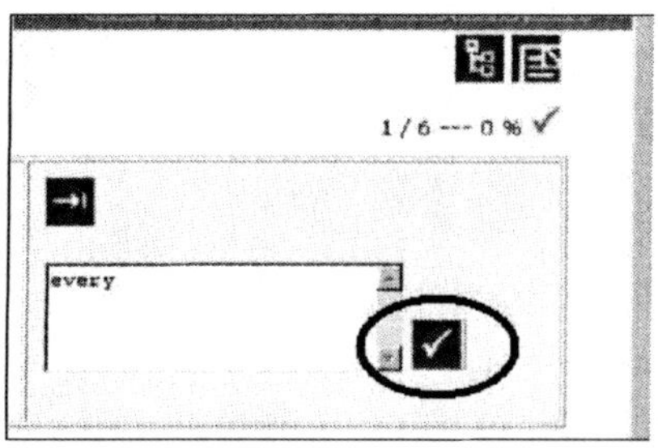

Figure 15. Move to next question icon

Figure 16. Text completion exercise and system feedback

6. Text completion associated with a recording. Students are expected to write some data (immediate response on answer correctness; if the answer is wrong, the right answer is displayed).
7. Translation exercise (Figure 17). Students are asked to translate a number of words, expressions, sentences or full text. The program's feedback on the correctness of students' answers is different here, due to the numerous possible translations, especially in sentences and texts, and the most appropriate translation is suggested.

The system allows students to always have full control of exercise performance. On the top right-hand corner, students can find information on the total number of questions

Figure 17. Translation exercise and system feedback

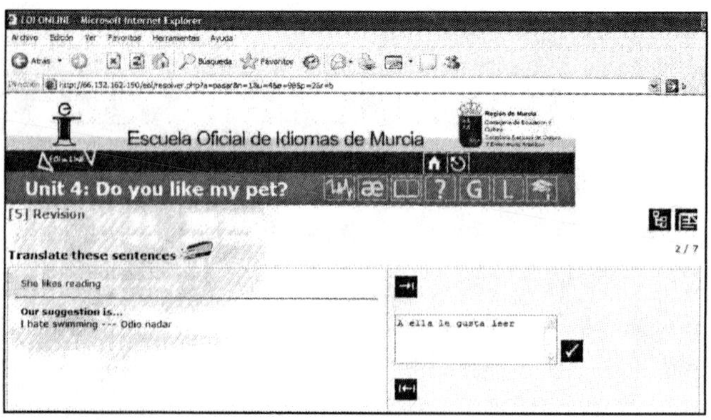

Figure 18. Information on exercise performance

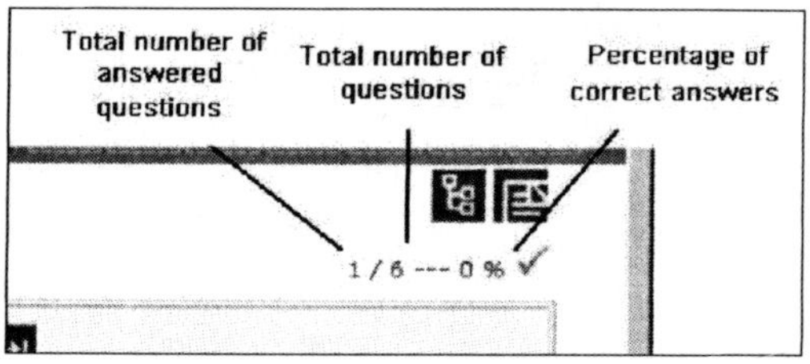

Figure 19. Feedback on correctness

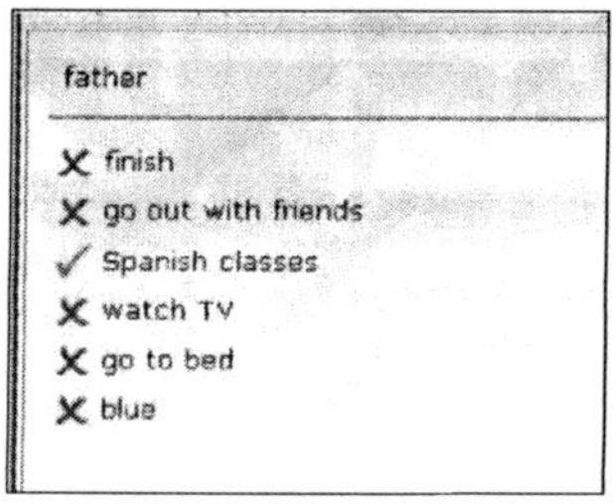

in each exercise, the number of questions answered and the percentage of correctly answered questions (Figure 18).

Regarding correctness feedback, the system offers three types (Figure 19):

1. Green tick: correct answer
2. Red cross: wrong answer
3. Grey cross: unanswered question

Online Help and Learning Facilities

The whole system has been designed in a very robust way, keeping in mind that the main goal was to design an autonomous distance-learning course. Therefore, we tried to incorporate a number of online help and learning facilities. These facilities can be accessed by clicking on the blue icons (Figure 20).

1. *Students' performance*: Any learner can graphically view his or her own learning progress, either reviewing all units (Figure 21) or any unit in particular with a

Figure 20. Online help and learning facilities

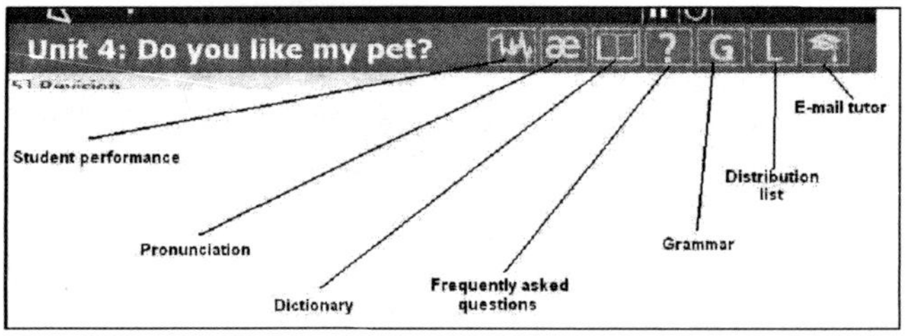

Figure 21. Course overview of student's performance

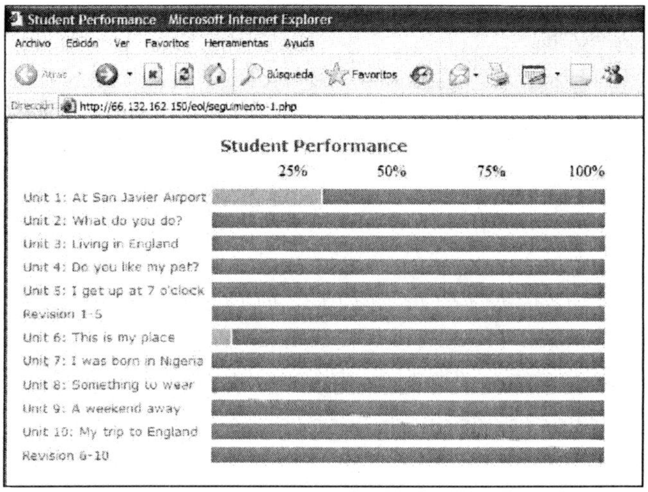

Figure 22. Unit performance

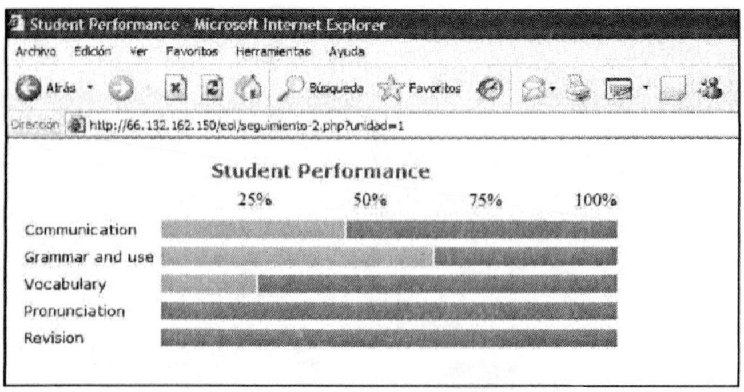

Figure 23. English sounds

Figure 24. Vowel sounds

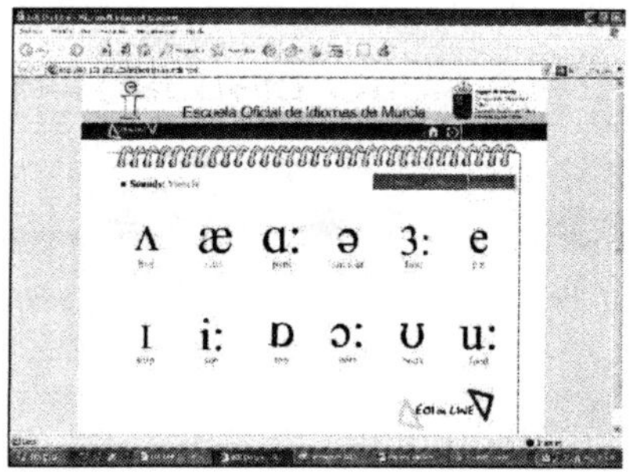

detailed description of the various content blocks (*Communication*, *Grammar and Use*, *Vocabulary*, *Pronunciation* and *Revision*; Figure 22).

Furthermore, students can also overview which exercises, activities or tasks they have successfully performed. These can be checked in the unit exercise window (see Figure 3). Exercises marked with a green tick have been done satisfactorily (above 60% of correctness), and those followed by a red cross are below the 60% success rate.

2. *Pronunciation*: This provides information on all English sounds. It is structured into vowels, diphthongs and consonants (Figure 23). Each sound comes with its corresponding phonetic symbol and is illustrated with an example, which can be heard by clicking on it (Figure 24).

Figure 25. Dictionary: browsing for words starting with "H"

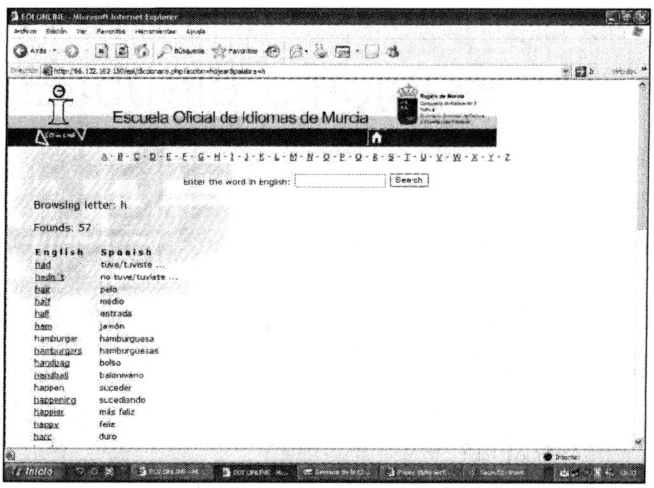

Figure 26. Dictionary: search result for "house"

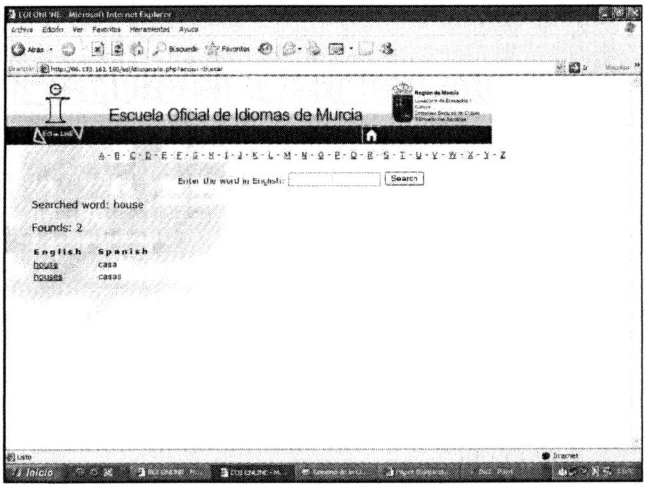

Figure 27. FAQs

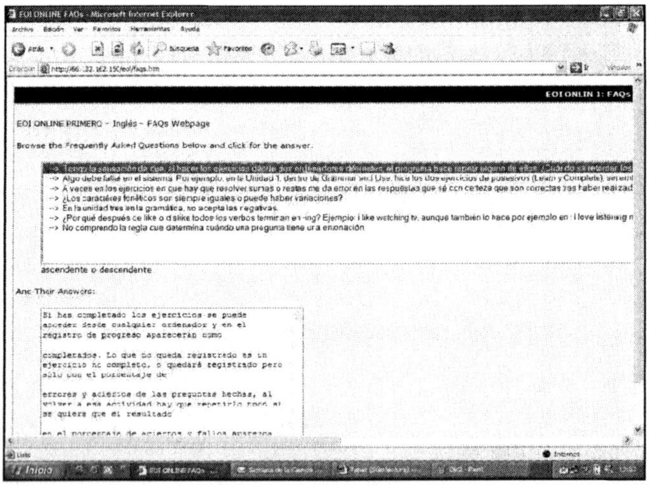

3. *Dictionary*: an online bilingual English-Spanish dictionary containing only the word forms present in the course. Instead of lexemes or headwords, we have included word forms. So, for example, *house* and *houses* are typified as different entries. The dictionary can be consulted in two ways: by clicking on any of the letters (A-Z), displaying all word forms under this letter (Figure 25), or searching

Figure 28. Online grammar

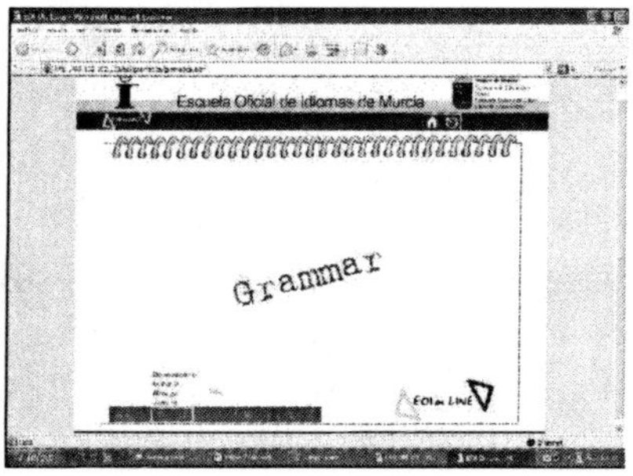

Figure 29. Online grammar: demonstratives

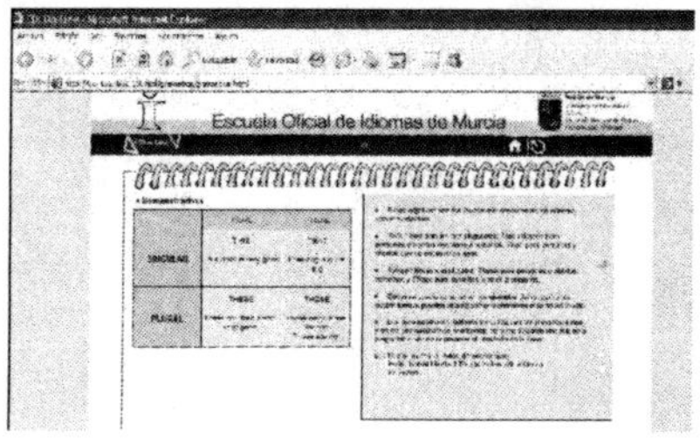

Figure 30. Exercise headings: possibility of translating them

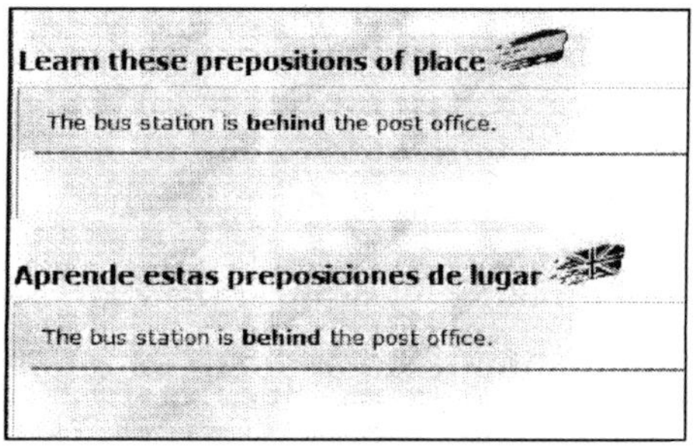

for a specific word or word form (Figure 26). In addition, students can listen to the browsed words by simply clicking on them.

4. *Frequently asked questions*: Students can access this facility and look for solutions or answers to their uncertainties or problems. This facility deals essentially with software problems (Web browser, etc.) and doubts related to the course interface (Figure 27).

5. *Grammar*: This facility contains only grammar points dealt with in the course. All explanations are in Spanish, to facilitate understanding, and are illustrated with numerous examples. The organization of the grammar contents is in alphabetic order, using exactly the same headings and expressions as in the units (see Figures 28 and 29).

6. *Exercise headings*: All headings have been translated into Spanish. By clicking on the Spanish flag, students can read the exercise heading translated into Spanish (Figure 30). To go back to English headings, they click on the English flag.

Figure 31. E-mail tutor icon

Figure 32. E-mailing tutor

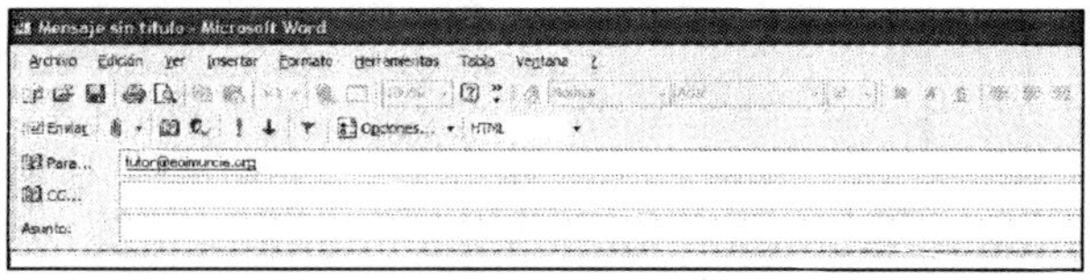

Tutoring

Much attention and care has been taken to tutoring and assisting students. This is also one ofthe reasons why the selected tutors are highly qualified and experienced language teachers at the EOI.

Apart from the FAQs facility described above, which is mainly about software and interface functionalities, students can access their tutor in various ways:

1. E-mail, asking for help (grammar, lexicon doubts, interface problems, etc.). This facility can be accessed by clicking on the top blue button (see Figure 31), and the system opens the installed e-mail browser with the tutor's e-mail copied in (Figure 32).
2. Alternatively, students can also contact their tutor via telephone or personally at the tutor's office (all students are supplied at the beginning ofthe course with their tutor's attendance timetable at the EOI of Murcia).
3. Whenever students have the same or similar doubts, the tutor can either incorporate the answer in the FAQs or use the distribution list facility (Figure 33). A click on this icon pops up the e-mail browser with the distribution list e-mail (eoiline@eoimurcia.org). This distribution list can also be used by students to ask their course mates for help and so forth, or just comment on various issues related to course contents or course performance.

Similar to the *Students' Performance* facility (see Figures 21 and 22), tutors can also assess students' performance. This is done by means of a special Web address only supplied to tutors involved in the course. Tutors can access a Web site that summarizes

Figure 33. Distribution list icon

Figure 34. E-mailing to the distribution list

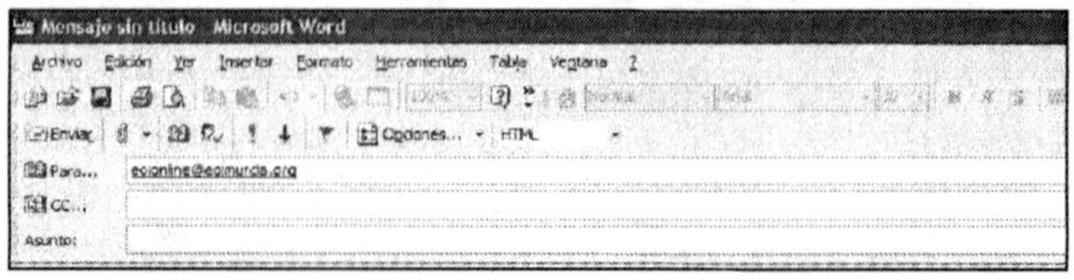

Figure 35. Tutor's student-performance overview

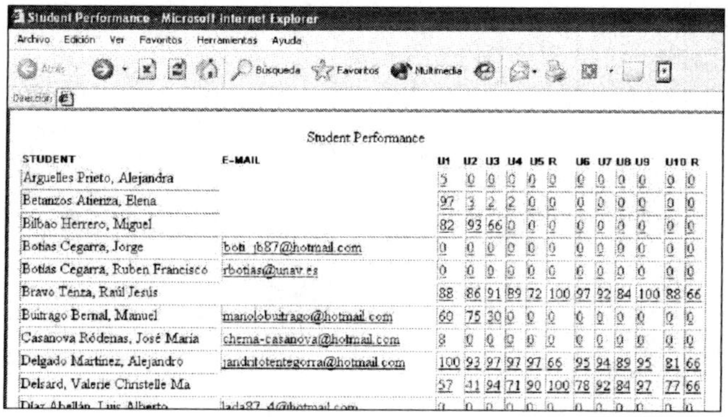

Student Performance

STUDENT	E-MAIL	U1	U2	U3	U4	U5	R	U6	U7	U8	U9	U10	R
Arguelles Prieto, Alejandra		5	0	0	0	0	0	0	0	0	0	0	0
Betanzos Atienza, Elena		97	3	2	2	0	0	0	0	0	0	0	0
Bilbao Herrero, Miguel		82	93	66	0	0	0	0	0	0	0	0	0
Botias Cegarra, Jorge	boti_jb87@hotmail.com	0	0	0	0	0	0	0	0	0	0	0	0
Botias Cegarra, Ruben Francisco	rbotias@unav.es	0	0	0	0	0	0	0	0	0	0	0	0
Bravo Tenza, Raúl Jesús		88	86	91	89	72	100	97	92	84	100	88	66
Buitrago Bernal, Manuel	manolobuitrago@hotmail.com	60	75	30	0	0	0	0	0	0	0	0	0
Casanova Ródenas, José María	chema-casanova@hotmail.com	8	0	0	0	0	0	0	0	0	0	0	0
Delgado Martínez, Alejandro	jandritotentegorra@hotmail.com	100	93	97	97	97	66	95	94	89	95	81	66
Delsard, Valerie Christelle Ma		57	41	94	71	90	100	78	92	84	97	77	66
Díaz Abellán, Luis Alberto	lada87_4@hotmail.com	0	0	0	0	0	0	0	0	0	0	0	0

their students' performance, expressed in percentages (Figure 35). In addition, a quick glance at these statistics allows the tutor to have full information as to the working pace of each student, and check which units have been performed and the success rate of these units. Tutors can then, according to the data supplied by each student, encourage any individual student to speed up or slow down. Furthermore, if the tutor wants or needs more specific information on a particular unit performance, he or she can click on the unit and look for the performance of the specific learning blocks (*Communication*, *Grammar and Use*, *Vocabulary*, *Pronunciation* or *Revision*; see Figure 22). This information is most valuable, as the tutor can then recommend students to work over the same unit or block again, or encourage students to do specific remedial work (see *Section III.7*).

Additional Non-Compulsory Attendance Lessons

Though this online course aims to be an autonomous and autosufficient language course, it cannot overcome one major aspect any language course invariably needs: practice of oral skills, particularly speaking. The course lacks actual speaking skills activities. To solve this problem, parallel to the course, students can attend non-compulsory 1-hour speaking sessions, run weekly by the tutor and native conversation assistants. At the beginning of the course, students are supplied with a time schedule for these optional conversation classes, highlighting the topics that will be dealt with and the materials and readings they need to prepare beforehand.

Additional Materials

Apart from all the learning facilities, the course is fitted with:

1. Online grammar

Figure 36. Free accessible resources

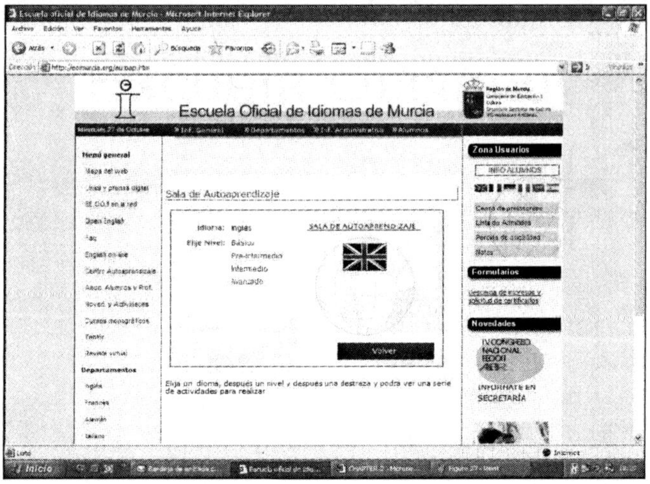

Figure 37. EOI Online resources

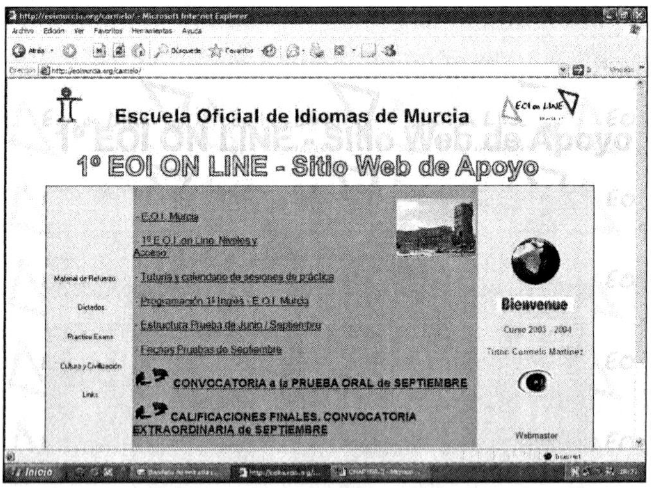

2. Online dictionary
3. Pronunciation
4. Exercise heading translation

In addition, at the additional non-compulsory 1-hour speaking sessions, students can also access free additional working materials. Students can either access the free follow-up materials that are accessible to any students of the EOI of Murcia (Figure 36), or those materials restricted to EOI online students (Figure 37). The latter materials have been selected and elaborated on by the tutors and refer specifically to contents dealt with in the online course. These complementary materials contain not only remedial exercises but also former examinations, texts and Web sites on British culture and civilization and so forth related to the course contents.

Course Performance and Evaluation

The first official course performance was carried out during the 2003-'04[14] academic year. Once registered, students were supplied with an instruction booklet, explaining all system functionalities, software requirements and so forth. In addition, students were given all academic and administrative information (syllabus, recommended course pace schedule, timetable for optional oral sessions, tutorial timetable, etc.).

E-Mail

The most common form of communication between students and tutor was e-mail. A noteworthy finding was that most e-mails were about computer-related issues (hardware and/or software configuration problems, wrong e-mail addresses, students who used free e-mail accounts with a limited space capacity, etc.). More than 5% of all e-mails sent to students were rejected because of wrong or expired addresses or because the space capacity had been exceeded.

The remaining e-mails (around 300) were related to academic issues: 45 students sent a total of 180 compositions. These essays were corrected by the tutors, using a word processor and highlighting the errors in a different color, without any further specification. The essays were e-mailed back to the students and students were asked to think about the errors and correct and improve their compositions. Two days later, the tutor e-mailed a second message with full explanations on the errors.

A further 15 e-mails were sent to the tutor containing oral recordings in response to a limited number of oral exercises present in the course.

Students' Performance

The total number of registered students was 106. Not all students fully worked on all units, as we found a gradual decline in the student number. This is actually quite common in vocational studies and also happens in the normal attendance course, where the course abandoning rate is about 50%. The figures (Table 3 and Figure 38) show the most dramatic decline after the first two units.

Table 3. Students' attendance

UNIT	1	2	3	4	5	Rev	6	7	8	9	10	Rev
STUDENTS	106	80	61	58	50	42	40	38	35	32	30	30

Figure 38. Students' attendance

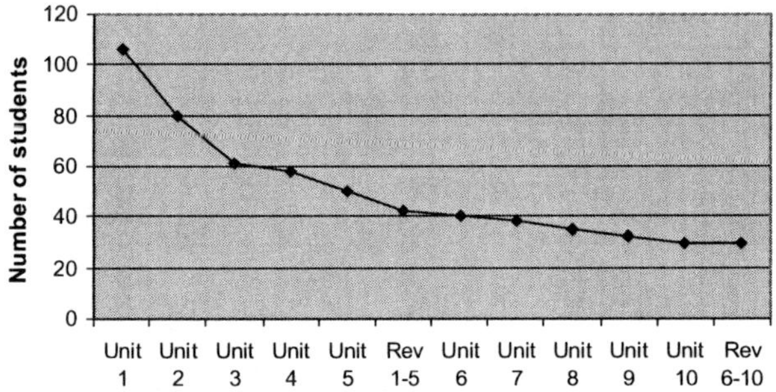

Table 4. Students' performance

	Number	%
Registered students	106	100,00
Students sitting exam	77	72,64
Students passing written exam	57	53,77
Students passing oral exam	50	47,17
Successful students	50	47,17

Figure 39. Students' performance

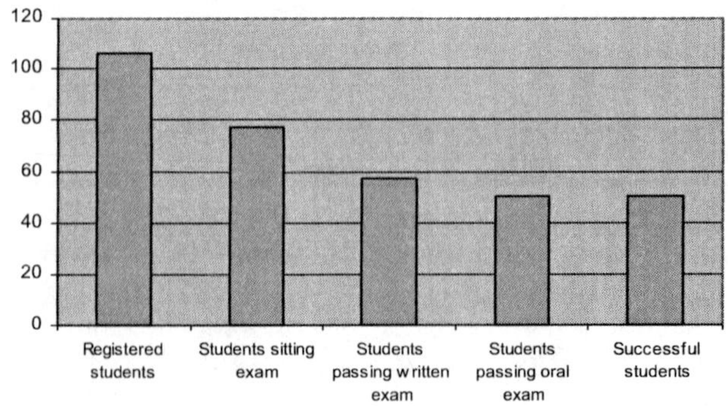

Table 5. Average marks

		Average score	Max. score
Written part	**Use of English**	26.10	40
	Writing	11.53	20
Oral part	**Speaking**	9.95	20
	Listening	13.58	20
Total score		**61.16**	**100**

Table 6. Online vs. offline performance

	Online		Offline	
	Number	%	Number	%
Registered students	106	100	1.156	100
Students sitting exam	77	72,64	820	70,93
Successful students	50	47,17	482	41,69

However, irrespective of the students who did not complete the whole units, 77 of them attended the final examination (72.64%). Fifty-seven students passed the written exam (53.77% of overall students and 74.02% of the students who sat the written examination), and 50 students performed positively in the oral part (47.17% overall and 87.72% of those passed the written component; see Table 4 and Figure 39).

The average marks in the written and oral components are shown in Table 5.

A brief comparison between online students' performance and offline students' performance (normal attendance course) results into very similar figures regarding exam attendance and success/fail rates (Table 6).

Apart from this academic information, we also wanted students' feedback on the course structure, system interface and so forth. Therefore, an online questionnaire was designed and students were invited to access and answer it anonymously[15]. The information elicited by the questionnaire centered on three main issues:

1. Online course (questions 1-8)
2. Previous knowledge on English (9-10)
3. Internet connection and technical aspects of the course (11-17)

Online Course

1. *Question 1:* In general terms, 74% of the students considered the course as excellent or good; 26% as normal or not too good. In addition, students commented on the advantage of being able to study from home, without restricting themselves to any predefined timetable.

2. *Question 2:* contents; 58.5% of students said contents were excellent or good; 37.5% normal and 4% not too good.
3. *Question 3:* exercise performance; 48.5% excellent or good; 42.5% normal and 9% not too good. Students found pronunciation exercises as the most difficult, stressing the need of additional help or facilities.
4. *Question 4:* clarity of the exercise explanations; 41.5% excellent or good; 41.5% normal and 17% not too good.
5. *Question 5:* difficulty in following course contents and explanations; 66% did not find any problems or very few; 33% had some problems; 1% had serious problems.
6. *Question 6:* tutorial assistance; 80% excellent or good; 19% normal and 1% bad.
7. *Question 7:* optional oral sessions contents; 54% excellent or good; 34% normal; 7% not too good and 3% bad.
8. *Question 8:* optional oral sessions' frequency and timetable; 20% excellent or good; 51% normal; 22% not too good and 7% bad.

Previous Knowledge of English

1. *Question 9:* years of English study; 10% had never studied English before; 18% had studied it for 1-2 years; 27% for 2-4 years; 45% for more than 4 years.
2. *Question 10:* How would you define your level of English?; 10% absolute beginners; 49% elementary; 34% pre-intermediate and 7% intermediate.

Internet Connection and Technical Aspects of the Course

1. *Question 11:* type of processor; 20% had a computer with a 3.0 GHz processor or above; 21% 2.0-3.0 GHz; 12.5% 1.0-2.0 GHz; 8.5% less than 1GHz; 38% did not know the computer processing speed.
2. *Question 12:* type of Internet connection; 68.5 had DSL (broadband) connection. (The rest of the students did not answer this question.)
3. *Question 13:* usual working place; 78.6% at home; 7% out of home; 14.4% at home and outside of home.
4. *Question 14:* usual Internet connection time; 49% 1-3 hours a week; 33% 3-5 hours a week; 9% more than 5 hours a week.
5. *Question 15:* regularity in course performance; 49% very regular and quite regular; 51% not too regular.
6. *Question 16:* technical problems; 37% found some problems in connecting to the course server; 24% had Internet connection problems.
7. *Question 17:* computer literacy; 59.5% were habitual computer users; 26% had advanced or expert computer skills; 14.5% basic computer skills.

Future Trends

From the data above (academic information and students' feedback on course performance), we can extract useful consequences and ideas that can help us improve this online English language course. Probably the most urgent improvements are related to:

1. *Some exercise headings:* 17% of students stated that some explanations and exercise instructions were not too clear. This explains why 33% had some problems in following explanations and 9% when performing the exercises.
2. *Pronunciation exercises:* Some comments added to question 3 clearly suggest that either the exercise formats or typologies are not adequate, or that further pronunciation facilities should be added, such as Web-based voice solutions.
3. *Optional oral sessions:* 29% of students considered the timetable assigned and/or the frequency of these sessions as "not too good" or "bad." This is probably due to their way of working, as they have to switch from a completely flexible working schedule to a fixed and rigid course attendance schedule. Looking for greater timetable flexibility is bound to staff availability, and this is something that clearly exceeds our limits at present.
4. *Unbalanced grouping of students:* Students ranged from absolute beginners to intermediate. This could be solved applying a placement test before registering.
5. *Connection to the course server:* 37% of students said they had problems when they wanted to connect to the course. A possible solution is to have an alternative access or server so that two course accesses/servers are working simultaneously. Surprisingly enough, the server never went down during the whole course.
6. *Basic computer skills:* 14.5% of students were not very proficient in computer-related issues. This might have been one of the reasons for connection problems to the course server. A possible solution might be to plan an intensive pre-course seminar on basic Internet issues and, more specifically, on the online course functionalities.

The questionnaire revealed that although all exercise headings were translated into Spanish, some students still have problems understanding what they have to do. It is noteworthy to point out that in some cases, we suggested using the Spanish translated heading whenever they had problems understanding, and some of them were not even aware of this facility. However, action has already been taken in revising all exercise headings, particularly those on which students reported problems on the exercise performance.

A further issue is that students did take a placement test this year before deciding in which course to register. In academic year 2004-'05, *EOI Online-Inglés I* (level A1) and *EOI Online-Inglés II* (level A2) are available, apart, of course, from all the usual attendance-mode courses. This solution might ensure a more homogeneous learning group.

Figure 40. Wimba Voice Direct

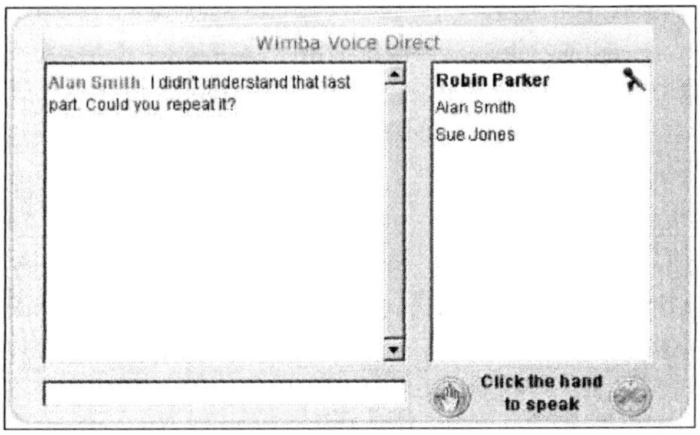

An alternative access has been implemented, a sort of mirror site, to ensure instant access to the course and its contents; though, we stress again, no student actually reported server problems, only in the questionnaire.

To ensure that students get familiar with all the course functionalities and facilities, instead of arranging an intensive pre-course seminar, a seven-page color booklet was created, with succinct and clear explanations, illustrated with numerous examples. In addition, this booklet also included the most used facilities on two CD-ROMs:

1. Dictionary
2. Grammar
3. Pronunciation

This saves unnecessary Internet connection time and use of computer resources. We are confident that this inevitably benefits in computer speed and encourages students to use these materials more extensively, not just as mere facilities but also as autonomous learning tools. This booklet was distributed to all students free of charge once registered in the *EOI Online-Inglés* course.

But the most challenging issue to solve or improve is the one related to the deficient pronunciation exercises. Obviously, the exercise formats were not satisfactory. A possible solution to this, which we have now started to explore, is using Web-based facilities that enable people to communicate, collaborate and learn vocally, with little training required. The Open University has developed Lyceum, which is unfortunately not commercially available yet, using it mainly for tutor-led sessions with materials that have been specially prepared for the online medium. At the beginning of the year, students are grouped and allocated to a tutor and tutorial dates are organized. In addition to these scheduled tutorials, some students use Lyceum for what they call "self-help groups."

Alternative commercial products are already available, such as Wimba[16] and FirstCall[17]. These Web-based voice solutions are lightweight and fast, and do not require high-performance computers or network connections. Apparently, they can be quickly and seamlessly integrated into online learning environments. Wimba Voice Direct (Figure 40), for example, allows vocal communication in real time. It is like a conference call through a computer and can be used for interactive discussions or "broadcasting."

In addition to the use of Web-based conferencing tools for pronunciation tasks, the integration of these applications into online learning environments, such as our online English course, would allow more flexible speaking opportunities, not just restricted to the optional oral attendance sessions. Students spread over the region of Murcia or Spain would not need to attend these sessions and could use these Internet-based, real-time audio conferencing facilities instead, thus making a groundbreaking move in distance learning and teaching of languages.

Conclusion

Unfortunately, there are no universal truths on how to design and develop online language courses. One of the major problems confronting us is that we are often reduced to using evidence, common sense or experience for important pedagogical decisions. We lack enough solid research on this field. However, one thing we can urge from start is the need of trialing prototypes with typical learners. Our experience is that this almost always provides interesting, and sometimes even surprising, results that lead to immediate and urgent adaptation(s) of the program.

"We need to know better what works!" (Bangs & Cantos, 2004, p. 234). This precisely has been our starting premise. The interface and contents of *EOI Online-Inglés I/II* have been designed and implemented with the potential necessities and difficulties distance-language learning students were likely to find in mind. Therefore, collaborative development was a must. The synergy of language teachers with sheer experience, experts in CALL and programmers was vital. The result was a user-friendly and easy-to-use tool, though the trade-off between complexity and ease of use is always a difficult compromise. The system integrates a number of tools and facilities always accessible to students. These tools range from linguistic ones (pronunciation kit, English-Spanish dictionary, English grammar in Spanish) to tutorial facilities (tutor e-mailing and distribution list), informative facilities on students' own learning progress and system functioning uncertainties (FAQs).

We always had in mind that the learner is the center of the learning process. The course (contents and interface) has been designed for learners, not for teachers; this links with the role of assessment, but assessment for learning. Students always have full control on their performance; and they can obtain information and feedback any moment in various ways, either from the tutor or from the system (answer correctness, translated exercise headings, further information on linguistic issues, progress, etc.). Great effort was made in looking for transparent and standard formats of assessment and progress able to supply feedback both to the learner and the tutor.

As mentioned above, there is a need of trialing prototypes with typical learners. This was done with the first version of *EOI Online-Inglés I*. The information elicited by means of the questionnaire (http://eoimurcia.org/carmelo/encuesta.htm) and the numerous e-mails received (tutor and distribution list) were very positive, with a high degree of satisfaction on course performance, course functioning and design. Students also highlighted some deficiencies related to the course and its contents, such as: 1) some exercise headings/instructions were not clear enough, and 2) poor/not enough practicing of oral skills (pronunciation and speaking). Other drawbacks had to do with some students' lack of computer literacy, unbalanced grouping (absolute beginners mixed with intermediate students), not too convenient schedule for oral sessions and server problems.

Of course all of the problematic issues raised by students need a detailed analysis and possible solution. However, those related to the course and its contents were most important and urgent for us, particularly the issue related to oral practice. We think that integrating Web-based voice solutions might be positive, improving the quality and quantity of oral practicing supplied so far with the course. Unfortunately, this will not happen overnight.

For some readers, all these solutions and improvements might just be immediate micro-level solutions. More ambitiously, Bangs and Cantos (2004, p. 236) propose that: "What we can do is to hold on to recognized principles, monitor new pedagogic developments, and lobby, through organizations such as Calico, EuroCall and WorldCall, etc., for the best interest of CALL on behalf of developers and learners the world over." However, this is presently beyond our scope.

References

Bangs, P. (2002). Why is feedback dying of starvation? — Let's try to revive it ... Retrieved from http://members.aol.com/bangspaul/EuroCall2002.htm

Bangs, P. (2003). Engaging the learner — How to author for best feedback. In U. Felix (Ed.), Language learning online: Towards best practice. Zurich: Sweet & Zeitlinger.

Bangs, P., & Cantos, P. (2004). What can computer assisted language learning contribute to foreign language pedagogy? *International Journal of English Studies, 4*(1), 221-239.

Boletín Oficial del Estado. (1988, September 10). *Real Decreto 967/1988, de 2 de septiembre, sobre ordenación de las enseñanzas correspondientes al primer nivel de las enseñanzas especializadas de idiomas.* Madrid: B.O.E.

Boletín Oficial del Estado. (1989, December 18). *Real Decreto 1523/1989), de 1 diciembre, por el que se aprueban los contenidos mínimos del primer nivel de las enseñanzas especializadas de idiomas extranjeros.* Madrid: B.O.E.

Boletín Oficial del Estado. (1992, February 5). *Real Decreto 47/1992 de 24 de Enero, por el que se aprueban los contenidos mínimos correspondientes a las enseñanzas especializadas de las lenguas españolas, impartidas en las Escuelas Oficiales de Idiomas*. Madrid: B.O.E.

Chun, D., & Plass, J. (1996). Research on text comprehension in multimedia environments. *Language Learning & Technology, 1*(1), 60-81.

Council of Europe. (2001). *Common European framework for languages: Learning, teaching, assessment*. London: Cambridge University Press.

European Union (1995, November 29) *White paper on education. Teaching and learning: Towards the learning society*. (COM (95) 590).

Heift, T. (2003). Multiple learner errors and meaningful feedback: A challenge for ICALL systems. *CALICO Journal, 20*(3), 533-549.

International Certificate Conference. (2001). *The impact of new technologies and Internet: On the teaching of foreign language and the role of teachers of a foreign language*. Retrieved from www.icc-europe.com/

Mayer, R. E. (1997). *Computer assisted language learning: Context and conceptualization*. Oxford: Oxford University Press.

Rösler, D. (2000). Foreign-language learning with the new media: Between the sanctuary of the classroom and the open terrain of natural language acquisition. *GFL-Journal, 1*(2002), 16-31.

Endnotes

1 MEC stands for *Ministerio de Educación y Ciencia* (Spanish Ministry of Education and Science).

2 Real Decreto (Royal Decree) 967/1988, 2 September 1988; and published in the B.O.E. (Boletín Oficial del Estado) 218/88 (State Oficial Bulletin), 10 September 1988.

3 The Common European Framework provides a common basis for the elaboration of language syllabi, curriculum guidelines, examinations, textbooks and so forth across Europe. It describes in a comprehensive way what language learners have to learn to do in order to use a language for communication and what knowledge and skills they have to develop so as to be able to act effectively in the target language.

4 *White Paper on Education*. Teaching and Learning: towards the Learning Society, COM(95)590; http://europa.eu.int/en/record/white/edu9511/

5 Proficiency in several community languages has become a precondition if citizens of the European Union are to benefit from the occupational and personal opportunities open to them in the border-free single market. This language proficiency must be backed up by the ability to adapt to working and living environments characterized by different cultures. Since March 1995, it is becoming necessary for everyone, irrespective of training and education routes chosen, to be able to acquire and keep up their ability to communicate in at least two community

languages in addition to their mother tongue. The Commission regrets that the importance of this commitment was reduced by some the member states (*White Paper on Education* 1995: 51).

6 International Certificate Conference (ICC, Frankfurt): "The Impact of Information and Communication Technologies on the Teaching of Foreign Languages and on the Role of Teachers of Foreign Languages". A report commissioned by the Directorate General of Education and Culture; http://www.icc-europe.com

7 http://www.thatsenglish.com/

8 http://eoimurcia.org/open.htm, http://www.eoicartagena.org/quesopen1.html

9 See Mayer (1997) and Rösler (2000) on multimedia learning.

10 See http://eoimurcia.org/programonline.htm

11 See http://eoimurcia.org/dingles.htm

12 See Bannerti et al. (2003) on requirements and infrastructure for CALL.

13 See Chun and Plass (1996) on text comprehension in multimedia environments.

14 See Bangs (2002 and 2003) and Heift (2003) on adequate system feedback.

15 An experimental performance with a limited group of students was conducted in the second semester of course 2002-'03, in order to fine-tune the course (find possible errors, typos, bugs, etc.).

16 The questionnaire can be accessed at http://eoimurcia.org/carmelo/encuesta.htm

17 http://www.wimba.com

18 http://www.softarc.com

Chapter X

Metacognition and Learners' Interactions with a Web-Based CALL Grammar Exercise

Wai Meng Chan, National University of Singapore, Singapore

Abstract

The nature of learners' interactions with the computer has received thus far relatively little attention in computer assisted language learning (CALL) research. In particular, few studies have investigated the role of metacognition, acknowledged in cognitive and constructivist learning theories as an important factor contributing to the learning outcome, in the processing of CALL tasks. This chapter reports on a qualitative study that examined the relationship between subjects' metacognition and their interactions with a German language CALL grammar exercise. The data collected seem to indicate that the effective use of interactive aids is dependent on the extent of learners' metacognitive knowledge. Conversely, it was observed that interactive aids had a positive effect on learners' metacognition by supporting their strategy use and helping them build new metacognitive knowledge. Excerpts from subjects' think-aloud reports and retrospective interviews will be presented to illustrate these insights.

Introduction

Kozma (1994) underlined the need to build media theory based on the study of how learners interact with the computer and how the attributes of computer media may influence learning. He wrote:

> *Understanding the ways in which students use the unique processing capabilities of the computer is essential to understanding the influence the computer may have on learning and to building media theory. The other half of media theory is understanding when and how to employ these symbolic and processing capabilities so that cognitive and social processes, so influenced, result in learning for certain students, tasks, and situations.* (pp. 13-14)

Despite this call and the increasingly significant role of computer technologies and media in today's foreign language learning environment, we still know relatively little about learner-computer interactions and how these influence or are influenced by the learner's cognitive and metacognitive processes. For instance, which processes are involved? Which strategies do learners employ? What role does metacognition play in CALL? How do these variables affect learners' interactions with CALL materials? Conversely, how is learning, and learners' metacognition, mediated or affected by technology and the specific features of CALL materials? Some studies in the last two decades, indicative of the growing interest in these questions, have investigated learners' strategies for CALL tasks and their use of online help (see Liou, 1997). In one such study, Chapelle and Mizuno (1989) studied English as a Second Language (ESL) students' use of cognitive strategies (resourcing and practice) and metacognitive strategies (self-monitoring, self-management and self-evaluation) while working on learner-controlled CALL grammar lessons. They uncovered that while some students used these strategies some of the time, they do not always employ optimal strategies. Another study (Hsu, Chapelle, & Thompson, 1993), based on the same CALL grammar lessons, showed that students do not always make full use of learning resources integrated into the CALL materials. While interest in the relationship between CALL, CALL-enabled cognitive support and strategy use is growing, there is still — as Liou (1997) points out — a sore lack of empirical data, and much research is needed to achieve more conclusive results.

This chapter reports on a study that seeks to contribute towards this growing body of literature. It is hoped that this qualitative study, which investigated the relationship between learners' metacognition and their interactions with a Web-based CALL grammar exercise, will lead to larger studies and the subsequent construction of hypotheses. It focused on the subjects' metacognitive processes and strategy use while performing the exercise, as well as how these affect or are affected by their use of interactive aids. It was underpinned by the constructivist theory of learning and instructional design (e.g., Wheatley, 1991; Jonassen & Reeves, 1996) and a model of metacognition in second-language learning proposed by Chan (2000).

Theoretical Foundation

The Constructivist View of Learning and Instructional Design

Constructivist pedagogy is based on the principle that knowledge does not represent an objective entity that exists independently of the human mind and can be transmitted as a complete and unadulterated body of information from one person to another. Wheatley sums up this view by stating that:

> *... knowledge is not passively received, but is actively built up by the cognizing subject. Ideas and thoughts cannot be communicated in the sense that meaning is packaged into words and "sent" to another who unpacks the meaning from the sentences. That is, as much as we would like to, we cannot put ideas in students' heads, they will and must construct their own meanings.* (1991, p. 10)

Constructivists view learning as an active and subjective process for the construction of meanings and knowledge. As the learner perceives new information through his senses, he attempts to interpret and make sense of this information on the basis of his pre-existing cognitive structures, including his personal experiences, beliefs and attitudes. New knowledge that is meaningful and relevant is created through this process, and constructivist pedagogy strives to create conditions that are conducive to and facilitate such construction of knowledge (see Rüschoff, 1999; Mandl & Reinmann-Rothmeier, 1998).

Many constructivists argue that technology and CALL materials can support these complex learning processes by providing various cognitive tools for learning (e.g. Rüschoff, 1999; Chun & Plass, 2000; Jonassen & Reeves, 1996; Issing, 1998). Jonassen and Reeves (1996) describe computers and software such as databases, spreadsheets and multimedia/hypermedia construction systems as important cognitive tools that help learners organize, restructure and represent knowledge. For language learners, cognitive tools are available in the form of word processors, electronic encyclopedias and dictionaries, spelling and grammar checkers, and concordancers (Rüschoff, 1999). As the above-mentioned resources represent tools that support learning in general and larger projects consisting of numerous learning units or tasks, this chapter will describe them as macro-level cognitive tools.

Support can also be provided at a micro-level; that is, at the level of individual learning tasks or applications, to aid learners' task processing. For instance, Brett (1995) cites the example of multimedia software for developing listening skills in English business communication with options for learners to determine the content, mode of delivery, activity and task type, degree of difficulty, level of support, sequence of activity, and time and pace of learning. He sees instantaneous feedback CALL materials can provide as an important cognitive aid, for it can encourage learners to self-correct and thus evaluate their own strategies. Chan and Kim (2004) believe that computer media make it easier to differentiate between learners of varying capabilities by providing interactive help and cognitive tools on demand (e.g., word explanations, lists of expressions, hints and strategy advice for task processing, and information on grammar rules). They point out that the specific nature of such media, which can draw upon the computer's immense processing capabilities, makes it possible to provide such help instantaneously and will greatly encourage the use of these options. Like Brett, they believe that this will encourage learners to adopt a more conscious approach to task processing and increase their metacognitive awareness. This is consistent with the constructivists' call for the development of reflective (or metacognitive) awareness among learners and for greater attention to the process of knowledge construction (Bednar, Cunningham, Duffy, & Perry, 1992; Müller, 2000).

Metacognition and Language Learning

Metacognition has long been considered a linchpin of effective learning. It is the mechanism in one's cognition that enables the conscious reflection and regulation of one's cognitive processes, including language comprehension and production, and language learning. It is thus considered to be central to the effective selection and use of learning strategies (see O'Malley & Chamot, 1990). Many studies have shown that good learners are often distinguished by their ability to match appropriate strategies to the tasks they are performing (see Chamot, 2001). Studies by Wenden point to a strong relationship between what learners know and how they self-regulate (1982, 1991). Wenden cites studies from cognitive psychology and second-language research that indicate metacognitive processes require a rich knowledge base to be successful and that self-regulated and autonomous learners show the ability to use their metacognitive knowledge flexibly (Wenden, 2001).

The study to be described is underpinned by a theoretical model of metacognition that seeks to explain the dynamic interactions between the various components of learners' metacognition during their second-language learning processes (Chan, 2000; see Figure 1). The following is an account of the salient features of this model, concentrating in particular on the role of metacognitive control processes and metacognitive knowledge.

The two main components of metacognition are metacognitive control and metacognitive knowledge[1]. Metacognitive control is the executive centre of all cognitive and metacognitive processes. Through it, learners direct their performance of learning tasks and make decisions pertaining to the way they process the task (including their strategy choice) and the distribution of available cognitive capacity. Brown (1987) identifies four main control processes. The initial task analysis allows learners to ascertain the objective(s) of the current task and to assess the task demands. During the planning phase, learners plan appropriate strategies for performing the task. The monitoring processes provide online feedback on their performance and enable ongoing evaluation of the effectiveness of their strategies. Where necessary, this could lead to modifications to their strategy choice and execution, and perhaps re-analysis and re-planning. Evaluation of task performance can take place after completion of the task and provides learners with an assessment of the effectiveness and appropriateness of their chosen strategies.

Figure 1. Theoretical model of metacognition for second-language task processing (Chan, 2000)

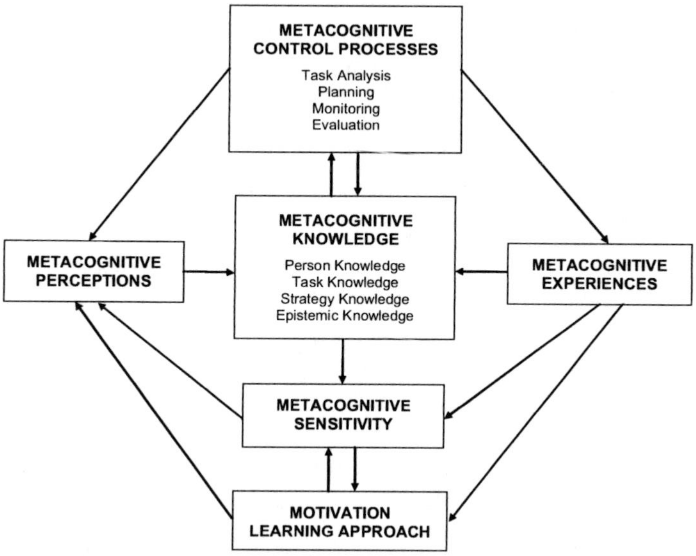

Metacognitive knowledge constitutes the knowledge base of the above control processes and enables learners to make the decisions necessary for the regulation of their learning. Flavell (1987) argues that metacognitive knowledge is declarative knowledge and defines three sub-categories of such knowledge: person, task and strategy knowledge. Person knowledge refers to the knowledge about one's individual characteristics as a learner (e.g., one's learning preferences, special aptitudes or weaknesses in learning) as well as knowledge about universal laws of human cognition and learning (e.g., the knowledge about the limitations of the human mind). Task knowledge refers to one's knowledge about various task forms, their characteristics and demands on learners (e.g., the knowledge that, in a typical multiple-choice task, only one of a number of given answers is correct). Strategy knowledge refers to one's knowledge about strategies available for the accomplishment of particular tasks or learning objectives, including knowledge about the application of these strategies. Hasselhorn (1992) adds a fourth category, epistemic knowledge, which refers to what one knows about the available knowledge in one's memory, including its contents, application possibilities and limitations.

However, metacognitive knowledge is not always automatically activated and applied during task processing. Learners' metacognitive perceptions have an important role to play. While working on a task, learners continuously register and interpret such perceptions, which can be emotive feelings such as anxiety or joy, or cognitive sensations such as confusion or certainty. The accurate interpretation of these perceptions is necessary for the activation of appropriate metacognitive knowledge. Conversely, an inaccurate assessment could result in the failure to apply the necessary knowledge for the metacognitive control processes (e.g., recalling the characteristics of a particular task type, or determining and using appropriate strategies for a task). How such perceptions are interpreted is dependent on one's sensitivity, which Hasselhorn (1992) defines as the intuitive feeling that a particular learning situation may require more strategic activities. The higher the sensitivity, the more likely it will be that learners will assess their perceptions accurately and activate the appropriate metacognitive knowledge. During task processing, the executive receives continuous feedback through monitoring processes. Such feedback constitutes metacognitive experiences — episodic knowledge that is essentially intuitive by nature. It is unanalyzed knowledge, which can become declarative metacognitive knowledge if learners analyze it through reflective, evaluative processes.

The Study

Objectives and Project History

The study was designed to examine the relationship between interactive aids and learners' metacognition, and was conducted over a 4-month period, from May to August 2003. Its objectives were:

- To seek insights into the cognitive and metacognitive strategies employed by learners when performing a Web-based CALL grammar exercise.
- To explore how learners' metacognition influences their interactions with the exercise.
- To explore if and how interactive aids included can support and improve learners' strategy use and metacognition.

Subjects

The subjects were 24 students of the National University of Singapore, who had completed about two-thirds (45 to 50 hours) of their German 1 course when the study began. As the individual interviews reveal, all 24 subjects had little or no CALL experience prior to the course.

Methodology

The data were collected using introspective and retrospective procedures as well as a tracking function built into the CALL grammar exercise performed by the subjects. There were three phases to the study:

Phase 1

In phase 1, the subjects attended a 90-minute briefing, during which the investigator introduced the think-aloud technique and provided pointers on how to "think aloud." They were also shown some video examples in which student assistants modelled the procedure while performing CALL exercises. The assistants had previously received instruction by the investigator and practiced the procedure before the recording. Finally, some arithmetic and language tasks were provided for the subjects to practice this technique.

Phase 2

In phase 2, the subjects were individually recorded on videotape while performing a Web-based CALL grammar exercise on the nominative and accusative case in the German language. A camera captured the subjects seated before a laptop PC, while another was used to record their mouse movements and keystrokes. The gapfill exercise requires subjects to fill in definite/indefinite articles or possessive pronouns matching the gender and case of nouns in the exercise items. It contains six items with two gaps each, organized on two pages. The nominative and accusative forms of the articles had been introduced in the German 1 course about 3-4 weeks prior to the video recording, while the possessive pronouns in nominative and accusative were taught about 7 to 10 days before the recording.

The subjects, divided into three groups of eight, were asked to "think aloud" while performing the exercise. A maximum of 25 minutes was allowed for the exercise. The first group worked on an exercise that offered no learning support, except for instructions for them to fill in the correct articles or pronouns and a correction function, which provides only evaluative feedback (i.e., "correct/incorrect" for each gap).

The second group was given the same six items, but several forms of interactive aids were included in the exercise: a glossary with English translations of selected vocabulary items (including genders of nouns); grammar notes on the nominative and accusative case; a correction function with hints for self-correction; and a "case computer," which guides the learner through the process of determining the right article or pronoun. The case computer asks learners for information required to solve an item (gender, number and the function of the noun in the sentence) and then produces the correct article or pronoun based on this information. While it appears to perform the task for the learners, it is actually designed to guide them through a systematic analysis of the tasks.

In addition to these aids, the third group received explicit metacognitive information on the learning objectives, the interactive aids available and their application possibilities. This information was displayed prior to the exercise and could also be accessed during the exercise on demand.

All interactive aids, including the correction function and the button to navigate between both pages of the exercise, were organized in a drop-down menu in the top right-hand corner of the exercise interface. This design allowed the investigator to determine if subjects 1) knew about typical features of CALL exercises, especially the availability of interactive learning support, and 2) applied any strategies to survey the exercise for such support.

The videos were transcribed for a qualitative analysis of the subjects' strategy use and metacognitive processes. In all three groups, a built-in tracking function recorded the subjects' use of the various aids and options as well as the frequency of use.

Phase 3

In phase 3, subjects attended individual interviews during which they were shown excerpts from the video recordings and were asked to explain some of their actions and statements. It serves to verify the investigator's analysis of the data from phase 2 and to provide a better understanding of the subjects' cognitive and metacognitive processes. The investigator also used the interviews to seek indications of the subjects' general metacognitive competence and computer literacy. The interviews were transcribed subsequently for a qualitative analysis.

Results and Discussion

The results of the qualitative analyses of the introspective and retrospective data can be organized under three broad categories, pertaining to the subjects' strategy use, the influence their metacognition had on their use of interactive aids and the effect of the interactive aids on their metacognition.

Strategy Use

The strategies were identified by studying the subjects' observable behaviours (including their mouse movements, keystrokes and use of interactive aids and other exercise options) and utterances made while thinking aloud. The strategies observed were referenced against the taxonomies proposed by Oxford (1990), and Bimmel and Rampillon (2000). However, the classification of the strategies can only be loosely based on these taxonomies, as both, insofar as direct strategies are concerned, describe essentially only strategies for the four skills, and not for the processing of a grammar task. Furthermore, the taxonomies did not make reference to strategies specific to or typical of CALL.

Strategies Most Commonly Observed

The 10 most commonly observed strategies and their frequency are summarized in Table 1. Select strategies will be described and discussed.

To solve the exercise items, subjects have to determine the gender (masculine, feminine or neuter), number (singular or plural) and function/case (subject-nominative/object-

Table 1. Ten most commonly observed strategies employed by subjects

Strategy (Ranked by Overall Mean Average)	Strategy Type	Mean Frequency			
		Non-Aided Group	Aided Group	Metacognitive Group	Overall
Analyzing	Cognitive	16.500	23.875	17.125	19.167
Applying Rules	Cognitive	13.000	20.125	17.250	16.792
Translating	Cognitive	6.875	14.000	10.250	10.375
Monitoring	Metacognitive	14.429	12.000	5.750	10.125
Guessing	Cognitive	12.375	6.000	1.500	6.625
Using Glossary	Cognitive	–	4.500	4.000	4.250
Using Feedback	Cognitive	3.125	6.250	3.250	4.208
Surveying Exercise Options/Aids	Metacognitive	2.143	2.125	2.875	2.292
Skipping	Affective/ Metacognitive	3.143	2.500	1.500	2.250
Determining Task & Task Demands	Metacognitive	2.143	2.125	2.250	2.083

accusative) of the noun following each gap. They must also decide if a definite or indefinite article, or possessive pronoun is required. This process of breaking down the elements of the sentence and studying selected elements (especially the nouns) constitutes the strategy of *analysing* and is necessary to successfully complete this exercise. Not surprisingly, analysing is the most frequently observed strategy in all three groups (non-aided, aided and metacognitive), with a mean of 19.167 attempts at this strategy per person. It is followed closely by *applying rules* (mean frequency of 16.792), which involves the recall and application of rules for the article and pronoun endings. The rules applied may in some instances be incorrect rules, arising from an imperfect recall of the rules. Excerpt 1 below illustrates how one subject, Wenqi[2], applied these strategies:

Excerpt 1 (Wenqi, metacognitive group):

> Hmm ... I see ... *sofort*, hmm ... *Polizei* ... I think it's *feminin*, so this is call, call, call the policemen, so it's eh ... definite or indefinite article? Ah, think it should be ... (types *die* into blank) this, OK, hmm ... *ich glaube, ich habe, ich glaube* is I think, and I hmm ... I don't know what is *Dieb*, uh ... hmm ... but I'm going to guess and hmm ... I think it's *feminin* and ... umm ... umm

> ... perhaps just indefinite hmm ... (types *eine* into blank) umm ... yup, so what do I do now? After I'm done, OK, umm ... (clicks on Glossary) let me try it ... Ah, *Dieb* is thief, so ... umm ... so *Dieb* is a thief, so I think *Dieb* should be *maskulin*, and because usually people they are *maskulin*, so umm ... OK, so and then it should be *Akkusativ* ...

Wenqi consciously analysed the exercise items and determined the sentence elements as well as the function/case and the gender of nouns following the gaps. Having established these parameters, she typed articles into the blanks by applying the appropriate rules she had learned previously.

Two other strategies were often observed in connection with analysing and applying rules. As Wenqi above, most subjects used the strategy of *translating* to aid their comprehension of the sentences, which is vital if the analysis is to yield positive and useful results. Frequently, Translating also enabled subjects to transfer L1 (English) structures to the target language to help determine if an article (definite or indefinite) or a possessive pronoun is required. Translating is, in fact, the third most commonly observed strategy (mean frequency of 10.375). To compensate for her deficits in lexical knowledge (not knowing the meaning of the noun "Dieb"), Wenqi made use of the built-in glossary. This strategy, *using glossary*[3], was used only by the aided and metacognitive groups (mean frequency of 4.250), as the glossary was not available to the non-aided group. Subjects also employed this strategy to look up the genders of nouns.

The most commonly observed metacognitive strategy was *monitoring* (mean frequency of 10.125). Typically, subjects would use the correction function to ascertain the correctness of their answers and thus their current progress. In all three groups, the correction function provides a feedback. For the non-aided group, the feedback informs subjects only about the correctness of their answers. For the aided and metacognitive groups, hints are provided, prompting the subjects about the nouns' genders and their functions (subject or object) as well as the article type (definite or indefinite). Many subjects made use of the feedback given (strategy of *using feedback*; mean frequency of 4.208) to assist in (re-) analysing and (re-) applying rules to correct their incorrect answers. Subjects in the non-aided group attempted the same strategy and tried to use the limited feedback available for the same purpose. Excerpt 2 shows how Wenqi applied the strategies monitoring and using feedback:

Excerpt 2 (Wenqi, metacognitive group):

> OK. (clicks on Previous Page) I'll check this too (clicks on Correction Button) ... umm ... OK, (reading feedback) die ... *leider ist die* two ... *Dieb ist Maskulin*. OK, *und Dieb ist Objekt*, OK (types *einen* into blank). This ... umm ... (reading feedback) *Freund ist Maskulin*, yeah, plural ... und *das Akkusativ* ... *Freund* is plural? Hmm ... I thought *Freunden* is plural (types *-e* into blank) ... Oh yeah, *Freunde* is plural, not *Freunden*. *Deine Freunde* is ... OK, so this should be correct (clicks on Correction Button). Yup, so I'm done?

The fifth most commonly observed strategy was *guessing* (mean frequency of 6.625). Subjects used this strategy to guess answers or to guess the nouns' genders or meanings. Knowing the gender is essential if one is to analyse and apply rules successfully. Though this strategy was observed in all three groups, there is a significant difference in the frequency of use across the groups. The data clearly show that this strategy is used most frequently in the non-aided group, both in absolute and relative terms. The mean frequency of this strategy in the non-aided group is 12.375, while the mean frequencies for the aided and metacognitive groups stand at 6.000 and 1.500, respectively. If the frequency of guessing is described in relation to the frequency of analysing in each group, we see that, in the non-aided group, for every attempt to analyse, the subjects made 0.845 attempt to guess (mean of all subjects in the group). In comparison, the aided and metacognitive groups made only 0.243 and 0.082 attempt at guessing, respectively, for every attempt at analysing. One plausible explanation for this would be the absence of interactive aids (especially the glossary and the hints accompanying the feedback), which forced the non-aided group to guess with far greater frequency when difficulties were encountered. Excerpt 3 shows Benson, who, after numerous attempts, made two correct guesses to complete the first page of the exercise:

Excerpt 3 (Benson, non-aided group):

> Umm ... (types *ein* into blank 1 of item 1 and clicks on Correction Button) ein, eh, hat *ein, eine* ... (types *eine* into blank) *ein* ... uh ... Nope, this is not. This is false. *Hat ... das ... neuen Sportwagen.* (types *das* into blank and clicks on Correction Button) It's still wrong. What can it be except *ein, eine, eine n*... (types *einen* into blank and clicks on Correction Button)? Aha, cause it's ... why? *Akkusativ. Nominativ, Akkusativ.* So, *Akkusativ, einen.*

It would appear he was at a loss after his previous incorrect answers and decided to chance a guess. In the retrospective interview, he confirmed that he was, in fact, merely typing answers randomly:

Excerpt 4 (Benson, non-aided group, interview):

Investigator:	You typed *einen*. So how did you manage to actually get the correct answers there? How did you actually ... uh ... arrive at the answer *einen* here?
Benson:	The part was random. I think it was random, right.
Investigator:	It was random.
Benson:	Yeah. I was trying.
Investigator:	Were you just trying, you were just guessing?
Benson:	Sort of. Yeah.

CALL-Specific Strategy Combinations

The most frequently used strategy combination of *analysing-translating-applying rules* represents perhaps the most effective procedure to process this exercise. It was the procedure the subjects would have learned in class. It is a strategy combination that could also be applied to printed or other non-CALL exercises; for example, worksheets. Some subjects, in fact, mentioned during the interviews that they had done some printed exercises (worksheets or textbook exercises) assigned by their instructors and gained some previous practice in the same procedure. While most subjects in the aided and metacognitive groups used an interactive aid, the glossary, to support this strategy combination, this course of action is not CALL-specific, as they can use a dictionary or vocabulary notes to the same effect in a non-CALL context. This strategy combination, thus, cannot be considered CALL-specific.

Two likely CALL-specific combinations of strategies were observed, however. The first of these was discussed above and is illustrated by Excerpt 2. The combination of *using feedback-(re-)analysing-(re-)applying rules* is dependent on the availability of informative hints in the computer feedback. Few learners working on a non-CALL exercise inside or outside of class would have constant access to the same instantaneous feedback typically available in a CALL exercise. This situation can only be replicated if learners have access to a form of instruction where the teacher works individually with a single or very small number of students. This, however, would be the exception rather than the rule. In Excerpt 5, we see how Adeline successfully used the feedback for self-correction. The feedback triggered a focused re-analysis of the exercise items and led to the re-application of rules to arrive at the correct answers.

Excerpt 5 (Adeline, metacognitive group):

> ... umm ... OK. (clicks on Correction Button) Let's close this first. (closes Glossary) How come I only get five correct? (reads feedback) *Leider ist die* two ... *leider ist die* two *Antwort falsch. Scanner ist* ... oops ... OK. Can I correct it now? Eh ... so this is masculine, should be *einen*. (types *einen* into blank and clicks on Correction Button) Oh, ok, aiyah. (laughs) I should have changed the answer for the other one. Umm ... what is *vorige Seite*? Something page. (clicks on Previous Page) Umm ... this goes back to the previous one, and since I got this wrong ... Eh, this menu is in the way. Umm ... (reads feedback) *Antwort falsch. Polizei ist feminin und das Objekt im Satz*. Arrgh (sighs) ... police is feminine and it's the object in the ... *Satz* ... wait, uh. *Ich habe einen* ... if it's the object, it's not the subject ... *Rufen Sie sofort* ... eine ... arrgh (sighs) ... umm ... wait ... umm ... *Ergänzen Sie* ... you can put article or possessive. So, maybe, I should put article here instead. (types *die* into blank) I don't know, try, lah. (clicks on Correction Button) Oh, OK, that's great.

During the interview, Adeline said she found the correction function with the feedback to be the most useful interactive aid, as it told her where she had gone wrong and yet did not reveal the answers altogether, providing only hints for self-correction.

The second CALL-specific strategy combination observed involves the use of *guessing and monitoring* with the help of the correction function. In Excerpt 3, we saw how Benson made guesses and then clicked on the correction button to monitor the correctness of his guesses. This combination can be regarded as CALL-specific, for it is the automatic correction function of a computer-based exercise that enables learners to instantly check their guesses and encourages them to make repeated guesses in quick succession. This combination was used most frequently in the non-aided group (a clear indicator is the very high frequency of the guessing strategy in this group), as the correction function was the only form of limited aid available to them. Excerpt 6 provides another example of this combination, as employed by Wanhui, who was bewildered and frustrated after many unsuccessful attempts to solve the items:

Excerpt 6 (Wanhui, non-aided group):

> Then I just go on to question two. Umm ... *ich glaube, ich habe ... Dieb gesehen. ... Ein ... ein...* (looks at assistant) uh ... *rufen Sie sofort ...* so I just try lah. *Ein* is not right, *eine, eine ...* (types *eine* in the blank and clicks on Correction Button) *eine* wrong, *einen ...* (types *einen* in the blank and clicks on Correction Button) Wrong, so it's not right. Then use *kein, keinen, keinen, keinen ... keinen.* Try *keinen.* (types *keinen* in the blank and clicks on Correction Button) Wrong. *Keine, keine.* (types *keine* in the blank and clicks on Correction Button) Wrong. Try *kein.* (types *kein* in the blank and clicks on Correction Button) Wrong. Oh, but then it's, then it's, then it's ... should put nothing here. Is it right? (clicks on Correction Button) Hmm ... *schreiben Sie in ...* so it asks me to fill the blank. Fill in blank. Called the police. Have you called the police? Should use the, so use *die ... Polizei.* Use *die.* I check my answer. (types *die* in the blank and clicks on Correction Button) OK, finally, got my answer right.

Wanhui typed, in an apparently random manner, five different answers (various forms of the indefinite article "ein" and the negation particle "kein") and made conscious use of the correction button to monitor the correctness of these guesses. Eventually she gave up guessing and translated the item instead. This allowed her to transfer structures in English to German and helped her solve the item (through analysing and applying rules).

It would appear easy to pass negative judgment on this strategy combination because of its reliance on guessing and to attribute it to weaker students with metacognitive and linguistic deficits. However, it was observed that some subjects, who apparently had a good grasp of the nominative and accusative case, systematically used this strategy to compensate for their deficits in lexical knowledge. For instance, Chunhong, who was in the non-aided group and completed the exercise successfully in 15 minutes, didn't know the meaning or gender of a word ("Dieb," or "thief" in English) and couldn't be sure if it is preceded by a definite or indefinite article. She consciously employed the combination of guessing and monitoring to narrow her options and arrive at the right answer. Believing that "Dieb" is either masculine or neuter, she first attempted the definite article for masculine and neuter nouns. When these guesses were returned as incorrect by the exercise, she switched to the masculine indefinite article and got it right. When interviewed, she confirmed that this was indeed a conscious strategy of hers, which she calls "trial and error." She explained that she uses this strategy sometimes to guess the correct answer and then reflect on the processes that led to it.

How Metacognition Affects the Use of Interactive Aids

The data seem to indicate that the effective use of interactive aids is greatly dependent on the level of the learners' metacognitive competence (which this chapter will define as learners' ability to use the components of their metacognition — e.g., their metacognitive knowledge and control processes — for the regulation of their learning). An example of a metacognitively competent learner is Boon Shao, who is apparently a proficient learner. His extensive metacognitive knowledge and effective metacognitive strategies helped him complete the exercise successfully in 7 minutes. Although he claimed in his interview that he does not usually do any planning prior to his learning tasks (an important metacognitive strategy), the excerpt below seems to suggest that he does analyse the tasks and take steps to prepare for them:

Excerpt 7 (Boon Shao, metacognitive group, interview):

Boon Shao:	Umm ... Actually I don't think I plan a lot before I do the exercise. Usually I ... umm ... when I want to do it, I look at the exercise then ... umm ... I try to ... umm ... I just look at it and see ... umm ... if I can do, I can, I will do it or if I don't know how to do, maybe I look up, I refer back to my textbook or maybe ask my lecturer.
Investigator:	OK.
Boon Shao:	So I don't really plan before hand how to do it.
Investigator:	But you do think about whether you know how to do it or you do not?
Boon Shao:	Yeah. And I ... I will look at the questions.

He was one of few in the metacognitive group who actually read and carefully considered the metacognitive information preceding the exercise (consisting of exercise instructions, objectives and information about the aids available). It would appear that, while doing so, he was determining the nature of the task and its demands, and preparing himself for the task – important strategies to facilitate metacognitive control of his task processing. Consequently, he was apparently well aware of the menu and the aids available in it, as Excerpt 8 shows:

Excerpt 8 (Boon Shao, metacognitive group):

> *Rufen, rufen Sie sofort Polizei. Rufen* is call. *Polizei* I think is feminine. *Die Polizei. Ich glaube, ich habe Dieb gesehen.* Oh, what is *Dieb gesehen*? Menu. *Glossar.* (clicks on Glossary) Whether there is a *Dieb, Dieb* or thief. Ok … umm … thief. I'll kind of bring this away. (drags the Glossary) *Dieb gesehen.* Thief is ... hmm ... (looks at the Glossary) I think it's masculine. Ich habe *ein, einen* Thief ... *einen*, oops, wrong button, *E - I - N - E - N, gesehen.* (types *einen* into blank)
>
> *Wann triffst du dein Freunde. Freunde* plural. *Deine Freunde.* (types *-e* into blank) *Ich treffe heute Abend mein Onkel.* I'm meeting my uncle today, this evening. *Mein ... heu-, ich treffe*, is *meinen.* (types *-en* into blank) It's *Akkusativ.* Umm … OK, so how do I go to the next one?
>
> Yeah, OK, menu. Umm … look for the *Kontrolle*, I think. (clicks on Correction Button) Umm … OK. So, OK, how do I go to the next page? (looks at the menu) *Neu starten*? Ah, *nächste Seite.* (clicks on Next Page)

Boon Shao looked into the menu and activated the glossary without hesitation to look for "Dieb" and "gesehen," words apparently new to him. And after completing all three items on that page in only 2 minutes, he looked consciously for the correction function ("Kontrolle" in German) and surveyed the menu for the button to proceed to the next page. He explained during the interview that the metacognitive information displayed before the exercise had pointed him to the menu and interactive aids. It also became evident that his extensive metacognitive task knowledge stemmed in part from his considerable experience with interactive Web-based exercises in "e-*daf,* "[4] the university's electronic self-access center for German language learners. By his own reckoning, he did these exercises regularly — twice a week on average — to supplement his classroom lessons. He appears to be highly metacognitive-sensitive as a result of the considerable metacognitive experiences and knowledge accumulated from this exposure. Excerpt 9 would appear to confirm the importance of the task knowledge gathered from his previous experience:

Excerpt 9 (Boon Shao, metacognitive group, interview):

Investigator:	How did you know that there was a *Glossar*?
Boon Shao:	Umm … I think it was in the instructions.
Investigator:	So you remembered it from the instructions?
Boon Shao:	Yeah. Then … umm … for most of the exercises in e-*daf* there were also *Glossar.* Like the … umm … some simulations in, in the *Lebensmittelgeschäft*, *das Glossar* and there, so I sort of expected a *Glossar.*

One example, of Vadi, seems to suggest that the metacognitive information alone was not sufficient to ensure that subjects will notice and be able to use the interactive aids effectively and appropriately. Like Boon Shao, Vadi was in the metacognitive group and had access to the same metacognitive information. It was probably this information that made him look into the menu when he encountered the unknown word "Dieb." In fact, he went on to survey the exercise for interactive aids and other options six more times during his task processing and tried two interactive aids (Case Computer and Grammar Information on Case) to determine their purposes and their usefulness. Despite applying appropriate metacognitive strategies (*surveying exercise options/aids* and *assessing purpose/usefulness of aids*), he was unable to make effective use of the aids and develop effective strategies for the exercise. He clarified later that he had never done any Web-based exercises in "e-*daf*," as he much prefers learning cooperatively with others to interacting with the computer and doing CALL exercises.

The above examples provide strong indications of the importance of metacognitive task knowledge for the use of interactive aids. It was observed that one-third of the subjects did not make use of the available aids and options, and did not even appear to have noticed the menu until the investigator or the attending assistant intervened and prompted them to scrutinize the exercise interface more closely or referred to the menu. Among them was Zhuni from the metacognitive group, who— despite the metacognitive information available and the investigator's instruction to look carefully at the menu — completely missed the correction button and left the exercise without correcting her answers, two of which were incorrect. Her apparent lack of CALL task knowledge can perhaps be explained by a combination of three factors: first, by her own admission, she did not read most of the metacognitive information, including the description of the interactive aids; second, she had done very few Web-based exercises in "e-*daf*," restricting herself only to the exercises that were made mandatory by her course instructor; and third, she did not make effective use of metacognitive strategies like surveying exercise options/aids or assessing purpose/usefulness of aids. Excerpt 10 would appear to support this conclusion:

Excerpt 10 (Zhuni, metacognitive group, interview):

Investigator:	Now, the introductory text was pretty long actually. And you seem to have read ... umm ... the instructions require you to fill in missing articles, or *Possessivbegleiter*, and you also read about ... a little bit about the objectives, you will learn more about the functions and usage of *Kasus*. OK, it can reinforce your grasp of arti ... the article and *Possessivbegleiter*, *Nominativ* and article ... uh ... uh ... *Akkusativ*. And you started, which means ... did you actually ignore this half of the information?
Zhuni:	Yes.
Investigator:	You did? You didn't read it at all?
Zhuni:	Yeah, yeah. I didn't read it at all. In fact, I don't think I even noticed it.
Investigator:	But ... why, why not?

Zhuni:	Huh?
Investigator:	Why? Why didn't you notice it?
Zhuni:	I don't know. Sometimes, I can be quite blind, for all you know.
Investigator:	It's quite ... it's quite big, actually.
Zhuni:	Yeah.
Investigator:	Were you impatient to get on with the exercise?
Zhuni:	No, I ... I really didn't notice it.

Like some others, Zhuni also said that she does not process CALL exercises any differently from paper-based exercises, nor does she see any differences between them.

How Interactive Aids Affect Metacognition and Strategy Use

Interactive Aids as Supporting Tools for Metacognitive and Cognitive Strategies

As discussed above, the data seem to suggest that the subjects' metacognitive knowledge and metacognitive strategies had a bearing on the way they used — or failed to use — interactive aids. There appears to be strong evidence that the converse also is true: The interactive aids look to have had a mediating influence on the subjects' metacognition and strategy use. The discussion above suggests that some of the interactive aids apparently supported the subjects' strategy use (see Figure 2). Excerpts 1 and 8 illustrate how the glossary provided important support for the strategy of translating and aided subjects' comprehension. The glossary was also frequently activated when subjects were unsure about the gender of nouns. Determining the gender constitutes part of the analysis necessary to solve the exercise items. Apparently, the glossary provided support, too, for the strategies of analysing and applying rules.

Another interactive aid, the correction function, was used by practically every subject across all three groups to support the metacognitive strategy of monitoring. Though a few subjects attempted to self-monitor by re-reading and checking their solutions, most apparently found the correction function to be a useful and welcome tool for self-monitoring. An example was Lee Shi, who checked her answers and monitored her performance twice without the correction function early in the exercise. After filling in the two gaps for item 1, she re-read the item (and translated it in the process) to check the answer and decided to change one of her two answers. Upon discovering the correction function at the prompting of the research assistant (she did not apparently notice it previously), she used it 16 times to check her answers and stopped all attempts to 'manually' monitor her own performance, for it provided much quicker and more reliable feedback on her performance and the correctness of her answers than her own unaided monitoring. On the basis of this and similar evidence, the author argues that the

Figure 2. Interactive aids as support for learners' cognitive and metacognitive strategies

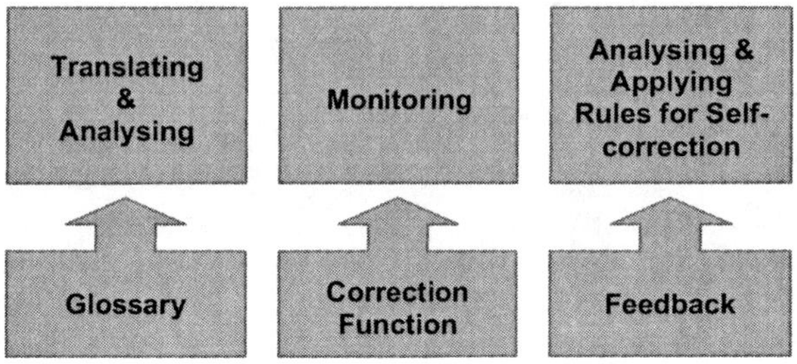

high mean frequency of 10.125 observed for monitoring is most likely attributable to the presence of the correction function.

Excerpts 2 and 5 provide clear indications of another form of strategy support through the interactive aids. In both excerpts, the feedback returned by the exercise when the correction button was clicked clearly supported the subjects' strategies of (re-)analysing and (re-)applying rules in their attempts to self-correct. Especially in the aided and metacognitive groups, the informative feedback with explicit hints contributed to their success in self-correction. The following statistics provide some indication of the usefulness of this and the other interactive aids: Of the eight subjects in the non-aided group with only evaluative feedback (correct/incorrect), four were unable to complete the six items successfully within the given time. In the aided and metacognitive groups, only one and two subjects, respectively, failed to do so.

Formative Effect of Interactive Aids

Use of the interactive aids appears to have had a formative effect on the metacognition of some subjects. These subjects, who had initially lacked the task and strategy knowledge to effectively use the interactive aids provided, appear to have profited from their experience with this exercise and the application of these aids. Especially subjects who had encountered difficulties and subsequently switched to a more conscious mode of processing, made frequent use of these aids and apparently developed some measure of skill in the use of these aids. For six subjects in the aided and metacognitive groups, it was observed that the increasing use of interactive aids seems to have brought about corresponding improvements in their metacognitive control and self-regulation.

Stephanie, in the metacognitive group, was one of these six subjects. She was given the same metacognitive information to read as Boon Shao, who was discussed previously. Unlike Boon Shao, Stephanie apparently read only the basic exercise instructions before proceeding to the exercise. Despite her assurance during the interview that she had done Web-based exercises in "e-*daf*" on a regular basis, she, in actual fact, did not apparently possess the appropriate task and strategy knowledge for effective CALL task processing. When asked if she approaches online and paper-based exercises differently, she replied in the negative, and Excerpt 11 suggests that she was not aware of the interactive aids and correction function:

Excerpt 11 (Stephanie, metacognitive group):

Stephanie: *Rufen Sie sofort* something *Polizei.* Hmm ... *ich glaube, ich habe* something ... *Sie*, you call ... the police? *Ich glaube* ... I know I have something *gesehen*. I have you ... should be talking about you. *Ich habe* something *Dieb gesehen.* I, I guess, tentatively it's you ... I think that is a noun. So it should be a *Possessivbegleiter*. I have a ... we're not talking about police, we're talking about *Dieb* now. This cannot be a police. Police ... police ... police is a ... his ... no, plural ... uh ... if it's a male, then ... I have his, *sein, sein*. (types *sein*, smiles wryly and switches to another item)

Wann triffst du dein ... You met with ... your friend. *Ich treffe*, I meet my ... uncle this evening, ok. Hmm ... uh ... what am I supposed to do? (looks at the assistant)

Assistant: Uh ... OK, try the menu button.

Stephanie: OK... oh! (opens and reads the menu) OK ... hmm ... (clicks on Glossary) ... Scrolling down the glossary. I have, oh, I saw a thief! Heh! Thief ... (clicks on Glossary) clicking on the glossary again ... and ... yeah, I think ... I saw, I saw a thief. I think I saw a thief. (types *einen* into the blank) *Einen* ... that should be *Akkusativ*.

OK ... and ... uh ... *wann triffst du dein Freunde*?

(Opens and looks at the menu) What is *Kasus-Computer*? (Clicks on Case Computer and laughs at the audio recording) OK, I want to close this. Uh ... Info about ... the exercise, *Info zur Übung*. (clicks on Information on Exercise) Uh ... this is the ... uh ... this is what I saw just now. (closes the text box without reading)

Although she did not know the meaning of the word "Dieb" ("thief"), she did not look into the menu until the assistant intervened, and she was surprised to find the glossary and other aids. Later, after completing the items on the first page, she again did not know there was a correction function or how to navigate to the next page. She thought she had finished and turned once more to the assistant, who again pointed her towards the menu (see Excerpt 12).

Excerpt 12 (Stephanie, metacognitive group):

Stephanie: ...OK ... eh ... Freunde is plural, so it should be *deine*. (types *-e* into blank) I think I'm done. (looks at assistant)

Assistant:	Are you sure?
Stephanie:	Uh ...
Assistant:	What other options are there?
Stephanie:	Options?
Assistant:	In the menu.
Stephanie:	Oh, there is *Kontrolle, neu starten. Neu starten* is start anew. *Kontrolle* is answer, is it? (clicks on *Kontrolle*) Oh! *Ich habe* ... I have four right answers?

Her ignorance can most likely be attributed to the lack of appropriate task knowledge. She did not, by her own admission, "look at the right side" of the metacognitive information. Although she had noticed the menu, she stated that she did not expect to find any help or exercise options there.

Like most other subjects, Stephanie relied a lot on translating into English. She analysed the sentence elements and applied her knowledge of grammar rules to solve the items. After discovering the interactive aids, she used these increasingly to compensate for deficits in her lexical knowledge (glossary) and to support the monitoring and self-correction of her errors (correction function and feedback). It appears that she started to develop some measure of skill in applying these aids to her task processing. As a result, her metacognitive control apparently improved as her time on task increased. It would seem that she has acquired new task and strategy knowledge for processing CALL tasks, something she herself was conscious of, as Excerpt 13 — in which she evaluated her own task processing — indicates:

Excerpt 13 (Stephanie, metacognitive group, interview):

Investigator:	OK ... umm ... Would you say that you are actually experienced in working on online exercises before this?
Stephanie:	Nah, not really.
Investigator:	Not really?
Stephanie:	Yeah.
Investigator:	But if you lacked that experience, did this experience working on this exercise help you in any way?
Stephanie:	Yeah, yeah. I will remind myself to read the whole instructions and ... yeah.
Investigator:	Uh ... huh ... and did you learn anything else about interactive online exercises?
Stephanie:	I think there are, more help are rendered than those ... uh ... worksheets. I'm pretty used to those worksheets so it's like I just didn't think of ... uh ... there's helping aids around.

Investigator:	So it has actually increased your understanding of interactive online exercises?
Stephanie:	Yeah.

Conclusion and Implications

The study described in this chapter examined learners' interactions with a Web-based CALL grammar exercise and how these relate to their metacognition, including their strategy use, and the interactive aids available. The data collected suggest that some interactive aids provide vital support for learners' strategy use. For example, the built-in glossary was an important tool for the strategy of translating and also supported the strategies of analysing and applying rules. The correction function was used frequently to aid subjects' attempts at monitoring and provided accurate and reliable feedback on the correctness of their answers and progress. The hints within the feedback in the aided and metacognitive groups supported the self-correction of incorrect answers. The presence of such learning support would appear to provide a reasonable explanation for the higher rate of success and lower levels of negative affects observed in these two groups. Another significant indication of the impact of these aids lies in the much greater reliance on the strategy of guessing, observed in the non-aided group. The absence of learning support meant that subjects in this group had little choice but to resort to guessing when analysis fails because of deficits in lexical, grammar and strategy knowledge.

Interactive aids appear to have played a pivotal role in two CALL-specific strategy combinations observed. Both strategy combinations can be considered CALL-specific, as their application is enabled or encouraged by the presence of particular interactive aids. The instantaneous feedback with hints (using feedback) was used in combination with the strategies of (re-)analysing and (re-)applying rules for self-correction. The subjects, especially those in the unaided group, also used the correction function consciously as a quick monitoring tool (monitoring) in combination with guessing to complete the items, usually as a means to overcome their helplessness.

These findings are certainly significant when one considers that many CALL materials found on the Internet still provide little or no learning aids. It is not uncommon to find exercises on the Internet purportedly intended to enable learning, but are, in actual fact, much more like tests or quizzes, with minimal or no learning support. This is, perhaps, not surprising, given that authoring software, such as the popular Hot Potatoes suite, still do not provide means of constructing and integrating interactive aids, such as vocabulary help, grammar information or strategy hints. Indeed, the provision of appropriate interactive aids requires careful planning and deliberate design, and thus places greater demands both on specialist developers or teaching practitioners — demands that these are not always able or prepared to satisfy.

While the study has shed some light on learners' strategy use and interactions with the computer, more data need to be collected on learners' interactions with other forms of

CALL tasks and in other areas of language learning (e.g., speaking, reading, writing, listening and vocabulary learning). This will contribute towards a more complete picture of the strategies employed by learners, including CALL-specific strategies, and the kind of aids that would make a positive difference. It would be beneficial to study how these relate to individual learner variables (such as learning styles, motivation, beliefs and attitudes). Generally, CALL researchers have favored quantitative research designs, relying heavily on questionnaires administered to large sample sizes. Such studies, while valuable, will need to be balanced by more studies of a qualitative nature, which usually produce richer data and afford a more insightful look at learners' interactions and cognitive and metacognitive processes.

The results also suggest that some form of guidance is necessary to help learners make optimal use of available interactive help. Integrating metacognitive information into the materials may not be an adequate or appropriate measure, as some subjects in the metacognitive group did not seem to perceive the information provided before the exercise as useful or even notice it without intervention. The lack of appropriate task and strategy knowledge for processing CALL tasks meant that many subjects failed to take advantage of the aids available to devise effective strategies for the CALL grammar exercise. This implies that some form of strategy instruction for CALL may be necessary to ensure optimal performance. This raises further questions, such as: Which strategies should be taught and how should such instruction be structured? Can it be implemented online? Is self-instruction appropriate, and can it be implemented? Or must it necessarily be classroom-based and teacher instructed? Certainly, further research is needed to provide the answers to these and other questions.

Acknowledgment

The study described in this chapter was supported by an Academic Research Grant (No. R-127-000-004-112), awarded by the Faculty of Arts and Social Sciences of the National University of Singapore in 2003.

References

Bednar, A. K., Cunningham, D., Duffy, T. M., & Perry, J. D. (1992). Theory into practice: How do we link? In T. M. Duffy & D. H. Jonassen (Eds.), *Constructivism and the technology of instruction: A conversation* (pp. 17-34). Hillsdale: Lawrence Erlbaum Associates.

Bimmel, P., & Rampillon, U. (2000). *Lernerautonomie und Lernstrategien*. Berlin: Langenscheidt.

Brett, P. (1995). Multimedia for listening comprehension: The design of a multimedia-based resource for developing listening skills. *System, 23*, 77-85.

Brown, A. L. (1978). Knowing when, where, and how to remember: A problem of metacognition. In R. Glaser (Ed.), *Advances in instructional psychology* (pp. 77-165). Hillsdale: Erlbaum.

Brown, A. L. (1987). Metacognition, executive control, self-regulation and other more mysterious mechanisms. In F. E. Weinert & R. H. Kluwe (Eds.), *Metacognition, motivation and understanding* (pp. 65-116). Hillsdale: Erlbaum.

Chamot, A. U. (2001). The role of learning strategies in second language acquisition. In M.P. Breen (Ed.), *Learner contributions to language learning* (pp. 25-43). Harlow: Longman.

Chan, W. M. (2000). *Metakognition und der DaF-Unterricht für asiatische Lerner. Möglichkeiten und Grenzen.* Münster & New York: Waxmann Verlag.

Chan, W. M., & Kim, D. H. (2004). Towards greater individualization and process-oriented learning through electronic self-access: Project "e-daf." *Computer Assisted Language Learning, 17*(1), 83-108.

Chapelle, C., & Mizuno, S. (1989). Student's strategies with learner-controlled CALL. *Calico Journal, 7*(2), 25-47.

Chun, D. M., & Plass, J. L. (2000). Networked multimedia environments for second language acquisition. In M. Warschauer & R. Kern (Eds.), *Network-based language teaching: Concepts and practice* (pp. 151-170). Cambridge: Cambridge University Press.

Flavell, J. H. (1971). First discussant's comments: What is memory development the development of? *Human Development, 14*, 272-278.

Flavell, J. H. (1987). Speculations about the nature and development of metacognition. In F. E. Weinert & R. H. Kluwe (Eds.), *Metacognition, motivation and understanding* (pp. 21-29). Hillsdale: Erlbaum.

Flavell, J. H., & Wellmann, H. M. (1977). Metamemory. In R. V. Kail & J. W. Hagen (Eds.), *Perspectives on the development of memory and cognition* (pp. 3-33). Hillsdale: Erlbaum.

Hasselhorn, M. (1992). Metakognition und Lernen. In G. Nold (Ed.), *Lernbedingungen und Lernstrategien* (pp. 35-63). Tübingen: Günter Narr.

Hsu, J., Chapelle, C., & Thompson, A. D. (1993). Exploratory learning environments: What are they and do students explore? *Journal of Educational Computing Research, 9*(1), 1-15.

Issing, L. J. (1998). Lernen mit Multimedia aus psychologisch-didaktischer Perspektive. In G. Dörr & K. L. Jüngst (Eds.), *Lernen mit Medien: Ergebnisse und Perspektiven zu medial vermittelten Lehr- und Lernprozessen* (pp. 159-178). Weinheim & München: Juventa.

Jonassen, D. H., & Reeves, T. C. (1996). Learning with technology: Using computers as cognitive tools. In D.H. Jonassen (Ed.), *Handbook of research on educational communications and technology* (pp. 693-719). New York: Macmillan.

Kozma, R. B. (1994). Will media influence learning? Reframing the debate. *Educational Technology Research and Development, 42*, 7-19.

Liou, H. (1997). Research of on-line help as learner strategies for multimedia CALL evaluation. *CALICO Journal, 14*, 81-96.

Mandl, H., & Reinmann-Rothmeier, G. (1998). Auf dem Weg zu einer neuen Kultur des Lehrens und Lernens. In G. Dörr & K. L. Jüngst (Eds.), *Lernen mit Medien: Ergebnisse und Perspektiven zu medial vermittelten Lehr- und Lernprozessen* (pp. 193-205). Weinheim & Munich: Juventa.

Müller, K. (2000). Constructivism in education. In M. Wendt (Ed.), *Konstruktion statt Instruktion. Neue Zugänge zu Sprache und Kultur im Fremdsprachenunterricht* (pp. 43-54). Frankfurt: Peter Lang.

O'Malley, J. M., & Chamot, A. U. (1990). *Learning strategies in second language acquisition*. Cambridge: Cambridge University Press.

Oxford, R. (1990). *Language learning strategies. What every teacher should know.* Boston: Heinle & Heinle.

Rüschoff, B. (1999). Wissenskonstruktion als Grundlage fremdsprachlichen Lernens. *Fremdsprachen lehren und lernen, 28*, 32-43.

Salomon, G. (1979). *Interaction of media, cognition and learning*. San Francisco: Josey-Bass.

Wenden, A. (1982). *The process of self-directed learning: A study of adult language learners* (masters thesis). Teachers College, Columbia University.

Wenden, A. (1991). *Learner strategies for learner autonomy*. Englewood Cliffs: Prentice-Hall International.

Wenden, A. (2001). Metacognitive knowledge in SLA: The neglected variable. In M.P. Breen (Ed.), *Learner contributions to language learning* (pp. 44-64). Harlow: Longman.

Wheatley, G. H. (1991). Constructivist perspectives on science and mathematics learning. *Science Education, 75*, 9-21.

Endnotes

1. Metacognitive knowledge and metacognitive control are the two most intensively investigated and discussed aspects of metacognition. Arguably, the most significant contributions to research on metacognitive (or declarative) knowledge came from Flavell and his associates (e.g., Flavell, 1971; Flavell & Wellmann, 1977; Flavell, 1987). Extensive work on metacognitive (or executive) control was carried out by Brown (e.g., 1978, 1987).

2. The subjects are identified by pseudonyms assigned randomly by the investigator.

3. Under the category of cognitive strategies, Bimmel and Rampillon (2000) identify the strategy of Using Aids. Using Glossary represents a variant of this strategy specific to the exercise in this study. It is useful for the current discussion to differentiate between the aids used by subjects. Another variant of the strategy Using Aids observed with some frequency is Using Feedback.

4 See Chan and Kim (2004). "E-*daf*" is an acronym that stands for "Elektronisches Selbstlernzentrum für Deutsch als Fremdsprache" (in English: Electronic Self-access Centre for German as a Foreign Language); http://courseware.nus.edu.sg/e-daf/.

Chapter XI

The Effect of a Native-Language Interface vs. a Target-Language Interface on Students' Performance

Jay Melton, Prefectural University of Kumamoto, Japan

Abstract

The Internet is being used more often to help teachers of second and foreign languages to create activities for language learning and assess their students' progress. One kind of computer package used to manage various types of online course work is being used ever increasingly in language learning environments: course management systems (CMS). The choice of which language, native or target, to use in a CMS is a source of debate. This chapter details an experiment conducted to determine the effect of an English and a Japanese interface on a CMS quiz module. The participants were 48 Japanese students of English. To control for internal sources of invalidity, random assignment was made and the design was a post test-only control group. The results showed no significant difference in the scores; the English interface may be an acceptable choice for the interface language of the quiz module for those whose native language is not English.

Introduction

As computers and the Internet come to be used more and reach farther into institutions of higher education, they are increasingly being used in new ways in courses not often associated with Internet-linked computers. One form of technology, placed into the all-encompassing term computer-assisted language learning (CALL), has been used for years, but this format is often associated with "kill-and-drill" exercises, where learners pit themselves against the computer to study grammatical and/or vocabulary features of the target language. The Internet has opened new opportunities for language education, enabling learners to conveniently communicate with their teachers and other course members, complete homework assignments and test their knowledge and understanding of course material (Clark & Meyers, 2003; Wood & Smith, 2001).

E-mail was one of the first Internet modalities to allow learners to move beyond traditional CALL activities. Warschauer (1997) examined several studies detailing the uses of e-mail to improve class discussions with both classmates and teachers. The asynchronous characteristic of e-mail allows for learners to think more constructively during actual class meetings.

More recently, the use of CMS (not to be confused with content management systems), also known as learning management systems (LMS), are being explored as a means of connecting students in a variety of courses. CMS modalities are helping teachers create a wide variety of activities that can help learners with the goals of learning a second or foreign language (Catterick, 2001; Thornton, 2002). CMS provide instructors with powerful tools for organizing their courses. The tools included with CMS can help create opportunities for promoting interactive communication, encouraging productive collaboration and developing methods of evaluation and/or assessment.

Two of the most popular CMS are Blackboard (2005) and WebCT (2005). These are powerful packages, but are known to be associated with high costs and occasional maintenance problems. Open-source software is noted for its no-cost pricing structure and dynamic development structure. Although there are some CMS dedicated to e-learning, such as Segue (Schine, Chapin, Franco, & Radichkov, 2005) and Claroline (De Praetere, 2005), one recently developed CMS stands above the rest in the open-source community: moodle (Dougiamas, 2005). Moodle is a fully featured CMS and incorporates most tools associated with robust CMS. Thanks to the dynamism of the open-source community, moodle is under constant development and refinement. This development is bringing new features, such as multilingual interfaces, which are being requested by the users most responsible for putting moodle into practice: the teachers.

Since the merging of language teaching and learning through the use of CMS is a fairly new innovation, much has yet to be researched about CMS and how their use can be optimized for language programs. Since the debate continues on whether to allow use of students' native language or the target language exclusively (Storch & Wigglesworth, 2003), a parallel question that arises is, which language should be used in the CMS interface to help foreign- or second-language students: their native language or the target language?

Statement of the Problem

The purpose of this study was to compare the effect of a native-language CMS interface on Japanese university students of English with the effect of a target-language CMS interface.

Putting the Study into Context

Computers are being used more often in courses — such as those related to language teaching and learning — that have been taught in traditional ways (Field, 2002). CALL systems have been in place for some time now. These systems allow language learners to know what grammatical or vocabulary features they need to study and provide these learners the activities that will help them improve (Egbert, 1999). In addition, networked modalities like e-mail, bulletin boards and chat systems, for example, are being put to use to help language learners communicate with real people, both other learners and native speakers (Egbert & Hanson-Smith, 1999; Warschauer & Kern, 2000). More recently, complete packages — called CMS — for conducting courses online are starting to be used for language teaching (Abrams, 2003; Lee, 2002; Smith, 2003).

Educators looking to take their courses online, whether completely or partially in a hybrid format, can now turn to CMS for many of their needs. CMS that are truly course management systems can provide organizational tools for courses from start to finish (Catterick, 2001). Learners and teachers can work together to build a knowledge base to keep track of key concepts and vocabulary. Instructors can create synchronous activities using text chat functions, bringing learners together in real time. Learners can communicate with each other as well as their teachers through the use of asynchronous discussion forums, also known as bulletin boards. Students can collaborate together on projects using community work areas and wikis. Students can also submit assignments electronically for evaluation by their instructors. In addition, instructors can design tests to be taken by learners who can, in turn, get immediate feedback on the results of those tests.

Well-known commercial packages include Blackboard (2005) and WebCT (2005), but these CMS require much money and often much support (Pain & Heron, 2003). Not as well-known, but growing in popularity by language educators, are no-cost, open-source CMS packages, such as moodle (Dougiamas, 2005). Moodle is a robust CMS and is localized in more than 65 languages at this writing. This is made possible by the design of open-source software; any willing user who can translate from English, or another language, into the target language can participate in localizing moodle. In addition, it includes components for handling e-mail, conducting synchronous chat and asynchronous forum discussions, journal writing, submitting assignments, creating glossaries, conducting polls, gathering information through surveys, holding workshops and, finally, writing and administering quizzes. It is this final component, quizzes, that is the subject of this investigation.

Obviously, an English course with Japanese university students does not need all the languages available. However, the question remains, should the Japanese module be activated for students with lower levels of English to give them a head start? One researcher's experience (MacAuley, 1995) suggests that the use of a native language may indeed help learners in the early days of a new target-language course.

Smith, Alvarez-Torres and Zhao (2003) examined the effect of different computer-mediated communication (CMC) technologies on learners of English. While theirs was a preliminary study and the number of participants was small, the authors concluded that a multi-user, object-oriented system with sound allowed users to experience more social presence than is typical of CMC in addition to communicating more with others than in a text-based chat. They also found that in the text-based chat system, learners were more focused on the task, producing less text overall.

In an experiment to determine students' attitudes towards using WebCT (2005), Burgess (2003) discovered that package was easy for students to learn to use in a variety of modalities. That population, however, was made up of technology students, who, presumably, were already somewhat comfortable with using computers. Conducting experiments on the various components of moodle with a variety of student populations could bear fruit. The results of such studies, for example, could determine whether problems using technology exist because of computer anxiety, unfamiliarity with computer interfaces, poor interfaces or language difficulty.

In human-computer interaction (HCI) research, studies show that interfaces designed well and with a consistent look make it easy for users to navigate (Colace, Santo, & Vento, 2002; Krug, 2000; Ozok & Salvendy, 2004; Wang & Beasley, 2002). The results of Wang and Beasley's work also suggest that having some help available in the form of glossaries can help learners of another language who have little experience with computers or Web navigation. Although moodle appears to pass Nielsen's (1994) list of 10 major heuristics (Melton, 2004), there is no help screen or list of glossary terms within the quiz module.

Statement of the Hypothesis

Since there was no prior research in the area of the effect on users of language in the interface of CMS, a non-directional hypothesis is appropriate: There will be a significant difference in the scores on a syllabus quiz of Japanese first-year university learners of English using a Japanese moodle interface and learners using an English moodle interface.

Methodology

Participants

Participants for this study were selected from the population of science students enrolled in Basic English I, a one-semester, required course for first-year students in the Faculty of Environmental and Symbiotic Sciences (FESS) at the Prefectural University of Kumamoto (PUK) in Kumamoto, Japan. The vast majority of the population was middle class, between the ages of 18 and 19. All of the participants were Japanese. The FESS is made of three divisions: Environmental and Ecological Sciences, Human Habitat, and Food and Health. In the first year of study, starting in April 2004, there were 21 Environmental and Ecological Sciences students, 42 Human Habitat students and 42 Food and Health students. The FESS divided these 105 students into three groups of 26 students and one group of 27 students. Since it was impossible to adjust these groups because of scheduling conflicts, these groups had to remain intact. For this preliminary study, two of the groups of 26 students were used as participants.

Of the two groups in this study, one was made up of 26 Human Habitat students, who study rural and urban planning, design, architecture, structural materials and engineering for housing. The other was made up of 26 Food and Health students, who study nutrition, food chemistry, dietary management and lifestyle-related diseases. The female-to-male ratio of the Human Habitat group was 16:10, and that of the Food and Health students, 25:1. The English level for both groups was average for matriculating university students in Japan because of their concentration on science and math studies during their high school years. However, the scores on the FESS English entrance exam showed that the Food and Health students scored slightly higher than those of the Human Habitat. Because of the differences in gender ratios and English abilities, and the biases these differences present to the study, all of the participants in each of the two groups were randomly assigned to either a Japanese or English interface. It is believed that the design of the study, based on a true-experimental, post test-only control group design, made for a high-quality preliminary study (Gay & Airasian, 2003). However, the sample of this study is small, so it will be difficult to generalize far beyond the participants in this sample and others who might fit a similar profile.

Instruments

An instrument (Appendix A) was created to test the students on information about their English course, called Basic English I. This instrument assessed the knowledge participants retained concerning course syllabus information delivered primarily in English during the first class meeting. The quiz used a variety of question types: multiple-choice, true/false, short answer and matching; the quiz module in the CMS moodle was the method of delivery. In addition to this modality being a major part of this study, moodle's quiz feature allowed for instant feedback for the students and fast data collection for the researcher. The quiz was written in English; only the language of the interface was different for the participants.

To ensure test validity, the quiz was developed first on paper, then it was distributed to two Japanese associate professors of the FESS. These faculty members also received copies of both the course syllabus (Appendix B) and the PowerPoint file supporting the syllabus. Both members read the syllabus and viewed the PowerPoint file at their leisure. Then they were asked to take the quiz, also at their leisure. The comments they made on the quiz were incorporated into the final version of the quiz.

Prior to the administration of the first quiz, a questionnaire (Appendix C) was given to the participants. This questionnaire was used to collect basic background information, including, but not limited to, the participants' English abilities and experience with computers and the Internet.

Materials and Apparatus

To access the Internet, participants were provided with accounts to use the computers in one of the university's computer labs. In addition, participants needed accounts at one of the two moodle sites: one with a Japanese interface or one with an English interface. These accounts were provided at the beginning of the testing session.

Experimental Design

The goal of this preliminary research was to examine whether an interface using the participants' native language (Japanese) or target language (English) had an effect on the outcome of their scores on a quiz testing their retention of knowledge of their course syllabus. The design of the study was a post test-only control group, with the independent variable the language of the interface. The two levels were Japanese and English language of the interface, and the dependent variable the participants' scores on the syllabus quiz. This design was used because of its ability to control for sources of internal invalidity (Gay & Airasian, 2003). Although random selection from a large population was not possible because of the fixed size of the participant pool, random assignment was possible. The 52 participants in the two courses were divided into four subgroups, and the design was to administer a post test based on the Basic English I course syllabus. Mortality occurred, and four students were eliminated from the study. Fortunately, the balance of the treatments was maintained, and the final number of participants for the study was 48 (Table 1). The scores of the A and C subgroups were combined, as were

Table 1. Experimental design

Group		Assignment	*N*	Treatment	Posttest
Human Habitat	A	Random	11	Syllabus & Presentation	Quiz (English Interface)
	B	Random	11	Syllabus & Presentation	Quiz (Japanese Interface)
Food and Health	C	Random	13	Syllabus & Presentation	Quiz (English Interface)
	D	Random	13	Syllabus & Presentation	Quiz (Japanese Interface)

those of the B and D subgroups. To determine if there were any significant differences, the scores of the A and C subgroups were compared with those of the B and D subgroups using an independent *t* test.

Procedure

As soon as the course numbers were determined, the 48 participants were randomly assigned to one of four subgroups (A, B, C or D) by drawing student numbers. During the study, the A and C subgroups had an English interface for their moodle accounts, and the B and D subgroups one with Japanese. In other words, half of the participants in the Human Habitat group were randomly chosen to have an English interface (A) and the other half Japanese (B); the same subgroups were assigned in the Food and Health group (C and D, respectively).

The participants in this study were all given a course syllabus in English (Appendix C) on the first day of their Basic English I courses. The syllabus was explained verbally in simple English with occasional explanations in Japanese for difficult words or concepts. This explanation was supplemented with a PowerPoint presentation written in English and a question-and-answer period. For homework, participants were given a questionnaire in English (Appendix C) that elicited their English language background as well as their experience using computers and the Internet. The participants were not told that they were part of an experiment, nor were they told that they would have a quiz in the following class session.

In the second class, held in a computer lab, participants were given sheets of paper with instructions to register for accounts on one of the two moodle installations to which they had been pre-assigned. Participants were asked to sit in assigned seats. Participants with English interfaces were seated at computers facing the window side (with the blinds closed) of the computer lab, and those with Japanese interfaces were facing the side of the lab with a wall. A short PowerPoint presentation was shown to demonstrate how to register for moodle. Then those assigned to groups A and C logged into the moodle installation with English as the default language, and those assigned to groups B and D registered in Japanese. To facilitate ease of checking that participants were using the correct interface, the English interface was colored blue (see Figure 1) and the Japanese interface pink (see Figure 2).

Figure 1. English log-in screen

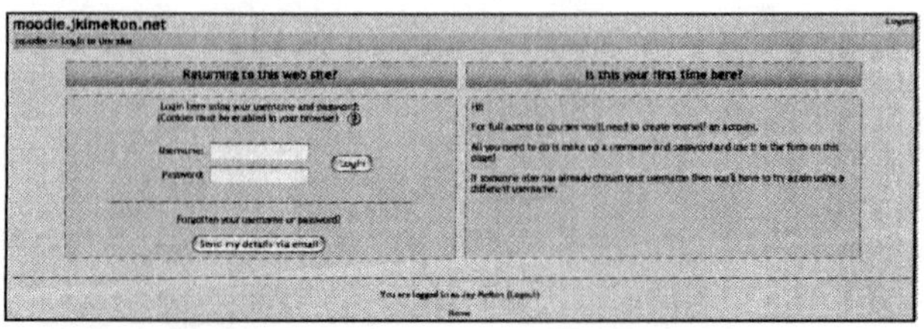

Figure 2. Japanese log-in screen

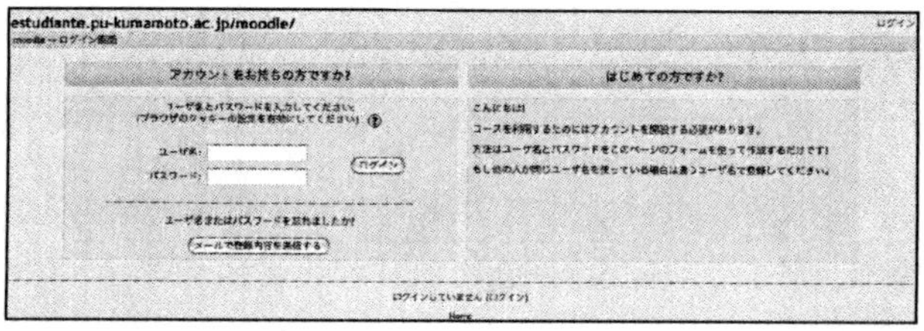

Two graduate students and one third-year student from the FESS were present to assist with registration to the system. After registering in moodle, participants were directed to the course quiz; they needed to start the quiz by clicking on the *attempt quiz now* buttons (see Figures 3 and 4).

The quizzes for both groups were identical; only the interface differed. Examples of how the interfaces differed can be seen in Figures 5 and 6. Although the content of the quiz is in English in both versions, the attempt number, the number of points for the question, and the word for *answer* are in the language of the interface. In addition, for true/false questions, the Japanese responses are listed as *X* and *O*, and for matching questions, the word for *choose* is in Japanese.

Figure 3. English attempt quiz now

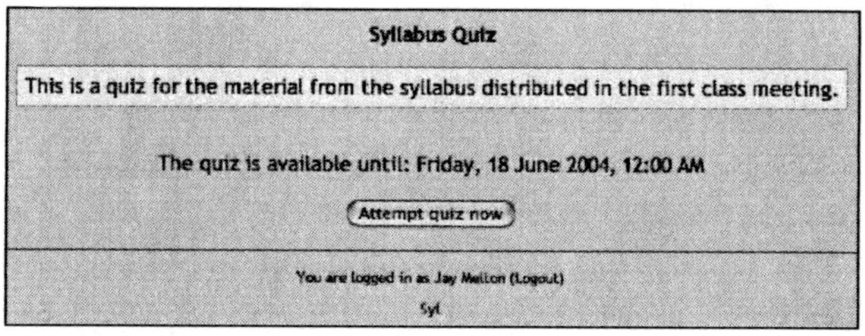

Figure 4. Japanese attempt quiz now

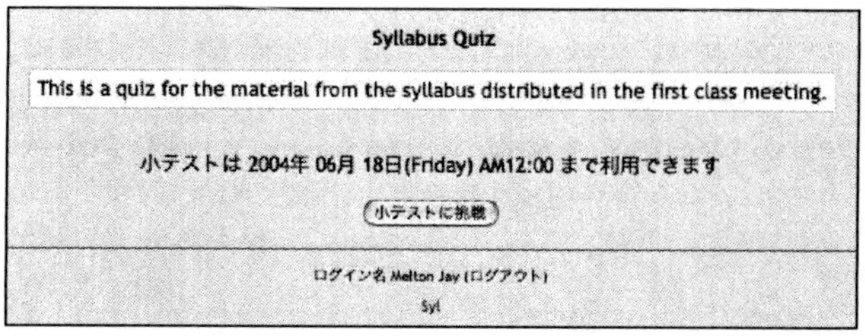

Figure 5. English quiz example question

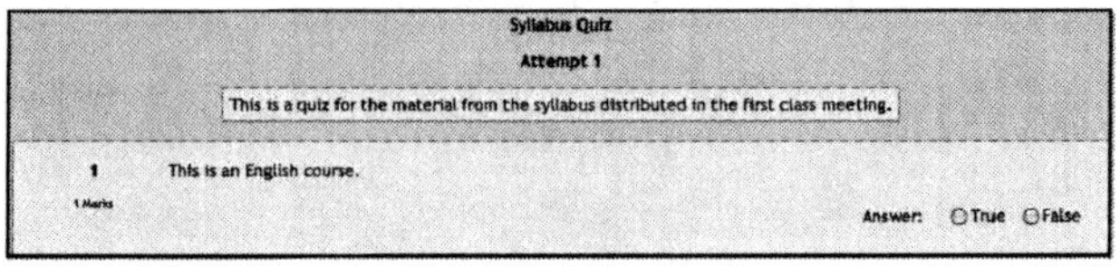

Figure 6. Japanese quiz example question

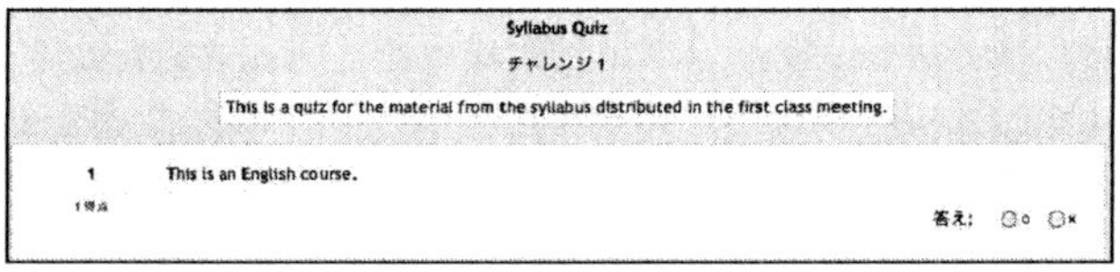

Figure 7. English save my answers

Figure 8. Japanese save my answers

After the participants finished the quiz, they were required to save their answers. This was accomplished by a click on the *save my answers* button (see Figures 7 and 8).

The data were collected after the testing session and adjusted to account for correct answers on open-ended questions that were not or could not be anticipated.

Data Analysis

There was one independent variable involved in this study — the language of the interface — and it had two levels: Japanese and English. The dependent variable was the score on the quiz on the course syllabus. According to Gay and Airasian (2003), the independent samples *t*-test was appropriate under such circumstances. The collected and adjusted data were input into a statistical package for social science (SPSS) file and analyzed using that software. Because of the two-tailed hypothesis, the level of significance for this study was set at $P < 0.05$.

Results

The Questionnaire

Because three participants missed the first day of the course, and another missed the second, the data collected represent 48 of the 52 original participants assigned to this study. In addition, of these 48 participants, 45 submitted the questionnaires (Appendix B) that were assigned as homework during the first class meeting. These questionnaires reveal that 20 of the 45 respondents subjectively rate themselves knowledgeable about using computers (see Figure 9).

Similarly, 17 respondents noted that they owned computers (see Figure 10).

Interestingly, although 20 respondents claim that they know how to use a computer, 35 responded that they use the Internet in a variety of ways, such as browsing, searching for information, playing games and using e-mail (see Figure 11). Presumably, these other 15 participants consider their computer skills to be low. More likely, however, is that at least some of them are using their cell phones for Internet use, and they do not equate their cell phone usage with computer usage (Yoneoka, 2001). Some research acknowledges that many university students in Japan do not yet have computers at home (Jarrell,

Figure 9. Computer knowledge

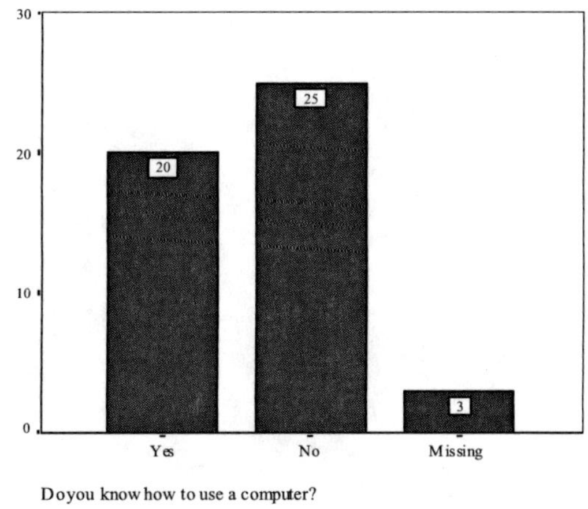

Figure 10. Computer owners

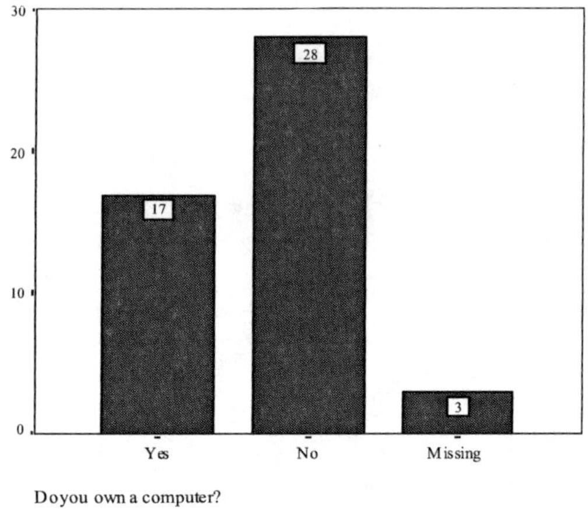

2002). This data, along with the fact that computer training in secondary schools in Japan is often on a case-by-case basis (Kitao, 2002), suggests that the participants had a fairly low level of computer literacy when this study was conducted.

Data Collection

Moodle kept the entire responses of each participant in its databases. It was possible to access completed quizzes for each participant through a single page. This made a

Figure 11. Uses of the Internet

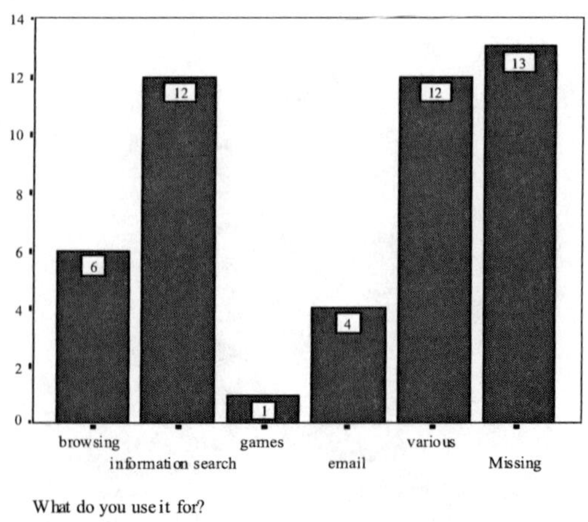

review of the responses simple and helped ensure that the data were accurately recorded. Moodle also records the responses and scores into a spreadsheet format that can be downloaded and read in Excel. This function is both powerful and convenient, and it provides a complete list of the results of quizzes with answer types, such as multiple-choice, true/false and matching.

However, this function proved to be problematic for the embedded-answer (cloze) questions, because the participants' responses did not show up in the automatic results. Since these questions required participants to type in responses as text, it was important to check that mere spelling or grammatical mistakes were not preventing participants from receiving proper scores on their quizzes. These responses needed to be checked by hand from the Excel file output.

Another problem occurred in the short-answer format. Moodle's quiz module provides 10 possible answers for this question type. Those chosen as possible answers for question 20 on the syllabus quiz were not enough, as several participants wrote responses that were not among the 10 predicted responses.

In both cases above — the embedded-answer (CLOZE) and short-answer questions — all of the responses on these question types were checked by hand and rescored. Participants were given the benefit of the doubt on reasonable spelling errors or if the answers given were technically correct.

The Data

The descriptive statistics can be seen in Table 2. Both the skewness and kurtosis were between -1.00 and 1.00, which indicate that the distribution of the data was normal.

By interface language, the distribution of the scores can be seen in Figures 12 and 13.

Given that the distribution of the scores was normal, a parametric independent samples *t* test was used to determine if there were any significant differences in the scores on the

Table 2. Descriptive statistics

	N	Range	Minimum	Maximum	Sum	Mean	
	Statistic	Statistic	Statistic	Statistic	Statistic	Statistic	Standard Error
Test Scores	48	14	15	29	1064	22.17	.52
Valid N	48						

	Standard Deviation	Variance	Skewness		Kurtosis	
	Statistic	Statistic	Statistic	Standard Error	Statistic	Standard Error
Test Scores	13.121	13.121	-.023	.343	-.779	.674

Figure 12. Distribution of English scores

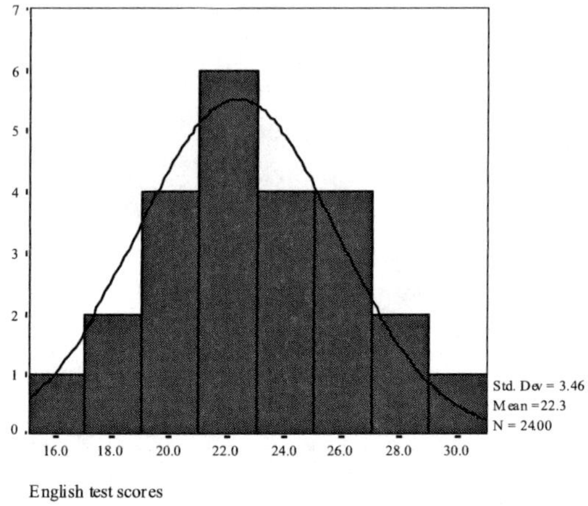

Figure 13. Distribution of Japanese scores

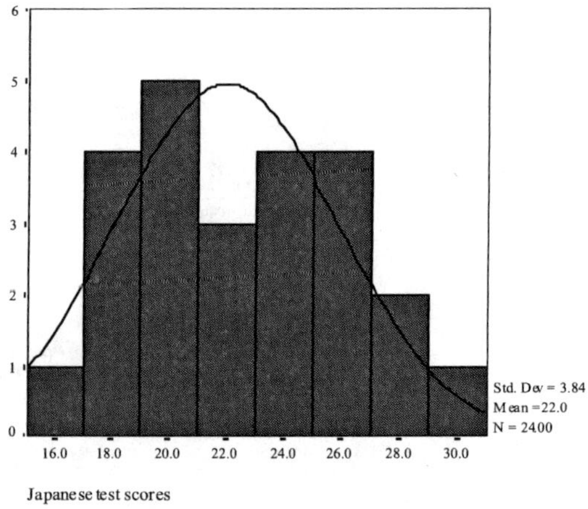

syllabus quiz. An examination of the group statistics showed an average of 22 with the Japanese interface and 22.33 with the English interface (see Table 3); these scores are out of a possible 37 points. This gave a preliminary indication that there was very little difference between the scores.

In addition, a graph (see Figure 14) of the data indicates no differences in the scores.

An independent samples *t*-test was run with an *alpha* value of .05; this value was halved to .025 in the analysis because of the non-directional hypothesis. The output from this test can be seen in Table 4.

Table 3. Group statistics

	Interface Language	N	Mean	Standard Deviation	Standard Error Mean
Test Scores	Japanese	24	22.00	3.845	.785
	English	24	22.33	3.460	.706

Figure 14. Test scores

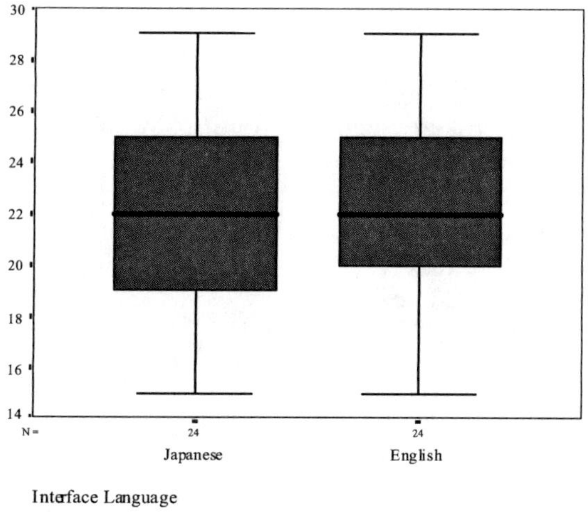

Table 4. Independent samples t-test

		Levene's Test for Equality of Variances		t-test for Equality of Means						
		F	Sig.	t	df	Sig. (2-tailed)	Mean Diff.	Std. Error Diff.	95% Confidence Interval of the Difference	
									Lower	Upper
Test Scores	Equal variances assumed	.697	.408	-.316	46	.754	-.33	1.056	-2.459	1.792
	Equal variances not assumed			-.316	45.498	.754	-.33	1.056	-2.459	1.793

Because the *p* value of .754 is greater than the two-tailed *alpha* value of .50, the null hypothesis — there will be no significant difference in the scores — was not rejected. Therefore, there was no significant difference in the scores. These results show that the English and Japanese interfaces were not enough to create differences in the scores of the participants of this study.

Conclusion

The Current Study

The first issue to consider is the overall low scores on the syllabus quiz; the mean of 22.17 represents an average of 60%. The presence of the assistants allowed the researcher some freedom to observe participants during the data collection. The participants seemed somewhat nervous that they were taking a test so soon in their new term. It is very possible that they were suffering from anxiety from this, from the stress of logging into a new account on an unfamiliar computer, from taking a test in English, or a combination of these factors.

The main issue to consider is the lack of a significant difference in the scores on the syllabus quiz. It is very possible that the number of language prompts in the quiz module was not enough to affect how the participants interact with the interface. Perhaps the quiz itself was the main concern of the participants, and the interface did nothing to influence that objective. The quiz module is very straightforward to use, so its simplicity itself may have been a factor in the outcome.

The bottom line here is that the results of this study suggest that the use of the English interface with moodle's quiz module is an appropriate choice, even for students with fairly low-level English skills. These students need as much English input as possible; the quiz module in moodle is one more tool that can be used to further that aim.

However, one caveat needs to be stressed for these results. The size of the sample must be taken into consideration. Because of its small size, far-reaching generalizations cannot be made. These results may generalize to other relatively low-level Japanese learners of English, and perhaps to other similar learners of English from different language backgrounds. To extend those generalizations further will require more testing with more and different learner types.

Future Directions

Moodle has several modules, many of which require more interaction through their interfaces. A strong case can be made easily to thoroughly test them. A preliminary usability study (Melton, in press) discovered that the assignment module of moodle was difficult for 50% of the Japanese participants to use in English. It is quite possible that learners' first languages should be used in these instances. Without a doubt, there are more aspects of moodle and the language of the interface to explore. Because of the dearth of research on the topic, there is much more to be examined concerning these issues. However, designing an evaluation will require careful planning and much work.

It is important to note that careful preparation is critical when planning and conducting an experiment like this. A number of variables, some of them beyond the control of the researcher, could have made data collection impossible. Either of the connections to the moodle package could have gone down due to network, server or computer troubles. To minimize the chances of this occurring, it is recommended that the channels of communication be kept open with those in charge of computer labs and the servers running the software. Other factors to consider are that the quizzes should be tested thoroughly before the data collection session goes live. This includes creating dummy participants to test that the registration and quiz-taking processes run smoothly and in a timely manner.

For the future, the key issue is that further evaluation and assessing additional moodle modules with more participants over a longer period of time could help answer questions concerning which language or languages should be activated for second- or foreign-language study.

References

Abrams, Z. I. (2003). The effect of synchronous and asynchronous CMC on oral performance in German. *The Modern Language Journal, 87*(2), 157-167.

Blackboard. (2005). Blackboard. Retrieved April 13, 2005, from http://blackboard.com/

Burgess, L. A. (2003). WebCT as an e-learning tool: A study of technology students' perceptions. *Journal of Technology and Education, 15*(1), 6-15.

Catterick, D. (2001). An academic writing course in cyberspace. In L. E. Henrichsen (Ed.), *Distance learning programs* (p. 208). Alexandria: TESOL.

Clark, R. C., & Meyers, R. E. (2003). *E-learning and the science of instruction.* San Francisco: John Wiley & Sons.

Colace, F., Santo, M. D., & Vento, M. (2002). *Evaluating on-line learning platforms: A case study.* Paper presented at the 36th Hawaii International Conference on System Sciences, Big Island.

De Praetere, T. (2005). Claroline. Louvain-la-Neuve, Belgium. Retrieved April 13, 2005, from www.claroline.net/

Dougiamas, M. (2005). Moodle. Retrieved April 13, 2005, from http://moodle.org/

Egbert, J. (1999). Classroom practice: Creating interactive CALL activities. In J. Egbert & E. Hanson-Smith (Eds.), *CALL environments: Research, practice and critical issues* (pp. 27-40). Alexandria: Teachers of English to Speakers of Other Languages.

Egbert, J., & Hanson-Smith, E. (Eds.). (1999). *CALL environments: Research, practice and critical issues.* Alexandria: Teachers of English to Speakers of Other Languages.

Field, M. H. (2002). Towards a CALL pedagogy: Students use and understanding. In P. Lewis (Ed.), *The changing face of CALL: A Japanese perspective* (pp. 3-17). Lisse: Swets & Zeitlinger.

Gay, L. R., & Airasian, P. (2003). *Educational research: Competencies for analysis and applications* (7th ed.). Upper Saddle River, NJ: Merrill Prentice Hall.

Jarrell, D. S. (2002). Network-based language teaching in the Japanese context. In P. Lewis (Ed.), *The changing face of CALL* (pp. 175-186). Lisse: Swets & Zeitlinger.

Kitao, K. (2002). Teaching cultural awareness through writing: Student Web page projects. In P. Lewis (Ed.), *The changing face of CALL: A Japanese perspective* (pp. 203-215). Lisse: Swets & Zeitlinger.

Krug, S. (2000). *Don't make me think! A common sense approach to Web usability.* Indianapolis, IN: New Riders.

Lee, L. (2002). Synchronous online exchanges: A study of modification devices on non-native discourse. *System, 30*(3), 275-288.

MacAuley, M. (1995). The students' mother tongue: Should it be used in the EFL classroom? *Language Issues, 1*(1), 49-56.

Melton, J. (2004). *The CMS moodle: A heuristic evaluation.* Paper presented at JALTCALL 2004, Mito, Japan. Retrieved April 13, 2005, from http://jklmelton.net/2004/jaltcall/

Melton, J. (in press). Moodle: A usability evaluation. *Language Issues, 11*(1).

Nielsen, J. (1994b). *Ten usability heuristics.* Retrieved April 13, 2005, from www.useit.com/papers/heuristic/heuristic_list.html

Ozok, A. A., & Salvendy, G. (2004). Twenty guidelines for the design of Web-based interfaces with consistent language. *Computers in Human Behavior, 20*, 149-161.

Pain, D., & Heron, J. L. (2003). WebCT and online assessment: The best thing since SOAP? *Educational Technology & Society, 6*(2), 62-71.

Schine, G., Chapin, A., Franco, A., & Radichkov, D. (2005). *Segue.* Middlebury, Vermont. Retrieved April 13, 2005, from http://segue.middlebury.edu/index.php?&action=site&site=segue

Smith, B. (2003). The use of communication strategies in computer-mediated communication. *System, 31*(1), 29-53.

Smith, B., Alvarez-Torres, M. J., & Zhao, Y. (2003). Features of CMC technologies and their impact on language learners' online interaction. *Computers in Human Behavior, 19*, 703-729.

Storch, N., & Wigglesworth, G. (2003). Is there a role for the use of the L1 in an L2 setting? *TESOL Quarterly, 37*(4), 760-770.

Thornton, P. (2002). Web-based learning environments. In P. Lewis, C. Imai, & K. Kitao (Eds.), *The Proceedings of JALTCALL 2002 Hiroshima Jogakuin University* (pp. 15-22). Nagoya: The Japan Association for Language Teaching.

Wang, L.-C. C. & Beasley, W. (2002). Effects of learner control and hypermedia preference on cyber-students performance in a Web-based learning environment. *Journal of Educational Multimedia and Hypermedia, 11*(1), 71-91.

Warschauer, M. (1997, Winter). Computer-mediated collaborative learning: Theory and practice. *The Modern Language Journal, 81*, 470-481.

Warschauer, M., & Kern, R. (Eds.). (2000). *Network-based language teaching: Concepts and practice.* Cambridge: Cambridge.

WebCT (2005). *WebCT.* Retrieved April 13, 2005, from http://webct.com

Wood, A. F., & Smith, M. J. (2001). *Online communication: Linking technology, identity, & culture.* Mahwah, NJ: Lawrence Erlbaum.

Yoneoka, J. (2001). *Blending computers and English using student PowerPoint presentations.* Paper presented at the 2nd International Conference on Information Technology Based Higher Education and Training, Kumamoto, Japan. Retrieved October 31, 2005, from http://www.eecs.kumamoto-u.ac.jp/ITHET01/proc/031.pdf

Appendix A: Syllabus Quiz

1. *This is an English course.*

   □ True □ False

2. *How many times a week does this course meet?*

   □ One □ Two □ Three □ Four

3. *In how many rooms does this course meet?*

   □ One □ Two □ Three □ Four

4. *What names will your teacher use for you and your classmates?*

   □ Our given names □ Our family names

   □ Both given and family names □ Our family names and titles

5. *What name should you use with your teacher?*

   □ Jay □ Melton □ Mr. Melton □ Mr. Jay

6. *How can you contact your teacher to tell him something or ask a question? (please select all the correct answers)*

   □ Go to his office during his office hour. □ Call him at the office.

   □ Fax him. □ Call his cell phone. □ Send him e-mail.

   □ Go to his house □ Use the moodle system

7. *Please match the following **uses** with their required and optional course **materials**:*

   □ Vocabulary and phrases study □ TALK Learning System Set 1-A

   □ Writing important information □ An MO disk

   □ Your main textbook □ A way to find out more about words

   □ Basic Vocabulary in Use □ How to keep your computer data

   □ A dictionary □ A notebook

8. *Fill in the blanks with the correct words:*

The main objectives of this course will be to help _________ improve their _________ skills, as well as their knowledge of English-speaking and other cultures. This course will be different from any other __________ class you have taken before. The main focus will be on you and your classmates and what you want to _________. You will choose the pace of the _________ and what material you study during each __________. Your ___________ will act more as a facilitator than a teacher.

9. *You will have one TALK test this semester.*

□ True □ False

10. *Choose the correct work to complete the sentence:*

The TALK test(s) will count toward your ___________ grade.

□ Attendance & participation □ Quizzes, in-class & homework

□ Exam(s)

11. *How many vocabulary units will you complete each week?*

□ One □ Two □ Three □ Four

12. *How will you be tested on your vocabulary knowledge? (please select all the correct answers)*

□ A quiz in every class meeting □ A quiz from time to time

□ Your moodle discussions □ Your final exam

13. *What will you be doing on the moodle system? (please select all the correct answers)*

□ Making phone calls □ Keeping a journal □ Writing e-mail messages

□ Conducting chats □ Discussing topics with your classmates and teacher

□ Making presentations □ Writing book reports □ Doing extensive reading

14. *Choose the correct work to complete the sentence:*

Your moodle work will count towards your __________ grade.

□ Attendance & participation Quizzes, in-class & homework Exam(s)

15. *What is the minimum number of extensive reading books you will read each week?*

□ Zero □ One □ Two □ Three □Four

16. *Choose the correct words to complete the sentence:*
    Your book reports will count towards your ______________ grade.
    □ Attendance & participation □ Quizzes, in-class & homework
    □ Exam(s)

17. *What percentage is your attendance and participation grade?*
    □ 25% □ 50% □ 75% □ 100%

18. *What percentage is your quizzes, in-class assignments and homework assignments grade?*
    □ 25% □ 50% □ 75% □ 100%

19. *What percentage is your exams grade?*
    □ 25% □ 50% □ 75% □ 100%

20. *What should you do if you ever have a question?* ______________________

Appendix B: Basic English I-b

1st Year Science Students – First Semester, 2004

Day & Time: Mondays, 5th period (16:10-17:40) & Thursdays 1st period (8:40-10:10)
Room: 小7 (Mondays) & Computer lab #2 [情2] (Thursdays)
Teacher: Mr. Melton (メルトン)
Office: New Science Building, 5th floor
Office Hour: Tuesdays, 3rd period, and by appointment
Telephone: 383-2929, ext. 787
Fax: 384-6765
E-mail: jay@pu-kumamoto.ac.jp
moodle URL: http://moodle.jklmelton.net/
Jay Melton's URL: http://www.pu-kumamoto.ac.jp/~jay/jay.html
Course URL: http://www.pu-kumamoto.ac.jp/~jay/class/beI/

Required Materials:

TALK Learning System — Set 1-A, by Junge, Johann; Creative Services International

AND

Basic Vocabulary in Use, by McCarthy & O'Dell; Cambridge

AND

A notebook to keep class notes in (any size you like)

AND

An MO disk to use with the computers in the lab.

AND

There may be other materials for you to bring in during the year.

Optional (but recommended) Materials:

A good English learner's dictionary like:

Oxford Wordpower Dictionary, Oxford

Oxford Advanced Learner's Dictionary, Oxford

Dictionary of English Language and Culture, Longman

International Dictionary of English, Cambridge

Objectives:

The main objectives of this course will be to help students improve their English skills, as well as their knowledge of English-speaking and other cultures. This course will be very different from any other language class you have taken before. The main focus will be on you and your classmates and what you want to study. You will choose the pace of the course and what material you study during each class. Your teacher will act more as a facilitator than a teacher.

The material for this course will come from four main areas: the TALK Learning System, your vocabulary textbooks, the material we use on the computers and the Internet, and extensive reading books.

In the TALK system, you are responsible for what you learn. At first, you will spend some time learning how to use the system. Your facilitator will help you get started by carefully showing you how to use the system. The whole idea is to talk a lot and have fun doing it! You will have two TALK tests during the semester. In the tests, you will need to show me what you studied and learned from the TALK system. These tests will count towards your exams grade.

The vocabulary study will come from a textbook designed to increase your vocabulary as well as give you phrases that are useful. You will be able to study the words and phrases using many useful examples. Then you can try out what you learned with the exercises at the end of each unit. To check that you are learning important vocabulary, you will have a quiz from time to time (quiz grades) and a final exam at the end of the semester (exams grade).

You will also be doing many things on the computer. You will have an opportunity to read and write on the moodle system that your teacher has prepared. You will be able to discuss topics with your classmates, keep a journal with your teacher, write book reports and conduct chats. All of this will count towards your homework grade.

There are many, many extensive reading books to choose from. There are at least 6 levels from each publisher and many titles in each level. We will all read together in the beginning. Then you will choose the level that fits you and the titles that you are interested in. After you read each book, you will be required to write a book report. These reports will be written on the moodle system and will count towards your homework grade.

Grading:

Your grade will be based on the following criteria:

25% attendance & participation

50% quizzes, in-class assignments, and homework assignments

25% exams

Notice that most of your grade is based on what happens in the course during the academic year. If you do not attend class regularly, it will be impossible to pass this course. In addition, for the purposes of grades, coming to class late three times will be counted as one absence.

Appendix C: Basic English Students Questionnaire

Personal Major ______________________ Date ______________

Name (*romaji*) ______________________ (*kanji*) ____________

Nickname (If you want, I can help you choose a Western name) ______________

E-mail address ____

Home/cell phone # ____________________________________

Where is your hometown? ______________________________

Study questions (Please answer the following questions about studying English.)

1. What kind of English do you need to learn? ______________________________

2. What kind of English do you want to learn? ______________________________

3. What are your strong skills in English? ________________________________

4. What are your weak skills in English? _________________________________

5. What do you like to watch (TV or videos, for example) or read (books, magazines, newspapers, etc.) when you study English? _____________________________

6. How do you like to study? ____

7. Do you know how to use a computer? _____ If yes, what kind of computer and what do you do with it? ____

8. Do you own a computer? _____ If yes, do you have an Internet connection? _____

8a. If you have used the Internet before, what do you use it for? _____________
____

9. Have you ever been to an English-speaking country? _____ If yes, where?
____

10. Do you want to travel to an English-speaking country? _____ If yes, where?
____

11. What is your area of interest in science? ________________________________

12. What do you plan to do when you graduate? _____________________________
____

13. Please write any additional comments (You may also use the back of this paper).
____

Chapter XII

Reading and Learning from Screen

Miriam Schcolnik, Tel Aviv University, Israel

Sara Kol, Tel Aviv University, Israel

Abstract

Electronic texts are playing an increasing role in education in general and in language courses in particular. Computer-assisted language learning (CALL) tasks utilizing authentic texts on the Web require extensive screen reading. The flexible nature of electronic text encourages customization, which is important for effective screen reading and learning. For users to read comfortably and effectively, attention must be paid to the way electronic text is presented. Presentation includes factors related to the screen (e.g., contrast), to the reader (e.g., familiarity with the medium) and to the text layout (e.g., number of lines per screen). Navigation method (e.g., scrolling or paging) may also affect reading and learning from screen. Two studies conducted by the authors show that not everyone performs well with the same presentation mode and that preferences also vary. Designers of user-centered CALL materials should, therefore, allow for choice of presentation mode.

Introduction

Electronic texts are playing an increasing role in education, and teaching and learning are moving in the direction of digital formats (Davidson, Shields, & Biscos, 1997; Wilson & Landoni, 2002). As a result, students are reading more from screen in both content and language courses. Yet, many of these students find reading on screen more difficult than reading on paper, even in their native language (O'Hara & Sellen, 1997). CALL tasks utilizing authentic texts on the Web require extensive screen reading in a second or third language. Since text display is an important factor, it is important for language students and teachers to be aware of the ways in which text is displayed on screen, of their own preferences and of the options available for changing the display. CALL developers should pay attention to screen presentation so as to facilitate screen reading for language learners.

The *Background* section of the chapter begins with a comprehensive survey of the literature on reading and learning from screen, including the differences between reading on paper and reading on screen, the special features and structures of digital text, and the concept of reading to learn. In addition, the section includes an in-depth discussion of the variables that affect the appearance of digital text and a description of various navigation methods.

The section *Learning from Screen: Two Studies* focuses on studies conducted by the authors that explored the effect of screen presentation mode on learning among advanced learners of English. This investigation can inform the design, development and use of digital text in CALL courses as well as other Web-enhanced courses.

The chapter ends with recommendations for on-screen text presentation to enhance reading and learning from screen. In addition, an outline of future trends related to reading and learning on screen is presented.

Background

Reading on Screen vs. Reading on Paper

Studies comparing performance when reading on screen and on paper have not been conclusive. For example, one study (Muter, 1996) found no difference on comprehension scores between the group that read on screen and the group that read on paper. A number of other studies that looked at reading comprehension support this finding (McKnight, Dillon, & Richardson, 1990; Muter & Maurutto, 1991). However, a study that offered subjects online reading assistance (Reinking, 1998) found that students who read expository passages from screen performed better on a comprehension test than those reading on paper. On the other hand, Heppner, Anderson, Farstrup and Weiderman (1985) found that students reading from paper performed better on a standardized test than those reading on screen; Kellogg (1999) also reported on better test performance when reading from paper.

In a pilot study comparing reading on paper and on screen (Kol & Schcolnik, 1997), the authors found that students who were not experienced computer users could neither scan nor skim texts effectively on screen. In a subsequent study (Kol & Schcolnik, 2000), students were taught to use facilitating tools, like a hyperlinked outline, the highlighter, the Find feature and an online bilingual dictionary. The results of a reading comprehension test administered after the training showed that those students reading from screen performed as well as those reading from paper.

In a study comparing the processes involved in reading on screen and on paper, O'Hara and Sellen (1997) found that while subjects reading on paper could easily annotate their texts, those reading from screen found the process to be cumbersome and distracting. They also found that whereas both groups agreed that moving through documents was important, the group reading from paper found navigation to be fast, automatic and seamless; for the online readers, navigation was slow, difficult and distracting. Moreover, those reading on paper felt that laying out pages on a desk was important to help them gain a sense of the structure of the texts and allow them to visualize a great deal of information. Those reading online could not easily see a number of pages simultaneously; they either used overlapping windows or minimized the size of the documents, which, in both cases, restricted their visible field.

Kellogg (1999) reports on a study with English as a foreign language (EFL) students at a Japanese university. In this study, the students preferred reading on paper to reading on screen, explaining that reading on paper was easier. According to Thurstun (2000), the basic problem in reading online texts is the lack of a traditional schema or text structure. This deficiency limits readers' capacity to make assumptions and predictions about the text and hampers their ability to search for specific information and understand the main ideas in the text.

The Features and Structure of Digital Text

Features

In the Interquest report (Davidson et al., 1997), the researchers predicted that long academic texts would continue to be read from paper until screen image quality and readability improved. Today, even though long documents are still commonly read from paper, there are many features of digital text that can facilitate screen reading.

Digital text can be highlighted and annotated, just as with printed text. In addition, digital text has features unique to the electronic medium. Readers can manipulate and edit digital text. For example, they can add or link to textual or multimedia elements to enrich or update a document. Readers can also delete parts of the original text when creating a summary for their own use. The dynamic and flexible nature of digital text encourages customization, thereby creating a kind of combined ownership that blurs the distinction between reader and writer.

Readers of digital text can change font, font size and color, and background color. These options are useful for all readers but crucial for readers with reading disabilities. For the latter, the options are essential for allowing access to information. Moreover, digital text can be read aloud by a text-to-speech program. This makes digital texts accessible to both visually impaired and dyslexic readers. An option offered by most text-to-speech programs is automatic highlighting of the sections being read.

Digital text is searchable. Information can be located quickly by using the Find feature available in browsers, text editors and e-book reading programs. In addition, the availability of online dictionaries increases the usability of digital text, especially for language learners.

The abovementioned features are common to all digital text. In addition, other features can be implemented in digital texts, especially to aid, teach or practice reading comprehension. Reinking (1992) identifies unique characteristics of digital text that can be exploited for instructional purposes. He notes the possibility of structuring text differently, for instance, as a hypertext. In addition, he points out that with digital text, readers' access to text can be controlled, allowing selective or gradual display, for example, to practice prediction. Digital text can also adapt itself to the reader's needs. These customized texts can offer readers a wide range of features, including definitions of difficult words, additional background information, an outline of the structure of the text, and an easier version of the text. The hyperlinked outline of the main sections of a digital text can help readers grasp the organization of the text and help them reach the various sections quickly. The outline, therefore, compensates for the inability to leaf through a digital document as is done with a paper text (Kol & Schcolnik, 2000). The outline can also help overcome orientation difficulties within the text.

Gillingham (1996) suggests the option of providing readers with assistance in reading strategies. In a study donc in 1989 (Gillingham, 1996), Gillingham, Garner, Guthrie and Saywer compared the effect on text comprehension of online background knowledge on the one hand and reading strategy instruction on the other. They found that whereas background knowledge had no significant effect, the strategy resources offered with the digital text were effective in improving readers' comprehension. In other words, help with how to read was more effective than help with the content of the text. Gillingham cautions that if digital text is presented the same way as paper text, it will not be filling its potential. The features of the text should not only help readers comprehend the content, but also help them become more competent readers of digital text in general.

Van der Weel (n.d.) discusses the notion of an "intelligent text"; that is, a text created by a database capable of generating Web pages that answer a particular information need. Such digital texts would be made to order according to each reader's specifications.

Structure

A digital text can be structured as a single linear document, similar to a paper text, or it can be structured as a hypertext, where some information is presented on screen and additional information is accessed through links. When first created, hypertext was expected to be the technology that would allow access to an extensive network of information at the click of a mouse. However, since then, empirical findings have shown that reading and learning from hypertext is not always effective (Dillon, 1996). Thurstun

(2000) suggests a possible explanation: Hypertext does not always give readers the systematic patterns of information needed for effective reading. Nevertheless, the hypertext structure can be effective for learning in certain situations, as in the Blake Project (http://virtual.park.uga.edu/wblake/home.html), in which annotations and interpretations are linked to each stanza of Blake's poetry.

Appearance of Digital Text

For reading on screen to be as unconscious as reading from paper, certain conditions need to be met (Hill, 2001). According to Hill, good online typography must make the reading process as transparent as possible for the reader. Presentation and appearance play a crucial role in allowing users to read and use text in electronic form. Guidelines for the production of good electronic text need to take into account issues related to style and layout (Landoni, Wilson, & Gibb, 2000).

However, Grabinger and Osman-Jouchoux (1996) point out that research into typography elements is problematic for several reasons, such as the fact that there are many combinations of text format variables and it is difficult to investigate all possible interactions among them. Moreover, the contribution of each single variable may be too small, and thus, it will be difficult to assess its contribution to the readability or learnability of a text. The researchers suggest focusing on users' perceptions of different displays to find out how they assess them in terms of readability and "studyability."

Many factors may affect reading on screen. Some factors relate to the screen, such as resolution, sharpness, chromaticity, polarity, contrast between characters and background, interference from reflections, curvature of screen and distortion in corners. Other factors relate to the reader, such as posture, distance between the reading material and the reader, angle of the reading material and the reader's familiarity with the medium; while still other factors have to do with the characters. These include character shape, inter-character spacing, width of characters, size of characters and characters per line. Layout factors include words per page, lines per page, inter-line spacing and margins (Muter, 1996). In addition, the font type and size, and the presence or absence of page numbers may also affect reading, and consequently, learning from digital text.

The following section discusses some of the abovementioned factors that can affect screen reading.

Length and display of text. Hill (2001) points out that when the text is short (e.g., a short e-mail message), problems of display are not crucial. However, for longer texts and tasks requiring deeper processing — for example, learning for a test — poor display of text can have a serious effect on performance.

Words on screen and screen size. According to Muter (1996), reading speed decreases as the number of words per page decreases. He also says that large screens enhance the processing of text, possibly because of the greater number of words on the screen. For example, de Bruijn, de Mul and van Oostendorp (1992) found that learning times are shorter when larger screens are used, and thus concluded that it is easier to study a text when there is a large amount of text on the screen. Kilgour (1998) claims that future electronic readers should have a minimum of 500 words per screen.

Line length. Gordon (2001) explains that if the user can process information easily and quickly, comprehension and concentration will improve. If the line is too long, the eye will have to travel too far, and there will be an interruption of the flow of comprehension or the wrong line may be picked up. If the line is too short, the phrases will lack continuity and comprehension will suffer.

Landoni et al. (2000) found their users had trouble reading lines spanning from one edge of the screen to the other. Their guideline regarding line length is to use lengths similar to those of the printed page (10-15 words).

In a study on the effect of line length on readability, Dyson and Kipping (1998) showed that lines of 100 characters (rather than the accepted 45-60) were actually read more quickly, but readers were less comfortable with these longer lines, preferring the more normal line lengths. They suggest that the difference between readers' perceptions and actual performance makes it difficult to make practical recommendations on optimal line length. Dyson and Haselgrove (2000) had similar results.

Dyson and Haselgrove (2001) found that a medium line length (55 characters) resulted in faster reading and a higher level of comprehension than very long line length (100 characters per line). The researchers suggest the reduction in comprehension with long lines may have to do with eye movement and the difficulty of locating the beginning of the next line. With very short line length, they did not find a difference in comprehension, but they did find a lower speed of reading.

Inter-line spacing. Poor line spacing produces problems similar to those caused by poor line length. Lines that are too spaced out will make the process of moving down the page longer, and this may be tiring and uncomfortable. When lines are too close, the eyes may drift. According to Muter (1996), research suggests that in clear and comfortable text, lines are not too close together and characters are not too far apart.

Inter-character spacing. Hill (2001) recommends tight letter spacing that is not so tight as to cause collisions, but tight enough to enable easy word recognition, and around 66 characters and spaces per line.

Fonts. Fonts affect readability (Dix, Finlay, Abowd, & Beale, 1998). For digital text, Nielsen (2000) recommends the use of Verdana, a sans serif font developed by Microsoft for online reading.

Figure 1. Serif and sans serif fonts

Examples of serif fonts	Examples of sans serif fonts
Courier: user-centered	Arial: user-centered
Georgia: user-centered	Verdana: user-centered

A lot has been written about the difference between serif and sans serif fonts. Serifs are small lines at the ends of characters (see Figure 1). These are present in serif fonts and absent in sans serif typefaces. Examples of commonly used sans serif fonts are Arial and Verdana. Examples of commonly used serif fonts are Times Roman, Courier and Georgia.

Serif fonts are easier to read than sans serif fonts because the serifs make the individual letters more distinctive and easier to recognize. The commonly used convention for printed work is to use a serif font for the body of the work and a sans serif font for the headings.

However, printed works generally have a resolution of at least 600 dots per inch, whereas computer monitors are usually only 72 dots per inch. This lower resolution can make very small serif characters harder to read than the equivalent sans serif characters because of their more complex shapes. Therefore, according to the tips given by Scribe Consulting (www.scribe.com.au/tip-w017.html), for small on-screen fonts it is better to use a sans serif font like Verdana or Arial.

In contrast with that view, Boyarski, Neuwirth, Forlizzi and Regli (1998) found that the Georgia font was more readable than Times New Roman, but regarding Verdana, their results were mixed. Weisenmiller (1999) compared four typefaces: Georgia, Verdana (designed to optimize on-screen readability), Times and Arial (both designed for print). The purpose of the study was to determine whether sans serif and serif typefaces optimized for on-screen viewing significantly improve reading rate and reading comprehension. No significant difference among the four typefaces was found for either reading speed or reading comprehension scores.

Bernard, Mills, Peterson and Storrer (2001) compared the 12 most common Web font types and found no significant difference in legibility. However, they found significant differences in reading time (the fastest reading time with Tahoma).

Page numbers. According to McCusker (1998), page numbers are a clue that readers are used to; thus, it is helpful to have page numbers even in running electronic text. Landoni et al. (2000) point out that readers gain a sense of their place via page numbers and that the page metaphor should be respected.

Page orientation. According to Hill (2001), portrait orientation displays lines of a better length than landscape. Wearden (1998) reports on two studies conducted in 1997 and 1998 that checked what screen orientation media consumers prefer. In the first study, the results showed a strong cultural bias in favor of portrait orientation for periodicals. In the case of books, the data seemed to suggest a preference for landscape, but it later became clear that those who chose the latter orientation did so because they expected the device to display two facing pages of a book. Education, gender, race and age did not affect preferences. However, the expectations of those who spend more time watching television and using online services than reading from paper were influenced by their viewing. The results of the second experiment showed that the portrait, page-based design was considered preferable. Wearden hypothesizes that portrait text orientation is so firmly fixed in human experience that most people prefer it. However, he feels that perhaps continued viewing of landscape-oriented electronic displays will alter the historic cultural bias with regard to the orientation of documents.

Color. According to Muter (1996), color has many disadvantages for text presentation, many of which have been mentioned in the literature. For example, approximately 8% of males are at least partly colorblind; overuse of color can create confusion; some colors have expected meanings, which may contradict the intended meaning; and so forth. In spite of this, he points out that people often prefer color, and color can be useful to highlight, categorize or improve aesthetics.

Polarity. Muter (1996) points out that most users prefer positive polarity (dark characters on a light background). Positive polarity reduces optical distortion and increases visual acuity, contrast sensitivity, speed of accommodation and depth of field. It also decreases the problem of interfering reflections of external light. A disadvantage of positive polarity is an increase in the risk of perceived flicker, although this can be overcome with a high refresh rate.

Navigation in Digital Text

Navigation refers to the way in which people move through a document. When reading digital text, the navigation method is usually determined by the characteristics of the program used for reading (e.g., browser, pdf reader) and its interface. For example, when reading on the Web, users usually use a combination of methods: for a long article that is divided into several "pages," the user will probably scroll down to read one page, then click an arrow to go to the next page and repeat the scrolling process.

Navigation aids can promote learner control. Two studies (Armitage, Wilson, & Sharp, 2004) investigated the effects of navigation aids like maps on ownership for learning. They found that overall, navigation aids influence ownership for learning. However, not all aids contribute equally: A-Z indices and maps led to significantly higher feelings of control than paging buttons and hypertext.

Navigation method may affect reading and, consequently, learning. Many studies on the way readers move through a text on screen have compared scrolling and paging (e.g., de Bruijn, de Mul, & van Oostendorp, 1992; Piolat, Roussey, & Thunin, 1997; Dyson & Kipping, 1997, 1998). Dyson and Kipping (1998) found that participants read through paged documents faster than scrolled documents but showed no differences in reading comprehension.

In their study of the influence of reading speed and line length on the effectiveness of reading from screen, Dyson and Haselgrove (2001) investigated scrolling patterns as well. They found that scrolling patterns associated with better comprehension (more time in pauses and more individual scrolling movements) are different from scrolling patterns used in faster reading (less time in pauses between scrolling). They concluded that effective readers can only be defined in relation to the aims of the reading task, which may favor either speed or accuracy. Moreover, how a document is navigated appears to be critical for recall in situations like reading at a fast speed or reading documents with long lines.

Two studies assessed the effects of two navigation methods, paging and scrolling, on participants' performance while reading and revising texts (Piolat et al., 1997). In both studies, the page-by-page presentation facilitated the task. This is consistent with the findings reported by Muter (1996), that paging is superior to scrolling in terms of performance and user preference. In a study checking preference and performance in a learning task (see Screen Presentation Studies section), the authors found that some users performed better with scrolling but preferred paging. Moreover, users may prefer different navigation modes depending on the purpose of reading.

In a study of dedicated e-readers (Schcolnik, 2001), 90% of the respondents preferred paging to scrolling. This finding is consistent with the findings reported in the literature (Muter, 1996; Piolat et al., 1997; McCusker, 1998; Hill, 2001). It is important to point out, however, that the majority of subjects used their e-readers to read for pleasure. In reading to learn, they may have had a different preference. The advantage of paging can be attributed to the ability to remember the text by its appearance and arrangement, and to remember details by their location on the page (Severinson Eklundh, Fatton, & Romberger, 1996). The reader's internal representation of the organization of the text can be facilitated by the elements on the screen or page (Grabinger & Osman-Jouchoux, 1996). McCusker (1998), discussing the Rocket eBook developers' decisions concerning paging, explains that paging was chosen over scrolling to help users keep their place on the page.

However, scrolling is now commonly used when reading or skimming Web pages (Nielsen, 1997). As a result, people are now familiar with this navigation method and may, therefore, prefer it. In a pilot study (see Screen Presentation Studies section), the authors found that most students in the sample preferred scrolling to paging for learning.

Baker (2003) examined the use of paging vs. scrolling and their effect on reading comprehension. He found reading time in the paging condition to be significantly slower than in the scrolling condition. However, performance was not significantly different. Similarly, he found no significant differences in the perception that a particular condition was better suited for reading or that information was easier to find. He suggests that participants were able to read the documents more quickly when scrolling because of previous scrolling experience. Some participants said that when they paged they had little on the screen, had to "go back and forth" and found it hard to scan.

In a study of efficiency and preference of scrolling vs. paging when seeking information in long passages (Parsons, 2001), subjects who used paging for extended passages used significantly less time to find the information to answer questions than did those who used scrolling. Parsons found no gender differences in accuracy, quickness or preference.

Reading to Learn

Reading to learn is one of the many purposes for reading. It is not the fragmented reading that occurs as readers of digital text move from window to window in an effort to locate pieces of information as quickly as possible. Rather, reading to learn implies comprehending a text in-depth and trying to remember the important content. It involves understanding the author's ideas, following the logical development of the text, reflecting on the ideas and critically analyzing the text. Such reading demands great concentration, mental effort and time.

In an effort to characterize different kinds of reading, Lorch, Lorch and Klusewitz (1993) studied the reading habits of college students. After compiling a list of reading purposes common to all of the students, the researchers constructed a reading profile for each purpose. These profiles confirm that the way students read varies with their purpose. The profiles also show that reading to learn in preparation for an exam is significantly different from other kinds of reading. It is slower and requires more attention to detail, more reflection and memorization. Such reading also involves more use of supporting materials and is characterized by frequent rereading and checks of understanding.

Reading to learn is also associated with other supporting skills and strategies that aid readers as they strive to comprehend text. When good readers are confronted with a new text, they usually begin with an initial survey of the text — to identify purpose, main ideas, structure, genre and organization. While reading, they may take advantage of such study skills as underlining, note-taking, annotating, outlining, summarizing and representing information in graphic form (flowcharts, tables, etc.). As a final step, good readers will most likely review the material studied.

For generations, these skills have helped learners who read from printed texts. Are the same skills also useful when reading digital texts? The answer depends on the type of digital text considered. If the digital text was originally formatted for print and subsequently displayed as such on screen, the above skills are still relevant, but their implementation will be adapted to the new medium. For example, when text is formatted for print, pages are in portrait layout, but when displayed on the screen, the reader is confronted with a landscape surface. When dealing with such digital text, the initial survey will be done by scrolling. The *find* feature will be used to locate specific information, and annotating will be done with colors, the use of upper case or a different font, or a note-taking feature. However, the digital text is not always a linear text on screen but is often a hypertextual network, and to deal with that type of text the reader will need to learn new enabling skills. Readers will probably be able to survey the text in the usual fashion, but will need the additional skill of deciding which links to follow and when to do so; that is, how to create their own path through the network of texts. In short, readers will have to learn how to construct their own texts from the information available in the original (Coiro, 2003).

Paper supports reading to learn because it is "markable, flexible, tangible and moveable within space" (O'Hara & Sellen, 1997, p. 16). Most people also find paper easy on the eyes and possessing physical warmth. They may also feel attached to their irregular text markings and perhaps even to the coffee stains on the page. These markings can aid remembering (and hence learning) and allow for a kind of text ownership. With paper, readers can annotate and underline easily, leaf through the text to sense the organization and feel the flow of the text, and move through the text in non-linear fashion without getting lost. The visual features of paper texts, such as page numbers and location of information on the page, endow the text with both context and reference points that can help readers develop a sense of the text.

Digital text also supports reading to learn. A host of features have been developed and studied in an effort to make such texts more useful for learning. For their study on the effectiveness of Web-based learning, Landoni, Wilson and Gibb (2000) revised a text chapter to make it more scannable. They divided the chapter into separate files, according to the sub-headings in the original text, and presented each sub-section on a separate page. Moreover, a chapter contents page was created to list and provide links to each section. Extra headings, colored and sized, were inserted in the text to divide it into even smaller, more digestible chunks. The results showed that the subjects who used the revised chapter made fewer errors on an information retrieval task and reported higher satisfaction than those who read the original text on screen. Similarly, Reinking (n.d.) reports on a number of studies in which student comprehension increased when electronic texts provided a variety of options for readers. In one of the physics texts Reinking used in his research, the following options were available: (1) assistance with difficult words or phrases; (2) illustrations related to the content; (3) useful background information; (4) a map of the text structure; and (5) an easier, less technical version of the text. In addition, Reinking described situations where the program not only adapts to the characteristics of the reader and presents suitable texts, but also determines which part of a text the reader is permitted to see. In doing so, the computer program is able to guide reading by influencing what a reader focuses on.

Dyson and Haselgrove (2000) used a range of question types to check comprehension after subjects read from screen at both a normal and a fast reading speed. In addition, by automatically recording how readers scrolled through each document, reading patterns were explored. A speed-accuracy tradeoff was found and, in general, the recall of specific details was less accurate than responses to higher-order questions. Questions that addressed the structure of the text were hardest. Analysis of the scrolling movements showed that the overall time spent pausing between movements was the best predictor of comprehension. At a normal reading speed, the most effective readers — in terms of higher comprehension scores — were those who spent more time between scrolling movements.

Dyson and Haselgrove (2001) investigated the effects of two reading speeds (normal and fast) and different line lengths on comprehension, reading rate and scrolling patterns. They found a reduction in overall comprehension when reading fast. A medium line length (55 characters per line) produced the highest level of comprehension.

Reading to learn involves heavy cognitive processing on the part of the reader, whether the reader is reading in his or her native language or a second language. If we consider reading as an interactive process involving the reader and text in top-down and bottom-up processes (Rumelhart, 1977, reprinted in 1994), we can understand that in the decoding processes, the second-language reader has a greater cognitive load than the native speaker. Therefore, the supports that can be added to digital text should be especially useful to second-language readers. If various support features are available, users can choose those most useful to them, and read to learn according to their own learning styles and preferences. Leu, Gallo and Hillinger (1995) found that when learners are given a number of supportive features, there is differential exploitation of these features by students of different reading achievements. This study supports the need to offer many different options. Going one step further, instructional materials could be designed as adaptive systems that could automatically identify and support learners' different traits (Chun & Plass, 1997; Reinking, n.d.).

Learning from Screen: Two Studies

Today it seems more relevant to deal with screen modes, or "post-typographic surfaces," (Reinking, 1998) than with the comparison of paper and screen presentation. This section focuses on two studies conducted by the authors to investigate the effect of screen presentation on learning. According to Reinking (1992), new formats can increase comprehension. Duchastel (2001) claims that learning involves interacting with information, and the design of that information is crucial to learnability.

In the two studies, the texts for screen presentation were prepared for browser display and MS Reader (the Microsoft e-book reader) display. In browser display, the Hyper Text Markup Language (HTML) text was presented in one piece, so the subjects needed to scroll up or down to view the various sections. The MS Reader text (presented on the same desktop computer monitors as the HTML text) appeared one page at a time, and the subjects moved forward or backward to view the various pages (see Figure 2).

According to Hill (2001), MS Reader has no distractions from reading: no menu bars, no menus, nothing between the reader and the content. The MS Reader was created to offer on-screen reading that is similar to reading a printed book.

In the first study, which was a pilot, the subjects read a text on screen in one of the two modes. After reading, the students turned off the monitors and wrote everything they learned from the texts. No significant difference in recall scores was found between the two modes.

The subjects also answered an attitude questionnaire. Contrary to the findings in the literature, most of the students (61.7%) preferred the browser presentation to the MS Reader presentation, particularly students in the exact sciences. When grouped by major (exact science vs. health professions), 72% of the exact sciences preferred the HTML text, while only 44% of the health professions preferred HTML. The majority of the students (59.5%) preferred scrolling to paging for learning. No significant difference between males and females was found for preferences of navigation mode or reading mode.

The second study built upon these findings and further investigated the influence of reading mode on learning. The research questions were:

Figure 2. Browser and MS Reader text layout

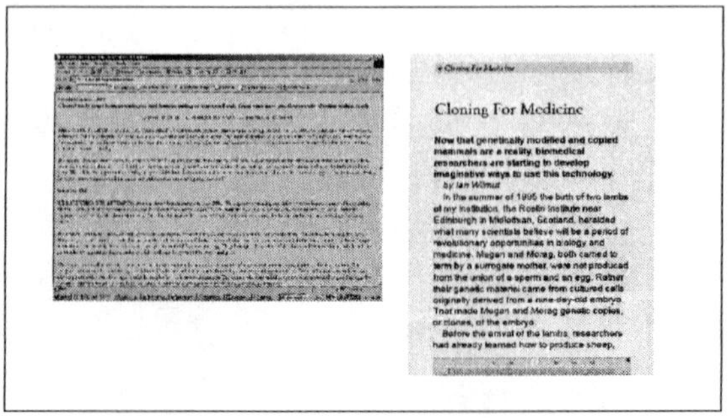

1. Does the mode of text presentation on screen affect test performance?
2. Do students prefer scrolling or paging, short lines or long lines?
3. Are there differences in preference and performance between men and women?
4. Are there differences between exact science and health science students?

Method

Subjects

Ninety-four undergraduate students (57 females and 37 males) from five intact advanced classes for English for Special Academic Purposes participated in the study. The majority were native speakers of Hebrew, and the others speakers of Russian or Arabic. The students in three of the classes were from the exact sciences (math, physics and chemistry), and in the other two classes students were from the health professions (physical and occupational therapy). The subjects' ages ranged from 18 to 24 years.

Instruments

Three instruments were used in the study: A text on cloning presented in two modes — browser and MS Reader; a test on paper (Cronbach Alpha 0.65) with closed questions (fill-in or multiple choice), checking learning of the content; and a short attitude questionnaire tapping student attitudes towards the two reading modes.

The cloning text was a full-length text of about 1,100 words (with a Flesch-Kincaid grade level of 12.0). Wherever possible, text display features (e.g., font, font size, background color) were held constant in the two modes. The differences that remained between the two modes were those that were mode dependent, mainly navigation method and amount of text on screen. See Table 1 for a comparison of the two modes used.

Table 1. Text presentation modes

Feature	Browser	MS Reader
page layout	landscape	portrait
navigation	scrolling	paging
# of words per line	9	6
# of words per screen	about 200	about 110
background color	off-white	off-white
font size	11 pt	11 pt
font	Verdana	Verdana
spacing between characters	condensed	condensed

Procedure

In preparation for the study, the subjects were trained in the use of the two modes. During the practice session in the computer room, the subjects studied a text of the same type and length and on a similar topic as the one to be used for the experiment and were allowed to use an online dictionary and take notes. Then they took a practice test (with monitors off) to become familiar with the style of test questions they would get and with the experience of reading on screen and being tested right after.

The students in each class were randomly assigned to two groups — one for each screen-reading mode. Students were told that this was to research how well they could learn from texts presented on screen. They were also informed that the grade on the test would be a part of their class mark. This was important so students would do the activity mindfully.

At the beginning of the experimental session, the students were informed that they would have 1 hour to study the content of the text, and that after that they would take a test to check what they had learned. The students studied the text for an hour in the assigned mode. While studying the text, they were allowed to use an online dictionary and to take notes to help them understand and remember the information. Then, the computer monitors were turned off, the notes put away, and the students took the test. This procedure simulated typical "cramming" for a test. The attitude questionnaire was administered immediately after the test.

Results

Performance

The test results showed that students who learned from the HTML text performed significantly better than students who learned from the MS Reader text. Mean score for HTML was 88 and mean score for the Reader was 84 ($p = 0.04$). No significant difference was found between men and women nor between the exact sciences and the health professions.

Preferences

Results of the student attitude questionnaire are presented in Table 2. These results show that about two-thirds of the students felt that learning mode affected their learning, and about two-thirds of these students expressed a preference for HTML text. Only one-third of the total number of students felt that reading mode did not influence how well they learned. In addition, the majority of students preferred scrolling to paging, and those who expressed a preference for line length preferred short lines to long lines. Both of these preferences were consistent across majors (exact sciences and health sciences).

No significant correlation was found between gender and preference of learning mode. In addition, more men than women said mode did not make any difference. A t-test for

Table 2. Results of attitude questionnaire (in percentages) (N= 94)

Preference	Browser display	MS Reader display	No difference
Learned better from ...	44	21	35
Amount of text on screen better in ...	42	34	24
Navigation mode better in ...	54 (scrolling)	24 (paging)	22
Line length better in ...	32	42	26

independent samples showed that women were more likely than men to choose the Reader for learning (p=.005).

Preference for short lines. 42% of the students expressed a preference for short lines over long lines. Thirty-two percent preferred long lines, and 26% said that line length makes no difference.

Preference for reader by female students. A t-test for independent samples showed that female students were more likely than male students to choose the Reader for learning (p=.05). A higher percentage of women (29% women vs. 11% men) felt they understood better with the Reader and a higher percentage of women (46% vs. 36%) preferred short lines.

Discussion

The results of the study show that students who had more text on the screen were able to learn better. Muter (1996) claims that large screens enhance the processing of text, possibly because the number of words per screen is large. The number of words per screen may affect learning as well as reading. In the authors' research, reading mode affected learning for both groups of students: Students from both the exact sciences and the health sciences performed better after studying the HTML text. These results contradict Piolat et al.'s (1997) findings that page-by-page presentation facilitated learning. According to Piolat et al., readers build a better mental representation of the task and remember more when paging. In the authors' research, better student performance with HTML may have been due to familiarity with the browser display, or to the fact that more text on screen helps students grasp the universe of the text and thereby facilitates learning.

The preference for HTML text is not consistent with Piolat et al. (1997), who found paging superior to scrolling in terms of preference as well as performance. However, this preference for scrolling is consistent with recent research (Nielsen, 2000) and with the preferences expressed in the first study. This result may be explained by familiarity with scrolling. Another explanation may be that when reading for learning, preferences may be different from preferences when reading for pleasure.

Recommendations for User-Centered CALL

Electronic presentation of text gives the reader control over text appearance (Chartier, 2001-2002). This is in line with Muter's (1996) recommendation that designers of online texts try to accommodate individual differences. Internet sites in which texts are presented in more than one mode reflect a user-centered approach. One way of accommodating individual differences is to allow readers to choose a font style and size to suit their preferences (Landoni, 2000).

The Open eBook organization (www.openebook.org) has developed a series of specifications for electronic readers. All of them start with "Let the user." For example, "Let the user resize the window. Let the user choose the font. Let the user change the font size. Let the user specify the background color. Let the user specify the text color."

The authors' findings also support this flexible approach to text presentation. Since not all students perform equally well with a given presentation mode, and since preferences vary as well, learners should be offered choices. We recommend that whenever possible, designers of CALL materials provide more than one mode of text presentation, and provide options for line length and navigation. In addition, learners should be allowed to customize font size, font color and background color. Every learner should be able to choose a reading mode that suits his or her learning style and preferences. This is particularly important for language learners, who have to cope with language difficulties in addition to new content in a new reading medium.

Future Trends

Screen Presentation and Ergonomics

1. More attention will be paid to ergonomic issues, such as angle of the screen and room illumination.
2. Screen resolution will improve even more and will aid screen reading.
3. Since one mode of screen presentation does not fit all users and all purposes, a variety of modes will be available.

Language Teaching

1. Language teachers will take into account the new ways of writing and new genres available as well as ways to read them.
2. More language teachers will exploit online texts as up-to-date readings for their courses (e.g., newspapers, newsletters, encyclopedias, blogs, textbooks, academic journals).

3. Language teachers will incorporate digital reading skills in their courses. This will empower students and help them become more effective readers who can take advantage of digital texts.

Reading and Learning

1. Most texts for educational purposes will continue to be printed until portable computers become commonplace.
2. There will be more online publications of all kinds.
3. Libraries will make more digital texts available.
4. Students will demand digital texts for several reasons:
    - Working with digital information will be commonplace.
    - The value of online tools (such as bilingual dictionaries or "Find on this Page") that facilitate reading will be recognized.
    - Students will be aware that certain presentation formats enhance learning.
5. CALL courses will allow electronic text selection and customization, and as a result, the courses will become more user-centered.
6. For students with reading disabilities, customization options together with text-to-speech software will make reading from screen better than reading from paper.

Conclusion

This chapter has surveyed screen presentation and its effect on reading and learning. One size no longer fits all, and therefore, options of text presentation need to be provided and exploited. This conclusion is relevant to Web designers, publishers, educational materials designers and developers, developers of online tests, teachers, learners and readers of digital texts in general. In particular, the field of CALL can benefit from an increased awareness of the new needs arising from the electronic medium.

References

Armitage, U., Wilson, S., & Sharp, H. (2004). Navigation and ownership for learning in electronic texts: An experimental study. *Electronic Journal on e-Learning, 2*(1), 19-30.

Baker, J. R. (2003). *The impact of paging vs. scrolling on reading online text passages.* Wichita: Wichita State University, Software Usability Research Laboratory, Department of Psychology. Retrieved May 2004, from http://psychology.wichita.edu/surl/usabilitynews/51/paging_scrolling.htm

Bernard, M., Mills, M., Peterson, M., & Storrer, K. (2001). *A comparison of popular online fonts: Which is best and when?* Wichita: Wichita State University, Software Usability Research Laboratory. Retrieved July 2002, from http://psychology.wichita.edu/surl/usabilitynews/3S/font.htm

Boyarski, D., Neuwirth, C., Forlki, J., & Harkness Regli, S. (1998). A study of fonts designed for screen display. *Proceedings of CHI'98* (pp. 87-94).

Chartier, R. (2001-2002, October 15-March). *Readers and readings in the electronic age.* Paper presented at the text-e, Virtual Symposium.

Chun, D. M., & Plass, J. L. (1997). Research on text comprehension in multimedia environments. *Language Learning & Technology, 1*(1), 60-81.

Coiro, J. (2003). *Reading comprehension on the Internet: Expanding of understanding of reading comprehension to encompass new literacies.* Retrieved November 2004, from www.lite.iwarp.com/compint.html

Davidson, K. T., Shields, M. A., & Biscos, G. (1997). *Network, screen and page: The future of reading in a digital age.* Torrance, CA: The Electronic Document Systems Foundation.

de Bruijn, D., de Mul, S., & van Oostendorp, H. (1992). The influence of screen size and text layout on the study of text. *Behaviour & Information Technology, 11*(2), 71-78.

Dillon, A. (1996). TIMS: A framework for the design of usable electronic text. In H. van Oostendorp & S. de Mul (Eds.), *Cognitive aspects of electronic text processing* (Vol. LVIII, pp. 99-120). Norwood: Ablex Publishing.

Dix, A., Finlay, J., Abowd, G., & Beale, R. (1998). *Human-computer interaction* (2nd ed.). Hemel Hempstead Hertfordshire: Prentice Hall Europe.

Duchastel, P. (2001, September 15). *Learnability.* Retrieved October 2002, from http://home.earthlink.net/~castelnet/info/learnability.htm

Dyson, M. C., & Haselgrove, M. (2000). The effects of reading speed and reading patterns on the understanding of text read from screen. *Journal of Research in Reading, 23*(2), 210-223.

Dyson, M. C., & Haselgrove, M. (2001). The influence of reading speed and line length on the effectiveness of reading from screen. *International Journal of Human-Computer Studies, 54*, 585-612.

Dyson, M. C., & Kipping, G. J. (1997). The legibility of screen formats: Are three columns better than one? *Computers & Graphics, 21*(6), 703-712.

Dyson, M. C., & Kipping, G. J. (1998). The effects of line length and method of movement on patterns of reading from screen. *Visible Language, 32*(2).

Gillingham, M. G. (1996). Comprehending electronic text. In H. van Oostendorp & S. de Mul (Eds.), *Cognitive aspects of electronic text processing* (Vol. LVIII, pp. 77-98). Norwood: Ablex Publishing.

Gillingham, M. G., Garner, R., Guthrie, J. T., & Sawyer, R. (1989). Children's control of computer-based reading assistance in answering synthesis questions. *Computers in Human Behaviour, 5*, 61-75.

Gordon, B. (2001). *Making digital type look good.* London: Thames & Hudson.

Grabinger, R. S., & Osman-Jouchoux, R. (1996). Designing screens for learning. In H. van Oostendorp & S. de Mul (Eds.), *Cognitive aspects of electronic text processing* (Vol. LVIII, pp. 181-212). Norwood: Ablex Publishing.

Heppner, F. H., Anderson, J. G. T., Farstrup, A.E., & Weiderman, N. H. (1985, January). Reading performance on a standardized test is better from print than from computer display. *Journal of Reading,* 321-325.

Hill, B. (2001). *The magic of reading.* Microsoft Corp. Retrieved March 2001, from http://slate.msn.com/ebooks/00-09-26/ebooks.asp

Kellogg, G. (1999). Students' reactions to reading electronic vs. printed documents. *Proceedings of the Fourth International Conference of Language and Development.* Retrieved November 2004, from www.languages.ait.ac.th/hanoi_proceedings/kellogg.htm#top

Kilgour, F. G. (1998). The electronic book. *The evolution of the book* (pp. 151-160). New York: Oxford University Press.

Kol, S., & Schcolnik, M. (1997). Reading from screen vs. reading from paper: A pilot study. *CAELL Journal, 8*(1), 10-14.

Kol, S., & Schcolnik, M. (2000). Enhancing screen reading strategies. *Calico Journal, 18*(1), 67-80.

Landoni, M., Wilson, R., & Gibb, F. (2000). From the visual book to the WEB book: The importance of design. *The Electronic Library, 18*(6).

Leu, D. J., Jr., Gallo, M. J., & Hillinger, M. J. (1995). Reading comprehension in hypermedia environments: Reconsidering considerate text in dynamic electronic environments. Cited in Leu, D. J., Jr. & Reinking, D. (1996), *Bringing insights from reading research to research on electronic learning environments.*

Lorch, R. F., Jr. , Lorch, E. P., & Klusewitz, M.A. (1993). College students' conditional knowledge about reading. *Journal of Educational Psychology, 85*(2), 239-252.

McCusker, D. (1998). *The design of the Rocket eBook.* Rocket eBook. Retrieved December 2000, from www.zippublishing.com/abstracts/rocket_ebook_ergonomics.htm

McKnight, C., Dillon, A., & Richardson, J. (1990). A comparison of linear and hypertext formats in information retrieval. In R. McAleese & C. Green (Eds.), *Hypertext: State of the art* (pp. 10-19). Oxford: Intellect.

Muter, P. (1996). Interface design and optimization of reading of continuous text. In H. van Oostendorp & S. de Mul (Eds.), *Cognitive aspects of electronic text processing* (Vol. LVIII, pp. 161-180). Norwood: Ablex Publishing.

Muter, P., & Maurutto, P. (1991). Reading and skimming from computer screens and books: The paperless office revisited? *Behaviour and Information Technology, 10*(4), 257-266.

Nielsen, J. (1997). *Changes in Web usability since 1994*. useit. Retrieved November, 2004, from www.useit.com/alertbox/9712a.html

Nielsen, J. (2000). *Designing Web usability*. Indianapolis: New Riders Publishing.

O'Hara, K., & Sellen, A. (1997). *A* comparison of reading paper and on-line documents. *Proceedings of CHI'97* (pp. 335-342).

Parsons, C. G. (2001). *The efficiency and preference implications of scrolling versus paging when information seeking in long text passages* (doctoral dissertation). Greeley: University of Northern Colorado.

Piolat, A., Roussey, J. Y., & Thunin, O. (1997). Effects of screen presentation on text reading and revising. *International Journal Human-Computer Studies, 47*, 565-589.

Reinking, D. (1992). Differences between electronic and printed texts: An agenda for research. *Journal of Educational Multimedia and Hypermedia, 1*, 11-24.

Reinking, D. (1998). Introduction: Synthesizing technological transformations of literacy in a post-typographic world. In D. Reinking, M.C. McKenna, L. D. Labbo & R. D. Kieffer (Eds.), *Handbook of literacy and technology: Transformations in a post-typographic world* (pp. xi-xxx). Mahwah: Lawrence Erlbaum Associates.

Reinking, D. (n.d.). *Electronic literacy*. Retrieved November, 2004, from http://curry.edschool.virginia.edu/go/clic/nrrc/reinking.html

Rumelhart, D. E. (1977, reprinted in 1994). Toward an interactive model of reading. In R.B. Ruddell, M.R. Ruddell & H. Singer (Eds.), *Theoretical models and processes of reading* (pp. 864-894). Newark, NJ: International Reading Association.

Schcolnik, M. (2001). *A study of reading with dedicated e-readers* (doctoral dissertation). Fort Lauderdale, FL: Nova Southeastern University.

Severinson Eklundh, K., Fatton, A., & Romberger, S. (1996). The paper model for computer-based writing. In H. van Oostendorp & S. de Mul (Eds.), *Cognitive aspects of electronic text processing* (Vol. LVIII, pp. 137-160). Norwood: Ablex Publishing.

Thurstun, J. (2000). Screenreading: Challenges of the new literacy. In D. Gibbs & K.L. Krause (Eds.), *Cyberlines: Languages and cultures of the Internet* (pp. 61-78). Albert Park: James Nicholas Publishers.

van der Weel, A. (n.d.). *The concept of markup in digital text and the Gutenberg heritage*. Retrieved November, 2004, from www.let.leidenuniv.nl/English/B&P/eltext/Ch03%20Concept%20of%20markup.fn.pdf

Wearden, S. (1998). *Landscape vs. portrait formats: Assessing consumer preferences*. Kent State University. Retrieved October, 1999, from www.jmc.kent.edu/futureprint/1998summer/wearden.htm

Weisenmiller, E. M. (1999). *A study of the readability of on-screen text* (doctoral dissertation). Blacksburg: Virginia Polytechnic Institute and State University.

Wilson, R., & Landoni, M. (2002). *Electronic textbook design guidelines.* JISC Project. Retrieved November 2004, from http://ebooks.strath.ac.uk/eboni/guidelines.pdf

Chapter XIII

Evaluating Students' Perceptions of *Online Counselor* for Independent Language Learning

Yoko Hirata, Hokkai-Gakuen University, Japan

Abstract

This chapter outlines the Online Counselor *computer program, which has been designed to assist students in planning and organizing their learning using appropriate resources, and evaluating their work. Based on the results of a study implemented for students who lack previous independent learning experience, it argues that* Online Counselor *is effective in guiding their learning and developing their initiative, responsibility, self-awareness and independence in language learning while giving a considerable amount of freedom to them in performing tasks. Furthermore, the author argues that different levels of support are important if online learning is intended to play a major role in curriculum and teaching programs. Online independent language learning is best achieved by developing both learner and teacher autonomy and providing extensive teacher development activities that encourage instructors to adopt self-reflective attitudes.*

Introduction

Recent academic interest in the idea of autonomous self-directed language learning and new technology has promoted the development of a variety of Web-based online independent language-learning systems throughout the world. However, it has been proven that simply providing students with the variety and flexibility to work at their own level and pace through the technology is not sufficient to make a significant improvement in their language proficiency levels (Gremmo & Riley, 1995; Kelly, 1996). Many computer novices and students are not culturally predisposed to being independent language learners. Also, it is clear that as people have more choices, they need more support and constant guidance to handle them. Although online educational approaches need to be adapted to suit local circumstances, little research has been conducted so far to determine how to provide these students with a variety of language materials and resources electronically. In addition, many off-the-shelf computer programs tend to have been developed without taking into account the users' perceptions of online language learning and their learning contexts. It is important to determine how students can adopt self-access learning approaches effectively and how they can be supported in the process of their language learning. To maximize the quality of students' online learning experiences, the development of a comprehensive learner support system is necessary.

Research Background

Autonomous and Independent Language Learning

The development of students' autonomy and independence within their own learning environments has been widely acknowledged as a valuable aspect of learning that aims to achieve long-term academic success (Gremmo & Riley, 1995; Littlewood, 1997; Sheerin, 1997). The emphasis of teaching lifelong learning techniques and the shift from a teacher-centered to a more learner-centered approach has also contributed to this growing awareness of the importance of autonomous and independent learning. This new focus on language learning and an increasing number of multimedia-based facilities has led to an appraisal of effective teaching approaches in self-access resource centers, where students are able to choose and use independent language-learning materials on their own and take charge of their own learning without the direct control of an instructor (Gardner & Miller, 1999; Gremmo & Riley, 1995; Sheerin, 1989). In addition, a variety of Web-based or computer-assisted language learning (CALL) programs, which seem to be a favorable option in terms of providing a language-learning environment based on students' choice, claim to be highly appropriate for autonomous learning needs, and a number of potential benefits of these autonomous learning approaches have been reported (Levy, 1997; Warschauer, Turbee, & Roberts, 1996). Both self-access centers and CALL programs are regarded as effective in dealing with the diversity of language learners. They address the wide range of their proficiency levels, learning strategies, individual preferences, goals and previous language-learning background, as well as improve their language skills outside the classroom (Aston, 1993; Esch, 1996). Many organizations have invested a large amount of money in developing and maintaining these self-access and independent learning systems (O'Dell, 1992)

Recent studies on autonomous and independent language learning have indicated that students' more active involvement with respect to the learning process leads to successful understanding of the language (Aston, 1993; Dickinson, 1995). According to another study that focused on students' attitudes and beliefs about their own learning capacities, incorporating autonomous learning is more useful than class work alone (Jones, 1998). It has also been suggested that language learning is best facilitated by the development of students' responsibility to learn by themselves (Dickinson, 1987; Sturtridge, 1997). Students can take initiative and assume responsibility for their learning when they have some control over the learning process (Little, 1991). All of these studies indicate that self-access and independent learning approaches do not necessarily work well when students are offered too many opportunities to explore their various options outside the classroom (Galloway & O'Brien, 1998). In spite of this recent surge in academic interest, however, the effectiveness of independent approaches has not yet been fully examined. In particular, further examination needs to address the effectiveness of these approaches in meeting the needs for which they were developed.

Influence of Cultural Values

As stated in the previous section, there is a prevailing view on independent learning that the provision of a self-access mode of learning is "the practical solution to many language teaching problems, such as mixed-ability classes and students with different backgrounds and needs" (Sheerin, 1989, p. 7). However, in the context of specific cultures, there are some major constraints. In many educational systems in Asia, there is a general perception that the concepts of autonomy and individual learning approaches have come from the West and they are totally different from students' previous learning experiences (Ho & Crookall, 1995).

Japan is no exception. In Japanese traditional educational contexts, the teacher-centered methods are still highly valued. There is a power-distance dimension, defined by Hofstede (1991), in "the hierarchical, social, and educational structure, which originates from the tradition of Confucian morality" (Koike & Tanaka, 1995, p. 23). As in many other Asian countries, the instructor's role in Japan is to be in charge, take the initiative and "transmit knowledge to the student, who is the passive recipient of a product" (Kennedy, 1991, p. 63). It is evident that, in this less favorable context for autonomous language learning, the Japanese students are not capable of taking responsibility for their learning and, thus, they are neither independent nor self-motivated learners (Galloway & O'Brien, 1998). It is also important to note that there is "a major characteristic of the Japanese social psychology" (Koike & Tanaka, 1995, p. 23) in that students do not tend to express themselves strongly as individuals.

These culture-specific styles of language learning have resulted in some major limitations on implementing online independent learning. For example, this traditional teacher-directed educational mode tends to impose inflexible external goals and structures on the student. Even at a university level, students do not "see learning as exploration, but instead wait for the teacher to lead them" (Galloway & O'Brien, 1998, p. 5). It can be difficult for the student to understand that there are many different pathways to success in learning a language and, as a result, in an online environment they may feel disoriented by the maze of huge resources (Smith, 2003). In addition, the "cultural reticence of Japanese students to self-disclose" (Galloway & O'Brien, 1998, p. 5) makes it difficult for the instructor to incorporate an online project successfully into the classroom. It is difficult to understand students' different needs, interests and preferences for this new teaching approach if they do not self-disclose.

Although "teaching is an activity which is embedded within a set of culturally bound assumptions about teachers, teaching and learners" (Richards & Lockhart, 1994, p. 107), there is a lack of literature that focuses on the development of academic approaches sensitive to certain cultural traits in online education. To promote students' online learning strategies, the importance of the culturally determined nature of support systems should be emphasized, which, until now, has been given only peripheral attention in educational settings.

Lack of Consideration for Students' Needs and Preferences

Another problem of integrating independent language learning into the traditional language-learning environment is that program designers and resource administrators often fail to focus on how students learn with the resources available. Instead, people involved with these environments concentrate on high-tech equipment and materials rather than the learners that use these resources. They tend to introduce such resources without considering students' personal histories and needs (Little & Dam, 1998) or deciding how to connect independent language learning to an existing language program (Barnett, 1993). One of the reasons for this tendency is that the introduction of self-access approaches in educational institutions has often resulted from a nationwide academic re-organization of universities and their policies on publicity. Instructors are often required to fulfill the demands of the school curriculum, and the demands must take precedence over individual students' needs. In addition, as Jones (2001) points out, because of a lack of time, most instructors "only manage to recommend to their students CD-ROMS or Internet sites which are relevant to the syllabus, not having enough time to properly integrate CALL into their regular teaching, or help learners individually" (p. 366).

Without the proper supervision of instructors, many students are unlikely to know how to work effectively. It is often the case that students are not even sure about what to learn. In particular, for those who are not highly motivated to develop their language skills, simply providing a variety of language materials and high-level technology does not guarantee that they will use them to maximum effect (Gremmo & Riley, 1995; Kelly, 1996). Because of these factors, the resources provided in such independent learning settings are not used to their full potential and the facilities may become underused by students.

As Benson (1997) claims, for students who have not developed appropriate learning skills, the use of self-access resources does not necessarily promote their independence in language learning. As a result, independent study is not promoted as well as it should be. The instructor should understand that successful independent learning depends not only on the availability of a variety of excellent resources and high-level technology, but also on the provision of a wide range of professional support.

Previous Studies on Learner Support Systems

Support Tools

Dickinson (1992) argues that in order to develop students' autonomy and promote their independence in language learning, both "methodological preparation" and "psychological preparation" are important. "Methodological preparation" includes knowledge about the target language, whereas "psychological preparation" focuses on "changing attitudes and building the learner's confidence in his/her ability to learn independently" (p. 60). Research has identified some of the major psychological components of autonomy, such as the importance of students developing their capacity to set their learning objectives, designing appropriate study plans, reflecting on their own learning process and evaluating their progress in a variety of learning contexts (Little & Dam, 1998; Victori & Lockhart, 1995; Voller, 1997). These metacognitive strategies have been supported by a variety of means. For example, a number of researchers have been using powerful learner-directed support tools to focus these strategies, such as reflective written journals or diaries (Barnett & Jordan, 1991; Dam, 2000; Dickinson, 1993), portfolios (Nunes, 2004; Statman, 1998) and language-learning logs (Martyn, 1994). These descriptive devices for the reflection process are widely considered effective in keeping a record of the materials students have used and the language problems they have faced during the language activities. They are regarded highly beneficial in that they give an indication of a student's learning styles and preferences. Therefore, they are useful in helping students articulate what they have learned and in encouraging them to consider how they can approach the target language more effectively.

However, there are some drawbacks. Students feel that evaluating their learning process and making comments through writing journals or diaries is cumbersome and time-consuming. If students are monitored through diaries and portfolios, it is extremely difficult to identify students' goals, their execution of study plans, their engagement of self-monitoring and their modification of learning styles and beliefs. These methods do not automatically keep track of the ongoing process of students' language learning. In addition, implementing these methodologies in a large class, which is common in many non-Western educational settings, can be very challenging. There is a strong need to overcome these constraints and create more efficient support systems that can promote individual development of independent language learning.

Human Support Systems

Effective learning support in successful independent language-learning environments depends not only on the descriptive devices stated in the previous section, but also on human resources (Miller & Rogerson-Revell, 1993). In the self-access center, for example, various levels of human support structures have been widely used for the purpose of improving students' language abilities effectively and managing the center efficiently. Library staff or resources managers are usually responsible for the management and supervision of the center on a day-to-day basis, such as filing and entering stock details. They play an important role in classifying and indexing the self-access materials in a user-friendly way (Sheerin, 1989).

Students who use such open-learning, self-access facilities frequently require different kinds of human support; that is, professional advice and counseling, which goes beyond administrative and technical assistance. These people are language advisors or counselors who help students find out which materials and equipment are most appropriate for their language proficiency levels. They give students specific advice on their language learning skills and strategies or offer solutions to their technical problems on the spot. They are also required to deal with students' own academic problems, such as a lack of motivation, poor grades and so forth, and therefore, these face-to-face tutorials or advisory sessions are considered to be beneficial (Gremmo & Riley, 1995; Riley, 1997; Victori & Lockhart, 1995; Voller, 1997).

In online and CALL environments, some limitations can impede efforts towards incorporating such counseling services in the regular language course. For example, the range of counseling services, which often vary by language course, depends largely on the availability of adequate counseling staff. If the number of counseling staff is limited, counseling services become an additional workload for instructors. University budgets are under increasing pressure and, because of substantial financial liability in language teaching settings, there are usually few counselors available. Even if trained counselors were employed, they often have difficulties in dealing with students' different aptitudes and learning styles towards self-access language learning. It has now become necessary to consider the different kinds of counseling systems required to solve these problems.

The Study

Purpose of the Study

The primary aim of this study was to determine how students, who lack independent learning experience both online and in the traditional classroom, perceive a counseling system computer program called *Online Counselor*. The *Online Counselor* program was developed with the dual aims of enhancing Japanese students' English proficiency levels and promoting their self-access and independent language learning. This program assisted students in planning and organizing their learning, using appropriate resources and evaluating their work. *Online Counselor* was based on the five criteria for effective self-access language learning support systems that were proposed by Esch's study (1996): Choice, Flexibility, Adaptability/Modifiability, Reflectivity and Shareability. *Online Counselor* was set up on a server with a task database called *Resource Bank* for students to access as a record-keeping system of their learning progress as well as a support for independent language learning. The entire process followed throughout this system was designed to encourage students to take control over their study management.

The present study was also aimed at determining how students are encouraged to discover for themselves effective ways of learning that work for them and develop independent study skills with the aid of *Online Counselor*. The study focused on the following issues:

1. How is *Online Counselor* effective for students to observe the process of reflection indirectly and get them to understand different pathways to success in language learning?
2. How do the students who rate *Online Counselor* highly and those who do not rate it highly differ in perception of online independent language learning?

Answers to these questions will help instructors determine how to integrate online learning into their language course in a way that maximizes the specific student's learning opportunities.

Project and Participants

Seventy-four Japanese university students ages 18 to 20 years participated in this study. They were used to the traditional textbook-based, teacher-directed, language-learning approach taken in a large lecture-type classroom, where the teacher tended to adopt a predominantly transmission mode of instruction (Cooker & Torpey, 2004). In addition, the participants lacked a sense of value in their learning (Doyon, 2003). This was due to their prior learning experiences in secondary school, where memorization and rote learning had been emphasized. The students had no experience in online independent learning in or beyond the conventional classroom. Approximately one-half of the students were novice Internet users, but almost all of the students expressed great interest in undertaking the project *Online Counselor* was incorporated into. All of the students had learned English for 6 years and had attained a lower-intermediate level of proficiency. Although they were highly motivated to improve their English proficiency levels, they needed some support to find out how they could best improve their English skills outside the classroom.

The project was implemented in a half-term English reading course that the students were required to take as one of their compulsory classes. The reading course was designed to mainly focus on the understanding of a variety of texts, sentence structures and paragraph organization, as well as lexical patterns. The classes were all scheduled for 1-

1/2 hours each week. Before the project started, there was a period of guidance and adjustment offered by the instructor for the purpose of making students understand the nature and major benefits of the project. During the course, students were encouraged to try *Online Counselor* as part of their study in the reading course, in their own time and at their own pace, either on campus or at home. Students were also required to use *Online Counselor* only when they needed to do supplementary classroom activities or assignments individually.

System Structure

Resource Bank

The *Resource Bank* includes a large variety of English-language teaching tasks that cover a wide range of topics intended to enhance the quality of the students' language experience. These tasks are extensively used in English classrooms, and include, for example, open-ended tasks that do not have correct answers. The tasks include a variety of recently published English language teaching (ELT) photocopiable exercises, as well. Some of these materials have not been prepared solely for the sake of students' independent language learning. They are indexed according to targeted skills, such as grammar, reading and vocabulary; proficiency levels required, such as elementary and intermediate; and preferred learning styles, such as group and individual. Each task is separately color-coded and labeled. These easily recognizable groups and labels are designed to help students locate the materials and understand how the particular type of tasks, language exercises and activities they are advised to engage in are arranged. This multiplicity of tasks is designed to accommodate students' specific needs and make the most of their opportunities to study English by themselves. Focus is also placed on the quality and quantity of the tasks and the accompanying language instruction. The tasks provided by the program are presented in a well-ordered fashion, similar to that in which they might be taught by an instructor in the classroom.

Online Counselor

The *Online Counselor* computer program is written for the Microsoft Windows operating system. Having clear instructions, guiding symbols, navigation buttons and icons that have been adopted by most computer-based applications, this program enables students to easily access the tasks by themselves in any order in the area they wish to study. This user-friendly program can handle the incorporation of a variety of media formats: graphics, audio and video. All the explanations on the screen are given in Japanese, so students clearly understand how to use this system.

When first accessing the system by clicking on an *Online Counselor* icon from Windows, students come to the "Introduction" page, which shows them how to navigate through the program. This introductory page then opens to the second page, which requests the student's identification number and password (see Figure 1).

Figure 1. Introduction

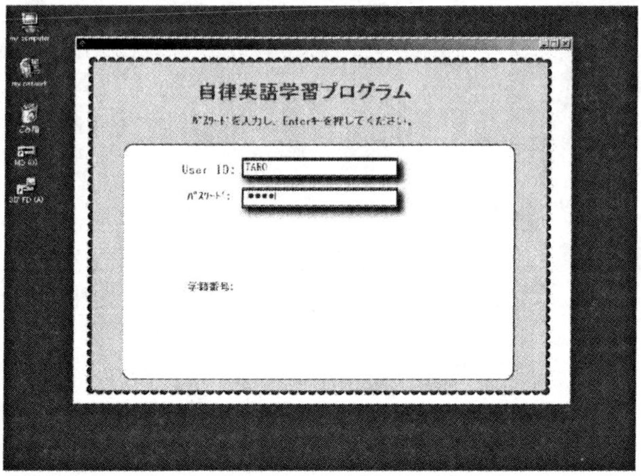

Students then come to the "Goal Setting" page by clicking on the icon from the second page (see Figure 2). From here, students are required to identify their short-term as well as long-term learning goals and select one of the goals from the list. These goals, which are specially formulated for students who participate in the project, include "taking part in overseas language programs in English-speaking countries," "preparation for standardized English examinations such as TOEFL/TOEIC," "completion of class assignments" and so forth. The system has great flexibility in that it allows students to reassess their goals for language learning and check whether the process they are following is continuing to meet their goals.

Figure 2. Goal setting

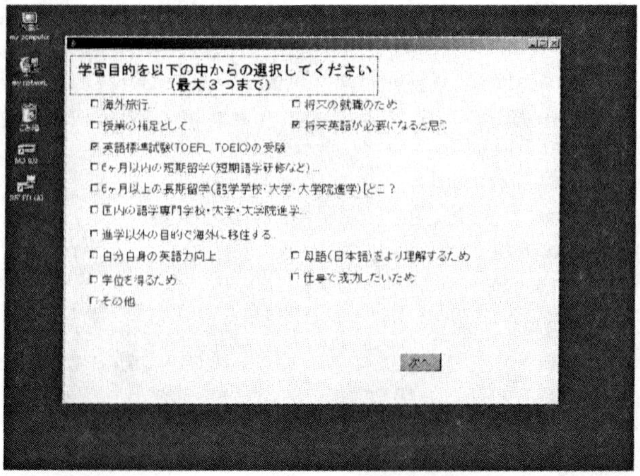

Figure 3. Skills

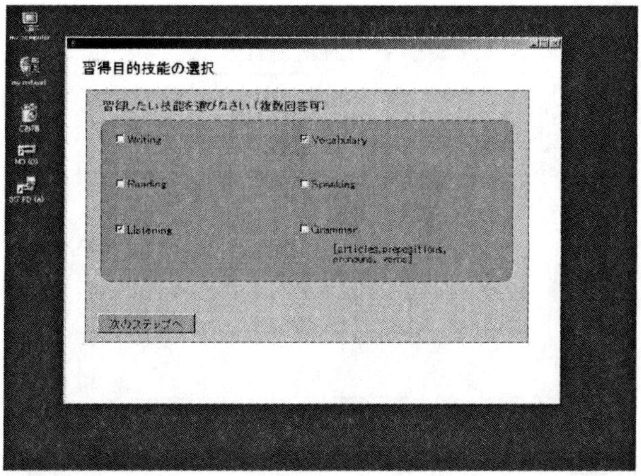

The "Goal Setting" page is followed by "Skills" (see Figure 3) and "Language Levels" (Figure 4) pages. This stage is designed to encourage students to identify their own learning problems and rate their present language proficiency levels. By this stage of their learning process, the system has helped students understand their strong and weak points and enabled them to plan the directions of their own learning. Students are then guided to select target skills from among listening, reading, writing, speaking, vocabulary and grammar.

Subsequently, by selecting one of the language skills and the students' language proficiency levels, students are guided to the "Selection of Tasks & Exercises" pages,

Figure 4. Language levels

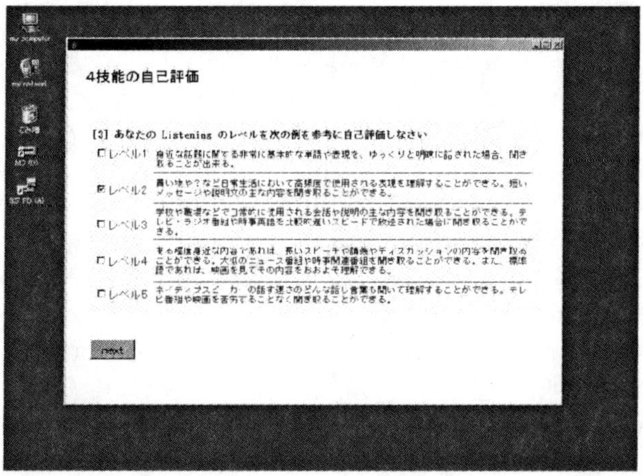

Figure 5. Selection of tasks and exercises

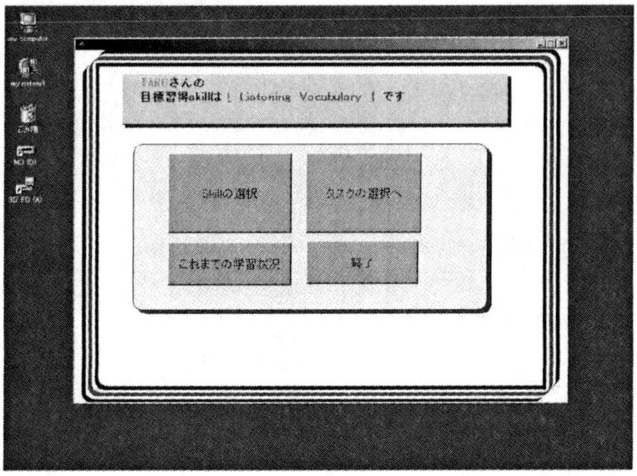

Figure 6. Self-assessment

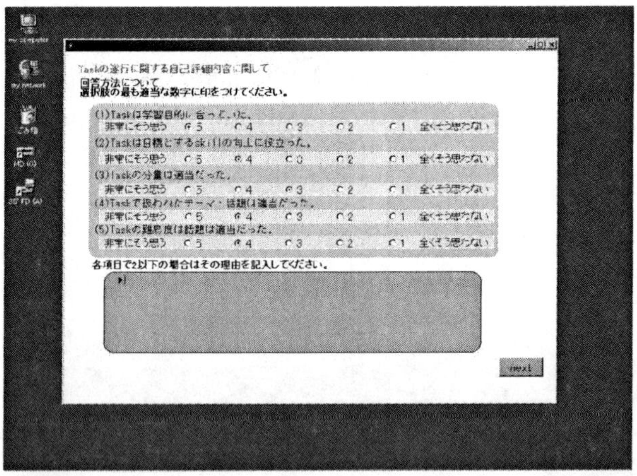

as illustrated in Figure 5. Here, students are provided with a table of tasks and exercises. Rows of buttons, labeled according to the type of task, enable students to access a particular task type. On the left side of the name is the number of the task being displayed. When the task is selected from the list, the page appears. The button at the bottom of the screen takes students back to the "Introduction" page.

When students have completed the task they selected, they can check with the answer key and follow-up suggestions. By clicking on the answer button, the answer is loaded automatically. The button next to the answer button takes students back to the "Selection of Tasks & Exercises" pages. That is, this program allows students to jump back and forth to any task at any time. Students have a considerable amount of freedom in selecting and doing the tasks repeatedly. Every time students work on this program, they are given an opportunity to determine whether the content of the tasks they have chosen is appropriate to their needs.

After each task has been completed, students are required to go on to the "Self-Assessment" page (see Figure 6). This final stage of the system provides students an opportunity to review what they have done and evaluate the learning process they have gone through. This retrospective process includes completion of a questionnaire concerning their level of satisfaction with the content and the usefulness of various features of the page layout. In addition to the closed questions, this page contains open-ended questions in which students are asked to write down their honest opinions on any aspect of this project; for example, the success or failure of their performances. This page also assists them in communicating with the instructor by writing the problems they have faced while using this system. For example, if a student finds it hard to improve his or her listening skills or struggles with increasing active vocabulary, the instructor provides the student with suggested strategies for dealing with these problems.

Once the task has been completed, each student can easily access his/her own records. This awareness-raising process gives students more detailed information on what skills and strategies have been successfully acquired and what needs further work. In other words, this evaluation process enables them to monitor their progress and helps them judge their own work more objectively. After completing the questionnaire, there are two options for students: exit from the program or continue to work on other tasks.

Procedure of Data Analysis

After the course had been completed, data was collected from students in the following ways.

1. A 28-item questionnaire was distributed to the students to gauge their opinions, attitudes and perceptions of the system, including the advantages and disadvantages of the system and the role of instructors. The questions were based on research conducted by Reid (1987), but some information was added to make it more relevant for Japanese participants. The students were required to answer the questions anonymously. A 10-point Likert Scale was used in the questionnaire, with 1 representing "strongly disagree" and 10 representing "highly agree." Some of the questions are shown in the Appendix. For students to fully understand the questions, the questionnaires were written in Japanese. To attain a mean response for each question, the responses were totaled and averaged. Standard deviation was then obtained, to examine statistically significant differences between students' responses. The data is presented in this chapter as mean ±SD. The questionnaire was also analyzed by using Spearman's correlation to determine correlations between responses and significant factors underlying their responses. Correlation is significant at the .01 level (2-tailed).

2. A follow-up interview was done to clarify students' individual comments on the possible benefits and problems of the project they had completed and their thoughts and feelings concerning the use of technology in learning. The interview was done in Japanese so they could fully explain even their abstract thoughts without any difficulties. The translation was then checked for accuracy.

The following section outlines results based on a summary of the responses.

Findings

The results of the questionnaire revealed the students' different perceptions of *Online Counselor*. The students had various goals and preferences for improving their English reading abilities and they differed from one another in their needs, interests and learning styles. Although their needs differed, a large proportion of students stated that they felt the project was valuable and found *Online Counselor* useful. The average (±SD) of this response was 8.21 (±1.66). In addition to the fact that many respondents highly valued flexible language-learning settings provided by this system, they felt that the system was effective in stimulating their motivation and capacity to control their own learning. The average (±SD) of this response was 6.58 (±1.42). The tasks were generally considered appropriate to their proficiency levels. As shown in Table 1, the correlation of .465 is significant between those who evaluated the effectiveness of *Online Counselor* and those who thought this system provided sufficient academic support to language learning. Those who highly rated this system as an educational tool to provide sufficient support to language learning had a weak correlation with those who rated this system

Table 1. Correlation between factors for effectiveness of Online Counselor

	Provide academic support to language learning	Effectiveness of *Online Counselor*	*Online Counselor* as an aid of regular language course
Provide academic support to language learning	1.00	-----	-----
Effectiveness of *Online Counselor*	.465**	1.00	-----
Online Counselor as an aid of regular language course	.370**	.609**	1.00

Note: **$p < .01$.

highly as part of their course, as well ($r = .370, p < .01$). In addition, there was a significant correlation between those who rated *Online Counselor* highly as part of their regular English course and those who rated the effectiveness of the system highly ($r = .609, p < .01$).

Qualitative data analysis also suggested that the students felt they would benefit from the system in that it assisted them in formulating a number of factors they had not been previously aware of. Some representative comments have been taken from the students' anonymous responses to the questionnaire.

> "This system was sufficiently simple to manage for people, like me, who had no previous online experience. Although the system was used as a complement to my reading class, I wanted to keep using this system after I completed this course. It's a totally new learning experience for me."

> "*Online Counselor* helped me identify the appropriate tasks and showed the type of language exercises and activities I should engage in. This system provided me with useful tips and strategies on how I could improve my language skills. One thing that I would like the instructor to consider is that more attention should be placed on engaging us in more active and realistic language tasks so that we are able to acquire the language more effectively outside the classroom."

> "I didn't realize how much I was conscious about my language learning until I worked on this project. I think the grammar exercises were a bit difficult for me. More detailed explanations of each task should be offered with the answer key."

> "In the beginning of the project, I couldn't see the point of using *Online Counselor* and I felt overwhelmed by the number of tasks. But after a few weeks, I began to like this system because it gave me the freedom to choose what I wanted to work on and enabled me to identify my learning process and personal learning strategies. The tasks were displayed in such a way as to facilitate individualized choice."

> "While I was engaging in different types of tasks with the help of *Online Counselor*, I thought setting my own learning goals was very important for me and realized that there were many different ways to achieve my learning goals. What I liked about this computer program was that it provided me with support for my language progress."

As is evident from the statements above, students were given responsibility for reflecting on their own learning process while determining their own needs. They did not have any difficulty in accepting the idea of autonomous language learning.

"While I was using this system, I was able to consider for myself questions regarding the kinds of language skills I needed to develop, the tasks that I should do, and the best way to start working on those tasks. *Online Counselor* provided help to answer these questions. I like this system because I don't have to wait for my instructor to tell me what to do next."

"I think that the mere accumulation of learning materials is not sufficient for effective learning in online learning. Unlike other programs in which the instructor gives us a compulsory appointment to attend an advisory session in his/her office, this system is effective in that I can ask my instructor questions through the system and this is given on an ad hoc basis."

The majority of students commented that they thought they could learn more systematically if they used *Online Counselor*. Also, as the comments indicate, through helping students identify their own language learning needs as well as strengths and weaknesses, this system raises their awareness of themselves as independent language learners.

Table 2 shows that there was a weak correlation between those who highly valued this system as part of their regular language course and those who preferred neither guidance nor supervision provided by the instructor ($r = .362$, $p < .01$).

As shown in Table 3, the correlation of .550 was significant between those who did not value the effectiveness of *Online Counselor* at all and those who needed constant step-by-step instructions offered by the instructor. In addition, there was a weak correlation between those who had previous online experience and those who did not value the effectiveness of *Online Counselor* at all ($r = .387$, $p < .01$). There was no correlation between those who had previous online experience and those who needed constant step-by-step instructions offered by the instructor.

Table 2. Correlation between factors for supervision and instruction

	Online Counselor as an aid of regular language course	No need for guidance or supervision by the instructor
Online Counselor as an aid of regular language course	1.00	----
No need for guidance or supervision by the instructor	.362**	1.00

*Notes: Correlation Matrix (N = 74), **p < .01*

Table 3. Correlation between factors for perceptions of Online Counselor

	Need for constant instructions by the teacher	*Online Counselor* not valued	Previous online experience
Need for constant instructions by the teacher	1.00	-----	-----
Online Counselor not valued	.550**	1.00	-----
Previous online experience	.049**	.387**	1.00

*Correlation Matrix (N = 74), **p < .01.*

Some students stated that they needed educational and technical assistance during the project rather than being left alone:

> "I found it difficult to work on this computer system. I needed step-by-step instructions, general advice on my language learning at different levels, and ideas for developing specific linguistic skills at all times."

> "Sometimes I had problems in finding how best to utilize this system and felt I was left alone in my own learning. I think this system is a good communication tool, because I don't have to talk with my instructor in the classroom. But, instead ofa computer system, I need someone who can assist me in doing the tasks on any point in my study."

> "I like this system because I was able to choose my own materials. But I don't like the fact that my instructor was not available to provide help and advice while I was working on the tasks. I need more direct teacher contact time to benefit fully from the system."

Discussion of Findings

Personalized Pathways

During the project, the students' computer anxiety (Benson, 1994) and resistance to the idea of independent learning were anticipated. However, the comments given by the students indicate that, overall, they were satisfied with their independent study using *Online Counselor*, which was designed based on Esch's (1996) five criteria defined as important features of effective support systems. Although the number of participants in this study was relatively small, the results suggest that application of *Online Counselor* can be educationally beneficial to students in two major ways.

First, it can be asserted that, despite the fact that many students had extremely limited computer competency with no previous experience of independent learning, *Online Counselor* stimulated their motivation and enhanced their capacity to take charge of their own learning. One major innovative feature of this computer system is the personalized pathways tailored to each student's goals. At the beginning of the project, a substantial number of students were unaware of their own language problems and proficiency levels. However, with assistance from the pathways, as time went by, these students seemed to gradually gain the ability to diagnose realistically their own problems and select appropriate resources.

Students' comments have shown that another advantage of *Online Counselor* is that by using the system, which promotes exploration, revision and control over learning, students have developed self-awareness and independence in their language learning. The page layout and buttons offered by the system were well signposted so that students were guided through the diverse menus, having a considerable amount of freedom in performing tasks without suffering from information overload. The system also deals with individual students' requests and issues, ranging from everyday problems regarding language learning to individual students' study interest. The multiplicity of support systems that *Online Counselor* can perform is particularly beneficial for students. Unlike various computer programs that only monitor students' attendance and keep records of which materials have been accessed, *Online Counselor* acts as a real language advisor. It is also important to note that this system is financially viable, since it is a potential tool in coping with a wide range of users' needs and attitudes, even with minimal levels of staffing and a limited budget.

Self-Evaluation Process

Among Esch's five criteria (1996), Reflectivity, offered by the last self-evaluation process of *Online Counselor*, forms an integral part of this system, and works in addition to Flexibility and Adaptability/Modifiability, which were discussed in the previous section. As Wenden (1995) claims, this self-evaluation process encourages students to focus on whether the tasks they have completed and the skills they have practiced through the program met the goals they had set for themselves. In addition, the records accessible to students help them consider not only what and how they have learned but also how they will be able to approach the target language learning more effectively (Dickinson, 1987). As constructive feedback from the students suggests, communication between students and the instructor through the evaluation pages also encourages them to "identify and utilize their preferred learning styles" (Reid, 1987, p. 101). The students' opinions confirm the idea that this dialog enables students to develop their own learning strategies, enhance their self-confidence and, therefore, develop their autonomy in language learning. As stated in the comments made by students, some students are more likely to prefer expressing personal opinions via writing rather than in an open-class atmosphere. Since Japanese students in general do not voluntarily ask questions in front of other students (Smith, 2003), this exchange between students and the instructor would provide vital individual consultation (Jones, 1995).

Another important finding of this study is that the information about the students' perceptions and critical evaluation of their entire online experience gives many advantages to the instructor, as well. This data retrieved from the self-evaluation sections helps the instructor understand the basic ideas of how students interact with the system. It includes students' understanding about the effectiveness of certain learning strategies and their individual attitudes towards specific aspects of language learning. Also, some students had opinions to offer to the instructor on what they thought they needed in terms of tasks and teaching methodologies. These resources have a valuable contribution to the greater success of both technology-based and traditional classroom teaching.

Role of Instructors

The findings of the present study indicate that some of the students did not prefer being guided and supervised by the instructor, even though they wanted this system fully integrated into their regular language classroom. Comments made by the students suggest that those who valued *Online Counselor* did not rely on the instructor's guidance, but rather preferred the flexibility in choosing what and how they wanted to improve their reading skills. In addition, the results show that those who had some previous online experience tended not to value *Online Counselor*, suggesting that this computer system is more likely to be suitable for computer novices. The data seem to imply that, for computer novices, this system is likely to be an effective substitution for the instructor.

The results of the questionnaire also provide valuable insights into how instructors should implement online language programs. Some students, who stated that they did not value *Online Counselor*, preferred being guided and supervised by the instructor, and it should be clear that the instructor's constant guidance and helpful advice to maintain students' motivation in online learning is a compelling need for some students. Other students, no matter how much online experience they had, seemed to need support to some extent, whether it was on-site support from the computer system or human support for directing their independent study. This is in accordance with the findings of Jones (2001), that the effectiveness of any technology-based language learning largely depends on close supervision and support by the instructor, regardless of educational context.

It is also important to note that some students expected to be spoon-fed and perceived instructors as those who should give step-by-step detailed instructions on how to tackle the tasks and improve their target skills. These students seem to prefer traditional teacher-centered methods, which are taken directly from their cultural contexts and transplanted to an online learning environment, so that the relic from the traditional authoritarian view of the instructor's role is still alive even in the online environment. As is evident from these various comments, students expected *Online Counselor* to be a system combining many roles, and the degree of support needed varied enormously from student to student. This implies that some might already have a set of skills and knowledge essential to develop independent learning strategies. Different levels of instructor support are particularly important if online learning is intended to play a major role in the whole language curriculum.

Implications and Future Modifications

Leadership

Although there is a widespread belief that Asian students are passive figures who lack critical thinking skills, Littlewood's recent study on Asian students' beliefs and attitudes towards language learning (2000) indicates that many students do not see the effectiveness of traditional methods of teaching, where instructors are the transmitters of knowledge and students are being spoon-fed by them. He suggests that these students have potential abilities to express themselves and a strong desire to "explore knowledge themselves and find their own answers" (p. 34). Another finding also casts doubt on the stereotypical image of passive Asian students and suggests that giving an opportunity to take responsibility for their own learning "enables them to develop the certain knowledge, skills and attitudes which are characteristic of learner autonomy" (Ho & Crookall, 1995, p. 242). The results of the present study also support these research findings. With the aid of *Online Counselor*, students can be trained to discover what works and what does not work for their own language learning and express their distinct opinions about both advantages and disadvantages of the project without unnecessary hesitation. It would be reasonable to assume that if *Online Counselor* was introduced in the classroom, even students who are accustomed to teacher-directed approaches would gradually take a more active role in directing their own study and achieve greater success in their language learning.

Cotterall (1995) claims that innovation and change are often motivated by external factors and the instructor tends to subvert the goal of developing students' autonomy by excluding them from planning and evaluating language programs. As is evident from the results of the present study, however, students' practical ideas and recommendations are helpful in improving their classes, and they will substantially contribute to the development of online language learning. It is important to acknowledge that students, who are the most important resources at all levels of an innovation process, need to be actively encouraged to acquire a sense of "leadership" (Carey & Dabor, 1995). Although it is difficult to change the existing system where the idea of self-access and independent learning is at variance with the local culture, this "leadership" provides students with "a sense of vision and clarifies organizational objectives" (Carey & Dabor, 1995, p. 38). A recent study that focuses on the role of student contribution to the development of independent learning as a part of their language program suggests that students' active cooperation with instructors through the management of innovation is an essential component for any type of autonomous learning (Malcolm, 2004). It is still unknown to what extent instructors' and students' collaborative activities successfully promote students' independence in a certain educational context, even if students are well motivated to do so. However, it is vitally important to provide students, who are "active agents of change" (Benson, 2000, p. 117), with an opportunity to take a leadership role in evaluating critically and contributing to make some positive changes in the process of innovation.

Teacher Autonomy and Development

The findings from the present study suggest that various teaching approaches adopted by the instructor are fundamental to the success or failure in the implementation of online language learning. Although these approaches and aims of innovation should be consistent, the instructor's capacity to manage this innovation is often constrained by a range of factors (Benson, 2000), and these factors make it difficult to achieve innovation in the long term. For example, there often exists a gap between decisions made by the people who initiate innovation and the teaching policy formulated by instructors. It is now a prevailing view that the administrative top-down approach to innovation results in an instructor's reluctance and lack of enthusiasm for learning new skills and various teaching strategies (Vieira, 2003). These instructors are, for example, more likely to implement online programs only as a panacea for various problems they have in the classroom. It is also often the case that, when instructors are required to change their methodologies, some instructors are uncertain to what extent new methodologies can be successfully introduced in the existing classroom, and are more concerned about anticipated failure. Other teachers, having resistance to change, insist that the traditional methods they employ have been successfully maintained and apply only normative approaches to teaching (Osburne, 1989; Vieira, 1999).

To address these problems and provide instructors with a sense of ownership of their new teaching approaches, Thavenius (1999) focuses on the importance of developing teacher autonomy, which she defines as the instructor's "ability and willingness to help learners take responsibility for their own learning" (p.160). McGrath (2000), arguing that not only students but also instructors have "insecurity, uncertainty and discomfort" in the practice of autonomy, points out the importance of instructors' "self-directed professional development" and their "freedom from control by others" (p.103). Little (1995) also claims that development of learner autonomy depends entirely on the development of teacher autonomy, and suggests that "learner autonomy and teacher autonomy are interdependent" (p. 179). Benson (2001), arguing the importance of instructors' own experience of autonomy as learners, points out that teacher autonomy should be developed based on the similar principles to the development of learner autonomy.

Wallace (1991) claims that instructors are more likely to teach students based on their "received knowledge," such as "research findings, theories and skills" (p. 15). This knowledge includes expectations based on cultural perceptions or an institutional basis of how education is supposed to proceed. For instructors to maintain and improve the quality of teaching, they should base their practices on "experimental knowledge," which is defined as "knowledge in action" (Wallace, 1991, p. 13). This knowledge encourages reflection and helps them "make judgments and take action in the classroom without articulating the underlying rules, criteria or procedures they know work" (Kennedy & Edwards, 1996, p.78). An important consideration for the management of any educational change is the introduction of teacher development activities in their regular teaching routines (Wenden, 1991). Such activities should focus on both "received knowledge" and "knowledge in action." In addition, there has been a great deal of discussion about the need for instructors to introduce reflective practices as "knowledge in action" development (Lamb, 2000; Richards & Nunan, 1990; Riley, 1997). As data retrieved from the project using *Online Counselor* suggests, surveys, questionnaires, peer observation and action research are effective tools for anyone who intends to implement successful training for online teaching (Richards & Lockhart, 1994). Such tools help instructors reflect critically and aid them in becoming more sensitized to their teaching methodologies. These teacher development activities encourage transition from the confines of the classroom to the reality of experiencing independent learning, which benefits both instructors and students. Such activities are an essential component for the future design of successful online language learning.

Conclusion

It can be concluded that *Online Counselor* caters for individual needs and preferences and helps students make the right choices to suit their personal learning styles. Ongoing optimum support can be achieved and learner autonomy can be facilitated through a student's learning process. The results of this study provided valuable insights into what instructors should do when intending to set up online independent learning programs tailored to students' needs and interests. The results also suggested that the relationship between a student's inner process of learning and an effective online system should be investigated in future research. In certain educational settings, independent language learning is still a relatively new development, and the transition from student dependence to independence is not likely to be an easy process. Since it is still unknown to what extent online activities successfully promote students' language skills, various possibilities for the effective implementation of online approaches, such as teacher development, should be fully explored. It is hoped that this system will help students acknowledge the benefits they can derive from online environments and contribute to the development of a positive attitude and initiative with regards to language learning.

Acknowledgment

I am extremely grateful to Yoshihiro Hirata for his tremendous help in developing *Online Counselor* and his valuable comments about the present project.

References

Aston, G. (1993). The learner's contribution to the self-access center. *ELT Journal*, *47*(3), 219-227.

Barnett, L. (1993). Teacher off: Computer technology, guidance and self-access. *System*, *21*(3), 295-304.

Barnett, L., & Jordan, G. (1991). Self-access facilities: What are they for? *ELT Journal*, *45*(4), 305-312.

Benson, P. (1994). Self-access systems as information systems: Questions of ideology and control. In D. Gardner & L. Miller (Eds.), *Directions in self-access language learning* (pp. 3-12). Hong Kong: Hong Kong University Press.

Benson, P. (1997). The philosophy and politics of learner autonomy. In P. Benson & P. Voller (Eds.), *Autonomy & independence in language learning* (pp.18-34). London: Longman.

Benson, P. (2000). Autonomy as a learners' and teachings' right. In B. Sinclair, I. McGrath, & T. Lamb (Eds.), *Learner autonomy, teacher autonomy: Future directions* (pp. 111-117). London: Longman.

Benson, P. (2001). *Teaching and researching autonomy in language learning*. Harlow: Longman.

Carey, J., & Dabor, M. (1995). Management education: An approach to improve English language teaching. *ELT Journal*, *49*(1), 37-43.

Cooker, L., & Torpey, M. (2004). From the classroom to the self-access centre: A chronicle of learner-centred curriculum development. *The Language Teacher*, *28*(6), 11-16.

Cotterall, S. (1995). Developing a course strategy for learner autonomy. *ELT Journal*, *49*(3), 219-227.

Dam, L. (2000). Why focus on learning rather than teaching? From theory to practice. In D. Little, L. Dam, & J. Timmer (Eds.), *Focus on learning rather than teaching: Why and how?* (pp. 18-37). Dublin: CLCS.

Dickinson, L. (1987). *Self-instruction in language learning*. Cambridge: Cambridge University Press.

Dickinson, L. (1992). *Learner autonomy 2: Learner training for language learning*. Dublin: Authentik.

Dickinson, L. (1993). Talking shop: Aspects of autonomous learning. *ELT Journal*, *47*(4), 330-336.

Dickinson, L. (1995). Autonomy and motivation. A literature review. *System*, *23*(2), 165-174.

Doyon, P. (2003). Enhancing value perception in the Japanese EFL classroom. *Asian EFL Journal*. Retrieved March 28, 2004, from www.asian-efl-journal.com/march_03_ind.html

Esch, E. (1996). Promoting learner autonomy: Criteria for the selection of appropriate methods. In R. Pemberton, E. S. L. Li, W. W. F. Or, & H. D. Pierson (Eds.), *Taking control: Autonomy in language learning* (pp. 35-48). Hong Kong: Hong Kong University Press.

Galloway, I., & O'Brien, D. (1998). Learning online: Choosing the best computer-mediated communication activities. *The Language Teacher*, *22*(2), 7-9.

Gardner, D., & Miller, L. (1999). *Establishing self-access: From theory to practice*. Cambridge: Cambridge University Press.

Gremmo, M. J., & Riley, P. (1995). Autonomy, self-direction and self-access in language teaching and learning: The history of an idea. *System*, *23*(2), 151-164.

Ho, J., & Crookall, D. (1995). Breaking with Chinese culture traditions: Learner autonomy in English language teaching. *System*, *23*(2), 235-243.

Hofstede, G. (1991). *Cultures and organisations*. London: McGraw-Hill.

Jones, F. R. (1998). Self-instruction and success: A learner-profile study. *Applied Linguistics*, *19*(3), 378-406.

Jones, J. F. (1995). Self-access and culture: Retreating from autonomy. *ELT Journal*, *49*(3), 228-234.

Jones, J.F. (2001). CALL and the responsibilities of teachers and administrators. *ELT Journal*, *55*(4), 360-367.

Kelly, R. (1996). Language counselling for learner autonomy: The skilled helper in self-access language learning. In R. Pemberton, E. S. L. Li, W. W. F. Or, & H. D. Pierson (Eds.), *Taking control: Autonomy in language learning* (pp. 93-112). Hong Kong: Hong Kong University Press.

Kennedy, J. (1991). Perspectives on cultural and individual determinants of teaching style. *RELC Journal*, *22*(2), 61-78.

Kennedy, J., & Edwards, D. (1996). *ELT management*. Birmingham: Birmingham University Press.

Koike, I., & Tanaka, H. (1995). English in foreign language education policy in Japan: Towards the twenty-first century. *World Englishes*, *14*(1), 13-25.

Lamb, T. (2000). Finding a voice: Learner autonomy and teacher education in an urban context. In B. Sinclair, I. McGrath, & T. Lamb (Eds.), *Learner autonomy, teacher autonomy: Future directions* (pp. 118-127). London: Longman.

Levy, M. (1997). *Computer-assisted language learning: Context and conceptualization*. Oxford: Clarendon Press.

Little, D. (1991). *Learner autonomy 1: Definitions, issues and problems*. Dublin: Authentik.

Little, D. (1995). Learning as dialogue: The dependence of learner autonomy on teacher autonomy. *System*, *23*(2), 175-181.

Little, D., & Dam, L. (1998). Learner autonomy: What and why? *The Language Teacher*, *22*(10), 7-8.

Littlewood, W. (1997). Self-access: Why do we want it and what can it do? In P. Benson & P. Voller (Eds.), *Autonomy & independence in language learning* (pp.79-91). London: Longman.

Littlewood, W. (2000). Do Asian students really want to listen and obey? *ELT Journal*, *54*(1), 31-36.

Malcolm, D. (2004). Why should learners contribute to the self-access centre? *ELT Journal*, *58*(4), 346-354.

Martyn, D. (1994). Self-access logs: Promoting self-directed learning. In D. Gardner & L. Miller (Eds.), *Directions in self-access language learning* (pp. 65-77). Hong Kong: Hong Kong University Press.

McGrath, I. (2000). Teacher autonomy. In B. Sinclair, I. McGrath, & T. Lamb (Eds.), *Learner autonomy, teacher autonomy: Future directions* (pp. 100-110). London: Longman.

Miller, L., & Rogerson-Revell, P. (1993). Self-access system. *ELT Journal*, *27*(3), 228-233.

Nunes, A. (2004). Portfolios in the EFL classroom: Disclosing an informed practice. *ELT Journal*, *58*(4), 327-335.

O'Dell, F. (1992). Helping teachers to use a self-access centre to its full potential. *ELT Journal*, *46*(2), 153-159.

Osburne, A. G. (1989). Situational leadership and teacher education. *System*, *17*(3), 409-420.

Reid, J. M. (1987). The learning style preferences of ESL students. *TESOL Quarterly*, *21*(1), 87-111.

Richards, J. C., & Lockhart, C. (1994). *Reflective teacher in second language classroom.* Cambridge: Cambridge University Press.

Richards, J. C., & Nunan, D. (1990). *Second language teacher education.* Cambridge: Cambridge University Press.

Riley, P. (1997). The guru and the conjurer: Aspects of counseling for self-access. In P. Benson & P. Voller (Eds.), *Autonomy & independence in language learning* (pp.114-131). London: Longman.

Sheerin, S. (1989). *Self-access.* Oxford: Oxford University Press.

Sheerin, S. (1997). An exploration of the relationship between self-access and independent learning. In P. Benson & P. Voller (Eds.), *Autonomy & independence in language learning* (pp. 54-65). London: Longman.

Smith, R. C. (2003). Pedagogy for autonomy as (becoming-) appropriate methodology. In D. Palfreyman & R. C. Smith (Eds.), *Learner autonomy across cultures. Language education perspective* (pp.129-146). New York: Palgrave Macmillan.

Statman, S. (1998). Tester and testee: Two sides of different coins. *System*, *26*(2), 195-204.

Sturtridge, G. (1997). Teaching and language learning in self-access centres: Changing roles? In P. Benson & P. Voller (Eds.), *Autonomy & independence in language learning* (pp. 54-65). London: Longman.

Thavenius, C. (1999). Teacher autonomy for learner autonomy. In D. Crabbe & S. Cotterall (Eds.), *Learner autonomy in language learning: Defining the field and effecting change* (pp. 159-163). Frankfurt: Peter Lang.

Victori, M., & Lockhart, W. (1995). Enhancing metacognition in self-directed language learning. *System, 23*(2), 223-234.

Vieira, F. (1999). Pedagogy for autonomy: Teacher development and pedagogical experimentation – an in-service teacher training project. In D. Crabbe & S. Cotterall (Eds.), *Learner autonomy in language learning: Defining the field and effecting change* (pp.149-163). Frankfurt: Peter Lang.

Vieira, F. (2003). Addressing constraints on autonomy in school contexts: Lessons from working with teachers. In D. Palfreyman & R. C. Smith (Eds.), *Learner autonomy across cultures. Language education perspective* (pp.129-146). New York: Palgrave Macmillan.

Voller, P. (1997). Does the teacher have a role in autonomous language learning? In P. Benson & P. Voller (Eds.), *Autonomy & independence in language learning* (pp. 98-113). London: Longman.

Wallace, M.J. (1991). *Training foreign language teachers*. Cambridge: Cambridge University Press.

Warschauer, M., Turbee, L., & Roberts, B. (1996). Computer learning networks and student empowerment. *System, 24*(1), 1-4.

Wenden, A. (1991). *Learner strategies for learner autonomy*. Englewood Cliffs, NJ: Prentice Hall.

Wenden, A. (1995). Learner training in context: A knowledge-based approach. *System, 23*(2), 183-193.

Appendix

Online Counselor Evaluation Questionnaire

This questionnaire has been designed to help you express your opinions and perceptions concerning the online language learning you have just completed. Read each statement below and rate it according to the scale, and then write the number in the brackets.

Strongly disagree 1 — 2 — 3 — 4 — 5 — 6 — 7 — 8 — 9 — 10 Strongly agree

- *Online Counselor* was quite effective in improving English language skills.[ ]
- The project was valuable for me and I found *Online Counselor* useful. [ ]
- The system provided sufficient academic support to my language learning. [ ]
- The system was effective because I could work on the tasks in my own time and at my own pace. [ ]
- The system was useful because I could engage in the project both on campus and at home. [ ]
- I liked the system because I could give the instructor my opinions and make a request. [ ]
- The system was effective because there were a wide variety of tasks to choose from. [ ]
- The record-keeping system for the students' evaluation and learning process was very useful. [ ]
- I needed step-by-step detailed instructions given by the instructor when I used this system [ ]
- The system helped stimulate my motivation and capacity to control my own learning. [ ]
- I would like to use *Online Counselor* as part of my English study at school. [ ]

Chapter XIV

Language Learning and User-Centered Design: The Development of the Electronic European Language Portfolio

Charalambos Vrasidas, CARDET - Intercollege, Cyprus

Elena Landone, University of Milan, Italy

Niki Christodoulou, Intercollege, Cyprus

Michalinos Zembylas, CARDET - Intercollege, Cyprus

Abstract

This chapter will discuss the rationale behind the development of the electronic version of the European Language Portfolio (ELP), its technological and pedagogical aspects, and its advantages over print-based counterparts. The electronic European Language Portfolio (e-ELP) has been developed following a user-centered design (UCD) framework. This framework will be discussed in detail. The e-ELP is part of a Minerva project funded by the European Union (EU) with the main goal to adapt the paper-based ELP in an electronic format. Some ELPs have already been validated and edited in a hardcopy format. These hardcopy editions present several limitations, such as maintenance and long-term updating. In this chapter, emphasis will be placed on discussing the affordances of the electronic environment in supporting language teaching and learning and the user-centered approach in developing the prototype.

Introduction

Emerging technologies and their affordances require that educators rethink their fundamental assumptions about teaching and learning (Vrasidas & Glass, 2002). Technology affordances played a major role in reshaping teaching and assessment and have revolutionized the use of portfolios as a pedagogical, reflective and assessment tool (Mason, 2002; Vrasidas & Glass, 2004). International organizations, such as the International Society for Technology in Education, UNESCO and the European Commission (EC), have established guides, plans and standards for the use of technology in education and training. In light of these developments brought about by rapid technology growth and use in education, the digital e-ELP was developed to examine the ways in which technology can support reflection and language learning.

The Common European Framework of Reference for Languages underlines the need for the European citizen to have a personal document describing all his or her linguistic experiences and certifications. This need for a language passport, called European Language Portfolio - ELP (see http://culture2.coe.int/portfolio) has been recognized by many European institutions that have already accepted the suggestions put forward by the Framework regarding the ELP. The EC encourages individual institutions to adapt the ELP to their specific needs and to submit their new ELP to a validation procedure to verify its conformity to the requested format. Several ELPs have already been validated and published in hardcopy format. Nevertheless, these existing hardcopy editions present several limitations (e.g., difficulties in life-long updating and maintenance). One of the main objectives of this project is to overcome such barriers and take advantage of the affordances of technology in serving the needs of language teachers and students alike.

Definition and Description of the ELP

The ELP is part of the EC language policies and suggestions to support European mobility and cohesion among its citizens through the development of multilingualism and multiculturalism. The ELP aims at helping European citizens understand and appreciate the cultural and linguistic richness of Europe. Furthermore, the ELP is an EC initiative to support life-long learning as a way of responding to economic, social and cultural changes in Europe. It is a personal document in which the owner can record and reflect on his or her scholastic and non-scholastic language learning and cultural experiences. Its aims include:

1. To motivate learners to improve their ability to communicate in different languages and to enhance their multilingual and intercultural experience.
2. To encourage learners to reflect on their objectives and ways of achieving autonomous language learning.
3. To provide a record of the linguistic and cultural skills of learners.

4. To document, report and attest the learners' competence in a detailed and internationally comparable manner.

To fulfill these functions, the ELP consists of three parts:

1. A *language passport,* a document where the owner/learner can describe his or her language competence according to common criteria accepted throughout Europe. This passport can serve as a complement to customary certificates.
2. A *biographical note (biography)* describing the owner's experiences in each language. It is designed to guide the learner in planning and assessing progress.
3. A *dossier*, where examples of personal work can be kept to illustrate one's language competence.

The ELP, being a self-assessment tool, is meant to help the user report and assess his or her language learning. For this reason, it is strongly linked to the *Common European Framework of Reference for Languages: Learning, Teaching, Assessment* and its common reference levels of competence (Christ et al., 1997).

Description of the e-ELP and Comparison with the Paper-Based ELP

The e-ELP is currently being developed according to the EC-defined standard format, following all the detailed parameters given by the *Guide for Developers*. It consists of a standalone application that the user can download from the Web and use to develop his or her personal portfolio, which will demonstrate the user's language proficiencies. Figure 1 illustrates the opening screen of the prototype e-ELP. From this screen, users can choose to modify their personal data, learn about the ELP, begin developing their own portfolio and export the portfolio for sharing with others.

More specifically, the system has the following technical aspects:

1. *A global structure.* The global structure of the e-ELP is a group of files of different type (multimedia, text file, etc.) grouped in a folder and indexed in a file *manifest* (see the last IMS specifications on e-learning contents standards). The manifest declares the metadata and descriptors of the portfolio, and describes and relates the folder's resources. The preferred language to define the manifest is XML/RDF. The manifest structure follows open-source (and not proprietary) standards and its protocols allow for further cooperative developments.
2. *A standalone application.* We developed standalone software for the authoring of the portfolio because the final output will be for the students' personal use. This

Figure 1. Opening screen of the e-ELP prototype

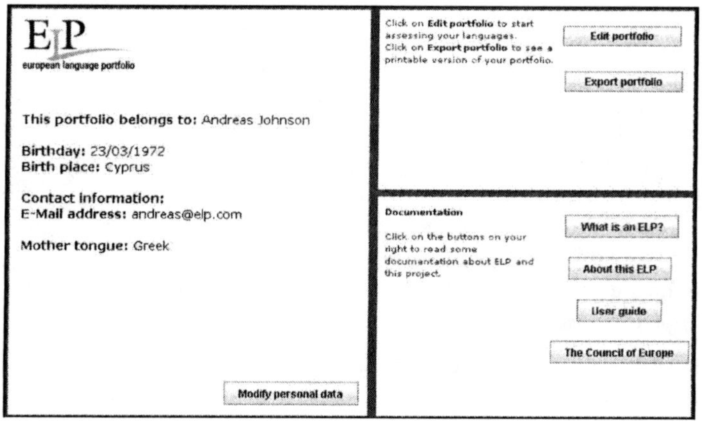

allows for portfolio creation and updating, and satisfies the need of operating system interoperability as well as the necessity of user-friendliness and usability.

3. *Web-based system.* The software for the management, storing and maintenance of the e-ELP is a Web-based system on an open-source platform. It has functions such as user authentication, portfolio compilation, portfolio updating, portfolio transfer and statistics data regarding use of and access to the site. It will be distributed under general public license (GPL) to allow access to the system code and allow for further modifications and updates.
4. *Multilingualism.* In accordance with the instructions of the ELP *Guide for Developers*, the e-ELP was developed in multiple languages, including Spanish, English, Italian and Greek.

The specific objectives of this project in developing the e-ELP are to:

1. support language learning through the use of technology;
2. take advantage of what technology can do to innovate and propose a new way for working with language portfolios;
3. produce an ELP specific for university language students in view of their entrance into the EU job market;
4. make the ELP available in English, Italian, Greek, Spanish and Swedish; and
5. give institutions a tool to monitor the students' language-learning process.

The educational context of the e-ELP is comprised of higher-education institutions (mainly, universities), and the subjects involved are adult students and teachers of second and foreign languages. Nevertheless, the potential target group is wider, since the overall aim is to put the e-ELP at the disposal of every educational institution willing to use it. As the ELP improves the student's self-consciousness of the progressive development of his or her learning, it can also contribute to language evaluation at K-12 level.

An important aspect of this project is that the ELP, being the European "flexible standard" for language portfolio, permits an alignment to the language curricula that not all language portfolios guarantee (Gibson & Barrett, 2002; Mariani, 2001a, 2001b; Orsini-Jones, n.d.). The ELP reports language learning in a transparent and reliable way, without penalizing the student's creativity in describing his or her personal language and cultural experience. In its electronic version, it will require students and teachers to also improve their technological literacy.

Once the user chooses to "edit" the portfolio, a screen is presented prompting the user to select the language in which to complete the work. Once the language is selected, the user enters the portfolio that is divided in four parts:

1. Language competence
2. Language experiences
3. Learning competence
4. Objectives and priorities

These four parts were chosen instead of the three parts that are components of the paper-based ELP (biography, passport, dossier). Technology helped us innovate in this aspect and create a more comprehensible structure through which users can move from one part to the next with the click of a mouse and, in the process, see the connections between the various components of the portfolio. The users can develop, update and maintain their portfolio individually. Once the portfolio is updated, the user can choose to publish or share parts or the whole portfolio with others electronically, via the Web or after printing. Table 1 presents a comparison of the structure of the paper-based ELP with the e-ELP structure. Note that all parts of the paper-based coded (P1, P2, etc.) are matched with the appropriate sections of the e-ELP.

As already discussed, the *passport* is a record of language skills, qualifications and experiences that provides an overview of the user's proficiency in all the languages he or she knows. It allows for a global self-assessment of the student language skills, summarizes the owner's language and intercultural experiences, and records formal qualifications. This agile structure and layout is identical in all editions of the ELP.

In addition to the reporting function, the ELP has the fundamental pedagogical function to motivate learners in improving their ability to communicate in different languages and to enhance their plurilingual and intercultural experiences through reflection. The tools used to fulfill this pedagogical function are the biography and the dossier.

The *biography* reports the student's learning history in great detail, complementing the information presented in the passport. It also facilitates the reflection on the past, current and future language-learning progress and enables the user to set goals for his or her future learning activities and cultural experiences. This section is considered a valuable tool for the teacher and the student. Its structure is quite flexible, and different ELPs have interpreted it introducing different grids (following the needs of their target students). These grids are used as scaffolds to help users think about their language learning in a deeper and more organized manner. The most common subsections of the biography are:

1. description of the student's learning history (or *language experiences*);
2. description of the most significant linguistic and intercultural experiences (or *language experiences*);
3. definitions of future language priorities, aims and objectives (or *objectives and priorities*);
4. a self-assessment detailed checklists (or "*can do descriptors*");
5. a section for self-awareness on how the student learns (the competence of "*learning to learn*"); and
6. a few ELPs also include pragmatic, sociolinguistic and strategic self-assessment grids (inside the *self-assessment checklists*).

Finally, the *dossier* offers the student the opportunity of selecting materials to illustrate the achievements and experiences recorded in the Passport or Biography (for example,

Table 1. The structure of the e-ELP vs. the paper-based ELP

ELP PAPER-BASED STRUCTURE	**e-ELP STRUCTURE**
Passport (P)	**Personal data (P1)**
P1. Personal data	
P2. Profile of language skills	**Language competence:**
P3. Self-assessment grid	Profile of language skills and self-assessment grid **(P2, P3)**
P4. Summary of language learning and intercultural experiences	Can do descriptors **(B5)**
P5. Certificates and diplomas	Strategic, pragmatic and sociolinguistic grids **(P3)**
	Language for specific purposes grid **(P3)**
Biography (B)	Intercultural competence grid **(P3)**
B1. My language learning history/biography	
B2. My most significant linguistic and intercultural experiences	**Language experiences (P4, B1, B2)**
B3. My current language learning priorities and targets	
B4. My language learning aims (and goal-setting grid)	**Learning competence (B6)**
B5. Self-assessment checklists	
B6. Learning how to learn grid	**Objectives and priorities (B3, B4)**
Dossier (D)	**Dossier (D, P5)**

any kind of text, audio and visual recordings, group works, digital projects, etc.). These reporting and pedagogical functions of the ELP have to be considered as the two faces of the same coin: One cannot exist without the other, since clear and well-organized information is important for reflection and language learning.

The e-ELP starts with a section where the personal data of the learner is supplied (*personal data*). A section called *language competence* follows, where the student can assess his or her language and cultural competence; that is to say, what he or she is able to do with the language in communicative contexts. The focus of this section is the linguistic and intercultural competence of the learner/user. It includes:

1. profile of language skills and self-assessment grid;
2. can do descriptors;
3. strategic, pragmatic and sociolinguistic grids;
4. language for specific purposes grid; and
5. intercultural competence grid.

In the *language experiences* section, the focus is on the linguistic *experience* and intercultural history of the learner. The subsequent sections are *learning competence* and *objectives and priorities*. In the first one, the student can identify strengths and future needs to improve the way he or she learns languages; in the second one, he or she can set goals and priorities for future language learning. Finally, the dossier has the same structure as described above.

From a pedagogical perspective, the result of the e-ELP is a more compact format that allows the user to:

1. have the *profile of language skills* (and the *self-assessment grid*) adjacent to the *checklists of Can do descriptors*;
2. have some grids on communicative competence (strategic, pragmatic, sociolinguistic and intercultural) along and integrated with more "linguistic" grids (*can do descriptors*);
3. treat experiences in a more holistic way;
4. underline the importance of the learning objectives and learning styles, and interpret them as autonomous sections; and
5. consider certificates and diplomas (formal documents) as learning evidence, at the same level of other, less formal documents.

The two structures meet exactly the same functions: to collect personal data, illustrate a profile of communicative language competence (in a concise and in a detailed way), describe language and intercultural experiences (in a succinct and detailed way), stimulate reflection on personal learning competence, aid future planning and collect concrete samples of competence and experiences.

Nevertheless, the standard three-part ELP structure presents some overlapping sections. This stems from the fact that its organization is based on the principle of having a documentary section followed by a pedagogical detailed section. For example, the student makes a global profile of his or her language skills in the Passport, but the detailed grids to refine it are in the biography. The same happens with the summary of language learning and intercultural experiences (passport*)* and language history (biography).

We decided to try another approach by having a *language*-focused section placed side by side with an *experiences*-focused section. From a usability point of view, this avoids having students report the same (or similar) data two times in different sections and check their congruence "manually." It must be underlined that this design choice does not sacrifice the ELP's substance, since the digital structure, when exported (printed or e-mailed), is recombined in an output conforming to the three typical parts (passport, biography and *dossier*). In other words, the e-ELP just changes its look in its interaction with the user; the interaction is not tailored after the ELP's functions (as in the paper-based structure), but is geared to better serve the users' needs and tasks. The decision to follow this is another aspect of the UCD approach, which came after several meetings with real users, teachers and students, who often get frustrated with the duplication of information in the paper-based ELP.

Having a *language competence* section followed by a *language experiences* section helps strengthen the usability of the e-ELP. This also means that a clear distinction between a documentary and a pedagogical function of the ELP is avoided. For example, if the student needs to prepare his or her ELP for a job application, he or she could be tempted to compile the passport only, which would fulfill the function of offering the owner's brief profile to the receiver. Biography and dossier risk to be postponed, and passport data (especially the global self-assessment) could not precisely mirror the owner's competence. On the contrary, if the student is using the ELP as pedagogical support to a language course, he or she will feel the ELP as a demanding tool and will underestimate its international-recognized mobility function.

For this reason, we defined a section focused on *competence* and one focused on *experience:* The former is more centered on the products and results, the latter is more centered on the progress and development of the language and intercultural learning. This does not mean that we are questioning the passport-biography-dossier structure (which is strictly maintained in the exported version), but rather, that we are attempting to have a more student-centered tool and a less tool-centered student.

Digital Portfolios and Reflection

Portfolios are widely applied at every school level, both as tools to document the learning outcomes and as instruments to reflect on the learning process. They support assessment aiming at a dynamic concept of learning, where the evaluation of the learning process is the focus of the assessment. Furthermore, a portfolio is a self-assessment tool that helps learners reflect autonomously on their ways of learning. Portfolios shift the ownership and mastery of the learning from the teacher to the student, building learner autonomy that is a fundamental requirement for the transition to subsequent school levels, as well as for a wider perspective of life-long learning (Glottlieb, 1995; Ciel, 2000).

As a pedagogical and assessment tool, portfolios are being used in a variety of ways in education and training. Activities can be integrated in portfolios to encourage students to review their own work; reflect on their learning; analyze their learning strategies, strengths and weaknesses; and assess their participation within a class context (Calfee & Perfumo, 1993; Glazer & Brown, 1993). With the growing use of the Internet in education, electronic portfolios have been used extensively by educators. Portfolios, in simple terms, are the collection of selected pieces of work by students. In the context of the ELP, the portfolio includes students' work, documentation and certifications that illustrate the students' language proficiencies. A major focus of a portfolio is to encourage students to reflect on their own work; thus, a portfolio can serve as a record of student learning and growth. A digital portfolio can include video, sounds, text and images.

An important aspect of portfolios is reflection. Reflection has been identified as a fundamental process that facilitates meaningful learning (Dewey, 1910; Schön, 1983, 1987). Dewey (1910), in his seminal work *How We Think*, defined reflection as "active, persistent and careful consideration of any belief or supposed form of knowledge in the light of the grounds that support it, and the further conclusions to which it tends" (p.6). Dewey also promoted reflective thinking as an educational aim and supported that it contributes to the intellectual and moral development of the person because it results in changes in one's perspectives.

The concept of reflection can be transferred to the context of language learners and the goals of the e-ELP. When learners reflect on their language learning and proficiencies, they engage in those processes essential for deep, meaningful learning. Here, portfolios can play an important role. By constructing, rearranging and evaluating their own digital language portfolio, students reflect on what they know and have achieved thus far, identify strengths and weaknesses, and establish clear goals for improving their language expertise.

Advantages of the e-ELP

Schneider and Lenz (2003), the authors of the official ELP guide for developers, acknowledged the importance of having an electronic ELP. However, despite the importance of ELP and the advantages of electronic portfolios, there is no electronic ELP available yet. In addition to the reflective component of a portfolio discussed earlier, some additional advantages associated with the e-ELP are:

1. The e-ELP is easy to update. During their language learning process, students can update and expand their ELP without having to buy new hardcopies or add extra photocopied pages. If a paper copy is needed, it is easy to print either the whole digital version of the ELP or part of it.

2. All the information of the e-ELP can be stored in a database that can be used by institutions for longitudinal studies on the language-learning process. On the other hand, the students themselves can have access to their ELP in progress to see the evolution of their language-learning process in a graphical, user-friendly form.
3. Once implemented, the e-ELP is widely accessible online by the students and can be customized in accordance with the user's language level thanks to the hypermedia nature of the project and selective access to the evaluation grids.
4. Considering that the e-ELP in its textual part is a multilingual document (e.g., all the instructions must be in at least three languages), the digital structure would permit the coexistence of many languages while avoiding graphical overload (e.g., with a change-language function).
5. An electronic version makes it possible to have multimedia integrated in the user's portfolio. In the dossier, the student could collect not only paper documents, but also audio and video samples of his work.
6. Another innovation is that the e-ELP is easy to share electronically (e.g., via e-mail), and it is quicker to fill in than its paper-based version (Barrett, 1994).

From a research and assessment perspective, the database underlying the digital ELP is an important instrument in getting longitudinal information on the language-learning process. This may bring considerable pedagogical innovations to evaluation. The e-ELP allows experimentation with new forms of assessment based on a dynamic concept of language learning. This concept of alternative evaluation would include evaluation of the process of learning (to integrate evaluation of product; e.g., tests and students' self-evaluation).

UCD and the e-ELP

The adoption of technology in education settings is a slow process for a variety of reasons, including lack of infrastructure, lack of teacher training, curriculum constraints, assessment practices and the resistance of education systems to change (Vrasidas & Glass, 2005). One of the most important factors for ensuring the use of technological tools within education contexts is UCD. Norman (1989, 1999) has argued that the philosophy behind UCD is to make products usable and understandable. In developing the e-ELP, we followed a UCD approach, placing emphasis on the user and not on the technology. We began placing an early focus on the users and the tasks they are to complete using the e-ELP. We followed an interactive design during which users participate throughout the design, modification, pilot testing and revision phases of developing the e-ELP.

Participants in this project were all experts in language teaching and learning and had worked for many years with students implementing the paper-based ELP. A detailed storyboard of the e-ELP was developed in collaboration with teachers and students who all had prior experience with using the paper version of the ELP. As paper-based prototypes of the e-ELP were developed, teachers from every country reviewed them and provided the design team with feedback. The focus group meetings were facilitated by a design expert, who worked closely with the language experts and students in reviewing the prototypes, identifying strengths and weaknesses, and offering suggestions for solutions.

Once the first electronic prototype was developed, teachers and students reviewed it under the guidance of the design team and discussed the various options provided on the screen and the functionality of the e-ELP. During the first round of pilot testing, the first draft was shared with one teacher and one student from each of the participating institutions. An instrument was developed that guided the users through the process of reviewing, testing and noting suggestions for improving the e-ELP. Users were

Table 2. Instrument used with users to evaluate the first prototype

		Strongly Agree	Agree	Disagree	Strongly Disagree	Not Applicable
		4	**3**	**2**	**1**	**NA**
1	The program uses simple language	4	3	2	1	NA
2	Links and buttons are labeled meaningfully	4	3	2	1	NA
3	The program places information, navigation, options and other features in a consistent manner	4	3	2	1	NA
4	It is easy use the e-ELP	4	3	2	1	NA
5	Features and functions are easy to remember	4	3	2	1	NA
6	Using the e-ELP helps the user reflect on his or her language learning	4	3	2	1	NA
7	As a user I'm always informed about the location I am in every section of the e-ELP	4	3	2	1	NA
8	The e-ELP provides the user sufficient control and freedom to accomplish tasks	4	3	2	1	NA
9	The user can easily locate information	4	3	2	1	NA
10	The interface is aesthetically pleasant	4	3	2	1	NA
11	Information is organized meaningfully	4	3	2	1	NA
12	The available help and documentation are helpful to the user	4	3	2	1	NA
13	The value for using the e-ELP instead of the paper ELP is clear	4	3	2	1	NA
14	The description of labels is informative and helps me make choices on the screen.	4	3	2	1	NA
15	Uploading material (images, files, audio, video, etc.) within the e-ELP is easy	4	3	2	1	NA
16	Modifying and updating the e-ELP is easy.	4	3	2	1	NA
17	Exporting the e-ELP is easy	4	3	2	1	NA
18	Browsing the e-ELP is easy	4	3	2	1	NA
19	The functions of the e-ELP are of high quality	4	3	2	1	NA
20	Rate the overall experience from using the e-ELP	4	3	2	1	NA

instructed to download the e-ELP from the project's Web site, run it on their personal computers, and complete a portfolio in a language of their choice. While they were completing the e-ELP, they were guided to note technical and language errors, suggestions for improvement and inconsistencies. Table 2 presents a part of the instrument that asked users to circle the numbers from each item that best described their experience with e-ELP.

In addition to the questions in Table 2, users were asked to rate their expertise in using computers as well as the paper version of the ELP. Additional open-ended questions included the following:

1. What are the technical errors you noted?
2. What are the language and pedagogical suggestions you have for improving the project?
3. What other aspects of the e-ELP need to change?
4. What are the things you feel work well?
5. Briefly list and discuss the most important criteria/conditions that need to be met so that students and teachers use the e-ELP.

We are currently in the process of preparing for the final tryouts of the last version of the prototype. During this stage, teachers in each country will work with five to 10 students each over a period of 4 weeks. Students will be developing their personal e-ELPs, saving them, maintaining and updating them, exporting them and sharing them with peers. Feedback from the tryouts will be collected from an assigned coordinator from each participating institution. At the end of the evaluation period, the coordinator will hold a focus group discussion with teachers and students to discuss with them issues, such as:

1. What are the major strengths and weaknesses of the e-ELP?
2. What are the major technical errors you noted?
3. What are the major usability issues?
4. How can the e-ELP be improved?
5. What needs to be done to support teachers and students in adopting the e-ELP?

All completed surveys, focus group minutes, and student and teacher reports will be collected by the principal evaluator, who will analyze and prepare the final report. The report will be shared with all participants, and the development team will implement the necessary revisions, following the recommendations put forward in the report.

Technological Issues in Using and Sharing the e-ELP

The digital nature of the e-ELP allows teachers and students to easily modify, update and share the portfolio that can demonstrate language proficiency using a variety of media. The ease of use and sharing of the e-ELP is crucial in spreading the use of portfolios among teachers, students and administrators. Following our project's main aim, the e-ELP is easy to get in a format that can be downloaded from the Web, and can easily be shared with others. The digital nature of the portfolio not only supports the use of the portfolio principles for language learning, but also promotes the social aspects of its use.

Even if the e-ELP is a customized system, a certain degree of "technical competence" is still required by users. For example, to compose their *dossier*, students must know word processing, be able to use a scanner to capture and edit graphic images, or know how to digitize sound files and video files. It will be important for institutions to provide students with the necessary technological support to enable them to integrate multimedia in their language teaching and learning.

One of our major goals is to design a product that is simple, shareable and usable. The real value of the e-ELP is to be very user-friendly, otherwise, teachers and students would not use it. Matters of usability are complex and, even if we can not make the interface completely "invisible" for the user, we can take advantage of the organizational and display flexibility that it offers. Several usability issues were addressed by our UCD approach, during which we engaged real users from the very beginning of the project and throughout the lifecycle of the final product.

An example of how our UCD approach addressed a challenge in the design of the e-ELP is presented here. One of the issues of the e-ELP is the distinction between writing the ELP and visualizing it, which is not possible in a paper format. In the paper-based ELP, what the student writes is what he or she gets. In a digital version, these activities can be differentiated, which is something that increases the facility of compiling the portfolio and the flexibility of sharing it with others. A customized access to the e-ELP is possible, so that, according to its updating needs (e.g., a quick update or a deep pedagogical reflection), the user can work following transversal paths in the e-ELP. It implies a more dynamic and less repetitive interface than having to enter — often similar — information for the passport, biography and dossier separately. Successively, the system takes charge of combining the entered input for visualization in a passport-biography-dossier format or other desired combination (such as a "reflective ELP" for pedagogical use, "assessment ELP" for summative evaluation or "marketing ELP" for job application).

Figure 2 illustrates the grid that the user has access to while working with the e-ELP. By clicking on the right cell (under the specified column) to rank the user's language proficiency, the cell gets colored and activates the right cell for the user to comment on the specific descriptor. When the user completes the portfolio and exports it, the grid is presented in color, along with the comments on each descriptor, allowing teachers and students to see their respective competencies at a glance.

Figure 2. Sample of language skills profile from the e-ELP profile

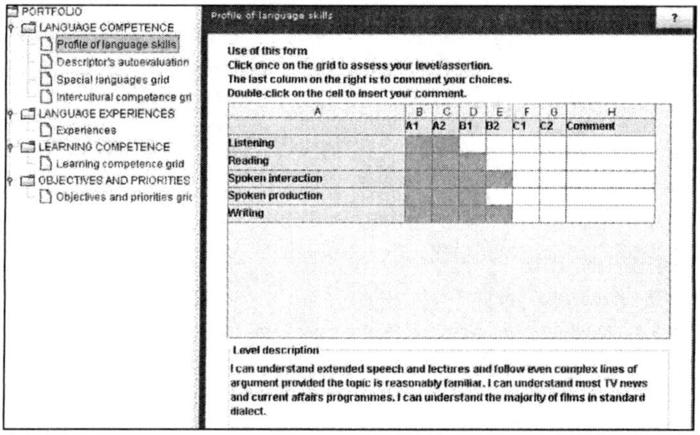

Another example of the flexible and usable nature of the e-ELP is that it allows the user to work in a single language. The e-ELP is a multilingual document, which means that all the languages the student knows are contextually documented and described. Nevertheless, sometimes teachers using the ELP as a pedagogical tool prefer to focus on just the language they teach. Therefore, the possibility to visualize one language at a time without compromising the ELP's multilingual nature is an added value of the digital version.

Pedagogical Issues in the Design and Development of the e-ELP

The project focused on the key points of foreign language learning and teaching that the ELP intrinsically supports. Our focus was to examine how digitalization could strengthen the ELP from the users' point of view (teachers and students). We concentrated on key issues, such as students' reflection and self-consciousness, self-assessment tools and learners' autonomy, transparency of the learning process, learning sharing and the provision for multimedia evidence of language learning.

The students' reflection and self-awareness are key characteristics of the active learner. The ELP has the fundamental pedagogical function to encourage students to reflect on their language learning and to set their own learning goals. In a portfolio, learners are asked to make their language competencies explicit and illustrate their growth over time, thus making the submerged competence evident that learners are not normally used to recognizing and capitalizing in their own learning process (Kohonen & Westhoff, 2003; Kohonen, 2000).

One of the goals of digitizing the ELP is to take advantage of what technology can do to support language learning. An initial idea in designing it was to create a net of digital links among the three parts of the ELP (passport, biography, and dossier) according to the documental-and-pedagogical interconnected double nature of the ELP. A good system of crossed references would make it easy for the student to fill or update the digital ELP in an integrated way. For example, from our experience as language teachers working with many students, we realized that having a link to a student's declared linguistic competence in the passport would make it easier for the student to update the objectives and goals in the biography section coherently.

Linking the dossier section to the passport and biography would give a higher pedagogical relevance to the dossier, which is sometimes considered just an appendix of representative artifacts (Kohonen & Westhoff, 2003). This first idea of making informative/formative links to allow for a transversal sailing in the ELP has been improved lately. In alignment with our UCD approach, and as discussed earlier, we have developed paper-based prototypes of the e-ELP and shared them with students who confirmed our design idea with some minor edits.

After some preliminary pilots with real users, we decided to free the student from the rigid three-section structure, and we opted for restructuring the e-ELP's interface in a way that the learner is required to deal with the three parts contextually. For example, first the student would insert his or her cultural and linguistic experience in a unique format, instead of writing it in a summarized form for the passport; then, he or she would rewrite it in a narrative form for the biography and, finally, he or she would select documents to attest it again for the dossier. It is apparent that the restructuring of the three parts implies a less repetitive interface for the student, which is supported by a modular digital structure that, at any time, is able to visualize and export the ELP in its three standard sections. In the paper format of the ELP, there is a partial overlap of the data. The electronic version offers a less redundant and tighter contiguity among its digital sections, thus avoiding a certain degree of dispersion found in the paper ELP.

Another key point of language learning, as conceived by the ELP, is student autonomy, which is especially intended as the ability of a mature and sensible self-assessment of the user's language competence (Kohonen & Westhoff, 2003; Little, 1999; Ciel, 2000). To make students better self-evaluators, the passport and biography sections are bounded by the clear language assessment criteria offered by the framework of reference, the common reference levels of competence and its descriptors. Descriptors itemize the various levels in terms of "I can do ..." statements that help the learner locate him or herself at a certain degree of competence. Therefore, the ELP offers detailed self-assessment grids that consist of a large list of descriptors like, "I can understand in detail what is said to me in standard spoken language even in a noisy environment" or "I can follow a lecture or talk within my own field, provided the subject matter is familiar and the presentation straightforward and clearly structured." The student is supposed to read these descriptors carefully, understand them in concrete terms and think if he or she owns the particular ability put forward by the descriptor. Even though the descriptors are often in an abstract language difficult for students to understand, the ELP is a powerful instrument for self-assessment (Kohonen & Westhoff, 2003). We also noticed that, in the paper version, sometimes the scaling is not very coherent and the self-assessment list presents a high risk of descriptors overload, since learners have to read many descriptors, which can result in confusion or boredom on the part of the learner.

For this reason, in the design of the e-ELP we tried to recombine the descriptors in a new format. We decided to adapt them in a syntactic combination that would allow the learner to focus on a reduced and relevant version of the descriptors. For example, if the student reads the descriptor "I can listen to public announcements and I can understand the gist," he or she can say: "Yes" or "No," or "Yes, with help." The latter choice would bring the student to a second step, where he or she is required to select a part of his descriptor (I need the translations, repetitions, etc.). In this way, the self-assessment is personalized thanks to a selective access and the student does not have to read the six or seven different descriptors found in the paper version of the ELP. In the digital version, not only is input overload reduced and descriptors scaled in a more coherent system, but it is also possible for the system to detect inconsistencies in the students' self-assessment. For example, the system can give notice when the learner says "yes" to a difficult descriptor and, at the same time, says "no" to an easier one. Again, self-assessment is a complex competence that requires "human training," but perhaps digitalization could at least assist this important function of the ELP.

In addition to the student's reflection and self-assessment is the transparency factor of the learning process. The ELP is a powerful tool of evidence, since the student should document his or her learning in a detailed and explicit way. Nevertheless, is the ELP able to show the change over time? Due to the "fixed" nature of papers, the limit of the hardcopy versions is that it is not very practical for the student to change, correct, add or integrate data to previous ones. One contribution of digitization is that the information of the e-ELP can be stored in a database that can trace a student's modifications and updates over time. Then, data can be represented in a user-friendly, graphic way to show the evolution of the language learning process in a sort of "historical function" that gives visibility to the recursive dynamism of learning (Kohonen & Westhoff, 2003).

Moreover, to empower the transparency of the learning process, the e-ELP allows for an easier way of providing feedback to the learners, as opposed to the paper-based version of the ELP. The introduction of free-writing areas, where the student or someone else (the teacher or a friend) can add his or her comments on the whole or on specific part of the ELP, is a very important source of feedback. In this way, the digital ELP is complemented by a collection of dated comments (written over months or even years by the student or others) that raise the student's consciousness on the fact that learning is a process that grows over time. This "feedback function" is also fundamental in encouraging the learner to share his or her experience with other learners or the teacher. Although the ELP is conceived as a personal document, it can be a very valuable pedagogical tool that also encourages the sharing of language experiences with peers. Such kinds of uses of the e-ELP that encourage "socialization" are issues well documented in technology and literacy studies (Kohonen & Westhoff, 2003).

Another relevant issue regarding technological literacy concerns the multimedia evidence of language learning in the e-ELP. As anticipated, the dossier is the part of the ELP where the student recollects evidence of his or her job experiences. This section is the most similar to non-linguistic portfolios and, in the ELP, it is intended to support the multimedia nature of language use and learning. Compared to the paper version, the digital version makes it easier to collect not only paper documents, but also audio and video samples of the learner's competence. In fact, since the dossier is particularly difficult to manage in the hardcopy version (because students do not know where to keep the non-paper materials), it tends to be undervalued and underused. Conversely, in the digital version, it can become a real tool for documentary evidence, not only because a wide range of language abilities can be fully demonstrated with multimedia, but also because it is directly integrated in the passport and biography.

Conclusion and Future Research

The ELP is in the core of a vast renewal European movement in the field of language teaching, and we hope that the adoption of the e-ELP on a regular basis by various institutions will stimulate an improvement in the quality of language teaching. However, we expect that the e-ELP will not be easily adopted in those educational contexts where a "portfolio culture" is not habitual (Guard, Ritcher, & Waller, 2002; Bilotto, 2000; Clark, 2002). Students' autonomy, self-evaluation, teaching transparency and learning sharing may come into conflict with those contexts where traditional forms of evaluation are highly valued.

The progress educational agencies make in the information society does not depend solely on having infrastructure; it also depends on the assimilation of digital technology into the prevalent pedagogical culture (Hodas, 1993). Following a UCD approach in developing the e-ELP is not enough in ensuring the use of the e-ELP across Europe. Several other factors also influence the adoption of technology in education settings.

A commonly cited obstacle to the use of technology in teaching and learning is the lack of teachers' content, technology and pedagogical knowledge. Because of a lack of pedagogical knowledge, teachers often fail to take advantage of what technology affords and instead use technology to teach in traditional ways. Most of the pressure of preparing teachers to use technology in their teaching lies on schools of education. Teachers are ill-prepared to integrate technology in education (CEO Forum on Educational Technology, 2000; Means, 2004; Moursund & Bielefeldt, 1999; Strudler, Archambault, Bendixen, Anderson, & Weiss, 2003). According to a recent report by McMillan Culp, Honey and Mandinach (2003), *A Retrospective on Twenty Years of Education Technology Policy,* "Teacher professional development has been one of the enduring themes across the past 20 years and is often highlighted … as the single most important step toward the infusion of technology into education" (p. 12). Focusing teacher training on simple technology skills is not enough. Teachers need to be given opportunities to experience technology in everyday practice, and then to try various approaches in the context of their own practice. If we want the e-ELP to be adopted, teachers need to be offered the training and support necessary. Furthermore, strong political will is essential for such innovative approaches to succeed and be adopted.

Acknowledgments

The project was funded by an EU grant under the MINERVA action, and coordinated by the University of Milan. The project participants are: Università degli Studi di Milano (coordinating institution), Europa Universität Viadrina Frankfurt (Oder), Universidad de Salamanca, GAP multimedia, Göteborgs Universitet, University of Skövde and Intercollege Cyprus. We would like to thank all members of the team for the valuable contributions to the success of the project.

References

Barrett, H. C. (March, 1994). Technology-supported assessment portfolios. *The Computing Teacher, 21*, 9-12.

Bilotto, A. F. (2000). Pilot experimentation of the European Language Portfolio at the University of Calabria. In A. Csillaghy & M. Gotti (Eds.), *Le lingue nell'università del duemila* (pp. 321-331). Udine: Forum.

Calfee, R. C., & Perfumo, P. (1993). Student portfolios: Opportunities for a revolution in assessment. *Journal of Reading, 36,* 532-537.

CEO Forum on Educational Technology. (2000). *School technology and readiness: A focus on digital learning*. Washington, D.C.: Author. Retrieved April 5, 2004, from www.ceoforum.org/downloads/report3.pdf

Christ, I. F., Debyser, F., Dobson, A., Schärer, R., Schneider, G., North, B., et al. (1997). *European language portfolio – Proposals for development.* Strasbourg: Council of Europe.

Ciel Language Support Network. (2000). *Assessment and independent language learning. The Guide to good practice for learning and teaching in languages, linguistics and area studies*. LTSN. Retrieved March 8, 2004, from www.lang.ltsn.ac.uk/resources/keywordresources.aspx?keywordid=548

Clark, C. (2002). Portfolio assessment as part of the teaching/learning process. In C. Taylor Torsello, M. Catricalà & J. Morley (Eds.), *Anno europeo delle lingue: proposte della nuova università italiana. Atti del II Convegno Nazionale AICLU* (pp. 191-197). Siena: Terre di Sienne Editrice.

Dewey, J. (1910). *How we think*. Boston: D.C. Heath and Co.

Gibson, D. & Barrett, H. (2002, November 30). Directions in electronic portfolio development, posted in ITFORUM, ITFORUM PAPER #66. Retrieved March 8, 2004, from http://electronicportfolios.org/portfolios.html

Glazer, M. S., & Brown, C. S. (1993). *Portfolios and beyond: Collaborative assessment in reading and writing,* Norwood: Christopher-Gordon Publishers.

Glottlieb, M. (1995). Nurturing student learning through portfolios. *TESOL Journal, 5*(1), 12-14.

Guard, N., Ritcher, U. & Waller, S. (2002). *Portfolio assessments*. In M. Fay (Ed.), *Learning from languages*. Preston: TransLang/University of Central Lancashire.

Hodas, S. (1993). Technology refusal and the organizational culture of schools. *Education Policy Analysis Archives, 1*(10). Retrieved May 15, 2004, from http://epaa.asu.edu/epaa/v1n10.html

Kohonen, V. (2000). *Student reflection in portfolio assessment: Making language learning visible. Babylonia, 1*/2000, 13-16.

Kohonen, V., & Westhoff, G. (2003). *Enhancing the pedagogical aspects of the European language portfolio (ELP)*. Strasbourg: Council of Europe.

Little, D. (1999). *The European language portfolio and self-assessment*. Strasbourg: Council of Europe.

Mariani, L. (2001a, March 15-17). *Documenting the curriculum: Process and competence in a learning portfolio*. Proceedings of the British Council 20th National Conference for Teachers of English. Venice.

Mariani, L. (2001b, Spring). Implementing language and cross-curricular portfolio projects: Some pedagogical implications. *Perspectives, a Journal of TESOL-Italy. XXVII*, 2.

Mason, R. (2002). Rethinking assessment for the online environment. In C. Vrasidas & C. V. Glass (Eds.), *Current perspectives on applied information Technologies. Volume I: Distance education and distributed learning* (pp. 57-74). Greenwich: Information Age Publishing.

McMillan Culp, K., Honey, M., & Mandinach, E. (2003). *A retrospective on twenty years of education technology policy*. Washington, D.C., U.S. Department of Education, Office of Educational Technology. Retrieved April 15, 2004, from www.nationaledtechplan.org/participate/20years.pdf

Means, B. (Ed.) (1994). *Technology and education reform*. San Francisco: Jossey-Bass.

Moursund, D., & Bielefeldt, T. (1999). *Will new teachers be prepared to teach in a digital age? A national survey on information technology in teacher education*. International Society for Technology in Education. Milken Exchange on Education Technology, Santa Monica, CA.

Norman, D. A. (1989). *The design of everyday things*. New York: Doubleday.

Norman, D. A. (1999). *The invisible computer*. Cambridge: MIT Press.

Orsini-Jones, M. (n.d.). Academic and professional skills for language learning. *The guide to good practice for learning and teaching in languages, linguistics and area studies*. LTSN. Retrieved March 8, 2004, from www.lang.ltsn.ac.uk/resources/keywordresources.aspx?keywordid=548

Schneider, G., & Lenz, P. (2003). *European language portfolio: Guide for developers*. Switzerland: University of Fribourg. Retrieved online on April 15, 2004, from http://culture2.coe.int/portfolio/inc.asp?L=E&M=$t/208-1-0-1/main_pages/../documents_intro/developers.html

Schön, D. (1983). *The reflective practitioner*. New York: Basic Books.

Schön, D. (1987). *Educating the reflective practitioner*. San Francisco: Jossey-Bass Publishers.

Strudler, N., Archambault, L., Bendixen, L., Anderson, D., & Weiss, R. (2003). Project THREAD: Technology Helping Restructure Educational Access and Delivery. *Educational Technology Research and Development, 51*(1), 41-56.

Vrasidas, C., & Glass, C. V. (2002). *Distance education and distributed learning.* Greenwich: Information Age Publishing.

Vrasidas, C., & Glass, C. V. (2004). *Online professional development for teachers.* Greenwich: Information Age Publishing.

Vrasidas, C., & Glass, C. V. (2005). *Preparing teachers to teach with technology.* Greenwich: Information Age Publishing.

About the Authors

Panayiotis Zaphiris is a senior lecturer at the Centre for Human-Computer Interaction Design, School of Informatics of City University, London. Before joining City University (in spring 2002), he was a researcher at the Institute of Gerontology at Wayne State University, where he also got his PhD in industrial engineering, specializing in human-computer interaction. His research interests lie in human-computer interaction with an emphasis in issues related to the elderly and people with disabilities. He is also interested in Internet-related research, such as Web usability, mathematical modeling of browsing behavior in hierarchical online information systems, online communities, e-learning and social network analysis of online computer-mediated communication.

Giorgos Zacharia is a PhD student in computer science at MIT (USA), and a member the Center for Biological and Computational Learning of the McGovern Institute for Brain Research, and the Computer Science and Artificial Intelligence Laboratory. His research focuses on multitask learning, and learning algorithms for ranking and conjoint analysis problems. He holds an SM from the Software Agents Group of the MIT Media Laboratory, where he did research in reputation mechanisms for online communities, dynamic pricing, and information retrieval. His research interests in human computer interaction include e-learning and quantitative methods for evaluating interactions of networked communities. Giorgos was the founder and chief scientist of Open Ratings Inc. where he lead research and development, to develop supply base risk management solutions using predictive data mining.

* * * * *

Chee Siang Ang is a PhD student at the City University London. He is particularly interested in studying computer games, not only as a tool for entertainment but also as a medium for other purposes, such as learning a domain of knowledge as well as conveying information and experiences. He obtained his master's degree at Multimedia University, Malaysia, by conducting research on educational technologies. His fields of interest include multimedia learning, computer games, interactive narratives, educational psychology, game engines and authoring systems. His PhD research is related to computer game-based language learning.

Beatriz de los Arcos, BA (USAL), MS (TCD), is a lecturer in Spanish at the National University of Ireland, Galway. She is an associate lecturer in Spanish with The Open University (UK), where she is involved in teaching languages implementing Lyceum, an online audio-graphical conferencing system. She is an active researcher in the field of computer-assisted language learning (CALL), and she is at present carrying out research on interaction and collaboration in virtual learning environments.

Pascual Cantos-Gómez received his BA and PhD degrees in the English language and literature from the University of Murcia (Spain); his MA in computational linguistics from Essex University; and a postgraduate diploma in multivariate statistics from UNED. He is a senior lecturer in the Department of English Language and Literature, University of Murcia, where he lectures English grammar and corpus linguistics. His main research interests are in corpus linguistics, quantitative linguistics, computational lexicography and computer-assisted language learning. He has published extensively in the fields of CALL and corpus linguistics, is co-author of various CALL applications (*CUMBRE Curso Multimedia para la Enseñanza del Español, 450 Ejercicios Gramaticales and Practica tu Vocabulary*, published by SGEL) and also is a member of the expert team for the design of EOI Online Inglés.

Wai Meng Chan received his MA and PhD degrees in the German language and literature from the German Universities of Würzburg and Kassel, respectively. He is currently deputy director of the Centre for Language Studies at the National University of Singapore. His research currently focuses on learner autonomy, metacognition and process orientation in foreign language education, and on new technologies and language learning. He is the author of numerous monographs, book chapters and journal articles on these areas of study.

Martha Christopoulou is a PhD student in art, craft and design education at Roehampton University. She is an art educator in primary education. Currently, she works for the Greek Education Office in London as a teacher of Greek language classes. Christopoulou is also a practicing artist (icon painter). Among her research interests is the importance of culture and cultural heritage in people's life; the ways that art reflects the culture that produced it; and the ways that art combines social and personal expression.

Niki Christodoulou received her BA in international relations and French (1985), and her Master of Education and TESOL (1987) from the American University in Washington DC, United States. From 1987 to 1992 she taught English as a second language (ESL) to immigrant students in New Jersey, U.S. Since 1993, she has been teaching English as a foreign language (EFL) at Intercollege, Nicosia, Cyprus, where she holds the position of assistant professor. Her research interests lie in the areas of bilingualism, bidialectalism, English language acquisition, English language testing, communication strategies, reflective teaching, learning styles and learning strategies, teaching of Greek as a foreign language and language-related problems returnees face in Cyprus.

Caroline Coit (caroline.coit@uni-koeln.de) has studied and taught German and English in both the U.S. and Germany. She is currently a lecturer for English at the University of Münster in Germany, where she specializes in academic writing and 19th century American literature. Her diverse experiences in both countries have awakened her interest in adapting uses of multimedia for online learning and cultural exchange. Over the years she has taught HTML, video editing, Photoshop and Web design. Her strong interest in collaborative learning has led her to develop the online course she introduces in her chapter.

Roderick A. Farmer is a PhD candidate in the department of computer science and software engineering at The University of Melbourne (Australia). Alongside a background in French and sociolinguistics, Farmer possesses a decade of experience in the information and communication technology (ICT) industry. In addition to lecturing in CALL software design and implementation at Melbourne, Farmer works as a consultant software engineer on multi-agent simulation environments for the Defence Science and Technology Office in Australia. His research interests include human-computer interaction, software engineering, CALL, philosophy of mind, spoken language technology, multimodal interaction and machine learning.

C. Ray Graham received his BA in Spanish linguistics (1967) and his MA in linguistics (1969) from Brigham Young University (USA). Following those, he directed language training programs and research projects for the Peace Corps in Escondido, Calif. (U.S.) and Ponce, Puerto Rico. He received his PhD in applied linguistics from the University of Texas at Austin, and subsequently taught at California State University at Northridge. Since 1980, he has been a faculty member of the linguistics department at Brigham Young University, conducting research in second-language acquisition and attrition and second-language pedagogy.

Silvia Gstrein is junior researcher at the ARC Research Studio eLearning Environments. Her main interests lie in e-learning and CALL, especially with emerging technologies. She has a degree in Spanish studies and economics from Innsbruck University (Austria). Since 2001, she has been teaching Spanish to adults at the Bildungs-Center Feldkirch (Austria). From 2002 to 2004, she took part in a university project aiming at implementing the Content Management System Manila/Frontier in Austrian schools (www.c3-

initiative.info). For the last 2 years, she has been giving lectures at the Institute for Organization and Learning (University of Innsbruck) in addition to her work for ARC Research Studio eLearning Environments.

Yoko Hirata is currently teaching English in engineering at Hokkai-Gakuen University in Sapporo, Japan. She has been teaching EFL for more than 10 years at secondary and tertiary levels. She formerly worked at Otaru University of Commerce as a language advisor, and was involved in the development of a self-access center. Her research interests include concordance-based material writing, computer-assisted language learning and the development of learner autonomy by means of self-access facilities. Her chapter is part of her research project which has been fully sponsored by the Japanese Ministry of Education, Culture, Sports, Science, and Technology as well as the Japan Society for the Promotion of Science.

Theo Hug is associate professor of educational sciences at the University of Innsbruck (Austria) and head of the ARC Research Studio eLearning Environments. He has studied psychology, pedagogy, mathematics and philosophy at Innsbruck University. His present areas of interest include media literacy, emerging forms of instant knowledge in new media culture, methodology of qualitative research in social sciences, e-learning and media communities, and philosophy of science and constructivist discourses. In addition to many other publications, he is editor of *Die soziale Wirklichkeit der Theorie* (Munich, 1990); *Erziehungswissenschaft als Lebensform* (Innsbruck, 1991); *Technologiekritik und Medienpädagogik* (Baltmannsweiler, 1998); and *Media Education and Globalization* (Frankfurt, M. et al., 2000).

Juan García Iborra got his BA degree in English studies from the University of Murcia (Spain). In 1990, he passed official professional examinations to become an English teacher at state secondary schools, and in 1992 to teach at state language schools. In 1993 and 1997, he was head of the English department of the Official Language School of Murcia. In 1998, he became head of studies of the school, and since 2002, he has been the director. Form 1997 until now, he has also been an associate lecturer at the University of Murcia. During these years at the Language School of Murcia, Iborra has developed several innovative language-learning programs and different European projects related to language learning, and also became a member of the expert team for the design of EOI Online Inglés.

Sara Kol teaches and coordinates English for academic purposes science courses at Tel Aviv University (Israel). She is a member of the pedagogical team of the Language Learning Center, develops online learning materials and course Web sites and recently coordinated an interuniversity project for Web-based materials development. Her research interests are learning from screen, digital text presentation and computer-mediated communication in EFL courses.

Niki Lambropoulos is an interaction design consultant and a Greek language teacher. She holds two BAs, a diploma and an MA in ICT in education, and she is finishing her PhD in learning technologies at the Learning Technology Research Institute, London Metropolitan University. Among her research interests is the combination of sociability and usability in interaction design for human-computer interaction, with a special interest in group-ware for online communities and e-learning environments, as well as their employment and effectives toward ubiquitous computing. She has published widely in the field and prefers working online.

Elena Landone graduated in Spanish language and literature at the University of Milan (Italy) and attended a post-graduate master of online learning and communication at the University of Florence (Italy). After a research grant for specialization in distance learning of Spanish at the Utrecht University (the Netherlands), she became a researcher at the University of Milan in 2000. Since then, she is professor of didactics of Spanish, educational technology, Spanish culture and Spanish language in the courses and masters of the University of Milan. Her research interests are in the areas of cooperative learning, collaborative electronic writing, alternative evaluation and portfolios. She is coordinator of the electronic European Language Portfolio (ELP) project.

Deryle Lonsdale received his bilingual BS from the University of Alberta in 1981. From then until 1990 he worked as a research computational linguist at ALPNET Inc. He received his MS (1992) and PhD (1997) degrees in computational linguistics from Carnegie Mellon University. Since 1998, he has been a faculty member at Brigham Young University (USA), where he teaches courses in morphology, syntax, semantics, speech applications programming and natural language processing. His research activities include language parsing and generation, speech processing, Web information extraction, machine learning and cognitive modeling of language use.

Rebecca Madsen earned her physics BS (2002) from Brigham Young University (USA), where she is currently completing her MS in computer science. She interned (2001) at the University of Southern California Information Sciences Institute, developing dialog for an interactive computer speech demo system to help train military officers. Further work in dialog developed into her undergraduate thesis, reviewing current approaches to dialog management systems. Rebecca researched commercial speech technologies and behavior modeling systems while at Soar Technologies (2003). Her current research interests include dialog modeling, natural language processing, speech processing and machine learning.

Rita de Cássia Veiga Marriott was a lecturer in Brazil at the Federal University of Paraná (UFPR) and at the Pontifical Catholic University of Paraná (PUCPR) (Brazil), where she attained her MA in education technology. She was responsible for teacher development programs related to computer-assisted language learning (CALL) and for providing support for the implementation of distance learning courses at the UFPR Language Centre. She was involved in the implementation of Web-based courses at PUCPR and has created modules for instructional media software for English-language learning. She has several publications on distance education, the teaching of English as a foreign language and concept maps. Now living in the UK, she gives teacher training courses while remaining a collaborator for the Research Group on Education, Communication and Technology at PUCPR.

Jay Melton has taught EFL, ESL and Spanish since the early 1980s. In the mid-'80s, he taught oral and aural English in Nagasaki, Japan. In 1991, after finishing his master's degree in linguistics at SDSU, he moved to Hikone, Japan, where he taught a variety of linguistics and English courses. In 1993, he began teaching at what is now known as the Prefectural University of Kumamoto, Japan. He has been implementing computing technology into a variety of his courses. Melton is a doctoral candidate at Nova Southeastern University in Fort Lauderdale, Fla. (U.S.); he is currently working on his dissertation.

Inmaculada Arnedillo Sánchez is a lecturer in ICT and education at Trinity College Dublin (Ireland), an invited lecturer in a number of international e-learning master programs and a senior researcher in the Centre for Research in IT in Education in Trinity. Arnedillo's research interests include CALL, mobile learning, enabling technologies and ICT and social inclusion. At present, she is leading two major research projects: TRUST-E: Teaching and Research in a Ubiquitous Secure Telecommunications Environment; and the Computer Clubhouse in Trinity College, in which technology-enhanced learning experiences are implemented. Prior to this, she has worked in EU projects and the evaluation of the integration of technology in Irish schools.

Miriam Schcolnik, PhD, is director of the Language Learning Center at Tel Aviv University, Israel, and she recently coordinated an interuniversity project for Web-based materials development. She also teaches and coordinates advanced English for academic purposes courses, develops online learning environments and has published EFL textbooks, teachers' resource books and courseware packages. Her research interests are e-reading and computer-mediated communication in advanced-language courses.

Patricia Lupion Torres, PhD, is a senior lecturer at the Pontifical Catholic University of Paraná (PUCPR) (Brazil), where she is a researcher/lecturer in the master's course in education and acting head of the School of Education. She is pedagogic coordinator for the National Rural Learning Service (SENAR-PR) and an ad-hoc consultant to the Ministry of Education (MEC) in Brazil for the accreditation of distance learning university courses. She has an MEd in education from PUCPR and a PhD in media and knowledge from the Federal University of Santa Catarina (UFSC), where she was lecturer in the master's courses on media and knowledge (1999-2002). She researches and publishes texts on distance education and ICT; and has authored, co-authored or edited 12 books on education and distance learning.

Kosmas Vlachos is a teacher of English who has worked in Greek state primary schools for 13 years. He holds a BA in English literature and civilization and a Master of Education in ELT. He is a PhD candidate at Aegean University (Greece). His research deals with computer-assisted language learning and, more specifically, with teaching English to young learners using network-based language teaching and computer-mediated communication. He has been engaged with pre-service and in-service teacher training, and has cooperated with the department of English of the University of Athens in its pre-service teacher training course. He has published widely in papers in conferences, conventions, seminars, workshops and ESL/EFL journals. He has also studied school management at Hellenic Open University. His interests include language learning and ICT, learners' and teachers' motivation, teacher education, language learning and intercultural awareness, evaluation within educational systems and European projects.

Charalambos Vrasidas is co-founder and executive director of CARDET – Centre (Cyprus) for the Advancement of Research & Development in Educational Technology (www.cardet.org) and associate professor of learning technologies at Intercollege. A former Fulbright scholar, he holds a PhD from Arizona State University (U.S.) in curriculum and instruction with emphasis on educational technology. His research interests include teacher education, e-learning and evaluation of educational technologies. He serves on the executive committee of the International Council of Educational Media, an UNESCO-affiliated organization. For more information, see www.cardet.org/vrasidas.

Michalinos Zembylas is associate professor of education at Intercollege, Cyprus, and director of curriculum development at the Center for the Advancement of Research and Development in Educational Technology (CARDET) (Cyprus). His research interests are in the areas of science and technology education, curriculum theory and philosophy of education. His recent articles have appeared in *Educational Theory*, *Journal of Curriculum Studies*, *Journal of Research in Science Teaching*, and *Teaching and Teacher Education*. His book, *Teaching with Emotion: A Postmodern Enactment* (Information Age Publishing, U.S.), is coming out spring 2006.

Index

K

L

M

N

O

P

X

Z